# Connections

## Writing, Reading, and Critical Thinking

# Connections

## Writing, Reading, and Critical Thinking

**Tammy L. Boeck**
*Cosumnes River College*

**Megan C. Rainey**
*Cosumnes River College*

New York • San Francisco • Boston
London • Toronto • Sydney • Tokyo • Singapore • Madrid
Mexico City • Munich • Paris • Cape Town • Hong Kong • Montreal

Editor-in-Chief: Joseph Terry
Senior Acquisitions Editor: Steven Rigolosi
Marketing Manager: Melanie Goulet
Supplements Editor: Donna Campion
Production Manager: Denise Phillip
Project Coordination, Text Design, and Electronic Page Makeup: Thompson Steele
Cover Designer/Manager: Nancy Danahy
Photo Researcher: PhotoSearch, Inc.
Senior Manufacturing Buyer: Dennis Para
Printer and Binder: Courier Corp.
Cover Printer: Phoenix Color Corp.

All photos property of Prentice Hall unless otherwise noted on page.

Library of Congress Cataloging-in-Publication Data

Boeck, Tammy.
    Connections: writing, reading, and critical thinking / Tammy Boeck, Megan Rainey.
        p. cm.
    Includes index.
    ISBN 0-321-04431-2
    1. English language—Rhetoric. 2. Critical thinking—Problems, exercises, etc. 3. Report writing—Problems, exercises, etc. 4. College readers. I. Rainey, Megan. II. Title.

PE1408.B573 2000
808'.042—dc21
                                          00-036211

Copyright © 2001 by Addison Wesley Longman, Inc.

All rights reserved. No part of this publication may be reproduced, stored in a retrieval system, or transmitted, in any form or by any means, electronic, mechanical, photocopying, recording, or otherwise, without the prior written permission of the publisher. Printed in the United States.

Please visit our website at http://www.awl.com/boeck

ISBN 0-321-04431-2

1 2 3 4 5 6 7 8 9 10—CRW—03 02 01 00

*This book is dedicated to*

*Our students at*
*Cosumnes River College*
*West Valley College*
*California State University, Sacramento*

*Bethany*

*John*

*The three graces—Brienna Faith, Keely Catherine, and Ann Marie*

# Contents in Brief

Contents  ix
Readings by Theme  xviii
Preface for Instructors  xx
A Note to Students  xxxiii

## SECTION I ▲ *ESTABLISHING THE CONNECTIONS*  1

Chapter 1  The Writing-Reading-Critical Thinking Connection  2
Chapter 2  The Structure of Writing and How to Summarize Texts  28
Chapter 3  Examining the Reading Process  72
Chapter 4  Examining the Writing Process  119

## SECTION II ▲ *EMPLOYING THE CONNECTIONS*  165

Chapter 5  Writing about Heroes  166
Chapter 6  Writing about Technology  221
Chapter 7  Writing about Television  286
Chapter 8  Writing about Music and Poetry  353

## SECTION III ▲ *SUPPLEMENTAL READINGS*  399

Reading Selections  400

## SECTION IV ▲ *SKILL BUILDERS*  431

Discovering Your Learning Style  432
Using the Dictionary  438
Building Your Vocabulary  444
Spelling Matters  449
Reading Aloud: A Trick of the Trade  458
Writing in Time  463

## SECTION V ▲ *EASY REFERENCE RULES*     475

    **Common Irregular Verbs**    476

    **The Right Word**    478

    **Capitalization**    480

    **Using Outside Sources**    481

    **Punctuation Rules**    485

    **Grammar Rules**    486

    **Glossary**    487

    **Acknowledgments**    491

    **Sources**    495

    **Subject Index**    499

    **Index of Authors and Titles**    503

# Contents

Readings by Theme  xviii

Preface for Instructors  xx

A Note to Students  xxxiii

SECTION I  ▲  ESTABLISHING THE CONNECTIONS

Chapter 1   The Writing-Reading-Critical Thinking Connection  2

Introducing the Connections  3
    The Writing Link  3  •  The Reading Link  5
    •  Making the Writing-Reading Connection  6
    •  The Critical Thinking Link  8
    •  Making the Writing-Reading-Critical Thinking Connection  10

Tools for Making the Connections  11
    Taking Notes  12  •  Keeping a Notebook  17
    •  Making the Most of a Good Tutor  19
    •  Using Computers  21  •  Using the Glossary and Index  21

Understanding the Text  22
    An Overview of the Text  22  •  Understanding the Assignments  23  •  Understanding the Sentence Work  26

*Summary of Chapter 1*  27

Chapter 2   The Structure of Writing and How to Summarize Texts  28

Understanding the Structure of Academic Writing  29

Examining an Essay  30

*Reading Assignment: "Romantic Love" by Frank D. Cox*  30

Contents

    A Closer Look at the Parts   32
        The Introduction Powers the Essay   32   •   The Thesis Guides the Essay   32   •   The Body Paragraphs Carry the Evidence   33   •   The Conclusion Signals Completion   34

    The Writer's Purpose and Audience   34

    Examining a Textbook Chapter   35

    *Reading Assignment: "Preparing for Marriage" by Alex Thio   36*

    A Closer Look at the Parts   38
        The Introduction and Thesis   39   •   The Body Paragraphs   39   •   The Conclusion   39

    The Writer's Purpose and Audience   40

    Understanding the Structure of Journalistic Writing   41

    Examining a Feature Story   41

    *Reading Assignment: "Modern Marriage" by William R. Macklin   42*

    A Closer Look at the Parts   45
        The Introduction Is Called the Lead   45   •   The Body Paragraphs Are Shorter   46   •   The Conclusion   47

    The Writer's Purpose and Audience   47

    Examining a Newspaper Column   49

    *Reading Assignment: "Women Play the Roles Men Want to See" by Maggie Bandur   49*

    A Closer Look at the Parts   51
        The Lead   51   •   The Body Paragraphs   52   •   The Conclusion   52

    The Writer's Purpose and Audience   52

    Learning to Summarize Essays and Textbook Chapters   53
        What Is a Summary?   54   •   Points to Remember about Summaries   54   •   A Sample Summary   54

    Summarizing Academic Writing   56
        Distinguishing between General and Specific Information   56

    *Reading Assignment: "Sexual Revolution, Cohabitation, and the Rise of Singles" by William E. Thompson and Joseph V. Hickey   58*

        Identifying the Main Points   60   •   Drafting the Summary   60   •   Revising the Summary   61

Summarizing Journalistic Writing   61
    Distinguishing between General and Specific Information   62

*Reading Assignment: "Sex Has Many Accents" by Anastasia Toufexis*   62
    Identifying the Main Points   64   •   Drafting the Summary   65
    •   Revising the Summary   65

Practicing Summary Skills   66

Time to Reflect   66

*Summary of Chapter 2*   67

> Understanding Verbs   68

## Chapter 3   Examining the Reading Process   72

The PARTS of an Effective Reading Process   73
    Preview   73   •   Anticipate   73   •   Read and Reread   73
    •   Think Critically   74   •   Summarize   74

Engaging in the Reading Process   74
    One Reader's Preview and Anticipation   74   •   One Reader's
    First Read   75

*Reading Assignment: "The Struggle to Be an All-American Girl"
   by Elizabeth Wong*   75
    Reread, Think Critically, and Summarize   77

Responding to Reading   78

Building Your Vocabulary   79
    Using the Dictionary to Find Word Meanings   79   •   Finding Definitions in
    the Writing   81   •   Recognizing Context Clues   81
    •   Keeping a Vocabulary Notebook   83

Practicing the Reading Process   84

Reading the Personal Narrative   84

*Reading Assignment #1: "Navigating My Eerie Landscape Alone" by Jim Bobryk*   84

Reading Textbook Chapters   88

*Reading Assignment #2: "Seventeenth Century Roles for Puritan Men, Women,
   and Children" by James Kirby Martin et al.*   89

*Reading Assignment #3: "Feminism: The Struggle for Gender Equality" by
   William E. Thompson and Joseph V. Hickey*   93

Reading Magazine and Newspaper Articles   96

*Reading Assignment #4: "In India, Men Challenge a Matrilineal Society" by Kavita Menon*   96

*Reading Assignment #5: "Not a Two-Bit Problem" by Dave Murphy*   101

Time to Reflect   105

*Summary of Chapter 3*   105

> Identifying Verbs   107
> More about Verbs   112
> Imposters   114
> Prepositional Phrases   116
> Manipulating Verb Tense   118

## Chapter 4  Examining the Writing Process   119

The Stages of an Effective Writing Process   120
- Discuss and Engage   120 • Read, Discuss, Think Critically   120
- Explore the Writing Assignment   120 • Draft   120 • Revise   120
- Edit   121 • Points to Remember about the Writing Process   121
- Developing an Effective Writing Process   121

*Writing Assignment #1: Analyzing Advertisements*   122

Discuss and Engage   122 • Read, Discuss, Think Critically   124

*Reading Assignment: Selected Advertisements*   124

Explore the Writing Assignment   131 • Draft   135 • Revise   137
- Points to Remember about Revision   137 • Edit   138

*Writing Assignment #2: Creating an Advertisement*   139

Discuss and Engage   139 • Read, Discuss, Think Critically   140

*Reading Assignment: "When Advertising Offends: Another Look at Aunt Jemima" by John J. Macionis*   140

Explore the Writing Assignment   142 • Draft   144 • Revise   144
- Edit   145

*Writing Assignment #3: The Most Evil Character*   145

Discuss and Engage   145 • Read, Discuss, Think Critically   146

*Reading Assignment: "The Most Evil Character" (Author Unknown)*   146

Explore the Writing Assignment   148 • Draft   150 • Revise   152
- Edit   153

Time to Reflect   153

*Summary of Chapter 4*   153

> Subjects   154
> Subject-Verb Agreement: Keeping Your Meaning Clear   156
> Revisiting Those *-ing* Words   159
> Subjects and the *There* Sentence   162

## SECTION II ▲ EMPLOYING THE CONNECTIONS

### Chapter 5   Writing about Heroes   166

Focusing Your Writing   167
    Focusing the Paragraph   168 • Focusing the Essay   169 • Points to Remember about Focus   172

Investigating Heroes   172
    Discuss and Engage   172 • Read, Discuss, Think Critically   176

*Reading Assignment: "Move Over, Barney" by Dennis Denenberg   176*

*Reading Assignment: "Rosa Parks Joins Children's Wall of Heroes" by Sandy Banks   184*

*Reading Assignment "How One Woman Became the Voice of Her People" by David Wallechinsky   187*

*Reading Assignment: "A Hero in My Family" by Megan Burroughs   192*

*Reading Assignment: "Florence Rena Sabin" by Darlene R. Stille   195*

*Writing Assignment #1: Defining Heroes   198*

    Explore the Writing Assignment   199 • Draft   202 • Revise   202 • Edit   203

*Writing Assignment #2: Analyzing a Film,* Hero   204

    View, Discuss, Think Critically   204 • Explore the Writing Assignment   205 • Draft   207 • Revise   208 • Edit   208

Time to Reflect   209

*Summary of Chapter 5*   209

> Pronouns   210
> Using Outside Sources   213
> Shaping Sentences   217

Chapter 6        Writing about Technology    221

Organizing Your Writing    222
Organizing the Paragraph    222   •   Organizing the Essay    226

*Reading Assignment: "Modernization and Women: A Report from Rural Bangladesh" by John J. Macionis    227*

One Approach to Organization    228   •   Points to Remember about Organization    230

Investigating Technology    230
Discuss and Engage    230

*Writing Assignment #1: Discussing Technology in Our Lives    233*

Read, Discuss, Think Critically    234

*Reading Assignment: "Stop the Clock" by Amy Wu    234*

*Reading Assignment: "Resistance to Internet Grows Weak" by Peter H. King    237*

Explore the Writing Assignment    240   •   Draft    242   •   Revise    242   •   Edit    242

*Writing Assignment #2: Arguing about Internet Access in High School    243*

Read, Discuss, Think Critically    243

*Reading Assignment: "Internet Access Puts Burden of Control on Schools" by Abby Goodnough    243*

*Reading Assignment: "On Web, New Threats to Young Are Seen" by Seth Schiesel    247*

*Reading Assignment: "School District Organizes Itself around Internet" by Tina Kelley    250*

*Reading Assignment: "Class Acts: How Three Schools Use New Technology to Empower Students" by Marie Faust Evitt and Joanne Cleaver    254*

Explore the Writing Assignment    258   •   Draft    262   •   Revise    262   •   Edit    264

*Writing Assignment #3: Internet Research vs. Traditional Research    265*

Read, Discuss, Think Critically    265

*Reading Assignment: "Reality Writes—Web Is but a Tool" by Susan Swartz    265*

*Reading Assignment: Quotation by Thiong'o    268*

Explore the Writing Assignment 268 • Draft 272 • Revise 273 • Edit 273

Time to Reflect 274

*Summary of Chapter 6* 274

> Sentence Boundaries 275
> Transitions and Concessions 281

## Chapter 7    Writing about Television   286

Developing Your Writing 287
    Examining Developed Paragraphs 288 • Examining a Developed Essay 290

*Reading Assignment: "Gender Role Images on Television" by Nancy Signorielli*   291

Developing the Focused Essay 293
    Points to Remember about Development 295

Investigating the Effects of Television 295
    Read, Discuss, Think Critically 296

*Reading Assignment: "The Trouble with Television" by Marie Winn*   296

*Writing Assignment #1: The Effects of Television*   307
    Explore the Writing Assignment 307 • Draft 311 • Revise 311 • Edit 313

*Writing Assignment #2: Television: Good, Bad, or Tolerable?*   313
    Read, Discuss, Think Critically 314

*Reading Assignment: "How TV Influences Your Kids" by Daniel R. Anderson*   314
    Explore the Writing Assignment 317 • Draft 321 • Revise 321 • Edit 322

*Writing Assignment #3: The TV Rating System and the V-Chip*   323
    Read, Discuss, Think Critically 323

*Reading Assignment: "V-Chip: Can It Protect Kids?" by Kathryn Doré Perkins*   323

*Reading Assignment: "What You Can Do about Violent TV" by Diana Griego Erwin*   327

*Reading Assignment: "V-Chip Will Add to Parental Chaos" by Michael Kilian*   330

Explore the Writing Assignment   333
   Draft   336   •   Revise   337   •   Edit   338

Time to Reflect   338

*Summary of Chapter 7*   339

Creating Expressive Sentences   340

## Chapter 8   Writing about Music and Poetry   353

Analysis and Inference in Your Writing   354
   Analyzing and Inferring in Your Essays   355   •   Analyzing and Inferring in Your Paragraphs   355   •   Analyzing Music Lyrics and Poetry   357
   Points to Remember about Analyzing Lyrics and Poems   360

*Writing Assignment #1: Analyzing Music Lyrics*   360
   Discuss and Engage   361   •   Read, Discuss, Think Critically   362

*Reading Assignment: "Time" by Pink Floyd*   362

*Reading Assignment: "Old 8 x 10" by Randy Travis*   363

*Reading Assignment: "Tangled and Dark" by Bonnie Raitt*   365

*Reading Assignment: "Perfect" by Alanis Morissette*   366

*Reading Assignment: "Silent Legacy" by Melissa Etheridge*   368
   Explore the Writing Assignment   371   •   Draft   372   •   Revise   372   •   Edit   373

*Writing Assignment #2: Analyzing Poetry*   373
   Discuss and Engage   373   •   Read, Discuss, Think Critically   374

*Reading Assignment: "What I Saw on the Bus" by Jessicah Pratt*   374

*Reading Assignment: "Take Wing" by Adria Conley*   376

*Reading Assignment: "Refugee Ship" by Lorna Dee Cervantes*   377

*Reading Assignment: "The Road Not Taken" by Robert Frost*   379

*Reading Assignment: "A Work of Artifice" by Marge Piercy*   380
   Explore the Writing Assignment   382   •   Draft   383   •   Revise   385   •   Edit   385

*Summary of Chapter 8*   386

Sentence Combining   387
Coordinator and Subordinator Review   396

End of Term Progress Journal   398

Contents **xvii**

**SECTION III** ▲ **SUPPLEMENTAL READINGS**

"Recipe for the '90s" (Associated Press)   400
"Spare the Rod? Maybe" by Michael D. Lemonick   403
"Spare the Chores, Spoil the Child" by Jennifer Bojorquez   406
"The Most Precious Gift" by Hank Whittemore   409
"Look Past Rapper for Real Heroes" by Fahizah Alim   414
"It's a Rap the Young Don't Deserve" by Donna Britt   416
"Who Is Great?" by Michael Ryan   418
"The Wrong Examples" by David L. Evans   423
"Child's Play" by Calvin Trillin   426
"Family Ties Put a Face on the Faceless Issue of Free Speech" by Eric Slater   428

**SECTION IV** ▲ **SKILL BUILDERS**

Discovering Your Learning Style   432
Using the Dictionary   438
Building Your Vocabulary   444
Spelling Matters   449
Reading Aloud: A Trick of the Trade   458
Writing in Class/Writing the Argument   463

**SECTION V** ▲ **EASY REFERENCE RULES**

Common Irregular Verbs   476
The Right Word   478
Capitalization   480
Using Outside Sources   481
Punctuation Rules   485
Grammar Rules   486

**Glossary**   487
**Acknowledgments**   491
**Sources**   495
**Subject Index**   499
**Index of Authors and Titles**   503

## READINGS BY THEME

### Families, Roles, and Relationships

"Romantic Love" by Frank D. Cox   30
"Preparing for Marriage" by Alex Thio   36
"Modern Marriage" by William R. Macklin   42
"Women Play the Roles Men Want To See" by Maggie Bandur   49
"Sexual Revolution, Cohabitation, and the Rise of Singles" by William E. Thompson and Joseph V. Hickey   58
"Sex Has Many Accents" by Anastasia Toufexis   62
"The Struggle to Be an All-American Girl" by Elizabeth Wong   75
"Navigating My Eerie Landscape Alone" by Jim Bobryk   84
"Seventeenth Century Roles for Puritan Men, Women, and Children" by James Kirby Martin, et al.   89
"Feminism: The Struggle for Gender Equality" by William E. Thompson and Joseph V. Hickey   93
"In India, Men Challenge a Matrilineal Society" by Kavita Menon   96
"Not a Two-Bit Problem" by Dave Murphy   101
"The Most Evil Character" (Author Unknown)   146
"Modernization and Women: A Report from Rural Bangladesh" by John J. Macionis   227
"Stop the Clock" by Amy Wu   234
"Old 8 x 10" by Randy Travis   363
"Tangled and Dark" by Bonnie Raitt   365
"Perfect" by Alanis Morissette   366
"Silent Legacy" by Melissa Etheridge   368
"Refugee Ship" by Lorna De Cervantes   377
"Recipe for the '90s" (Associated Press)   400
"Spare the Rod? Maybe" by Michael D. Lemonick   403
"Spare the Chores, Spoil the Child" by Jennifer Bojorquez   406

### The Power of Language

"Refugee Ship" by Lorna Dee Cervantes   377
"The Most Precious Gift" by Hank Whittemore   409

### Heroes and Role Models

"Move Over, Barney" by Dennis Denenberg   176
"Rosa Parks Joins Children's Wall of Heroes" by Sandy Banks   184
"How One Woman Became the Voice of Her People" by David Wallechinsky   187
"A Hero in My Family" by Megan Burroughs   192
"Florence Rena Sabin" by Darlene R. Stille   195

"Look Past Rapper for Real Heroes" by Fahizah Alim   414
"It's a Rap the Young Don't Deserve" by Donna Britt   416
"Who Is Great?" by Michael Ryan   418
"The Wrong Examples" by David L. Evans   423

## Technology and the Internet

"Stop the Clock" by Amy Wu   234
"Resistance to Internet Grows Weak" by Peter H. King   237
"Internet Access Puts Burden of Control on Schools" by Abby Goodnough   244
"On Web, New Threats to Young Are Seen" by Seth Schiesel   247
"School District Organizes Itself around Internet" by Tina Kelley   250
"Class Acts: How Three Schools Use New Technology to Empower Students" by Marie Faust Evitt and Joanne Cleaver   254
"Reality Writes—Web Is but a Tool" by Susan Swartz   265

## Television and the Media

"When Advertising Offends: Another Look at Aunt Jemima" by John J. Macionis   141
"Gender Role Images on Television" by Nancy Signorielli   291
"The Trouble with Television" by Marie Winn   297
"How TV Influences Your Kids" by Daniel R. Anderson   314
"V-Chip: Can It Protect Kids?" by Kathryn Doré Perkins   324
"What You Can Do about Violent TV" by Diana Griego Erwin   327
"V-Chip Will Add to Parental Chaos" by Michael Kilian   330
"Child's Play" by Calvin Trillin   426

## Music and Poetry

"Time" by Pink Floyd   362
"Old 8 x 10" by Randy Travis   363
"Tangled and Dark" by Bonnie Raitt   365
"Perfect" by Alanis Morissette   366
"Silent Legacy" by Melissa Etheridge   368
"What I Saw on the Bus" by Jessicah Pratt   374
"Take Wing" by Adria Conley   376
"Refugee Ship" by Lorna Dee Cervantes   377
"The Road Not Taken" by Robert Frost   379
"A Work of Artifice" by Marge Piercy   380
"Look Past Rapper for Real Heroes" by Fahizah Alim   414
"It's a Rap the Young Don't Deserve" by Donna Britt   416
"Family Ties Put a Face on the Faceless Issue of Free Speech" by Eric Slater   428

# Preface for Instructors

*Connections* is built on the premise that academic growth and communications require students to read, write, and think critically. While each activity—reading, writing, and critical thinking—can be discussed and even practiced in isolation, real progress occurs only when the three pieces are *connected*.

*Connections* takes an innovative approach as a developmental writing text, for it moves beyond traditional sentence and paragraph exercises and carefully weaves together reading, writing, and critical thinking. Instructors who use this text will find the support they require to engage students and guide them through chapters that integrate reading, critical thinking, writing, and sentence work. The result: Developmental writers who have often been relegated to the outskirts of academic discussion enter the multifaceted and challenging world of college where assignments are not simply busywork but, rather, support for authentic writing tasks.

The second text in a three-book developmental writing series, *Connections* would traditionally be called a "paragraph-to-essay text." However, as you will see, after journal assignments, critical responses, and summaries in Chapters 1–3, Chapter 4 begins with an essay assignment. Paragraphing is then taught in the context of essay preparation. Intuitively, students recognize this top-down method as an authentic college-level approach to improving writing skills. Many may be in courses requiring essays and reports, and students want to see the pieces of their writing instruction come together and apply to other courses. In addition, we have seen this top-down approach accelerate student progress when compared to discrete exercise programs. No time is wasted trying to get students to apply to their writing what they learned in drill/exercise work. With *Connections*, students engage in authentic essay assignments while learning about paragraphs, focus, organization, development, analysis, and sentence clarity.

## ▲▼▲ Goals of This Text

*Connections* aims to help developmental writers achieve their collegiate and workplace goals by sharpening their reading, writing, and critical thinking skills.

***Sharpen Study Skills*** For students to succeed in college, they must take notes, organize their work, seek tutorial help, use computers, understand the features of their textbooks, use dictionaries, and summarize other texts. *Connections* begins with a review of these basic study skills.

***Engage Students as Participants in College*** The thematic approach to each chapter in *Connections*—along with journal assignments, discussion questions, activities, readings, critical thinking questions, and writing assignments—makes students active participants not only in the classroom, but also in the learning community at large. Through the repeated reading and writing processes used in *Connections,* students learn to approach a subject critically and from an academic perspective. The students participate in the actual learning process, instead of pieces of it.

***Sharpen Reading and Critical Thinking Skills*** Although *Connections* is a writing text with a writing emphasis, reading and critical thinking are major components. Better readers and thinkers are also better writers. Students who use *Connections* will learn how to approach their readings (through an effective *process*), mark, discuss, and wrestle meaning out of difficult texts, imitate the readings (studying audience, purpose, development, focus, organization, and sentences), and, finally, use these outside sources to improve their own writing.

***Sharpen Writing Skills*** *Connections* emphasizes the writing process as key to generating meaningful text. Researchers such as Mina Shaughnessy (see "Beyond the Sentence" in *Errors and Expectations*) have shown that as inexperienced writers learn an effective process for completing writing assignments, they are able to create essays with improved focus, development, organization, and clarity. Individual elements (e.g., topic sentences) and skills (e.g., focus) must be taught and studied, but all the practicing and studying should be done within authentic writing tasks.

Chapter 4 outlines this writing process and Chapters 5–8 repeat it. As a result, students leave the text with a clear sense of the process writers follow to achieve clarity. Even the sentence work is woven into the writing process. In content, the grammar exercises connect directly to the topic of the chapters; in skill, the exercises help students troubleshoot the errors they tend to make with the various assignments.

## ▲▼▲ Content Overview

A resource for student writers, *Connections* provides tools and support in five sections of instruction. While promoting a progression of skill development, the text is designed to be flexible. Instructors can select from chapters or segments of chapters that address their students' particular needs. A collection of syllabi can be found in the *Instructor's Manual*.

***Section I establishes the writing-reading-critical thinking connection.*** Chapter 1 introduces the writing-reading-critical thinking connection and offers an overview of study skills, such as taking notes, keeping a notebook, and using the dictionary. It also explains the different types of assignments in the text—journals, activities, readings, discussion questions, and writing assignments. Because students will encounter a variety of texts in college, Chapter 2 introduces the unique characteristics of academic and journalistic writing and teaches how to summarize both types of text.

Chapter 3 summarizes the PARTS of the reading process: **P**review, **A**nticipate, **R**ead and **R**eread, **T**hink Critically About, **S**ummarize. Developing an effective writing process is the focus of Chapter 4, which takes students through the recursive process that leads from discovery to drafting, revising, and editing.

***Section II develops the writing-reading-critical thinking connection.*** Emphasizing a discreet writing skill per chapter—focus, organization, development, and analysis—Chapters 5 through 8 teach students how to construct coherent, unified paragraphs and essays. In each chapter, students engage in discussions, activities, and readings that lead directly to writing assignments. They investigate heroes in Chapter 5, then practice *focus* in their writing as they select particular heroes and *focus* on their heroic qualities in their essays. In Chapter 6, students explore technology and the Internet while developing their *organization* skills. They weigh the effects of television in Chapter 7 and focus on *development* in their writing. Finally, in Chapter 8, they *analyze* and write about music and poetry. Sentence work (appearing at the end of each chapter) encourages students to develop sentence skills within the context of their own writing and reinforces each chapter's focus and theme.

***Section III provides supplemental readings to complement writing assignments.*** Representing diversity in culture and thought, this collection of substantive articles and essays reinforces the themes presented in Chapters 2 through 8. Readings on the value of role models, education, and technology serve as alternates or additions to those in the chapters, offering students additional perspectives on issues and instructors greater flexibility in preparing assignments.

***Section IV offers additional skill-building instruction.*** Designed to enhance reading and writing instruction, this section contains chapters on study skills, basic skills, and timed writing. The chapters can be assigned to individuals needing extra help or to the entire class. In Discovering Your Learning Styles, students find out how they learn best and acquire study skills that complement their own styles. Mini-chapters—Using the Dictionary, Building Your Vocabulary, Spelling Matters, and Reading Aloud—offer instruction and reinforcement activities which lead to increased vocabulary as well as stronger reading and writing skills. Then, in a special section, Writing in Class/Writing the Argument, students examine the concerns of in-class writing and learn how to read a prompt, budget time, plan, draft, revise, and edit in a set amount of time.

***Section V contains easy reference charts and instruction on using outside sources.*** At a glance, students have access to irregular verb forms, right-word choices, capitalization, punctuation, and grammar rules. In Using Outside Sources, students learn how to integrate quotations and cite sources within the text.

## ▲▼▲ Features

The following features of *Connections* support students' development as writers and contribute to their writing success in college and the workplace:

*Academic Focus.* Students engage in the kinds of critical reading and writing activities—summarizing, discussing, and analyzing—they'll encounter in college classes.

*Flexibility.* Five distinct sections and eight distinct body chapters allow instructors to select writing skill instruction according to skill level and subject matter.

*Chapter Preview Pages.* Main topics for each chapter appear highlighted on the opening page of Chapters 1 through 8, providing an instant overview of the chapter and preparing students for what's to come.

*Coverage of Study Skills.* Skills such as taking notes, keeping a notebook, and using a dictionary appear in Chapter 1. Other helpful study skills in Section IV include instruction in vocabulary, spelling, and reading aloud.

*Learning Styles.* A variety of activities engages visual, auditory, and tactile learners. The segment Discovering Your Learning Style appears in Section IV.

*Integrated Sentence Skills Support.* Sentence work connects to each chapter's theme and readings and challenges students to inductively learn the parts of speech and basic rules of written language. In the sections entitled Your Own Work students create new sentences and apply instruction to current writing assignments.

*Reading Skills Support.* Students are taught effective reading strategies through the PARTS—Preview, Anticipate, Read and Reread, Think Critically About, Summarize—of the reading process. Prereading activities appear at the beginning of most readings, with questions for critical thought following the readings. Glossed vocabulary words occur at the end of readings in Chapters 1 and 2 as students develop their dictionary skills.

*Writing Assignments Linked to Readings.* Students read, analyze, and summarize articles from magazines and newspapers, textbook excerpts, and essays as they consider and develop their own perspectives on the issues presented.

*Level Appropriate, High-Interest Multicultural Readings.* Readings from academic and other sources reflect contemporary issues and diverse opinions on issues such as dating and marriage, the characteristics of a hero, the impact of technology and the Internet, the effect of television, and more. Representing a variety of styles and sources, these pieces vary in length and difficulty.

*Supplemental Readings.* An additional set of readings near the end of the text provides supplements or alternatives to those in the chapters.

*Student Writing Samples.* Examples of successful student writing appear as models throughout the text.

*Writing Skills Support.* Students engage in a step-by-step writing process. Journals, prereading questions, readings, questions for critical thought, and workshop activities assist students in moving from the discovery phase through the brainstorming, drafting, revising, and editing phases of this process.

*Opportunities for Collaboration.* Activities, journals, discussion questions, and draft workshops provide ample opportunities for group discussion and collaboration.

*In-Class Writing Support.* A special chapter—Writing in Class/Writing the Argument—shows students how to read a prompt, budget time, outline, draft, and revise under pressure.

*Easy Reference Rules.* Easy-to-read charts help students check grammar and punctuation rules, capitalization rules, right-word choices, and irregular verb forms.

*Using Outside Sources.* This unique chapter gives students basic instruction in integrating sources, using quotations, and citing source information in their writing.

*Glossary.* Definitions for terms appearing in bold are listed for easy reference.

## ▲▼▲ The Other Texts in This Series

*Connections* is the second text in a three-book developmental writing series.

Book One, *Expressions* (scheduled for publication in 2002), is for students three levels below Freshman Composition. Books at this level are traditionally created as sentence-to-paragraph books. *Expressions*, however, takes a more modern approach. This text initiates the developmental writer into the world of college by offering a survey of different types of written expression (from diaries to fairy tales to textbook chapters and essays). Immediately students are challenged to think critically about purpose, audience, and style as they read and write. They are presented with authentic pieces of written communication and are then called upon to respond as participants in this exchange.

As they enter this language give-and-take, students receive study skill and reading instruction in the opening chapters. In keeping with the top-down approach, *Expressions* offers a brief explanation of the essay early in the text and some essay assignments throughout the text, but the emphasis is on paragraphs and sentences. As added support, *Expressions* includes a reader at the end of the text with selections that allow the instructor to alternate readings or delve more deeply into topics covered in the body of the text.

Book Three in this series, *Interpretations* (scheduled for publication in 2002), is for the most advanced developmental writer. This essay-level book challenges students to read, write, and think critically as they study, summarize, and interpret current controversial issues, literature, and film. These more complex reading, writing, and thinking tasks are accompanied by more complex sentence-combining work that teaches not only sophisticated sentence structure but also punctuation and usage rules.

## ▲▼▲ Teaching and Learning Package

### The Instructor's Manual

The *Instructor's Manual* offers a discussion of the underlying pedagogy and an overview of features in *Connections*. The manual also offers diagnostic materials, sample semester syllabi, in-class writing assignments, and chapter-by-chapter support materials: chapter previews, preparation suggestions, overhead transparencies for class discussion activities, brainstorming and support activities, and a detailed, day-to-day lesson plan for one or two major assignments per chapter. (0-321-04583-1)

In addition to the *Instructor's Manual,* a series of other skills-based supplements are available for both instructors and students. All of these supplements are available either free or at greatly reduced prices.

### For Additional Reading and Reference

**The Longman Textbook Reader.** This supplement offers five complete chapters from AWL textbooks: computer science, biology, psychology, communications, and business. Each chapter includes additional comprehension quizzes, critical thinking questions, and group activities. Available FREE when bundled with this text. 0-321-07808-X

**The Dictionary Deal.** Two dictionaries can be shrinkwrapped with this text at a nominal fee. *The New American Webster Handy College Dictionary* is a paperback reference text with more than 100,000 entries. *Merriam Webster's Collegiate Dictionary,* tenth edition is a hardback reference with a citation file of more than 14.5 million examples of English words drawn from actual use.

**Penguin Quality Paperback Titles.** A series of Penguin paperbacks is available at a significant discount when shrinkwrapped with any Longman Basic Skills title. Some titles available are: Toni Morrison's *Beloved*, Julia Alvarez's *How the Garcia Girls Lost Their Accents*, Mark Twain's *Huckleberry Finn, Narrative of the Life of Frederick Douglass*, Harriet Beecher Stowe's *Uncle Tom's Cabin*, Dr. Martin Luther King, Jr.'s *Why We Can't Wait*, and plays by Shakespeare, Miller, and Albee. For a complete list of titles or more information, please contact your Addison Wesley Longman sales consultant.

***The Pocket Reader,* First Edition.** This inexpensive volume contains 80 brief readings (1–3 pages each) on a variety of themes: writing, nature, women, men, customs and habits, politics, rights and obligations, and coming of age. Also included is an alternate rhetorical table of contents. 0-321-07668-0

*100 Things to Write About.* This 100-page book contains 100 individual assignments for writing on a variety of topics and in a wide range of formats, from expressive to analytical. Ask your Addison Wesley Longman sales representative for a sample copy. 0-673-98239-4

**Newsweek Alliance.** Instructors may choose to shrinkwrap a 12-week subscription to *Newsweek* with any Longman text. The price of the subscription is 57 cents per issue (a total of $6.84 for the subscription). Available with the subscription is a free "Interactive Guide to *Newsweek*"—a workbook for students who are using the text. In addition, *Newsweek* provides a wide variety of instructor supplements free to teachers, including maps, Skills Builders, and weekly quizzes. To order the *Newsweek* program, please contact your Addison Wesley Longman sales representative.

## Electronic and Online Offerings

**The Writer's ToolKit Plus.** This CD-ROM offers a wealth of tutorial, exercise, and reference material for writers. It is compatible with either a PC or Macintosh platform, and is flexible enough to be used either occasionally for practice or regularly in class lab sessions. The Writer's ToolKit Plus may be packaged free with this text. CD-ROM 0-321-07894-2

**The Boeck/Rainey Web Site.** Both students and instructors can visit our free content-rich Web site for additional resources and exercises. From the Boeck/Rainey website, visitors can conduct Web searches, complete gradable quizzes, and engage in interactive chat. Stop by and visit us at **http://www.awl.com/boeck.**

**The Longman Electronic Newsletter.** Twice a month during the spring and fall, instructors who have subscribed receive a free copy of the Longman Developmental English Newsletter in their e-mailbox. Written by experienced classroom instructors, the newsletter offers teaching tips, classroom activities, book reviews, and more. To subscribe, visit the Longman Basic Skills Web site at **http://www.awl.com/basicskills,** or send an e-mail to Basic Skills@awl.com.

**Daedalus Online.** Addison Wesley Longman and The Daedalus Group are proud to offer the next generation of the award-winning Daedalus Integrated Writing Environment. Daedalus Online is an Internet-based collaborative writing environment for students. The program offers prewriting strategies and prompts, computer-mediated conferencing, peer collaboration and review, comprehensive writing support, and secure, 24-hour availability.

For educators, Daedalus Online offers a comprehensive suite of online course management tools for managing an online class, dynamically linking assignments, and facilitating a heuristic approach to writing instruction. For more information, visit **http://www.awlonline.com/daedalus,** or contact your Addison Wesley Longman sales representative.

***Teaching Online: Internet Research, Conversation, and Composition, Second Edition.*** Ideal for instructors who have never surfed the Net, this easy-to-follow guide offers basic definitions, numerous examples, and step-by-step information about finding and using Internet sources. Free to adopters. 0-321-01957-1

*Researching Online,* **Third Edition.**  A perfect companion for a new age, this indispensable new supplement helps students navigate the Internet. Adapted from Teaching Online, the instructor's Internet guide, *Researching Online* speaks directly to students, giving them detailed, step-by-step instructions for performing electronic searches. Available free when shrinkwrapped with this text. 0-321-02714-0

## For Instructors

**Electronic Test Bank.**  Available in December 2000, this electronic test bank features more than 5,000 questions in all areas of writing, from grammar to paragraphing, through essay writing, research, and documentation. With this easy-to-use CD-ROM, instructors simply choose questions from the electronic test bank, then print out the completed test for distribution. 0-321-08117-X

**Competency Profile Test Bank, Second Edition.**  This series of 60 objective tests covers ten general areas of English competency, including fragments, comma splices and run-ons, pronouns, commas, and capitalization. Each test is available in remedial, standard, and advanced versions. Available as reproducible sheets or in computerized versions. Free to instructors. Paper version: 0-321-02224-6. Computerized IBM: 0-321-02633-0. Computerized Mac: 0-321-02632-2.

**Diagnostic and Editing Tests, Second Edition.**  This collection of diagnostic tests helps instructors assess students' competence in Standard Written English for purpose of placement or to gauge progress. Available as reproducible sheets or in computerized versions, and free to instructors. Paper: 0-321-02222-X. Computerized IBM: 0-321-02629-2. Computerized Mac: 0-321-02628-4.

**ESL Worksheets, Second Edition.**  These reproducible worksheets provide ESL students with extra practice in areas they find the most troublesome. A diagnostic test and post-test are provided, along with answer keys and suggested topics for writing. Free to adopters. 0-321-01955-5

**80 Practices.** A collection of reproducible, 10-item exercises that provide additional practices for specific grammatical usage problems, such as comma splices, capitalization, and pronouns. Includes an answer key. Free to adopters. 0-673-53422-7

**CLAST Test Package, Fourth Edition.** These two 40-item objective tests evaluate students' readiness for the CLAST exams. Strategies for teaching CLAST preparedness are included. Free with any Longman English title. Reproducible sheets: 0-321-01950-4. Computerized IBM: 0-321-01982-2. Computerized Mac: 0-321-01983-0.

**TASP Test Package, Third Edition.** These 12 practice pre-tests and post-tests assess the same reading and writing skills covered in the TASP examination. Free with any Longman English title. Reproducible sheets: 0-321-01959-8. Computerized IBM: 0-321-01985-7. Computerized Mac: 0-321-01984-9.

*Teaching Writing to the Non-Native Speaker.* This booklet examines the issues that arise when non-native speakers enter the developmental classroom. Free to instructors, it includes profiles of international and permanent ESL students, factors influencing second-language acquisition, and tips on managing a multicultural classroom. 0-673-97452-9

## For Students

*Learning Together: An Introduction to Collaborative Theory.* This brief guide to the fundamentals of collaborative learning teaches students how to work effectively in groups, how to revise with peer response, and how to co-author a paper or report. Shrinkwrapped free with this text. 0-673-46848-8

*A Guide for Peer Response,* **Second Edition.** This guide offers students forms for peer critiques, including general guidelines and specific forms for different stages in the writing process. Also appropriate for freshman-level courses. Free to adopters. 0-321-01948-2

## ▲▼▲ Acknowledgments

We'd like to acknowledge those who've contributed to the writing of this text. Special thanks to Dr. Stephanie Tucker of California State University, Sacramento. Her knowledge of and enthusiasm for developmental writing encouraged us to write this text and continues to inspire our teaching. To Addison Wesley Longman and, specifically, Steven Rigolosi, senior acquisitions editor for Developmental English, we offer heartfelt thanks for believing in our approach and for supporting us through the stages of the writing and publishing processes. We also appreciate the guidance of David Cohen, our developmental editor, whose sound advice directed our revision of the text. And we're grateful for the perspectives offered by our colleague-reviewers:

- Alice Adams, Glendale Community College
- Alan Ainsworth, Houston Community College
- Dennis Chowenhill, Chabot College
- Robert Fuhrel, Community College of Southern Nevada
- Sugie Goen, San Francisco State University
- Susanmarie Harrington, Indiana University—Purdue University at Indianapolis
- Linda Houston, The Ohio State University Agricultural Technical Institute
- Peggy Karsten, Ridgewater College
- Laura Knight, Mercer County Community College
- Mary Ann Lee, Longview Community College
- Randall Popken, Tarleton State University
- Harvey Rubenstein, Hudson County Community College
- Valerie Russell, Valencia Community College
- Athene Sallee, Forsyth Technical Community College
- Mary Sauer, Indiana University-Purdue University at Indianapolis
- Nancy Taylor, California State University, Northridge
- Ben Thomserson, Crafton Hills College

We've implemented many of their suggestions in the revision of the text.

Our appreciation extends to Jennifer Krasula for responding to our every need, to Melanie Goulet for igniting interest in our project, and to Caroline Gloodt for securing permissions. Likewise, Denise Phillip, in-house production manager, and researchers Joanne Polster/Photo-Search, Inc., and Karen Pugliano deserve credit for their roles in the construction of the text. We're grateful, too, for the help of Tatiana Zaza, Donna Campion, Belinda Yong, and Christine White in the development of the Instructor's Manual. And we appreciate Nan Lewis-Schulz, senior production editor at Thompson Steele, Inc., for managing the production stage of the process. In addition, we'd like to thank

Mollie Burroughs for compiling the index, Lisa Abraham and Sean Colcleasure for helping pilot materials, Lisa Marchand for contributing a writing prompt, Milenko Vlaisvljevic for his photography/design contribution, and our colleagues, friends, and family members for encouraging us and believing in this project.

Finally, we'd like to thank our students at Cosumnes River College, West Valley College, and California State University, Sacramento, for being open to new materials and a new approach. We especially wish to acknowledge those students who've contributed essays, paragraphs, or sentences to the text: Jennifer Arch, Allison Baxter, Diony Fernandez, Paul Gregorio, Maria Gonzales, Keisha Harris, Ruth Hathaway, Doris Maysonet, Stacy Michel, Aura Northy, Parris Ray, Rector Sajor, and Miguel Viera. Your willingness to share your work with others makes this a better, more collaborative text.

Tammy Boeck<br>Megan Rainey

# A Note to Students

Dear Student,

Welcome to a challenging and dynamic textbook that will help you further develop your academic writing skills. If you are used to doing drill work and fill-in-the blank exercises in your English courses, you will be surprised by what you find here. We wrote this book to engage you in interesting, challenging topics. Our goal is to guide you through the realistic and productive reading and writing processes that help you write thoughtful essays. The title of the text is *Connections* because we have connected all the links of the communication chain—so that each piece of work you do makes sense and leads you to honest, meaningful communication.

## The Premise of this Book

This textbook is built on the premise that developing good writing skills requires you to connect three key elements:

## Writing—The First Link

It is obvious that developing strong writing skills requires you to write. But what should you write? For many years, students were asked to fill in blanks and do many, many sentence drills. However, research shows that such an approach only slightly improves a person's skill in writing essays, reports, summaries, and other work assigned in college and on the job.

Consequently, in this textbook, fill-in-the-blank work is used only as an occasional method of warming up. Instead, you will focus on journal assignments, summaries, and essay assignments. Even the sentence work usually requires you to write out whole sentences or paragraphs. This is the most productive approach to developing writing skills. Yet, these types of assignments aren't enough by themselves.

### Reading—The Second Link

Writing assignments must be linked to reading assignments. Working on both reading and writing skills at the same time will speed up your progress in developing stronger language skills. The reading work you do in this book will help you build your vocabulary, become more familiar with the forms of academic and journalistic writing, understand writing styles and techniques, and give you information you can use in your essays. You'll also work on your summarizing skills.

### Critical Thinking—The Third Link

The final link, critical thinking, connects to both reading and writing. Critical thinking work helps you make sense of the readings and analyze and develop ideas worth communicating in your essays. Critical thinking also helps you make important choices with your own writing.

### Connecting The Links

Of course, simply having each link present between the front and back covers of this book is not enough. The links must actually be joined. In Chapters 1 through 4, you'll learn more about each link and how they should connect when you are working on your reading and writing skills. In these chapters, you'll also learn about the reading and writing processes—the necessary steps for approaching and completing your reading and writing work successfully. The links are dynamically connected in Chapters 5 through 8—the essay chapters—as each chapter focuses on one theme: heroes, technology, television, poetry and music. All the discussion activities, journals, readings, writing assignments, and sentence exercises stay focused on the theme in the chapter. Each piece of work you do will connect to the next, and you'll be on your way to writing better essays.

### Goals

As you work on effectively connecting these links, you'll be working toward these specific goals:

### Writing Goals

- Develop an effective writing process.
- Write focused essays with clear thesis statements and topic sentences.
- Write well-organized essays.
- Write thoughtful, developed essays.
- Write clear, well-shaped sentences.

### Reading Goals

- Develop an effective reading process.
- Broaden your knowledge of how essays and other readings are shaped.
- Improve your vocabulary and your approach to vocabulary.
- Increase your knowledge of writing styles and techniques.

### Critical Thinking Goals

- Sharpen your questioning and thinking skills so that you better understand readings and analyze complex topics.
- Improve your ability to make good choices when writing your own essays.

Connecting the links and working toward these goals will be challenging, but this text offers you the tools and the guided steps to lead you to success.

Good luck!

Tammy Boeck and<br>Megan Rainey

## SECTION I

# Establishing the Connections

*This section of Connections will help you understand the writing-reading-critical thinking connection and will help you sharpen your study skills. You'll also study the shapes of essays and journalistic writing and then learn to summarize texts. The final two chapters explain the reading and writing processes and offer you many opportunities to practice these processes.*

**CHAPTER 1**
  The Writing-Reading-Critical Thinking Connection

**CHAPTER 2**
  The Structure of Writing and How to Summarize Texts

**CHAPTER 3**
  Examining the Reading Process

**CHAPTER 4**
  Examining the Writing Process

# The Writing-Reading-Critical Thinking Connection

**CHAPTER 1**

### Main Topics

- Making the writing-reading-critical thinking connection

- Considering audience and purpose in effective communication

- Reviewing your history as a writer, reader, and critical thinker

- Establishing reading, writing, critical thinking goals for the semester

- Taking notes, keeping a notebook, and working with a tutor

- Understanding the text, the assignments, and the sentence work

*Sacramento Bee*, Jan. 11, 1999, C:6

# Chapter 1   The Writing-Reading-Critical Thinking Connection

*Notes*

You may believe that the ability to write well is something that you're either born with or not. However, the fact is successful writers develop their writing skills in much the same way sculptors develop their artistic skills. Just as the sculptor begins with a lump of clay and then kneads, massages, and molds it into a vase or other object, so the writer begins with a cluster of ideas to explore, develop and shape into an essay.

Of course, with practice the sculptor becomes more adept at shaping the clay. In the same way, the writer becomes more adept at writing through practicing the craft. Like anyone learning a craft, the writer needs the right tools and techniques to fashion the work. This chapter will provide you with the tools. Future chapters will help you develop the techniques. While you read this chapter and those that follow, think in terms of sculptor and clay, writer and words, as you shape thoughts and ideas into expression.

## ▲▼▲ Introducing the Connections

This textbook may have surprised you. You may have expected it to begin with a series of grammar exercises or a description of how to start typing your first paragraph. While most writing textbooks start with writing sentences or paragraphs, this text is different. *Connections* was designed with the conviction that writing skills are developed through the linking of reading, writing, and critical thinking. Perhaps you've heard the saying, "A chain is only as strong as its weakest link." It's a reminder that each link must be strong enough to hold its share of the weight.

What does this comparison suggest in terms of your writing skills? To become an effective writer, you must strengthen not only your writing, but also your reading and critical thinking skills. In this section, you'll examine and practice the **writing-reading-critical thinking connection.**

As you read this chapter and those that follow, you'll need to keep a dictionary, loose-leaf notebook, pen, and highlighter ready. The margins throughout the text have been left blank so that you'll have room to write down any thoughts, questions, or notes as you read.

## The Writing Link

Writing serves many functions. In your personal life, it may help you reflect on your experiences, explore ideas, and discover new ones. It's also a form of communication. From office memos to e-mail, from

*Notes*

term papers to love letters, we often find ourselves writing. (Even the "Beetle Bailey" comic on page 2 has Private Bailey attempting to communicate with his sergeant through writing.) You've probably already discovered the need for strong writing skills. In fact, you may have discovered that writing well is one key to your future success.

> ### Journal Assignment
>
> The journal assignments in this text are opportunities for you to express yourself thoughtfully and freely. Concentrate on exploring ideas and don't worry about spelling, punctuation, grammar, or style.
>
> #### A Writer Today
>
> Think of some ways in which writing is a part of your life. How many things, personal or professional, have you had to write in the past few days or weeks? What might you have to write in the future? Respond to these questions in your notebook.

*Your History as a Writer* Although strong writing skills are required of both students and employees, many people lack confidence in their writing. If you don't enjoy writing, a look at your own history as a writer may show when, why, and how your apprehensions about writing developed. Or, if you're one of the lucky people who finds writing fun and easy, your history may show how you developed a more positive view toward writing.

> ### Journal Assignment
>
> #### Your History as a Writer
>
> In your notebook, trace your development as a writer. How far back can you remember writing? Try to remember what it was like to write in grade school for a teacher, parent, or friend. Explain what you were writing about and whom it was for. How did you feel about your writing at that time? What kind of feedback (if any) did you receive?
>
> Now answer the same set of questions for your writing in your middle school years and your high school years. Finally describe your writing experiences since high school. Overall, would you say your experiences have been positive or negative? Explain.

Chapter 1   The Writing-Reading-Critical Thinking Connection    5

## The Reading Link

Notes

Now let's take a look at the second link in our chain of connections: *reading*. Like writing, reading is a part of our daily lives. Even the most basic street sign is impossible to understand when you don't know how to read it (unless it's accompanied by a picture). If you've ever traveled to a country where you didn't speak the language, then you've probably discovered how much we rely on our reading skills.

We read all the time, often without even thinking about it. At the grocery store, for instance, we may stop to read a label to make sure a product doesn't contain too much fat. Or we may browse through a newspaper or magazine while waiting for a doctor or dentist appointment. In fact, if you've had the opportunity to surf the Web, then you may be reading e-mail or other documents from all over the world.

> ### Journal Assignment
> 
> **A Reader Today**
> 
> Think of some ways in which reading is a part of your daily life. How many things, personal or professional, have you read in the past few days or weeks? How important are strong reading skills for success in today's world?

*Your History as a Reader*   As you did earlier with "Your History as a Writer," take time now to consider your history as a reader. If you have always enjoyed reading, your history should show what you like to read and how you gained your love for reading. If you haven't enjoyed reading in the past, your history may show when, why, and how your apprehensions about reading developed.

> ### Journal Assignment
> 
> **Your History as a Reader**
> 
> Think about your own history as a reader. Did anyone (a parent, teacher, friend, or sibling) read to you as a child? How old were you when you first began to read on your own? Did you enjoy reading as a young person? Why? Why not? If you didn't read much, what activities probably took the place of reading in your life? Can you recall any book that you especially appreciated?

Notes

## Making the Writing-Reading Connection

To be a good writer, you must be a good reader. Reading helps you understand concepts and ideas while providing information to use in your writing. Reading also helps you learn the techniques of good writing. This joining of skills is what we call the writing-reading connection.

- **We often respond to reading through writing.**

  At work: You might be asked to read a report and write a summary of it for your supervisor.

  At school: Many exams require you to read a short article and then write an essay in response.

  At home: After reading an e-mail you've received, you might respond by writing and sending your own e-mail.

- **We read to gather ideas we might want to write about.**

  At work: Perhaps as a personnel manager, you need to write a memo explaining new laws concerning maternity/paternity* leave. You would first need to read government information about these new laws.

  At school: If your history instructor wants a research paper on an American hero, you would need to read books, essays, and articles to gather the necessary information.

  At home: Perhaps you want your medical insurance provider to pay for your X-rays. You would need to read your insurance plan materials before writing a letter to the company.

- **When we write, we expect to be read.**

  At work: If you write a proposal suggesting that the company pay the tuition costs for employees who take college courses, you expect someone to read your ideas.

  At school: After you've diligently worked on your English essay about music lyrics, you expect your instructor to read it.

  At home: When you leave a note reminding your roommate that rent was due two days ago, you expect her to read it (and also pay the rent).

---

*A slash (/) between words such as maternity/paternity usually means "or."

▼ **Activity**  Notes

Activities in the text are designed to help you practice new concepts. In this activity, you'll practice making the writing-reading connection.

### Even Abby Makes the Connection

This activity offers you an entertaining chance to practice the writing-reading connection. Whenever people write to advice columnist Abigail Van Buren, better known as "Dear Abby," they hope Abby will *read* about their dilemmas and *write* in response. Begin by reading the "Dear Abby" selection below, then follow the instructions after the reading.

> Dear Abby:
>
> I dated "James" for 18 months before he proposed. Our wedding is set for the fall of next year. James is loving, considerate, and honest. However, we're completely opposite in our tastes and interests. I am romantic, artistic, and impulsive. He is practical, predictable, and stable.
>
> I was happy with this relationship until a couple of months ago, when I went out to lunch several times with a single man I'll call "John." (We work together.) What began as a casual friendship seems to be developing into more. The attraction is mutual. We share the same values, the same likes and dislikes, and we often think alike. When I look at him, I see myself, so we're very compatible.
>
> John, however, has a less-than-perfect past. He's been in some bad relationships and is twice divorced. He has a troubled family history and two teenagers in therapy with numerous unresolved problems.
>
> Abby, we both realize we won't remain "just friends" if we continue going out to lunch, etc. John hasn't mentioned marriage, but he has told me that he wants me in his life.
>
> I think I love them both. James is safe, John is exciting. John knows about my fiancé, but James doesn't have a clue. Should I go through with the wedding because I'm certain that James would be a good husband, or should I take my chances that John and I will find happiness together?
>
> —Bewitched, Bewildered, and Bothered

Taken from the "Dear Abby" column by Abigail Van Buren. © 1966 Universal Press Syndicate. Reprinted with permission. All rights reserved.

*Notes*

1. Think about Bewitched's predicament and how she might solve it. Then respond in your notebook with a letter of advice. Begin your letter with the greeting "Dear Bewitched."

2. Compare your advice with a classmate's before continuing.

3. Now read Dear Abby's advice, which follows. Was your advice similar? Do you agree or disagree with her advice? What do you think Abby considers as she forms responses to letters like the one from Bewitched?

4. What was your classmate's response? How did you and your classmate arrive at your responses? Discuss the similarities and differences in advice.

> *Dear Bewitched:*
>
> *If you are attracted to John, it's obvious that you are not in love with James. You would be doing James an enormous favor if you broke the engagement and freed him to find a woman who would love and appreciate him. And the sooner the better.*
>
> —*Abby*

Taken from the "Dear Abby" column by Abigail Van Buren. © 1966 Universal Press Syndicate. Reprinted with permission. All rights reserved.

## The Critical Thinking Link

Although strong writing and reading skills are important to your success, your ability to **think critically** about issues or ideas is equally important. When you use your critical thinking skills, you look beyond the surface of an issue or action and examine the purpose or motivation behind it.

In terms of the "Dear Abby" activity, you used your critical thinking skills if you not only considered Bewitched's behavior, but also carefully examined and evaluated her motivations and desires. As you can see from Abby's response, Abby looked beyond the obvious symptom—Bewitched was attracted to another man—to what Abby believed is the main issue: Bewitched wasn't really in love with her fiancé. And although you may have judged Bewitched's motivations and actions differently, if you examined them carefully and took the time to consider the viewpoints of others *before* writing your response, you were thinking critically.

*Critical Thinkers*
- Consider different views and possibilities when looking at an issue or problem.
- Consider the possible reasons or motivations behind issues or actions.
- Question the ideas presented before agreeing, disagreeing, or seeking an alternative.
- Question ideas and seek new ideas.

Critical thinkers use their ability to reason—questioning, evaluating, and judging every issue or idea they read, discuss, and write about.

**Don't Believe Everything You Read or Hear**   It would be a scary and confusing world *if we believed everything we read or heard.* Sometimes even reliable sources have to be questioned.
- After reading only a few advertisements, we might believe that the only road to happiness, power, and beauty is to buy new cars, jewelry, and clothing.
- If we read one essay in favor of the death penalty and believed it, and then read another essay against the death penalty and believed it, we would be very confused.
- If we believed everything we heard, we might panic, as some 1.7 million people did on Halloween in 1938 during a radio presentation of H. G. Wells' *War of the Worlds*. (They believed Martians were invading Earth because they trusted the powerful medium of radio.)

**Think Before You Write**   Consider how difficult or even embarrassing it would be to write without carefully thinking through ideas first.
- A writer who dives into an essay on the death penalty without careful thinking (critical thinking) might waste significant time by writing things he doesn't believe or that don't make sense.
- A writer who reads about the death penalty, thinks about it, discusses it, and then takes a side on the issue is prepared to write what he believes.

**Consider Audience and Purpose**   With a few exceptions, most of your writing is directed at a specific audience for a specific purpose.

*Notes*

- Your **audience** includes anyone you intend to communicate to.
- Your **purpose** is your reason for writing and should be the driving force behind your writing.

Whether composing a letter to a loved one or writing a report for your employer, you use your critical thinking skills and consider your audience and purpose. Doing so ensures that you convey your ideas to your audience in a way that allows you to be heard.

### ▼ Activity

#### Analyzing Audience and Purpose

Review the "Beetle Bailey" comic strip from page 2 of this chapter. In it, Beetle Bailey, the main character, has presented to his sergeant a written list of reasons why he should be given the day off. With a partner, answer the following questions:

What is Beetle's purpose for writing? Who is his audience? Is he successful in getting his message across? Why? Why not? How might Beetle be more effective in his future communication with the sergeant? What advice about audience and purpose would you offer Beetle for the next time he tries to communicate in writing?

There's a simple message behind the "Beetle Bailey" strip that can help you with your writing: Think critically about audience and purpose to communicate effectively.

### Journal Assignment

#### Your History as a Critical Thinker

Reflect on times when you've used your critical thinking skills. Were any of them connected to reading and/or writing? Did any instructors or employers encourage critical thinking? How did they encourage you? What has been your response to activities requiring critical thinking? Write about your experiences as a critical thinker.

### Making the Writing-Reading-Critical Thinking Connection

Now it's time to use the writing-reading-critical thinking chain we've constructed. This chain can give you the power to learn new ideas and to say new things. Although the links can be separated and used individually, when connected they make your communication more interesting and powerful. The most important tasks in college and at work will require you to use this chain.

###  Activity

#### Making the Connection

In this activity, you will read, think critically, and write. With your classmates, review the following quotation:

> Writing is the act of saying "I," of imposing oneself upon other people, of saying listen to me, see it my way, change your mind.
> —*Joan Didion (1934–) American novelist and essayist*

Think about what Didion is saying about writing. Considering what she does for a living, why would she believe this?

Look up the word *imposing* in your dictionary to see what it means, then discuss your thoughts with classmates. Put Didion's idea in your own words.

Discuss with your classmates how you might use writing, "the act of saying 'I,'" in your future at college and work. Be sure to take notes.

---

#### Journal Assignment

##### Your Goals as a Writer, Reader, and Critical Thinker

Take time to re-*read* interesting sections of this first chapter, your journals, your class notes, and Didion's preceding quotation. *Think* about the skills you want to gain in this class and how you might use them. Consider what some of your classmates have said. Consider what past instructors have said. Consider, honestly, your strengths and weaknesses. *Write* down your goals as a writer, reader, and critical thinker.

---

### ▲▼▲ Tools for Making the Connections

Now that you've established your writing, reading, and critical thinking goals, you're ready to learn some strategies for achieving your goals. In this section, you'll learn how to

- take lecture notes,
- use the "Notes" column in the text,
- put together a notebook of your writing assignments,
- make the most of a good tutor, and
- use the computer to become a more efficient writer.

**Notes**

By applying these strategies, you'll not only strengthen your writing, reading, and critical thinking skills, but also your study skills.

## Taking Notes

You'll get much more out of your reading and lectures if you learn to take notes well, since taking notes is one way to be an active participant in the reading, writing, and critical thinking processes. By taking notes you aren't simply absorbing information. You're involved in the process of actively listening and identifying the most important points, then transcribing those points into writing that makes sense to you so that you can review the information later.

Sometimes taking notes is as simple as leaving a check next to an interesting idea in your reading. In other cases, taking notes involves writing out the speaker's main points while listening to a lecture. In this section, you'll learn how to take notes when reading and while listening.

***Writing in the Margins: Becoming a More Active Reader***   One simple way to become a more active reader is to make notes in book margins as you read. Does this suggestion surprise you? If so, you were probably taught *not* to write in your textbooks in elementary or secondary school. Since textbooks were usually passed down from one class to the next, or sold at the end of the school year, you may have been told to keep the margins clean. However, effective readers usually write in the margins of their textbooks. You should feel free to use the margins of your own books for restating main ideas, responding to what you've read, or making connections to other books or articles you've read.

In the following excerpt from his essay, "How to Mark a Book," Mortimer Adler, the founder of the Great Books Program, explains why marking up books is important.

> . . . Why is marking a book indispensable to reading? First, it keeps you awake. (And I don't mean merely conscious; I mean wide awake.) In the second place, reading, if it is active, is thinking, and thinking tends to express itself in words, spoken or written. The marked book is usually the thought-through book. Finally, writing helps you remember the thoughts you had, or the thoughts the author expressed.
>
> Saturday Review, *1940*

Adler suggests, as do other reading experts, that the act of writing in response to reading helps you think through and retain ideas. And if you've made notes next to important ideas in the text, you can easily refer back to these ideas when you review. For study purposes, marking your book makes sense. If you get into the habit of noting important points or ideas in your text, then you'll be a step ahead when it's time to study for an exam.

***Using the "Notes" Column in this Text*** Because we understand the importance of being an active reader, this text provides an ongoing "Notes" column in the margins. This column gives you a place to record your immediate reactions to a reading, jot down questions that come to mind as you read, identify main points, or brainstorm ideas for your writing. In short, the "Notes" column is meant to encourage you to become a more active reader.

To give you an idea of how you might use the "Notes" column, we've included the first three paragraphs of an essay that appears in the textbook *America and Its People*. Note the reader's comments in the margin of the text.

## The Modern Family
*by James Kirby Martin et al.*

This selection appeared in the American history book, *America and Its People*.

1. Does a father have the right to give his children his last name even if his wife objects? Can an expectant mother obtain an abortion without her husband's permission? Should a teenager, unhappy with her parents' restrictions on her smoking, dating, and choice of friends, be allowed to have herself placed in a foster home? Should a childless couple be permitted to hire a "surrogate mother" to be artificially inseminated and carry a child to delivery? These are among the questions that the nation's courts have had to wrestle with as the nature of American family life has, in the course of a generation, been revolutionized.

2. During the 1950s, the Cleavers on the television show "Leave It to Beaver" epitomized the American family. In 1960, over 70 percent of all American households were like the Cleavers: made up of a breadwinner father, a homemaker mother, and their kids. Today, "traditional" families with a working husband, [a homemaker], and one or more children make up less than 15 percent of the nation's households. And as

*Notes*

These are interesting questions. I wonder if all of them will be answered in the body of the essay. The essay appears to be about the American family.

"Epitomize": to be a typical example. Were the Cleavers really a typical American family? Maybe the writers mean simply that most families then had a father, mother, and children.

**Notes**

*True, the family has changed: divorce rate, single-parent households, couples living together are all higher now than in the '50s or '60s.*

3      America's families have changed, the image of the family portrayed on television has changed accordingly....

Profound changes have reshaped American family life in recent years. In a decade, divorce rates doubled. The number of divorces today is twice as high as in 1966 and three times higher than in 1950. The rapid upsurge in the divorce rates contributed to a dramatic increase in the number of single-parent households.... The number of households consisting of a single woman and her children has tripled since 1960. A sharp increase in female-headed homes has been accompanied by a startling increase in the number of couples cohabitating outside of marriage. The number of unmarried couples living together has quadrupled since 1970.

It's clear from the reader's margin notes that she engaged in her reading. She speculated about what the reading would cover, she looked up an unfamiliar term and put the definition where she will see it when she reviews, and she asked questions and made comments that show she had thought about the reading.

While this reader made extensive comments in the "Notes" column, this isn't always necessary. Let's look at another brief selection marked in a different way.

*—topic sentence*

*—support: facts and statistics*

*—creative wrap-up*

Television is the most popular of the popular media. Indeed, if Nielsen research and other studies are correct, there are few things that Americans do more than they watch television. On average, each household has a TV on almost fifty hours a week. Forty percent of households eat dinner with the set on. Individually, Americans watch an average of thirty hours a week. We begin peering at TV through the bars of cribs and continue looking at it through the cataracts of old age.

—Joshua Meyrowitz from "Television: The Shared Arena"

In this case, the reader used the "Notes" column to label the parts of the paragraph, as opposed to making comments on the reading. The point is to use the "Notes" column as needed. *You* are the one who decides how to use the margins.

### Additional Ideas for Engaging with Your Reading

Not every book comes equipped with a "Notes" column. However, most books have enough of a margin or some blank pages at the ends of chapters that you can use for notetaking. Here are some of Adler's pointers for marking not just your textbooks, but any book you may read.

1. *Underlining:* of major points, of important or forceful statements.
2. *Vertical lines at the margin:* to emphasize a statement already underlined.
3. *Star, asterisk, or other doo-dad at the margin:* to be used sparingly, to emphasize the... most important statements....
4. *Numbers in the margin:* to indicate the sequence of points the author makes in developing a single argument.
5. *Numbers of other pages in the margin:* to indicate where else in the book the author made points relevant to the point marked; to tie up the ideas in a book, which, though they may be separated by many pages, belong together.
6. *Circling key words or phrases.*
7. *Writing in the margin, or at the top or bottom of the page, for the sake of:* recording questions (and perhaps answers) which a passage raised in your mind; reducing a complicated discussion to a simple statement; recording the sequence of major points right through the books.

As you actively engage in your reading, you should freely adapt Adler's suggestions to fit your needs as a reader.

**Becoming a More Active Listener**   From the moment you walk into a classroom, you're expected to listen to and remember what the instructor says. But remembering everything the instructor says is quite a task. You've probably been told how important it is to take notes. But taking notes effectively is easier said than done. To take useful notes, you must first learn how to listen.

In his article "Learning to Listen," William H. Armstrong (who has taught history for over fifty years) briefly explains the history of lecture and the difficulties people have in listening.

> Before books and printing, the primary element in acquiring knowledge was listening. A "lecture" originally meant a "reading" from some precious manuscript. The reader read slowly and stopped to explain difficult passages to his listeners. The process has changed; reading is no doubt the primary element in acquiring knowledge, but listening remains the second most important element.
>
> Why is listening... the most difficult of the learning processes? The practices of seeing (reading), writing, and thinking are exercised within the person. But listening takes on the complexity of the listener having to coordinate their mental powers

*Notes*

with an outside force—the person or thing to which the listener is listening. This demands the discipline of subjecting the mind of the listener to that of the speaker.

The second problem in learning to listen arises from lack of associated control. When you learn to read, your eyes control the speed with which you read. When you write there is actual physical control in your hand. In thinking, the analysis of thought travels at exactly the speed capacity of your mind. But when you begin to train yourself to be a good listener, you are faced with a difficulty not unlike that of trying to drive a car without brakes. You can think four times as fast as the average teacher can speak.

Only by demanding of yourself the most unswerving concentration and discipline can you hold your mind on the track of the speaker. This can be accomplished if the listener uses the free time to think around the topic—"listening between the lines" as it is sometimes called. It consists of anticipating the teacher's next point, summarizing what has been said, questioning in silence the accuracy or importance of what is being taught, putting the teacher's thoughts into one's own words, and trying to discern the test or examination questions that will be formed from this material.

If you find your mind wandering after only a few minutes of class, you need to work on developing your concentration. Armstrong suggests that you begin by concentrating for the first ten minutes of every class period. As you focus on the instructor or task at hand, block out other sounds that might keep you from listening. Then, as your ability to listen develops, extend your period of concentration. Eventually, you'll be able to stay focused for the entire class period. Taking notes will help you stay focused.

*Taking Lecture Notes* This is the scenario in many classrooms: The instructor begins speaking when the class period starts and students write down the most important points. Later, they will review their notes when it's time to take the midterm or final. Sounds easy enough, doesn't it? But taking effective notes (as you may have discovered) can be quite challenging.

Here are some tips (from Armstrong and other instructors) for taking lecture notes:

- Be a good listener. If you aren't listening, you can't possibly take good notes.
- Be prepared. You need the tools with you, ready, in order to take lecture notes. This means blank paper, pencil, or pen in hand when class starts.
- Listen for clues in the lecture that suggest an important point is being made. Remember, you can't write down everything the instruc-

tor says. Trying to do so will only frustrate you. Listen for the repeated phrases, "the important point" or "we must remember." When you hear such clues, be ready to write.
- Watch the overhead or chalkboard. If the instructor displays or lists points, write those down. The instructor wouldn't write them down if they weren't important.
- Don't break your concentration to worry about spelling or grammar.
- If you miss an important point or need it clarified, ask the instructor before leaving class that day.
- After a lecture, find a quiet spot to review and fill in your notes so that you don't forget what you've heard.
- File your notes in an organized manner (in your notebook) so that they're in place when you need to study them.

### Journal Assignment
*Taking Effective Lecture Notes*

Taking effective lecture notes can help you get better grades. Reflect on how you've taken notes in the past. Then consider what you've learned about listening and taking notes in this chapter. Which strategies do you intend to use in your next class? How will you use these strategies to improve your reading, writing, and critical thinking skills?

## Keeping a Notebook

Being well organized is another key to success. The well-organized person carefully files away important papers and assignments so that they're easily found when needed. By learning to organize a notebook, you'll not only develop your organization and study skills, you'll simplify your life. The idea is to make your own life easier by keeping journal entries, reading questions, class activities, writing assignments, and other work handy.

To begin, you'll need a three-ring binder (1½ to 2 inch width), a package of dividers, and loose-leaf paper.

***Two Basic Methods of Organization*** There are many ways to organize a notebook, but we'll focus on two specific ways—organizing by process and organizing by assignment. No matter which method you use, your course syllabus should appear first in your notebook.

*Notes*

When one assignment builds on another it helps to ***organize your work by process.*** The idea is to organize assignments as you complete them so that you can see your writing develop through a chapter. Begin by filling out a divider for each chapter. Then, under each chapter divider, keep every assignment you complete—from activities to reading questions to journals to drafts—filed in order of completion. Also include any pages of your own: questions about the assignment, brainstorming activities, outlines, or any articles you discover and want to add to your body of research. Include your early rough drafts, developing drafts, and later drafts, again, in order. Also include a copy of your final draft as well as the graded draft returned by your instructor. As you complete each chapter, you'll be able to flip through the assignments and easily see how your essays developed.

Another approach is to ***organize your work by assignment.*** In this case, you store journal entries under one divider, reading questions under another, sentence work under another, and so on. If you choose this approach, consider using the following headings:

    A. Journal Assignments
    B. Reading Questions
    C. Class Activities
    D. Lecture Notes
    E. Writing Assignments
    F. Sentence Work
    G. Vocabulary
(other sections as needed)

If you use this approach, the "Writing Assignment" section should still store—from beginning to end—all the drafts of your essays.

As you store these drafts, you'll begin to understand and develop your own process for writing. Also in this section, jot down any thoughts or reactions you have to the assignment or any questions you have about the assignment so that you can ask your instructor. Feel free to include any pages of your own brainstorming—clustering, listing, freewriting—on the topic. Also include early outlines, rough drafts, developing drafts, and later drafts. Finally store a copy of your final draft as well as the graded draft returned by your instructor. As the semester progresses, this section of your notebook will become the largest. At a glance, you'll be able to see how your essays developed.

## Making the Most of a Good Tutor

Notes

As a supplement to your in-class writing activities we recommend that you see a tutor. Your reading and writing skills will improve much more quickly if you can discuss your work frequently outside of class. And, while study groups made up of students from your class are an excellent idea, too, it is important to discuss your work with a more experienced writer. This is where tutors come in.

Whether you are feeling secure or insecure about your reading and writing skills, you can benefit from tutorial assistance. (Even professional writers hire editors to help them rethink and revise portions of their writing.) However, it's extremely important that you have a clear idea about what you can expect from a tutoring session. A tutor who does too much for you can actually slow down your growth as a reader, writer, and thinker. You'll want to find a tutor who offers guidance and tools for success while encouraging you to do the work yourself. Here are things to look for in a good tutor:

### A Good Tutor Should
- be on time and ready to help you.
- listen carefully to you and your concerns about writing.
- ask you questions about your assignment, your deadlines, your concerns.
- probably comment first on the global aspects of your writing: focus, development, organization.
- respond honestly to your writing.
- discuss some possible ways to improve weak spots, but let you do the actual improvements.
- explain a grammatical error to you and different ways to correct it, but have you identify and fix it in your own work.
- tell you how many spelling errors he or she sees, but let you find the errors and fix them yourself.

### A Good Tutor Should Not
- waste your time by being consistently late or by talking about things unrelated to the writing task.
- rewrite sections of your paper or give you the "right words" to say. (Yours are the right words and ideas.)
- proofread your paper, mark and correct your grammar, punctuation, and spelling mistakes.

*Notes*

***Finding a Good Tutor***   To find a good tutor, go to the writing center, computer lab, your English instructor, or your college counselor to ask for a referral. Most colleges have some kind of tutorial service available at little to no cost. It's up to you, however, to use your school's system to your advantage. If you begin working with a tutor and discover that he or she isn't listening to or understanding your needs, then don't waste your time. Arrange to work with another tutor.

***Making the Most of a Tutoring Session***   The more enthusiasm and interest you put into your tutoring sessions, the more you'll get out of them. Think about it from the tutor's perspective for a moment. A tutor often works one on one with students for several hours in a single day. If you were a tutor, wouldn't you feel energized by those students who arrived at their sessions prepared to work? Here are some tips on how you can be a good tutee:

- See the tutor on a regular basis. Have a set appointment time, if possible, for once or twice a week. Be on time.
- Set goals with the tutor. Discuss and write down your strengths and weaknesses as a reader and writer. Prioritize your goals. Review this list with your instructor after your instructor has had time to evaluate some of your writing. Revise your goal list as your instructor suggests. (Review this list at midterm with your instructor.)
- Bring in and discuss readings. Discuss vocabulary words, main ideas, interesting points.
- Bring in the actual writing assignment and discuss the requirements of the assignment with your tutor.
- Brainstorm ideas for your writing assignments with your tutor.
- Show drafts to your tutor, and ask what is the strongest part of the draft and what is the weakest. (Consider your list of goals.)
- Leave the tutoring session with a short to-do list each week and an agreement about what you will bring with you next time.

Because your time with a tutor is limited, be *on time*—with materials organized—and ready to work. Plan to ask questions and share concerns about your writing with someone who can offer writing support. A tutor is such a person.

## Using Computers

In college and on the job, you will be expected to type most of what you write. You'll become a more efficient writer if you begin the practice of writing your essays on a computer. You don't need to know any fancy computer tricks to benefit from using a computer. You only need to know a few basic commands, which you can learn in the computer lab on your campus. You will also need to know how to type or be willing to learn. (Most college computer labs have computers equipped with typing tutorials.)

Here are a number of tasks that you can complete easily on the computer.

- Freely pour out ideas to discover what you're thinking.
- Move paragraphs and sentences with ease.
- Add and delete information without having to retype your entire essay.
- Check word definitions with the computer's dictionary.
- Check spelling with the computer's spell check program.

Overall, the computer is faster and more efficient than the typewriter. If you're unsure about where the computer lab is on your campus, ask your instructor or counselor. Both should be able to direct you to this important resource.

## Using the Glossary and Index

This book provides two additional resources for writers that you should know about. The first one is the **glossary.** Whenever an important term is mentioned for the first time, it will appear in boldface. The definitions of these boldfaced terms are listed alphabetically in the glossary (p. 487). In this chapter, you have encountered several boldface terms. Take a moment to look up the meaning of one of these terms in the glossary: **audience, purpose,** or **writing-reading-critical thinking connection.**

You can also find out information and the location of other terms, authors used in the text, or general subjects by looking in the general **index** (p. 496) or author-title index (p. 500). Terms in the index, as in the glossary, are listed in alphabetical order.

Notes

## ▲▼▲ Understanding the Text

Now that you've reviewed the tools and some basic strategies for college success, we'd like to explain how this text works.

### An Overview of the Text

This text is divided into five basic areas of instruction. The first section will help you understand how writing, reading, and critical thinking connect. The second will give you practice in making these connections. The third contains supplemental readings that will allow you to further explore these connections. The fourth and fifth will offer additional resources to help you refine these connections.

**Section I: Establishing the Connections**
    Chapter 1: The Writing-Reading-Critical Thinking Connection
    Chapter 2: The Structure of Writing and How to Summarize Texts
    Chapter 3: Examining the Reading Process
    Chapter 4: Examining the Writing Process

**Section II: Employing the Connections**
    Chapter 5: Writing about Heroes
    Chapter 6: Writing about Technology
    Chapter 7: Writing about Television
    Chapter 8: Writing about Music and Poetry

**Section III: Supplemental Readings**

**Section IV: Skill Builders**
    Discovering Your Learning Style
    Using the Dictionary
    Building Your Vocabulary
    Spelling Matters
    Reading Aloud
    Writing in Class/Writing the Argument

**Section V: Easy Reference Rules**
    Common Irregular Verbs
    The Right Word
    Capitalization
    Outside Sources

Punctuation Rules
Grammar Rules

## Understanding the Assignments

You'll encounter several types of assignments in this text: journals, activities, readings, and essays. Each type of assignment has been created to teach you something about the relationship between reading, writing, and critical thinking, and each offers you practice in applying what you've learned.

*Journal Assignments*   Usually consisting of a series of questions, **journals** are designed to get you thinking critically about a topic or issue. These are "freewriting zones." In other words, journal assignments provide you the opportunity to explore your ideas on paper. They're much like a diary in that you're allowed to write honestly without fear of judgment. Your instructor may write back in response to your journal, but will not judge your ideas or point out grammar errors.

To give you an idea of what a student journal entry looks like, two student journals on goals are reprinted below. You'll notice that each student's personal writing goals are different although both students are concerned with improving their writing.

> The skills I wish to gain from this class are simple. First of all, I would like to express myself better as a writer, so that I get good grades on essays and term papers. I know that I'm a good student, but English has always been a bit scary for me. I have a hard time writing ideas under pressure, but let me get in my car and ideas for writing seem to jump out of my head. As a reader, my goals are to continue reading for knowledge and pleasure. As a critical thinker, my goals are to consider a diverse amount of information and then make rational and intelligent decisions. For the larger part of my life, most of my decisions were made around my emotions or what I was feeling instead of thinking. Today I like to think things through.
>
> —*Allison Baxter*

*Notes*

> I know in fact that writing, reading, and critical thinking are the skills that I need to gain and improve in this class. I use these skills on my daily activities such as in school reading books and writing homework assignments and at work communicating with other employees to read and write procedures, reports, and instructions. In addition, reading and writing are very useful in some other ways such as when applying for a new job, writing a resume, traveling for directions, reading menus or labels, and so on. As far as the critical thinking, it may help me to organize things, solve problems and find solutions, and determine better ideas and make improvements.... My goal is to increase my knowledge in writing, reading, and most especially thinking to lead me to a higher career.
>
> —*Rector Sajor*

*Activities* Within the text, **activities** help you put into practice new writing concepts or ideas. In the "Dear Abby" activity earlier in this chapter, for instance, you were asked to practice the writing-reading connection. Future chapters include such activities as writing summaries, organizing ideas with cue cards, and making presentations on heroes. As you'll discover, this text offers a variety of individual and group activities all designed to help you practice new concepts.

Here's one student's response to the "Dear Abby" activity from pages 7 and 8. She read Bewitched's letter and responded as she believed Abby would have responded.

> Dear Bewitched,
> I believe you have quite a hard decision to make. But of all that you've told me, I have to wonder why you would even consider leaving a relationship with a man who is as loving, considerate and honest as James. John is just offering fun with no commitment.
>
> When the smoke clears, after all the fun you have had with John, you'll have to deal with two troubled teens, a history of divorces, and a man who believes in cheating.

> But if James doesn't turn you on anymore, it's obvious that you're not quite ready for commitment or marriage. James deserves someone who is honest, loving and considerate, too.
>
> —Maria Gonzalez

*Reading Assignments and Readings* Beginning in Chapter 3, readings are preceded by a **Reading Assignment.** This assignment will help you practice some of the steps of the reading process that you will learn about in Chapter 3: previewing, anticipating, reading, and rereading.

Then, following the Reading Assignment, you'll find a selected **reading** to complement the writing assignment and chapter theme. For instance, Chapter 5 focuses on heroes, so in that chapter you'll discover a selection of readings on heroes including an essay titled "Move Over, Barney" (which suggests we replace our children's cartoon heroes with real ones), a magazine article about Aung San Suu Kyi (leader of the Burmese movement toward democracy), a newspaper article on Rosa Parks (known as the mother of the Civil Rights Movement), a personal essay on a family war hero, and an essay on scientist Florence Rena Sabin. While these readings are tied directly to the writing assignments, there's no doubt that as you complete them, you'll be developing your reading skills also.

*Questions for Critical Thought* Following the readings in the text, **Questions for Critical Thought** help you understand and analyze what you've read. They help you think critically about the writer's message as well as the strategies used to convey the message to the reader. They also serve as springboards to class discussion. When responding to these questions, you may discover ideas to use in your writing assignments. Such questions bolster reading comprehension and strengthen critical thinking and discussion skills.

*Writing Assignments* You will practice several forms of writing in Chapters 1 through 3—journals, activities, and summaries. Then in Chapter 4 you'll encounter a more formal form of **writing assignment, the essay.** In brief, the essay is an organized, multi-paragraph piece of writing in which the writer focuses on and develops a particular issue or theme—for a specific audience, for a specific purpose.

Notes

Note: In Chapter 2, challenging vocabulary is listed before the readings. In later chapters, after some vocabulary instruction, you will become responsible for keeping your own vocabulary list for the readings.

*Notes*

Each writing assignment will take you through a series of stages that will help you develop and improve your writing. And you'll write essays on a wide range of contemporary issues and topics: advertisements, heroes, technology, television, music, and poetry.

## Understanding the Sentence Work

Throughout this text, sentence practice material will help you learn to develop and refine your sentences. You may find the work here different from the grammar exercises you've done before. For one thing, you'll be creating many of your own sentences as you practice what you've learned. Also, the practice segments are closely connected to the readings and issues discussed in the chapters. These grammar segments are designed to help you continue developing your writing, reading, and critical thinking skills.

*The How's and Why's*  When you learn how to drive a car, you don't have to know the names of all the parts of the car or how the car was assembled. You do, however, need to know a few key terms: emergency brake, hazard lights, high beams. You also need to know how to use these items. As you become a more experienced driver, you easily pick up more knowledge. For example, you learn how to check the fluids and change the oil. Many people who love cars and driving continue to learn even more about the technical aspects of cars: What is a flange gasket? How do you replace a flange gasket?

How does all of this apply to you as a writer? First, remember that you are a writer because you already know some important basics about writing. For example, you know thousands of words, and you've written these words in various forms—letters, essays, reports—over the years.

The exercises in this text will help you learn or get a better handle on *key writing terms* that will help you shape clear and effective sentences. You don't need to recite definitions of *all* the parts of speech, but knowing these terms *will* help you develop more control over your writing. That way, when you turn in essays to your instructor (or reports to your boss), you won't feel like someone who just turned over her prized car to a mechanic who knows everything when you know too little.

*Completing the Sentence Exercises*  You'll find that the exercises in this text call for you to read, research, create, discuss, and practice your reading-writing-critical thinking skills. These are the most effective methods for learning about sentences. You'll be exploring, and the more energy you put into your explorations, the better the results you will see.

As you complete the exercises, you'll discover that writing good sentences is becoming second nature, and you'll gain the ability to discuss your writing with others. Throughout this book, you'll continue to pick up more terminology and more ways of shaping sentences. In the end, you'll leave your class knowing that you have better control over your sentences and, consequently, the thoughts you choose to communicate.

## ▲▼▲ Summary of Chapter 1

In Chapter 1 you've learned about the Writing-Reading-Critical Thinking Connection. In particular, you've reviewed

- the importance of each connection as you've explored your history as a writer, reader, and critical thinker,
- the tools necessary for "making the connections" successfully this semester: taking and keeping notes, keeping a notebook, and making the most of a good tutor, and
- how the text works.

# The Structure of Writing and How to Summarize Texts

**CHAPTER 2**

## Main Topics

- Examining the structure of writing
- Building summary skills
- Reading, writing, and thinking about relationships
- Reviewing, supplying, describing, and defining verbs

Universal Press Syndicate, 1988

Your reading and writing assignments will become easier as you begin to understand the structure of writing and how to summarize. Let's begin by considering how the structure of an item reveals its function.

First, visualize a skyscraper and a sports stadium. Although both hold many people, these buildings have been designed for different reasons and to serve different functions. The skyscraper may have a small base since it must fit within a city block, but lack of ground space is made up for in the number of stories. Inside are offices and cubicles, allowing many people to work on individual jobs. The sports stadium, however, may take up several acres of land. With its stadium seating, it's designed to give the most people the best possible view of a game.

Just as the structures of these buildings suggest their functions, so the structure of a piece of writing tells you about its function. In this chapter, you'll examine several types of writing—essays, textbook excerpts, and news articles—and discover how their structures reveal their functions.

Once you've analyzed several forms of writing, you'll be ready to write a summary. When you summarize, you retell the main points and important supporting points of articles, textbook chapters, or essays. As you learn to summarize, you'll produce condensed versions of documents that express the author's meaning. In your classes, if you get into the habit of summarizing chapters as you complete them, you'll have a summary from each chapter to study when it's time for a test. In the workplace, if you have developed strong summary skills, you'll be able to summarize documents and present them in condensed form to your boss or colleagues. In this chapter, you'll develop the techniques for writing effective summaries.

## ▲▼▲ *Understanding the Structure of Academic Writing*

Academic writing, meaning an essay or textbook chapter, usually appears as a group of paragraphs working together to prove a point, explain an issue, describe a process, or relate an incident. Normally this group of paragraphs follows a specific organizational structure and may be broken into three basic parts: the introduction, the body, and the conclusion.

The **introduction** (the opening paragraph or two of the essay) explains what the essay will be about and suggests the order and direc-

*Notes*

tion of the paragraphs that will follow. The **body** of the essay (usually made up of several paragraphs) supports whatever claim has been established in the introduction. The **conclusion** (the final paragraph) summarizes the most important points made in the body or restates the writer's claim from the beginning of the essay, while at the same time drawing the essay to a close. Many textbook chapters and most of the essays you'll read and write in college follow this basic format.

It may help you to think of an essay or textbook chapter as a passenger train. In the same way that an engine pulls the various cars of the train toward a specific destination, an essay's introduction powers the body paragraphs and conclusion toward a specific point the writer is trying to make. And though a train's cars are different (there could be a sleeper car, a dining car, a baggage car), they are all being pulled in the same direction along the same track.

Each body paragraph of an essay, too, though proving different points and containing different kinds of evidence, is guided by the introduction. Finally, as the caboose signals the end of the train, the conclusion signals the end of the essay.

## ▲▼▲ Examining an Essay

Consider the structure of an academic essay and how it works as you read the following selection. This essay first appeared in a book entitled *Human Intimacy* by Frank D. Cox. In the essay, Cox explains America's fascination with romantic love. As you read, pay close attention to the essay's parts—introduction, body, conclusion—which are labeled.

In this chapter, words you may not be familiar with are listed before the readings by paragraph (par.) with their definitions.

Terms and definitions:

par. 1 *romantic love:* an idealized version of love involving perfect mates.

par. 5 *pithy:* forceful and brief.

*[handwritten: What is romantic love?]*

The *introduction* of an essay appears first. Here the writer introduces the subject and explains what the essay will be about.

### Romantic Love
*by Frank D. Cox*

1   For many Americans the idea of <u>romantic love</u> most influences their thoughts about attraction and intimacy. This concept of love encompasses

such ideas as "love at first sight," "the one and only love," "lifelong commitment," "I can't live without him/her," "the perfect mate," and so forth.

In essence the concept of romantic love supplies a set of idealized images by which we can judge the object of our love as well as the quality of the relationship. Unfortunately, such romanticized images usually bear little relationship to the real world. Often we project our beliefs onto another person, exaggerating the characteristics that match the qualities we are looking for and masking those that do not. That is, we transform the other person into an unreal hero or heroine to fit our personal concept of a romantic marital partner. Thus we often fall in love with our own romantic ideas rather than with a real human being.

For example, the traditional romantic ideals dictate a strong, confident, protective role for a man and a charming, loving, dependent role for a woman. A woman accepting this stereotype will tend to overlook and deny dependent needs of her mate. She will tend to repress independent qualities in herself. Love for her means each correctly fulfilling the proper role. The same holds true for a man who has traditional romantic ideals.

Those who "fall in love with love" in this way will suffer disappointment when their partner's "real person" begins to emerge. Rather than meet this emerging person with joy and enthusiasm, partners who hold romanticized ideals may reject reality in favor of their stereotypical images. They may begin to search again for a love object, rejecting the real-life partner as unworthy or changed. Dating and broad premarital experience with the opposite sex can help correct much of this romantic idealism.

When people fall in love with their romanticized expectations rather than with their partner, they may either reject the partner or attempt to change the partner into the romantic ideal. John Robert Clark has a pithy description of the first action:

> In learning how to love a plain human being today, as during the romantic movement, what we usually want unconsciously is a fancy human being with no flaws. When the mental picture we have of someone we love is colored by wishes of childhood, we may love the picture rather than the real person behind it. Naturally, we are disappointed in the person we love if he does not conform to our picture. Since this kind of disappointment has no doubt happened to us before, one might suppose we would tear up the picture and start all over. On the contrary, we keep the picture and tear up the person. Small wonder that divorce courts are full of couples who never gave themselves a chance to know the real person behind the pictures in their lives.[1]

---

[1] John Robert Clark, *The Importance of Being Imperfect* (New York: McKay, 1961), p. 18.

**Notes**

*The conclusion appears at the end of the essay. In it, the writer may summarize the main points of the essay or explain what he or she has learned. Its main job is to draw the essay to a close.*

Conclusion

6  ③ The second action, attempting to change one's spouse, also leads to trouble. Making changes is difficult, and the person being asked to do so may resent the demand or may not wish to change.

7  Generally, romantic love's rose-colored glasses tend to distort the real world, especially the mate, thereby creating a barrier to happiness. This is not to deny that romantic love can add to an intimate relationship. Romance will bring excitement, emotional highs, and color to one's relationship. From there one can move toward a more mature love relationship. As emotional, intellectual, social, and physical intimacy develops romance takes its place as one of several aspects of the relationship, not the only one.

## ▲▼▲ A Closer Look at the Parts

Now that you've read "Romantic Love" and have identified the three basic parts of the essay, you're ready to examine these parts more closely.

### The Introduction Powers the Essay

As we mentioned, most academic writing (essays and textbook chapters) starts with an introduction, a paragraph or two that establishes the subject of the essay, and the essay's route or direction—much like an engine powers the cars of a train along a track. Here you can tell your reader what to expect in your essay. Typically the introduction begins with general information and becomes more specific toward the end.

Look back to the introduction of Cox's "Romantic Love." Note how Cox first mentions romantic love in general, then describes it in more detail, and finally states his opinion on how ideas about love affect relationships.

### The Thesis Guides the Essay

At the very end of an introduction you'll often find a specific statement or two that convey the author's main idea for the entire essay or chapter. This is called the **thesis statement,** and its job is to keep an essay on track as it heads toward its destination.

▼ **Activity**

### Identifying the Thesis

Underline the thesis statement in "Romantic Love." In your own words, write in your notebook what the author intends to talk about in his essay. Share your ideas with a classmate.

## The Body Paragraphs Carry the Evidence

The middle paragraphs of an essay that follow the introduction are called **body paragraphs.** Body paragraphs, like the cars of a train, contain cargo or passengers in the form of evidence and support.

Body paragraphs have a particular structure, too. They usually start with a general statement—called a **topic sentence**—that introduces the main idea of the paragraph. (Sometimes it takes more than one sentence to tell what the paragraph will be about. A paragraph topic may be introduced in one or more sentences.) The rest of the paragraph supplies more specific pieces of information or examples that support the topic sentence.

▼ **Activity**

### Identifying Topic Sentences

Review the body paragraphs in "Romantic Love" and then complete the following tasks.

1. After reviewing, go back and highlight the topic sentences—general statements that begin the body paragraphs. In your notebook, write down the body paragraph numbers (3–6) and next to each number write down *in your own words* what the author says each paragraph will be about. Compare your ideas to a classmate's to see if you agree. Discuss any differences.

2. Further down your sheet of paper, make a separate list called "Specific Support." Then list any examples or details you find in the body paragraphs. How many specific pieces of support did you find? Which paragraph contains the most support? Compare your findings with a classmate.

*Notes*

## The Conclusion Signals Completion

Finally, at the end of the essay or chapter there is often a concluding paragraph or section that sums up what has been said earlier and helps the reader "make sense" of the entire piece. Here, as the writer, you can tell the reader what you've learned from writing the essay and what you want the reader to learn from your essay. In other words, the conclusion's job is to signal the end of the essay.

## ▼ Activities

### Examining the Conclusion

Look back at the conclusion of "Romantic Love." In your notebook, list the main points in the conclusion. Did Cox repeat all of the main points at the end of the essay? What does Cox want you to learn from his essay?

### Diagramming the Essay

With a partner or two, create a picture or diagram of an essay. Consider the structure of an essay. Besides drawing a train, how else might you illustrate an essay? You may want to use different colors and shapes to show where the general statements are and where specific information appears.

For Class Discussion: Share your diagrams.

## ▲▼▲ The Writer's Purpose and Audience

So far, you've considered the structure of an essay and how it works. But an essay's message is important as well. For instance, Frank Cox uses the essay form to explain to his audience (his readers) how Americans influenced by the notion of romantic love may "fall in love with their own romantic ideas rather than with a real human being." His purpose (reason) for writing the essay? To help people establish realistic expectations when choosing partners. Like Cox, every writer has a purpose for writing, as well as a message to convey to a chosen audience. The essay form that we've examined in this chapter is one of the possible ways for writers to send their messages.

## ▼ Questions for Critical Thought

*Notes*

Questions for Critical Thought help you examine the writer's message as well as the strategies used to convey that message to the reader. (Note that some questions contain more than one part.)

### "Romantic Love"

Respond in your notebook to the questions that follow. Be prepared to discuss your responses with classmates.

1. How does Frank Cox define *romantic love?*
2. a. Do you believe in "love at first sight" or a "one and only love"?
   b. Do you have an idealized view of your perfect mate? Or, if you don't *now,* did you *ever* have an idealized view of a perfect mate? What is/was this view?
3. Do you agree that *romantic love* influences most people when selecting a mate? Why? Why not?
4. What does Cox say is a more realistic view of a mate or marriage?
5. Who might be included in Cox's audience? How might his audience respond to his message?

---

### Journal Assignment

#### Making the Writing-Reading-Critical Thinking Connection

Now that you've read about and discussed the concept of romantic love and how it influences people's decisions when selecting their mates, you're ready to examine the "Calvin and Hobbes" cartoon from the beginning of the chapter.

In your notebook, restate (in your own words) Hobbes' explanation to Calvin about what it's like to fall in love. Then explain in writing the point cartoonist Bill Watterson is making about romantic love. Do you agree or disagree? Why?

---

## ▲▼▲ Examining a Textbook Chapter

Academic writing in the form of textbook chapters or sections often follows the same basic format as an essay. This is especially true in textbooks for courses such as history, sociology, anthropology, psychology,

**Notes**

and so on. These texts must include a range of important information in a form that is easy for students to follow.

In each segment of a textbook chapter, there should be an introductory paragraph or two, supporting body paragraphs, and a conclusion (or concluding remarks). The following textbook **excerpt** (selected passage) comes from the chapter, "Families," which appears in *Sociology: A Brief Introduction* by Alex Thio.

Terms and definitions:

par. 1 *diligently:* persistently.

par. 2 *chivalrous:* courteously attentive.

par. 3 *spontaneity:* impulsiveness; *seclusive:* isolated.

par. 4 *courting:* dating which leads to marriage; *"playing the field":* casually dating a number of people.

par. 5 *nuclear family:* a family consisting of a father, mother, and their children.

par. 6 *irrationally:* illogically; *intrinsic:* essential, inner; *extrinsic:* outer; *pragmatic:* practical; *overt:* open and observable.

par. 7 *fervent:* passionately sincere.

## Preparing for Marriage
*by Alex Thio*

In the *introduction,* the writer of the textbook section introduces the main ideas of the section.

1   Most people do not consciously prepare themselves for marriage or *diligently* seek a person to marry. Instead, they engage in activities that gradually build up a momentum that launches them into marriage. They date, they fall in love, and in each of these steps they usually follow patterns set by society.

The first *subsection* (which focuses on one of the main ideas) is identified by boldface. Clearly, the writer will focus on dating practices. This subsection is part of the body of the textbook selection.

2   **The Dating Ritual** Developed largely after World War I came to an end in 1918, the U.S. custom of dating has spread to many industrial countries. It has also changed in the United States in the last two decades. Before the 1970s, dating was more formal. Males had to ask for a date at least several days in advance. It was usually the male who decided where to go, paid for the date, opened doors, and was supposed to be *chivalrous.* The couple often went to an event, such as a movie, dance, concert, or ball game.

3   Today, dating has become more casual. In fact, the word "date" now sounds a bit old-fashioned to many young people. Usually you do not have to call somebody and ask for a date. "Getting together" or "hang-

ing around" is more likely. *Spontaneity* is the name of the game. A young man may meet a young woman at a snack bar and strike up a brief conversation with her. If he bumps into her a day or two later, he may ask if she wants to go along to the beach, to the library, or to have a hamburger. Males and females are also more likely today than in the past to hang around—get involved in a group activity—rather than pair off for some *seclusive* intimacy. Neither has the responsibility to ask the other out, which spares them much of the anxiety of formal dating. Getting together has also become less dominated by males. Females are more likely than before to ask a male out, to suggest activities, pay the expenses, or initiate sexual intimacies. Premarital sex has also increased, but it tends to reflect true feelings and desires rather than the need for the male to prove himself or for the female to show gratitude (Strong and DeVault, 1992).*

4   The functions of dating, however, have remained pretty constant. It is still a form of entertainment. More important, dating provides opportunities for learning to get along with members of the opposite sex—to develop companionship, friendship, and intimacy. Finally, it offers opportunities for *courting,* for falling in love with one's future spouse. "*Playing the field*" does not lead to a higher probability of marital success, though. Those who have married their first and only sweetheart are just as likely to have an enduring and satisfying marriage as those who have married only after dating many people (Whyte, 1992).

> Note the word "finally." This signals the writer's final point and concluding remark about dating.

5   **Romantic Love**   Asked why they want to get married, Americans usually say, "Because I am in love." In U.S. society, love between husband and wife is the foundation of the *nuclear family*. In fact, young people are most reluctant to marry someone if they do not love the person even though the person has all the right qualities they desire. . . .

> The second subsection (which focuses on a main idea from the introduction) is identified by boldface as well. This subsection is a part of the body of the textbook selection.

6   But does romantic love really cause people to choose their mates *irrationally?* Many studies have suggested that the irrationality of love has been greatly exaggerated. An analysis of these studies has led William Kephart and Davor Jedlicka (1988) to reach this conclusion: "Movies and television to the contrary, U.S. youth do not habitually fall in love with unworthy or undesirable characters. In fact, [they] normally make rather sound choices." In one study, when people in love were asked, "Does your head rule your heart, or does your heart rule your head?" 60 percent answered, "The head rules." Apparently, romantic love is not the same as infatuation, which involves physical attraction to a person and a tendency to idealize that person. Romantic love is less emo-

---

* The names and years appearing in parentheses (Strong and DeVault, 1992) are references to research used by Thio in the textbook.

*Notes*

*The writer wraps up this subsection with a concluding remark.*

tionalized, but it is expected to provide *intrinsic* satisfactions, such as happiness, closeness, personal growth, and sexual satisfaction. These differ from the *extrinsic* rewards offered by a *pragmatic* loveless marriage—rewards such as good earnings, a nice house, well-prepared meals, and *overt* respect.

7. In the United States over the last 30 years, the belief in romantic love as the basis for marriage has grown more *fervent* than before. In several studies in the 1960s, 1970s, and 1980s, college men and women were asked, "If a person had all the other qualities you desired, would you marry this person if you were not in love with him/her?" Today, as opposed to earlier decades, a greater proportion of young people say no (Simpson, Campbell, and Berscheid, 1986).

## ▲▼▲ A Closer Look at the Parts

Like the essay, the textbook chapter contains the basic elements of academic writing—introduction, body, and conclusion. However, there is a big difference between the essay "Romantic Love" and the textbook selection "Preparing for Marriage." Textbook chapters often contain section headings and subheadings in bold to keep information clearly organized. It's easy to see how such headings work.

Under the general heading of "Preparing for Marriage," the author gives a quick overview of the section. The two subsections, "The Dating Ritual" and "Romantic Love," which offer different aspects of the main topic, are presented in an organized manner—one topic at a time. Textbook headings and subheadings show the general topic of the section, give easy references to specific information, and help readers anticipate what sections will be about.

### ▼ Activity

**Examining Headings and Subheadings**

1. The heading of this textbook section is "Preparing for Marriage." Highlight the two subheadings. Notice that the two subheadings (or subsections) are introduced in the opening paragraph of the section. Explain how the writer sets up the two subsections in the introduction.

2. Examine the chapter of another textbook. (Look at a history, psychology, sociology, or other textbook that presents large sections of information.) Read the chapter, then write down the chapter's headings and subheadings. Explain how the writer has organized the information under headings and subheadings.

## The Introduction and Thesis

Notes

Textbook sections and chapters—like the essay—contain an introduction that lets the reader know what information will be covered. In fact, this information is clearly stated. Because textbook writers want students to follow the chapter discussion easily, they usually make the thesis or main idea of the chapter obvious.

### ▼ *Activity*

**Identifying the Thesis**

After *re*-reading the introduction, in your own words, write down the thesis of "Preparing for Marriage." What does the introduction tell us the excerpt will be about?

## The Body Paragraphs

The body paragraphs of a textbook chapter often begin with topic sentences like those in the essay. They are followed by support in the form of examples, details, quotations, and other evidence.

### ▼ *Activity*

**Identifying Topic Sentences**

Review the body paragraphs in "Preparing for Marriage" and then complete the tasks below.

1. Highlight the topic sentence(s) in each body paragraph. (Keep in mind that sometimes it takes more than one sentence to introduce the paragraph topic.) Then in your own words, write down what each paragraph is about.

2. Also in your notebook, make a "Specific Support" list. Go back through the selection and write down examples, details, quotations, and other forms of support. Which of the paragraphs contains the most support? Share your findings with a classmate.

## The Conclusion

Most textbook chapters end with a summary. You may have noticed, for example, that Chapter 1 of *Connections* ends with a summary of the entire chapter. However, within each section or subsection of a

*Notes*

chapter, you should be able to identify a concluding remark or two that draws that section or subsection to a close.

### ▼ Activities

#### Examining the Conclusion

Review the concluding remarks in each subsection of "Preparing for Marriage." Does Thio repeat all of the main points of the body paragraphs from "The Dating Ritual"? What does Thio want you to learn about dating? Does Thio repeat the main points of "Romantic Love"? What does he want you to learn about romantic love?

#### Comparing the Structure of Academic Writing

1. Compare the structures of "Preparing for Marriage" and "Romantic Love." How are their shapes similar? How are they different?

2. Compare the structure of "Preparing for Marriage" to a chapter or section in another college textbook. How are their shapes similar? How are they different? Does the section you've chosen contain headings and subheadings similar to those in "Preparing for Marriage"?

## ▲▼▲ The Writer's Purpose and Audience

While the essay "Romantic Love" was written to convince people to establish more realistic expectations when choosing partners, the textbook selection "Preparing for Marriage" was written to inform. If you look back through the selection, you will see that Thio has compiled source information (studies and research) and has presented concepts differently than Cox. As you respond to the questions that follow, consider why Thio's writing would serve a different audience and purpose than Cox's might.

### ▼ Questions for Critical Thought

#### "Preparing for Marriage"

1. According to Thio, do most people consciously prepare for marriage? What leads people to eventually marry?

2. How has dating in the United States changed in the last twenty years? What was it like before the 1970s? In what ways is it different today? What hasn't changed about dating? What's dating really for?

3. According to Thio, what is "the foundation of the nuclear family"?

4. What part, if any, does romantic love play in American marriages, according to Thio's findings?

5. Does Thio's presentation of romantic love agree with Cox's view in "Romantic Love"? Do both Thio and Cox think that people need to be more realistic in choosing partners? If so, why? If not, why not?

6. What is Thio's purpose in writing "Preparing for Marriage"? Who would be his audience?

> ### Journal Assignment
> **Making the Writing-Reading-Critical Thinking Connection**
>
> Compare dating, romantic love, and marriage in the past and present. Is dating today the same as it was in your parents' or grandparents' youth? Did romantic love play as big a part in their choices of mates? Do you consider romantic love to be important to your own relationships? In your notebook, write about what you believe to be the ideal approach to love and/or marriage based upon what you've read, as well as on your own personal experience.

## ▲▼▲ Understanding the Structure of Journalistic Writing

Besides academic writing, there are other forms of professional writing, such as **journalism** (news writing and reporting), that you probably encounter on a daily basis. If you read the newspaper or a weekly or monthly magazine, then you've already come across many different types of writing. In this section, you will examine two types of newspaper articles, the feature story and the column. As you read both, consider what the unique structure of each offers the reader.

## ▲▼▲ Examining a Feature Story

A **feature story** is a newspaper article that presents and discusses a timely issue. It does not follow the same format as the essay or textbook chapter. News writers know that they must "hook" their readers with an interesting opening statement. Once they snag their audience, they must provide manageable "bites" of information because busy readers are probably reading their papers over morning coffee. In fact,

Notes

that's one of the reasons the paragraphs are short, sometimes only a sentence or two in length.

Another reason for the short paragraphs has to do with the way a newspaper is laid out into **columns** (several long vertical rows of writing on a news page). Newspaper columns are long and thin, so paragraphs must be kept short. Otherwise, a paragraph might go on for an entire column, which could result in readers losing their place in the reading. Finally, journalistic style doesn't call for the same level of explanation and development that academic style requires, so shorter paragraphs are acceptable.

The feature story, "Modern Marriage" by William R. Macklin, appeared in *The Sacramento Bee* newspaper. In it, Macklin compares traditional matrimony, meaning marriage, to other forms of commitment.

Terms and definitions:

par. 1 *companionate:* harmonious; *marital fidelity:* faithfulness in marriage.

par. 2 *jibe:* agree; *archaic:* ancient.

par. 5 *mandate:* command; *diligent:* hardworking.

par. 8 *think tank:* group formed to solve a problem.

par. 14 *clans:* family groups united by common interests.

par. 15 *Industrial Revolution:* a surge in the economy in the late 18th century resulting from the use of machinery; *gender roles:* expected behavior for males or females.

par. 16 *socializing:* behavioral training for social situations.

par. 24 *protracted:* drawn out.

par. 28 *matrimonial contracts:* signed marriage agreements.

par. 29 *monogamy:* commitment to one partner.

par. 30 *unsavory:* offensive.

par. 31 *paradigm:* pattern, model, or example.

## Modern Marriage
*by William R. Macklin*

This feature story appeared in *The Sacramento Bee* newspaper, January 30, 1999.

1   In theory, at least, few things in modern life are as uncomplicated as traditional matrimony. A devoted couple take a vow to love, honor and

comfort, and then after champagne toasts and a toss of the bride's bouquet, they head off for a lifetime of *companionate* love and *marital fidelity.*

2   But theory and reality don't always *jibe,* and so it's no surprise that old-fashioned matrimony has its critics, observers who say that the institution of marriage is so *archaic* and unworkable that it's time to throw out the whole thing.

3   Nancy Saunders, a psychologist who has a family practice in the Philadelphia area, is one of them. . . .

4   "Society can no longer support what we think of as marriage," says Saunders. "When marriages come crashing to an end, as 50 percent of them do, there is a sense that the couple failed. That's not really true."

5   Saunders, who is divorced, says it's unrealistic to expect couples to balance contemporary work demands and heightened desires for personal happiness against a lifelong marital *mandate* to be faithful lovers, *diligent* parents and tireless helpmates.

6   That might have worked 100 years ago, when lifespans were shorter, or 50 years ago, when the majority of married women were economically dependent on their husbands, or even 30 years ago, when getting home on time for dinner was a daily priority, Saunders suggests. Now, she says, the traditional requirement that couples remain together "in sickness and in health . . . as long as you both shall live," often masks long years of bitter unhappiness.

7   Saunders believes that long-term, committed relationships still are the best hope for the care and support of children. But she favors doing away with traditional matrimony. Instead, she suggests individualized marriage contracts that would allow couples to custom-design their relationships with the full support and recognition of the state.

8   For Linda Chavez, head of a Washington *think tank* that studies family issues, however, the problem is not that traditional marriage doesn't work. It's that people don't work hard enough at traditional marriage.

9   The president of the conservative Center for Equal Opportunity in Washington, Chavez resents the suggestion that marriage is a failing institution.

10   "Perhaps what we really need is for people to rethink their sense of responsibility and consider more than their personal happiness," says Chavez, who has been married for 31 years. "I think that marriage as an institution has worked quite well, especially for raising children."

11   That's not surprising, given that marriage began as a way of protecting and supporting the young.

12   George Becker, a sociologist at Vanderbilt University in Nashville and

*Notes*

Notes

a specialist in the sociology of the family, says that early Western civilizations viewed marriage as a way to provide stability and safety for children during their long maturation period.

13   Not because people loved babies, but because children were a crucial source of labor.

14   "Early *clans* farmed the land and needed a lot of workers," Becker says. "And so you essentially needed a relationship that would ensure having children and make sure that they survived to provide the labor."

15   The concept of romantic love as the basis for marriage was virtually unknown to most working people before the 18th century, and the nuclear family emerged only in the 19th century, after the *Industrial Revolution,* Becker says. As a result, marriage has been slow to accommodate shifting personal expectations or to anticipate changes in *gender roles.*

16   "We are not adequately *socializing* men to pick up the slack around the house," Becker says. "It's a social lag. So many women are realizing, 'Hey, who needs this guy? I am doing everything by myself, earning a living, and then coming home and cleaning up the house.' It's no longer enough for a man to go out and get the bacon. He now has to cook it and help clean up after."

17   And what became of marriage as a public trust?

18   Becker says increased mobility and the growth of a national "cult of individuality" have left most marriages isolated from the cultural and societal pressures that have historically enforced the standards expressed in the traditional marriage vow.

19   That didn't happen to John and Vee Stanbach.

20   They were born one week apart in Wildwood Crest, N.J., met on the boardwalk when they were 17, and got married after a five-year courtship.

21   They believe, fiercely, in traditional marriage, indeed view it as a public trust, and say they would never do anything to lose the respect of their community.

22   The Stanbachs are 78 and have been married 55 years.

23   "A lot of our friends have been married 50 years and better," Vee says.

24   The Stanbachs say their marriage has survived because they avoid *protracted* arguments, rarely spend time apart, and never forget, as Vee says, that "marriage is forever."

25   And, they feel that the failure of a marriage, any marriage, is a cause for sadness.

26   "It breaks my heart that they couldn't persevere and work things out," says Vee.

27   What worked for the Stanbachs probably would work for most cou-

Notes

28. In the long run, though, the only way to help modern couples be happier is to "get rid of this huge muck we call marriage," Saunders says, and to allow couples to enter into *matrimonial contracts* that lay out the exact terms of their relationship.

29. Saunders says that such contracts—which might or might not include *monogamy,* lifelong commitment, or even living in the same home—should be entirely legal and that divorce action should take into account the terms of such contracts.

30. Saunders says that parenting contracts would be a strong start toward establishing a new type of marital bond based on the idea that couples have a right to dictate the terms of their marriages, even when those terms seem *unsavory* or troubling to those outside the relationship.

31. "We need a *paradigm* shift," she says. "We would do ourselves and society a tremendous favor if we would ask, 'What are the realistic tasks a committed relationship should accomplish? . . . What should a marriage have to do to last through all the changes?'"

## ▲▼▲ A Closer Look at the Parts

Although it doesn't have the same structure as the essay or textbook chapter, the newspaper article does contain some of the same components. All contain an introduction, body, and conclusion.

### ▼ Activity

#### Labeling the Parts

Go back through "Modern Marriage" and in the "Notes" column label the introduction, body, and conclusion. (Remember, an introduction may be longer than one paragraph.)

## The Introduction Is Called the Lead

While the essay contains a more formal introduction, a newspaper article begins with what is called the **lead.** The lead, the opening statement of an article, is often an intriguing or dynamic sentence or two designed to interest the reader. Other times, it is a statement of fact or the main point of the article. Without a clever or intriguing lead, newspaper writers risk

*Notes*

losing their audience. In "Modern Marriage," Macklin presents a lead with a twist.

### ▼ Activities

#### Examining the Lead

1. Review the opening two paragraphs of "Modern Marriage." How does Macklin attempt to draw in the reader? After reading paragraph one, what did you think the article would be about? When you read the second paragraph, how did your view change?

2. Read a front-page newspaper story from today's paper. Write down the lead. How has the writer tried to draw you into the article? What does the lead suggest the article will be about? Is the lead similar or different from the lead in Macklin's article?

#### Identifying the Thesis

Now that you've examined the introduction/lead, in your own words, write down the thesis of "Modern Marriage." What does the introduction suggest the article will be about?

## The Body Paragraphs Are Shorter

The body paragraphs of a newspaper article are shorter than those appearing in an essay. Some paragraphs, in fact, may be only a sentence long. As in the essay, there are paragraph breaks to identify when new ideas are presented. But there are paragraph breaks for other reasons as well:

- to set off a quotation or a set of facts,
- to transition the reader from one idea to another,
- to emphasize a certain point, or
- to simply keep the paragraphs short.

In "Modern Marriage" Macklin begins a new paragraph each time he presents someone else's point of view. He also begins new paragraphs to emphasize quotations and to help readers make the transition from one idea to another. Keep in mind, too, that paragraphs in journalistic writing don't always contain topic sentences. Instead of identifying topic sentences when you read a news story, you should identify main ideas.

### ▼ Activity

#### Identifying Main Ideas

Review the body paragraphs in "Modern Marriage." Complete the tasks that follow.

1. Macklin includes several people's points of view on marriage in his article. In the article, draw lines between each point of view presented. Then in your notebook, list the people Macklin refers to and their points of view. What does each believe about marriage?

2. In addition, make a Specific Support list. Read through the article again and jot down examples, quotations, and any other evidence used to support the main ideas of the article.

## The Conclusion

In the conclusion of a journalistic piece, writers try to bring their ideas full circle. Usually, the journalistic piece will end with a final thought or quotation, rather than with a summary of the main points.

### ▼ Activities

#### Examining the Conclusion

Review the conclusion of "Modern Marriage." Explain how Macklin concludes his feature story. Does Macklin's conclusion emphasize a particular point of view of marriage? Or does Macklin's article summarize the various views?

#### Comparing the Structure of Academic and Journalistic Writing

1. Compare the structures of "Modern Marriage" and "Romantic Love." How are their shapes similar? How are they different?

2. Now compare the structures of "Modern Marriage" and another newspaper article. How are their shapes similar? How are they different? What have you learned about newspaper articles that you didn't know before?

## ▲▼▲ The Writer's Purpose and Audience

The journalist has the same goal as any other writer—to convey a particular message to the reader. In "Modern Marriage," Macklin pre-

Notes

sents various sides of an issue to get readers to think about and perhaps reconsider their views on the issue of marriage. By quoting a variety of experts, it's clear that Macklin intends to present a range of views. Still, there may be a clue to his own perspective in the way in which he presents the "experts." Consider Macklin's perspective as you answer the questions that follow.

### ▼ Questions for Critical Thought
#### "Modern Marriage"

1. According to Macklin, what do critics say about marriage?
2. What does psychologist Nancy Saunders believe about traditional marriage? What does she suggest as an alternative?
3. Does Linda Chavez, President of the Center for Equal Opportunity, agree with Saunders? What does Chavez believe?
4. In the article, sociologist George Becker explains early Western views of marriage. How did early Western marriages differ from modern marriages?
5. Did romantic love play a part in the mate selection process in early Western civilization? Why? Why not?
6. What is John and Vee Stanbach's position on marriage? Do you agree or disagree?
7. Psychologist Saunders believes in marriage contracts. What might be negotiated in such a contract? How might the contract work?
8. Consider each of the experts and their perspectives. Who does Macklin quote most often? Which expert does he begin with? Which does he end with? Which does he emphasize most? What message do you think Macklin is conveying?

#### Journal Assignment
#### Making the Writing-Reading-Critical Thinking Connection

Consider the differing views on marriage in "Modern Marriage." Is marriage outdated as Saunders believes? Or is it worth keeping as the Stanbachs believe? Are there other ways to handle a long-term, committed relationship? Would any other options work just as well if not better than marriage? In your notebook write out your view on marriage.

## ▲▼▲ Examining a Newspaper Column

A **column** is an article in which a **columnist** (writer) expresses his or her own views on current issues, events, or concerns. Many newspapers have columnists who write opinion pieces on a daily or weekly basis for their papers. Some columnists—like the late Mike Royko—express strong opinions on controversial issues, like capital punishment or gun control. Others—like syndicated columnist Dave Barry—write humorous pieces on the human condition.

The newspaper column is shaped like other news articles, beginning with a lead that draws the reader into the story. It is followed by short paragraphs that usually contain a combination of discussion, dialogue, and evidence. Such articles are written to inform, explain, persuade, or sometimes simply to entertain. The column that follows appeared in *The Daily Northwestern,* a publication of Northwestern University. Writer Maggie Bandur offers a blend of discussion and dialogue laced with humor as she challenges women to defy female stereotyping.

Terms and definitions:

par. 1 *Victoria's Secret catalog:* a mail order catalog specializing in women's undergarments and lingerie; *objectification of women:* the treatment of women as objects; *scantily clad:* barely clothed.

par. 2 *antiquated:* outdated; *stereotypes of women:* oversimplified patterns of belief about women.

par. 3 *ogling:* staring; *not synonymous with:* not the same as; *fared:* done.

par. 4 *defy:* go against.

par. 5 *credence:* validity.

### Women Play the Roles Men Want to See
*by Maggie Bandur*

This column appeared in *The Daily Northwestern,* Northwestern University, January 23, 1996.

1   A favorite assignment of media courses is to have students analyze advertisements. Without fail, some boy will bring in a picture from the *Victoria's Secret catalog* as an example of the *objectification of women.* Does it objectify women? Considering how many sex-starved, male

Notes

dorm residents steal the mailroom's copies to check out the *scantily clad* women wearing submissive, come-hither looks, I would have to say "yes." The male-dominated society's lack of respect for women is alive and well!

2   What is not always pointed out, but should be, is that the catalog is marketed to women. And this type of marketing apparently works. The women are just as excited as the men on the day it arrives. Many *antiquated* attitudes and *stereotypes of women* persist because men still have a lot of power. But what makes it hard to destroy the stereotypes is that some women still go along with them.

3   Sometimes, I'm one of those women. As much as I hate the fact that men think women are stupid, I have on occasion played dumb to get male assistance. As much as I am offended by male *ogling,* there have been times when I have worn tight clothing and endured the agony of heels so that men would pay attention to me. (Keep in mind, of course, that attention is *not synonymous with* being touched.) As saddened as I am at how many women will let men treat them horribly, I haven't *fared* much better. As much as I try not to give in to all the stereotypes and societal expectations, I sometimes do, but I don't think I am alone.

4   In high school, when my friends and I would go out to dinner, none of the girls would want the guys to see us actually eating. Ordering anything more than a salad and a Diet Coke would supposedly insure that all the boys would think you were a cow. Every once in a while, the other girls and I would agree that this was ridiculous, that we were hungry, and that we would order whatever we darn well pleased. We'd get to the table and I, like a fool, would order first. "Hamburger and chocolate milk shake, please." And then those traitors would all order salads and Diet Cokes. If four or five girls can't work together on a trip to a restaurant, can all womankind join together to *defy* male expectations? If everyone dressed comfortably, let themselves reach the weight their bodies wanted, and stubbornly refused to give men the time of day until they treated women with the respect they deserved, men would come around a whole helluva lot faster. But there is always someone who is going to order that Diet Coke.

5   Sometimes it's easier to play along, and some people will; but in the long run it's better for all women if you don't. Every woman who embraces a stereotype—even if it is as a tool to get ahead in the world that men have made harder for women—is giving that stereotype more *credence.*

6   It may take a while before I have the strength to resist every dictate of male society, but I am trying. I have almost accepted the fact that I

will always be forty to fifty pounds heavier than supermodels my height, and I can almost get through a large meal with a man without apologizing for eating. Small victories, I will admit, but at least it's a start.

*Notes*

## ▲▼▲ A Closer Look at the Parts

The writer's column is shaped like the feature story or other news article. It contains a lead, short paragraphs, and a conclusion.

### ▼ Activity

**Labeling the Parts**

Read "Women Play the Roles Men Want to See" a second time. In the "Notes" column, label the lead, body paragraphs, and conclusion. (Remember, an introduction may be longer than one paragraph.)

## The Lead

"Women Play the Roles Men Want to See" contains a lead that "snags" the readers and compels them to read. In fact, if readers read only the lead, they might believe the article was going to focus on one issue when it is in fact concerned with another.

### ▼ Activities

**Examining the Lead**

1. Review the lead in "Women Play the Roles Men Want to See." How does Bandur "hook" the reader in the opening paragraph? If you had read just the opening paragraph but not the body, what would you have believed the author was writing about?

2. Compare the leads in "Women Play the Roles Men Want to See" and "Modern Marriage." How are the two approaches similar? How are they different?

**Identifying the Thesis**

After examining the lead, write down in your own words the thesis of "Women Play the Roles Men Want to See." What does the full introduction (first two paragraphs) suggest this column will be about?

Notes

### The Body Paragraphs

Because Bandur uses a conversational approach (as though she's talking directly to the reader), she relies on discussion and personal examples in the body paragraphs to make her points. Review the body paragraphs to see which ones contain topic sentences.

▼ **Activity**

#### Identifying Main Ideas

In her column, Bandur makes several points about stereotypes and women. Drawing from topic sentences and/or paragraph ideas, make a list of the main points.

### The Conclusion

As you discovered in "Modern Marriage," the writer's goal in the journalistic piece (as in the essay or textbook chapter) is to bring ideas full circle. Such a piece ends with a final thought or quotation. A column ends less often with a summary.

▼ **Activities**

#### Examining the Conclusion

Return to the conclusion of "Women Play the Roles Men Want to See." Consider Bandur's approach to her conclusion. Does she emphasize a particular point in the conclusion? Or does she summarize the points she's made in the article?

#### Comparing the Shapes of Journalistic Writing

Compare the shape of "Women Play the Roles Men Want to See" to "Modern Marriage." How are their shapes similar? How are they different?

## ▲▼▲ The Writer's Purpose and Audience

Writers must think about their message and how best to communicate their ideas to specific audiences. Consider, for example, what you might say and how you might express yourself if you were writing a cover letter for your resumé. If you are writing a letter to a close friend, however, you will discuss different topics and use different vocabulary.

Similarly, Bandur carefully considered the message she wanted to communicate to her readers, and she presented that message with words and examples her intended audience would find interesting.

## ▼ Questions for Critical Thought

*"Women Play the Roles Men Want to See"*

1. According to Bandur, what do men expect women to look like?
2. Does Bandur believe that men are the only ones who try to make women match this stereotype? Explain why Bandur believes it's so hard to get rid of stereotypical views of women.
3. Bandur admits to having played into some of these stereotypes herself. Do you believe that women in society today defy or follow the expectations encouraged by images such as the stereotypical supermodel? Explain.
4. What is the main message of Bandur's column? Mark parts of the text that point to this message.
5. Describe the readers in Bandur's audience. Consider these questions as you describe the readers: Where was this column published? Who would relate best to her examples? What specific words from Bandur's column give us clues about her audience? Your answers to these questions should help you make some thoughtful guesses about the ages and interests of her readers.

> ### Journal Assignment
> *Making the Writing-Reading-Critical Thinking Connection*
> Explain what Bandur means when she says that it's "easier to play along" but "better for all women if you don't." Would you say this is useful advice for women? Respond honestly to the article.

## ▲▼▲ Learning to Summarize Essays and Textbook Chapters

Now that you've learned how academic and journalistic writing works, you're ready to learn how to summarize these forms. As you learn to summarize, you'll begin to produce condensed versions of documents for study purposes, for work place reports, and your own writing.

Notes

## What Is a Summary?

A **summary** is basically a *concise retelling of the main points of a longer piece of writing.* Your job in writing a summary is to relay the author's most important points without including your own opinion on the subject. (Although your opinion isn't included when writing a summary, your opinion is a welcome and important part of reading questions, journal responses, essays, and other assignments.)

## Points to Remember about Summaries

- Summaries should be much shorter than what you are summarizing.
- Summaries should include all main points and important supporting detail—not just what you liked best. Nonessential details and examples should be left out.
- Summaries should include, when possible, the author's name and the title of what you're summarizing (and the date and place of publication, if available).
- Summaries should be written in your own words, paraphrased, not copied—to avoid plagiarizing* the author's work. (You may include an occasional quotation for impact.)
- Summaries should not include your reactions to the text.

## A Sample Summary

To give you an idea of what a summary looks like and how it works, reread "Romantic Love" on pages 30–32. Then study this list of important points.

- Many Americans are influenced more by the notion of *romantic love* than any other concept of love.
- Romantic love is an idealized version of love, a fairy tale–like view of love with expectations to match.
- The problem is that people who see love only from this perspective may "fall in love with their own romantic ideas rather than with a real human being."

---

*Plagiarism is the act of using someone else's words as your own without giving proper credit to the author. If you use a word-for-word phrase or sentence from the original, you must place it in quotation marks.

- These people will find it nearly impossible to be happy with a mate since no one can fulfill their romantic notions.
- A mate may be expected to fulfill a stereotypical role in order to live up to his or her lover's ideal image of a mate.
- A female lover may expect her male lover to be the strong silent type, whereas a male lover may expect his female lover to be the passive yet charming type.
- Lovers who expect their mates to live up to stereotypes are bound to be disappointed when the mate begins displaying characteristics that go against the stereotypes.
- If not careful, these lovers may reject partner after partner since no one will ever fit the idealized version.
- Or these lovers may expect their mates to conform to the idealized image, an impossible and painful task.
- Romantic love isn't all bad. It can add delight to a relationship, especially in the beginning. But it should exist in a balance with other attributes such as intellect.

*Notes*

***Summary*** In his essay "Romantic Love," author Frank Cox explains that Americans are more influenced by the notion of romantic love—a fairy tale version of love—than by any other concept of love. According to Cox, those who view love solely from this perspective may "fall in love with their own romantic ideas rather than with a real human being." These people will idealize their relationships and may even expect partners to fulfill stereotypical images like the strong, silent type for men, or the passive-yet-charming type for women. When partners inevitably begin to display characteristics that go against the stereotypes, these people can't help but be disappointed. They may even try to force mates to conform to their ideal images. If not careful, these disappointed lovers will reject partner after partner since no one ever fits the ideal. Still, Cox sees romantic love as a positive part of a new relationship. But he cautions that as the relationship matures, a couple should move toward balancing romantic love with emotional, intellectual, social, and physical intimacy.*

—Opening statement includes author, title, and main idea.

—Quotation emphasizes main idea.

—Important supporting point follows.

—Most important points appear through summary in logical order.

—Author's conclusions are relayed.

---

*Note: Summaries may be more than one paragraph depending on the length of the original document. However, most of the summary assignments in this text call for a single paragraph.

Notes

## ▲▼▲ Summarizing Academic Writing

As you examined how the typical essay or textbook chapter is constructed, you discovered that general information appeared in certain places and specific information in others. You learned, for instance, that in most cases the introduction offers an overview of the essay or chapter, so it contains mainly general information.

You've learned, too, that each body paragraph usually (though not always) begins with a topic sentence, a general statement that tells what the paragraph will be about. This topic sentence is followed by details and examples, specific information that helps prove the main point of the paragraph. Learning to tell the difference between the general and specific statements is the first step in learning to summarize a piece of writing.

### Distinguishing between General and Specific Information

Most of the academic writing you'll encounter contains both general and specific information. General statements usually give the reader an overview of the essay or a particular paragraph. Specific statements offer examples, statistics, quotations, or other forms of evidence to support the more general statements. Why is it important for you to be able to distinguish between general and specific information? As you develop this skill, you'll begin to see how main ideas appear in various forms of writing. This will help you understand your readings, prepare for exams, and summarize. Reread this paragraph from the essay titled, "The Modern Family." Note: General information has been identified by a "G" in the "Notes" column while specific information has been identified by "S."

G ⎡
  ⎣
S ⎡
  ⎣
G ⎡
  ⎣

During the 1950s, the Cleavers on the television show "Leave It to Beaver" epitomized the American family. In 1960, over 70 percent of all American households were like the Cleavers: made up of a breadwinner father, a homemaker mother, and their kids. Today, "traditional" families with a working husband, [a homemaker], and one or more children make up less than 15 percent of the nation's households. And as America's families have changed, the image of the family portrayed on television has changed accordingly. . . .
—James Kirby Martin et al. *from* America and Its People

The topic sentence of this paragraph offers a general statement about what the authors believe a typical American family used to be like. This statement is followed by specific information in the form of statistics, "In 1960, over 70 percent of all American households were like the Cleavers," and a definition of the traditional American family, a breadwinner father, a homemaker mother, and their kids. The statistical information and definition are followed by a final general statement suggesting that images on television reflect changes in the American family.

▼ *Activity*

### *Distinguishing between General and Specific Information in "The Modern Family"*

1. Reread the paragraph below. (This is another paragraph from the essay, "The Modern Family.")

   Profound changes have reshaped American family life in recent years. In a decade, divorce rates doubled. The number of divorces today is twice as high as in 1966 and three times higher than in 1950. The rapid upsurge in the divorce rates contributed to a dramatic increase in the number of single-parent households. . . . The number of households consisting of a single woman and her children has tripled since 1960. A sharp increase in female-headed homes has been accompanied by a startling increase in the number of couples cohabitating outside of marriage. The number of unmarried couples living together has quadrupled since 1970.

2. Write "G" beside general statements and "S" beside specific statements.

Now that you have identified general and specific information in the paragraph, you are ready to do it in the essay that follows. This textbook excerpt appears in a section titled "Contemporary Marriage and the Family in the United States." As you read the textbook excerpt, consider which statements introduce ideas and which offer support. Also look for clues such as "for example" or "for instance" that might help you identify specific statements. These phrases usually mean a specific piece of information follows.

Terms and definitions:

par. 1 *revolutions:* radical changes; *feminism:* movement toward equal rights for women; *proliferation:* rapid increase.

par. 4 *dispels:* disproves

*Notes*

*Notes*

## Sexual Revolution, Cohabitation, and the Rise of Singles
*by William E. Thompson and Joseph V. Hickey*

This excerpt is from the textbook, *Society in Focus: The Essentials*.

1   The twentieth century has witnessed several *revolutions* in sexual norms and behaviors that have brought dramatic changes to courtship, marriage, and family relationships. The first occurred in the Roaring Twenties, with greater sexual freedom and more diverse marriage and family forms. More dramatic changes occurred in the 1960s due to the widespread availability of birth control pills, the youth protest movement, the reemergence of *feminism* and a *proliferation* of mass media images and messages that proclaimed the "joy of sex" (Stengel, 1986; Masters et al., 1988).

2   These changes brought dramatic increases in the rate of premarital sexual intercourse, beginning at earlier ages for both boys and girls. In 1990, for example, by age 15, one-quarter of females and one-third of males had had sexual intercourse, and by age 19, the figure was over 80 percent for both sexes (Miller and Moore, 1990). Likewise, the double standard that once tolerated greater sexual freedom for men than women loosened considerably, and rates of pregnancy and out-of-wedlock childbearing among young women aged 15 to 19—especially white women—increased dramatically (Hofferth et al., 1987; Beeghley, 1994; Masters et al., 1994). For example, in 1990, "The percentage of children born to unmarried parents had risen to 28 percent" (Seltzer, 1994:235).

3   One impact of the sexual revolution has been a major increase in **cohabitation,** *two people living together as husband and wife without being legally married.* Since the 1960s, Americans have become more tolerant of alternative lifestyles; the fear of sexually transmitted diseases has also encouraged many people to opt for long-term relationships that include cohabitation. Likewise, greater employment and educational opportunities for young people, economic hardships, the decision of large numbers of women to delay marriage to pursue careers, and higher divorce rates also have contributed to an increase in the number of unmarried couples living together. . . .

4   Between 1970 and 1993, the number of unmarried couples who lived together quadrupled, and in 1993, approximately 3.5 million couples, or 6 percent of the population, lived in this type of relationship (Bumpass and Sweet, 1989; U.S. Bureau of the Census, 1993a). Research *dispels* several popular stereotypes about cohabitation and the people who practice it. For example, cohabitation is not confined to college campuses; it is in fact more common among working couples.

Most cohabitants are young adults aged 35 or younger, but almost 7 percent are aged 65 and older. Moreover, although 53 percent have never married, 34 percent are divorced, and 40 percent of all cohabiting couples have one or more children present in the household (Spanier, 1983; Bumpass et al., 1989; Surra, 1990).

5      Likewise, the belief that living together as a form of "trial marriage" results in happier and more stable marriages is not supported. In fact, research shows slightly higher divorce rates for cohabitants who later marry as compared to other couples—perhaps not because of some flaw in cohabitation but because people who cohabit tend to have less conventional ideas and are less attached to traditional beliefs about marriage and the family, including the view that marriage is "for life" (Surra, 1990).

6      Researchers have also found cohabitation unions to be brief and unstable; most last a little more than a year. About one-third of all men and women in their thirties have lived with someone before marriage, a statistic that supports the view that cohabitation has become a new stage in the courtship process, one that for about half of all cohabitants is the final step before marriage (Gwartney-Gibbs, 1986). When cohabitant relationships dissolve, however, many men and women enter or reenter the singles populations.

7      Over the past few decades, the number of single adults, including the never married, the divorced, and the widowed, has increased dramatically. In the late 1980s, for example, there were over 22 million single-person households in the United States—almost a quarter of all households. Some of the rise can be attributed to a growing tendency for young adults to postpone marriage. For example, in 1960, 28 percent of women and 53 percent of men aged 20 to 24 were unmarried; by 1990, more than 61 percent of women and 79 percent of men in that age group were still singles (U.S. Bureau of the Census, 1990b). . . .

8      Widowhood has contributed to the growth in the singles populations since the elderly have become better able to care for themselves and maintain independent households. Divorce, however, has been much more significant, with "6 million of the 26.8 million rise in the number of singles between 1960 and 1979 due to divorce" (Lamanna and Riedmann, 1988:149).

Notes

## ▼ Activity

### Distinguishing between General and Specific Statements

1. Read "Sexual Revolution . . ." again, keeping the following questions in mind: What are the main (or general) statements? What are the specific statements, those containing support for main ideas?

Notes

2. Working with a partner, decide which are the general statements and clearly mark each with a "G." Next, decide which are the specific statements and mark each with an "S." Are you and your partner in agreement?

3. Write down any words or phrases (such as "for example") which indicated that specific support would follow.

## Identifying the Main Points

What if you were asked by your instructor to summarize or retell what you had learned from "Sexual Revolution, Cohabitation, and the Rise of Singles"? What would you say? You certainly wouldn't want to repeat the whole thing. And you wouldn't just randomly choose a few sentences to read. You would need to pick out the most important statements and *put them in your own words*. Although this may seem hard to do, with practice it'll become easier.

### ▼ Activity

#### Identifying Main Points in "Sexual Revolution . . ."

1. Look back at how you've marked general and specific statements in "Sexual Revolution, Cohabitation, and the Rise of Singles." Which statements appear to be the most important, or main ideas? Highlight only these statements and review them carefully. Leave out details.

2. Now set the excerpt aside and from memory make a list of these main ideas. (You don't need to quote them exactly. In fact, you should put these main points in your own words.)

3. Go back to the excerpt and double check to see that you've included all of the main points. Add necessary information to your list.

## Drafting the Summary

Once you have made a list of the main points, you are ready to begin writing your summary. A summary should

- open with a statement that introduces what is being summarized (including author and title),
- provide an overview of the piece,

- include all of the main points (even those you may not agree with),
- end with the author's conclusions on the subject.

### ▼ Activity

**Drafting a Summary of "Sexual Revolution..."**

Drawing from your list of main ideas, write a summary of "Sexual Revolution, Cohabitation, and the Rise of Singles." First, include the author, title, and main idea of the piece. Follow with the most important points. End with the author's conclusions on the subject.

## Revising the Summary

Once you have prepared a draft of your summary, it's a good idea to look at the article a final time to make sure you have accurately explained the main ideas as the author intended. If you discover that you have not explained an idea correctly, then you need to **revise** (rewrite) parts of your summary to more accurately reflect the main ideas presented in the original piece.

### ▼ Activity

**Revising Your Summary of "Sexual Revolution..."**

Return to "Sexual Revolution, Cohabitation, and the Rise of Singles." Compare the main ideas that you highlighted to those you have relayed in your summary. Have you explained the most important points accurately? If not, revise your summary to reflect the main ideas in the original.

## ▲▼▲ Summarizing Journalistic Writing

Earlier in this chapter you discovered the ways in which journalistic writing differs from academic writing. Most newspaper or magazine articles begin with a lead that is followed by short body paragraphs that may or may not have topic sentences. Such articles often conclude with a final remark or a quotation that circles back to the lead.

Notes

## Distinguishing between General and Specific Information

Because the body paragraphs of articles do not always contain topic sentences, summarizing articles is made easier when you begin by identifying general and specific information. Consider the general and specific information in paragraphs 1–6 from the feature article, "Modern Marriage" which begins on page 42. Then complete the following activity.

▼ **Activity**

### Distinguishing between General and Specific Information in "Modern Marriage"

1. Reread the first six paragraphs from "Modern Marriage."

2. Write "G" next to general statements and "S" next to specific statements.

3. Also write down any clues that suggest that specific information follows.

---

Now that you've had more practice in identifying general and specific information in a newspaper article, you're ready to practice your summary skills on the magazine article that follows. It's important to note that some journalistic pieces do follow the essay form. "Sex Has Many Accents," for example, does contain the elements of the academic essay. It has an introduction with a thesis, body paragraphs with topic sentences (for the most part), and a concluding comment. While the paragraphs are short, they still contain both general and specific information. As you read, think about which statements are general and which are specific.

### Sex Has Many Accents
*by Anastasia Toufexis*
*with reporting by Ulla Plon and Hiroko Tashiro*

This article appeared as a 1994 *Time* magazine cover story.

1   Around the world, there are almost as many ways to teach sex as there are languages. At the two extremes are the conservative attitude in Japan and the bold approach in Scandinavian countries.

2. The Japanese seem embarrassed to discuss sex. Parents avoid the subject, though their offspring, like adolescents everywhere, are obsessed with it. "My parents aren't stiffs," allows Ayumi Suzuki, 17, from Togane, near Tokyo, "but it's just not something to talk about with them. I just talk about it with friends." Admits Yumiko Kaga, the mother of two adolescent daughters: "We never discuss sex at home. I feel we should, but . . . I do remember giving my children a book on where babies come from."

3. Schools are just as uncomfortable teaching about sex, though instruction is mandated beginning at age 10 or 11. But the curriculums resemble animal-reproduction lessons in biology class, with menstruation and ejaculation the primary topics. Teenagers say they learn about sex mostly from magazines and their peers.

4. Japanese teens are chaste compared with American youngsters. While a quarter of U.S. girls and a third of U.S. boys have had sex by age 15, in Japan it is just 4% for girls and 6% for boys.

5. "Why are Japanese children so good?" asks Hisayo Arai of the Japanese Association for Sex Education. "Partly because they're so busy with their college entrance examinations. Also, people are always keeping a watch on each other." While there are no religious taboos against premarital sex, Japanese culture has strongly urged youngsters, particularly girls, to wait until marriage. That tradition is slipping, however, because the average age for marriage among women has risen to 26, from 24 in 1970.

6. Whether adolescents become sexually active seems to depend to a large extent on peer pressure at a particular school. Some schools go so far as to ban dating, but at others "it's embarrassing if you haven't had sex, and you're under pressure to lose your virginity quickly," says Tsunetsugu Munakata, associate professor of health at Tsukuba University. "At one school I heard students would go to love hotels in their uniforms," declares Tetsuya Lizuka, 19, who lost his virginity four years ago, an experience "that made me the center of attention in high school."

7. In contrast to Japan's youngsters, Scandinavia's teens almost take sex for granted. "There is not much talk about sex between teenagers," notes Stefan Laack of the Swedish Association for Sex Information, "yet it is widely accepted that they sleep with their boyfriends or girlfriends in their homes."

8. Scandinavians believe that teens may be more receptive to sex education at school than at home. "When teenagers get in contact with their sexuality, they are about to break loose from their parents," says Laack. "This is only natural and shouldn't be disturbed."

*Notes*

Notes

9   Rather than confining instruction to special classes, schools integrate lessons throughout the curriculum. In Denmark sexual matters must be discussed whenever appropriate in any class. So too in Sweden, where sex education has been compulsory since 1956. Starting when the children are between ages 7 and 10, it is formally incorporated into different subjects. "In biology, for example, the physical side is discussed," explains Peter Karlberg of Sweden's Ministry of Education. Courses that cover geography, history or politics tackle ethics and gender roles. In Finnish schools, all 15-year-olds receive an introductory sexual package put together by the Population and Family Welfare Federation. Its contents: an information brochure, a condom and a cartoon love story.

10  The intense preparation has not pushed youngsters to having sex earlier. In Sweden youngsters typically lose their virginity at age 17, exactly the same age as 15 years ago.

### ▼ Activity

***Distinguishing between General and Specific Statements in "Sex Has Many Accents"***

1. Begin by labeling the basic parts—introduction, body, and conclusion.

2. Read the essay a second time, but as you read, mark general statements with a "G." Then identify the statements that contain specific information and mark each with "S."

3. Write down any clues that suggest that specific information follows.

### Identifying the Main Points

In distinguishing between general and specific information, you are preparing to write a summary. The main ideas in a journal article usually appear in general statements just as in academic writing.

### ▼ Activity

***Identifying Main Points in "Sex Has Many Accents"***

1. Look back at how you've marked general and specific statements in "Sex Has Many Accents." Which statements appear to be the most im-

portant, or main ideas? Highlight only these statements and review them carefully. Leave out the details.

2. Set the article aside and from memory write a list of the main points. (Don't worry about getting them down exactly. These should be in your own words.)

3. Return to the article and check to see if you've included all of the main points on your list. Add any you left out.

## Drafting the Summary

As you know, the next step in writing a summary is to put the main points into paragraph form. Once again, a summary should begin with a statement that gives an overview of the article and includes the article's author and title. In order for a summary to be effective, it must include all of the main points and end with the author's conclusions.

▼ **Activity**

### Drafting a Summary of "Sex Has Many Accents"

Working from your list of main ideas, write your summary. First, introduce the author, title, and overall main idea of the piece. Follow with the most important points. End your summary with the author's conclusions on the subject.

## Revising the Summary

After writing a draft of your summary, it's important to return to the article and check to make sure that you have explained the author's main ideas accurately.

▼ **Activity**

### Revising Your Summary of "Sex Has Many Accents"

Review "Sex Has Many Accents" again. Compare the main ideas you highlighted earlier to those that appear in your summary. Have you included the most important points? If not, revise your summary to agree with the original.

Notes

## ▲▼▲ Practicing Summary Skills

Knowing how to summarize will help you at work, at home, and in your classes. On the job, you may be asked to summarize documents and reports. At home, you might have to summarize the problems you have had with a product in a letter to the Better Business Bureau. In your classes, you will probably be asked to write summaries of textbook chapters or essays. Writing summaries of textbook chapters you have been assigned will also help you strengthen study skills and prepare for tests.

### ▼ Activity

**Put Your New Summary Skills to Work**

1. Choose a section from one of your textbooks from another class and then write a short summary. Be prepared to show your class/instructor the actual section in your textbook (and how you marked it up), and the summary. (This is a good way to get a jump on your reading for other classes.)

2. Choose a magazine or newspaper article, and then write a short summary. Be prepared to show your class/teacher the actual article (and how you marked it up) and the summary.

## ▲▼▲ Time to Reflect

### Journal Assignment

**Your Progress as a Writer, Reader, and Critical Thinker**

Spend a few minutes *reviewing* sections of the chapter that you found interesting or helpful. Look back at any notes you took, comments in the "Notes" column, journals, activities, and readings. *Think* about your summary skills and how they are improving already. *Write* down those things you've learned from this chapter that you hadn't known before. In what ways will you *apply* this new knowledge?

## ▲▼▲ Summary of Chapter 2

Notes

In Chapter 2, as you considered the themes of dating and marriage, you
- examined the structure of essays, textbook chapters, and newspaper articles,
- practiced distinguishing between general and specific ideas, and
- practiced summarizing essays, textbook chapters, and newspaper articles.

Notes

###  Understanding Verbs

*Reviewing Verbs*
*Supplying Verbs*
*Describing Verbs*
*Defining Verbs*

As you learned in Chapter 1, the sentence work in this text will probably be a little different from sentence work you've done before. The exercises in each chapter focus on the same topics discussed in the body of each chapter so that you can continue to think and learn about issues that relate to your writing. The exercises have also been organized so that you can gain the skills to tackle some sentence challenges unique to each writing assignment. For example, when you are working on the Hero essay in Chapter 5, you'll also be studying how to use pronouns since you'll need to use pronouns effectively when you discuss your hero.

To begin with, though, you'll be introduced to a few necessary basics: verbs (in this chapter and Chapter 3), subjects and subject-verb agreement (in Chapter 4). You don't need to memorize fancy grammar terms, but you should feel confident about a few key terms and few key points about sentence structure. The work in this text will help you do that.

### *Reviewing Verbs*

You might say that the **verb** is the heart of a sentence. It may tell what action is occurring, connect some descriptive information to the subject of the sentence, or tell you when the action is taking place.

> *Examples:* (verbs are underlined)
> The woman <u>wrote</u> to Dear Abby.
> Dear Abby <u>gave</u> advice.
> The woman <u>canceled</u> the wedding.
> The man <u>was</u> sad.

Practice supplying and identifying verbs.

Rewrite sentences 1–9 adding verbs that make sense. (Try not to add the same verb to more than one sentence.) Underline the verbs.

Chapter 2  The Structure of Writing and How to Summarize Texts

*"To Commit or Not to Commit"*

Notes

1. Mary and Joe ___*fell*___ in love when they met in Paris.
2. One day, Joe _____ at the top of his lungs, "Marry me, Mary!"
3. But Mary _____ having many boyfriends.
4. She _____ the idea of settling down right away.
5. Joe _____ this was strange.
6. He _____ all women wanted to get married as soon as possible.
7. Mary _____ Joe to wait for a few years and let her date for a while longer.
8. Joe _____ tired of waiting after about six months.
9. Mary and Joe _____ up.

Identifying and understanding verbs will help you talk about and gain better control over your sentences.

## *Supplying Verbs*

Write all the sentences in the following exercise (even the sentences that aren't missing any words), adding the necessary verbs. There is more than one way to complete some of these sentences. Experiment with verbs that fit the best. Your finished product should be three paragraphs. (Be sure to *indent* your paragraphs. This means that the beginning of each paragraph should be "pushed in" five spaces so that your reader will know that a new paragraph is starting. You can use your "tab" key on your computer keyboard to indent.)

   Some verbs consist of more than one part. If a part of a verb has been provided for you, it has already been underlined. And when complete verbs have been supplied, they have been underlined as well.

   Underline every verb in the paragraphs you write.

### *Monogamy vs. Polygamy*

Most people <u>think</u> monogamy <u>means</u> staying with one partner (a husband, a wife, a boyfriend, or a girlfriend). The opposite <u>would be</u> polygamy which <u>means</u> having more than one partner at a time (dating or being married to several people at one time). <u>Are</u> these definitions

Section I   Establishing the Connections

Notes

*scientifically* accurate? And <u>are</u> humans <u>meant</u> to be monogamous? According to Deborah Blum, a science writer, scientists <u>have made</u> a lot of interesting discoveries in this area.

   Blum _____ that monogamy <u>doesn't</u> necessarily _____ anything to do with sex. Monogamy _____ more about commitment. That <u>is</u>, according to scientists, monogamous animal couples <u>may</u> <u>sleep</u> around, but they always <u>come</u> home to each other. They _____ for the babies together. They <u>defend</u> their homes and babies together, etc. Interestingly, scientists _____ that only 3% of the world's mammals _____ monogamous. Blum <u>reports</u>, "Birds, lizards, and some loyal fish species a<u>re</u> the most likely to stay together." And she <u>adds</u>, "Before the rise of moralistic religions, such as Christianity, more than 70 percent of the world's societies <u>could be classified</u> as polygamous."

   You can often _____ which species <u>are</u> monogamous just by looking at them. Monogamous couples _____ alike, so much so that without looking at their sex organs, you probably <u>can't</u> _____ them apart! Polygamous animals, on the other hand, <u>will</u> _____ quite different. One example of a polygamous animal <u>is</u> the peacock. Male peacocks, for instance, _____ beautiful feathers whereas the females _____ quite plain feathers. And polygamous animals _____ very different roles. Females _____ care of the young. Males _____ their families from danger. Scientists <u>point</u> out that humans <u>don't look</u> monogamous. Men usually _____ larger bodies. Women <u>tend</u> to have softer curves and smaller frames. But consider this . . . our bodies <u>seem</u> to be more alike now than they <u>were</u> 300,000 years ago when "male skeletons <u>were</u> nearly twice the size of female ones." We <u>seem</u> to be becoming more alike!

**Your Own Work**   Copy part or all of a journal or summary you completed in this chapter. Then underline the verbs you find in your sentences. Exchange your sentences with a classmate. Have you underlined all the verbs? Have you underlined the correct words? Discuss any confusing sentences with your classmates and your instructor.

## Describing Verbs

Notes

Now that you've had some practice at identifying and supplying verbs, you'll work on describing and defining verbs.

**Quick Quiz:** (Be sure to look at your paragraphs in the sections "Reviewing Verbs" and "Supplying Verbs" when you are looking for the answers to this quiz.)

a. Can a verb be made up of more than one word?

b. Can a sentence have more than one verb?

## Defining Verbs

Try your hand at formulating the rest of the following definition:

Verbs are words which _____.

Don't look up the answer in a dictionary or grammar book! Look at what you've done in the sentence work in this chapter and develop a definition in your own words.

Share your definition with at least one classmate and see if you can improve your own definition.

This is your first attempt to define *verb* on your own. Consider this a "working definition." That is, you'll be changing and improving this definition in the next chapter.

# Examining the Reading Process

**CHAPTER 3**

*Main Topics*

- Examining the PARTS of the reading process
- Practicing the reading process
- Responding to texts
- Using the dictionary and building your vocabulary
- Reading about people's roles in society
- Identifying verbs and manipulating verb tense

## Calvin and Hobbes — by Bill Watterson

Calvin and Hobbes, Universal Press Syndicate, *There's Treasure Everywhere*, 1996

Reading is the process of gathering meaning from the letters, words, and sentences printed on a page (or a computer screen). In this chapter, you'll learn strategies that will help you better understand and remember what you read. In addition, as you read and absorb information about style, vocabulary, and writing technique, you'll begin to apply what you've learned to your own writing. Quite simply, the more you practice your reading skills, the better your reading and writing will become.

*Notes*

## ▲▼▲ The PARTS of an Effective Reading Process

Experienced readers aren't necessarily speed readers. In fact, they take their time when reading and often reread to reach understanding. They engage in a **reading process,** a series of steps that help them comprehend (understand) and retain (remember) what they have read. This process may be divided into five basic **PARTS,** or stages. As you begin to practice using the PARTS of the reading process, you will become a more effective reader.

### Preview

Experienced readers **preview** their reading by looking at author, title, length, and topic sentences. They also review any subheadings, charts, pictures, or diagrams that accompany the reading. This previewing helps prepare them for the information to come.

### Anticipate

Experienced readers know they will need to read the text more than once, so during the preview stage, they **anticipate** (expect or guess) what the reading will be about. Then as they read through the first time, they look forward to what will come next. Readers who have these expectations when they read stay interested and focused.

### Read and Reread

During their first **read,** successful readers move through the text quickly. They jot down questions and note words they don't recognize, although they won't answer these questions or look up definitions yet. Then they **reread** slowly, answer their own questions, and look up the meanings of any words they don't know or haven't figured out. At this stage, readers also take the time to highlight important points and make written comments in the margins of the reading or on note paper.

Notes

### Think Critically

Experienced readers also **think critically** about their reading. They discuss important points or answer critical thinking questions as they begin to "make sense" of the reading. These activities help readers understand the author's message and purpose, remember important ideas, and examine writing techniques which they can use in their own writing.

### Summarize

Finally, experienced readers take the time to **summarize** (in their own words) so that they can easily review the main points of their reading.

This process may seem like hard work if you've never done it before. However, as you become a more experienced reader, you'll begin to use the PARTS of the reading process without even thinking about them.

---

**Journal Assignment**

**Responding to Calvin and Susie**

Review Bill Watterson's "Calvin and Hobbes" comic strip on page 72. Which of the two characters, Calvin or Susie, appears to be the more experienced reader? How does each character feel about books? Are both views valid? What have you learned about reading and about readers from this strip?

---

## ▲▼▲ Engaging in the Reading Process

To help you see how the reading process works, you'll look at one reader's Preview, Anticipation, and first reading of "The Struggle to Be an All-American Girl," written by Elizabeth Wong. After reviewing the first two parts of the reading process, you'll read the article yourself. Then you'll complete the stages of the reading process by Rereading, Thinking Critically about, and Summarizing the writer's main points.

### One Reader's Preview and Anticipation

(The reader's thoughts are in brackets)

*Preview* [This column appeared in the newspaper, so I expect short paragraphs and few topic sentences. I'll look quickly at the *title, author, and the first two paragraphs to get an idea of what the column is about.*] The title suggests that the writer is struggling because she wants to be an "all-American girl." As I look over the column, I can see that the writer's mom made both of her children attend Chinese school. Also, the writer's first name is Elizabeth, but her last name is Wong. So her parents may be from China, but she was probably born in America. Maybe that's why there's a struggle.

***Anticipate*** Overall, Wong seems to be frustrated. She wasn't happy going to Chinese school.

[*As I read, I'll underline words that I plan to look up. I'll also place questions in the "Notes" column that I plan to answer when I read through the second time.*]

## One Reader's First Read

Following the preview and anticipation stages of the process, the reader reads through the column quickly, jotting questions in the margin and highlighting or underlining unknown words.

### ▼ Activity

#### The First Read

Read "The Struggle to Be an All-American Girl." As you read, look at one reader's questions in the "Notes" column and notice which vocabulary words the reader has underlined.

### The Struggle to Be an All-American Girl
*by Elizabeth Wong*

This column appeared in the *Los Angeles Times* in 1980.

1   It's still there, the Chinese school on Yale Street where my brother and I used to go. Despite the new coat of paint and the high wire fence, the school I knew 10 years ago remains remarkably, <u>stoically</u> the same.

2   Every day at 5 P.M., instead of playing with our fourth- and fifth-grade friends or sneaking out to the empty lot to hunt ghosts and animal bones, my brother and I had to go to Chinese school. No amount

**Notes**

stoically: seemingly indifferent to or unaffected by pleasure or pain

## Notes

*I'm wondering why Wong's mother insisted they learn Chinese against their will.*

of kicking, screaming, or pleading could <u>dissuade</u> my mother, who was solidly determined to have us learn the language of our heritage.

3   Forcibly, she walked us the seven long, hilly blocks from our home to school, depositing our defiant tearful faces before the stern principal. My only memory of him is that he swayed on his heels like a palm tree, and he always clasped his impatient twitching hands behind his back. I recognized him as a repressed maniacal child killer, and knew that if we ever saw his hands we'd be in big trouble.

4   We all sat in little chairs in an empty auditorium. The room smelled like Chinese medicine, and imported faraway mustiness. Like ancient mothballs or dirty closets. I hated that smell. I favored crisp new scents. Like the soft French perfume that my American teacher wore in public school.

5   Although the emphasis at the school was mainly language—speaking, reading, writing—the lessons always began with an exercise in politeness. With the entrance of the teacher, the best student would tap a bell and everyone would get up, <u>kowtow</u>, and chant, "sing san ho," the phonetic for "How are you, teacher?"

6   Being ten years old, I had better things to learn than <u>ideographs</u> copied painstakingly in lines that ran right to left from the top of a *moc but,* a real ink pen that had to be held in an awkward way if blotches were to be avoided. After all, I could do the multiplication tables, name the satellites of Mars, and write reports on "Little Women" and "Black Beauty." Nancy Drew, my favorite book heroine, never spoke Chinese.

7   The language was a source of embarrassment. More times than not, I had tried to <u>disassociate</u> myself from the nagging loud voice that followed me wherever I wandered in the nearby American supermarket outside Chinatown. The voice belonged to my grandmother, a fragile woman in her seventies who could outshout the best of the street vendors. Her humor was <u>raunchy</u>, her Chinese rhythmless, patternless. It was quick, it was loud, it was unbeautiful. It was not like the quiet, lilting romance of French or the gentle refinement of the American South. Chinese sounded <u>pedestrian</u>. Public.

*Why does Wong think Chinese is pedestrian? What does she mean by pedestrian?*

8   In Chinatown, the comings and goings of hundreds of Chinese on their daily tasks sounded <u>chaotic</u> and <u>frenzied</u>. I did not want to be thought of as mad, as talking gibberish. When I spoke English, people nodded at me, smiled sweetly, said encouraging words. Even the people in my culture would cluck and say that I'd do well in life. "My, doesn't she move her lips fast," they would say, meaning that I'd be able to keep up with the world outside Chinatown.

9   My brother was even more <u>fanatical</u> than I about speaking English. He was especially hard on my mother, criticizing her, often cruelly, for

her pidgin speech—smatterings of Chinese scattered like chop suey in her conversation. "It's not 'What it is,' Mom," he'd say in exasperation. "It's 'What is it, what is it, what is it!'" Sometimes Mom might leave out an occasional "the" or "a," or perhaps a verb of being. He would stop her in mid-sentence: "Say it again, Mom. Say it right." When he tripped over his own tongue, he'd blame it on her: "See, Mom, it's all your fault. You set a bad example."

10   After two years of writing with a *moc but* and reciting words with multiples of meanings, I finally was granted a cultural divorce. I was permitted to stop Chinese school.

11   I thought of myself as <u>multicultural</u>. I preferred tacos to egg rolls; I enjoyed Cinco de Mayo more than Chinese New Year.

12   At last, I was one of you; I wasn't one of them.

13   Sadly, I still am.

### Notes

*Why was Wong's brother so bothered by his mother's mistakes in English?*

*Why was she allowed to stop going to Chinese school? Why is she sad at the end? Didn't she get what she wanted?*

## Reread, Think Critically, and Summarize

***Reread*** Following a quick first read, the reader reads the column a second time, slowing down to consider the writer's meaning. Then the reader looks up meanings of unfamiliar terms, and answers her own questions from the first reading.

### ▼ Activity

#### Reread

Reread Wong's essay, looking up the meanings of any words you don't know or can't figure out. Write definitions in your notebook, in the "Notes" column, or on notecards. Also, write responses to the first reader's questions in the "Notes" column.

***Think Critically*** As you read through the article a second time, you should have begun to carefully consider the writer's message and purpose. This stage of the process also involves answering critical thinking questions and/or discussing important points with classmates after you have completed your second read.

### ▼ Questions for Critical Thought

#### "The Struggle to Be an All-American Girl"

1. Why would Wong's mother have wanted her children to attend Chinese school?

Notes

2. Why might Wong have rebelled against going to Chinese school? In your opinion, should she have been forced to attend? Why? Why not?

3. What are some of the reasons why Wong seemed to be embarrassed by her grandmother's Chinese? Are these the same reasons why Wong's brother became upset when their mother made mistakes in English?

4. The title of the article suggests that Wong was "struggling to be an all-American girl." What does she mean by this? Did she reach her goal? What evidence does she offer as proof?

5. What does Wong mean in paragraph 10 when she says, "I finally was granted a cultural divorce"? Does the word "divorce" accurately describe what happened?

6. Why does Wong use the word "sadly" in paragraph 13? In your opinion, does she have reason to be sad?

7. Because Wong's article appeared in a newspaper, we can assume that it was directed at a general audience. In your opinion, what message does she wish to share with her audience?

*Summarize* Finally, it's a good idea to summarize what you've read. As you discovered in Chapter 2, summarizing not only helps you remember what you've read, it can be a resource for your own writing.

### ▼ Activity

#### *Summarize*

Summarize Wong's article. Remember that when summarizing a newspaper article, you need to look for main ideas rather than topic sentences. Write a list of these main ideas. Then write a brief summary of the article. Be sure to include author, title, and place of publication.

### ▲▼▲ Responding to Reading

A **response** is a thoughtful reaction to what you've read. In a response, the writer refers back to the article, essay, or textbook chapter, and then comments on the most important or most intriguing ideas presented in the piece. It differs from the more organized summary, which requires the writer to include only the author's main points. Also, a response differs from the essays you'll be writing. In an essay, the writer states a thesis in the introduction and then supports that thesis in the paragraphs that follow. In a response, the writer has the freedom to move from one idea to another and back again, perhaps to explore several aspects of an issue or just to think on paper. You've been writing responses as you've worked your way through the first two chapters of this text. When you're asked to write your opinion in the form of reading questions, journals, or other assignments, you're writing a response.

> ### Journal Assignment
> **Respond to "The Struggle to Be an All-American Girl"**
> Write a ten to fifteen minute response to Wong's article. You might write about the importance of your own cultural heritage, an experience of your own that is similar to or different from Wong's, or another issue connected to the article.

## ▲▼▲ Building Your Vocabulary

One of the most important benefits of reading is improving your vocabulary. Your vocabulary will naturally grow as you look up new terms and figure out words as you read. But if you haven't had much practice using the dictionary, looking up words can be pretty frustrating, especially when there are several possible definitions listed for a single word. Also, new words are easy to forget if you don't have a plan for reviewing them.

## Using the Dictionary to Find Word Meanings

If you were unsure of what *pedestrian* means in paragraph 7 of Wong's article, then you probably looked it up in your dictionary.

> . . . The voice belonged to my grandmother, a fragile woman in her seventies who could outshout the best of the street vendors. Her humor was raunchy, her Chinese rhythmless, patternless. It was quick, it was loud, it was unbeautiful. It was not like the quiet, lilting romance of French or the gentle refinement of the American South. Chinese sounded *pedestrian*. Public.

*Notes*

This entry is from *The American Heritage Dictionary:*

**pe·des·tri·an** (pə-dĕs′trē-ən) *n.* A person traveling on foot; walker. —*adj.* **1.** Of, relating to, or made for pedestrians. **2.** Going or performed on foot: *a pedestrian journey.* **3.** Undistinguished; ordinary: *pedestrian prose.* [Lat. *pedester,* going on foot < *pedes,* a pedestrian < *pes,* foot.] —**pe·des′·tri·an·ism** *n.*

When you look at a dictionary entry you can't just pick any part of the entry and apply that information to the word and sentence you are interested in. *Pedestrian*, for example, can be a noun (person, place, or thing) or an adjective (a word used to describe a noun). The *n* (meaning noun) and *adj* (meaning adjective) in the entry tell us that. In order to choose the correct meaning, you have to figure out how the word you want to define is being used. In the quotation, *pedestrian* is being used as an adjective because it describes the noun "Chinese."

Once you know how the word is being used, then you can look at the possible definitions. Three are listed following *adj*. Numbers one and two relate to someone walking, but we can see that the sentence doesn't refer to walking. However, number three offers a different meaning, "Undistinguished; ordinary." These two words help describe how the grandmother's Chinese sounded to Wong. It sounded ordinary and unimportant. Remember, when looking up a word like *pedestrian,* you should think about how it works in the sentence.

You should also consider the words and sentences surrounding *pedestrian*. For example, look at the word *public,* which follows *pedestrian* in paragraph 7 (p. 76). When something is *public,* it's exposed to all. It's not special. Wong's use of *public* following *pedestrian* emphasizes the idea that the grandmother's Chinese sounded ordinary and unimportant to Wong. Then consider how Wong describes other languages and dialects in the same paragraph: "The quiet, lilting romance of French" and "the gentle refinement of the American South." Words such as *refinement* and *romance* contrast with *pedestrian* and *public,* revealing that Wong thought other languages were beautiful in comparison to her grandmother's. By considering the surrounding words and sentences, we're better able to understand what *pedestrian* means and how Wong felt.

▼ *Activity*

*Finding Meanings in the Dictionary*

The paragraph that follows is from a personal essay, "Navigating My Eerie Landscape Alone," in which writer Jim Bobryk talks about living with blindness. (You'll read the entire essay later in this chapter.) Practice your dictionary skills by finding definitions for the words in italics.

> . . . I was driving home for lunch on what seemed to be an increasingly foggy day, although the perky radio deejay said it was clear and sunny. After I finished my lunch, I realized that I couldn't see across the room to my front door. I had battled *glaucoma* for 20 years. Suddenly, without warning, my eyes had *hemorrhaged*.

Write down the definitions for these terms. Explain how knowing these terms helps you better understand what happened to Jim Bobryk.

## Finding Definitions in the Writing

Often, unfamiliar words in a reading are immediately followed by their definitions. This is particularly true in a textbook when the writer must introduce several new concepts within a single chapter. Note how the definition follows the term *feminism* in this example:

> The struggle for women's rights has been a long and hard-fought battle in the United States. The first major wave of **feminism,** *an ideology aimed at eliminating patriarchy in support of equality between the sexes,* was linked to the pre–Civil War abolitionist movement.
>
> —William E. Thompson and Joseph V. Hickey
> from "Feminism: The Struggle for Gender Equality"

## Recognizing Context Clues

In addition to using your dictionary or finding definitions in the text, you should try to figure out the meanings of unfamiliar words by looking at the **context** in which you find them. This means that you think about the entire sentence the unfamiliar word appears in, as well as the sentences before and after it. Nearby words and other sentences often give you clues about what the unknown word means.

For example, the word *patriarchal* in the following textbook excerpt on the Puritans might be unfamiliar to you. Consider what this word means by looking at the sentence which precedes it.

> . . . Families cared for the destitute and elderly; they took in orphans; and they housed servants and apprentices—all under one roof and subject to the authority of the father.
> The Puritans carried *patriarchal* values across the Atlantic and planted them in America. . . .
>
> —James Kirby Martin et al. from "Seventeenth Century Roles for Puritan Men, Women, and Children"

*Notes*

Notes

In this case, the last phrase of the first paragraph, "all under one roof and *subject to the authority of the father*," sets up the idea of *patriarchal* values. Now that you see this connection, it is clear that the term *patriarchal* connects to the idea that males were in charge of the family.

Also, look again at the excerpt that defines *feminism*.

> The struggle for women's rights has been a long and hard-fought battle in the United States. The first major wave of **feminism,** *an ideology aimed at eliminating patriarchy in support of equality between the sexes,* was linked to the pre–Civil War abolitionist movement.

Note that the word *patriarchy*—a form of the word *patriarchal*—appears in the definition of feminism. You recognize, then, that the term *patriarchy* has to do with males being in charge. So now you understand that feminism means eliminating male superiority (patriarchy) in favor of achieving equality between the sexes. When figuring out words in context, look for variations of words you already know.

## ▼ Activity

### Finding Meaning in Context

Read the paragraph that follows. Look at the context of the word *matrilineal*. What discussion follows the introduction of this term? Based on the sentences surrounding it, what do you think it means?

> Meghalaya, a district tucked away in the remote northeastern corner of India, is home to the Khasi, one of the largest surviving *matrilineal* societies in the world. In this hill tribe of nearly 650,000, descent is traced through the mother's line and women have an honored place in the society. Here, baby girls are quite welcome, and, some argue, even more highly prized than boys. Since the woman's family holds the cards when arranging a marriage, the question of dowry—paying a man's family for accepting the "burden" of a wife—would never even arise. No social stigma is attached to women, whether they choose to divorce, remarry, or stay single.
>
> —Kavita Menon from "In India, Men Challenge a Matrilineal Society"

Using the context to figure out what an unfamiliar word means is a critical reading skill. Figuring out a word in context will save you time and energy. However, the most important reason to develop this skill is so that you'll gain a better understanding of the meaning of the word and how it works in a particular sentence, paragraph, or essay.

## Keeping a Vocabulary Notebook

Notes

Assign a section of your notebook to vocabulary. Writing down new words, definitions, and other related information will help you build your vocabulary. However, just writing down such information is not enough. To help you make these terms a part of your life, you need to review your vocabulary section regularly. You must also practice using these new words in your own writing.

Use the vocabulary section of your notebook to write down and define unfamiliar words you come across in all of your classes—not just your English class. Your list should contain

- the sentence that the word appeared in,
- the meaning in context (if possible),
- how the word works in the sentence, and
- the dictionary definition.

Here is an example of how to list a word.

*dissuade* —— The new term

"No amount of kicking, screaming, or pleading could dissuade my mother, who was solidly determined to have us learn the language of our heritage." —— The sentence in which the term appeared

I know that "persuade" means to convince someone to do something. "Dissuade" seems to mean not being able to get someone to do it. —— Definition based on context

Verb —— Type of word

Pronunciation: dĭ-swād' —— Pronunciation

Definition: To deter from course or action. —— Definition

Other forms of the word: dissuader (noun) —— Other forms

Paraphrased: Nothing Wong did could keep her mother from insisting that Wong and her brother learn Chinese. —— Word meaning in context—in your own words

▼ *Activity*

### Vocabulary Notebook

Return to Elizabeth Wong's article, "The Struggle to Be an All-American Girl." Write any words that were new to you in the vocabulary section of your notebook. Be sure to include the definition as well as other related

**Notes**

information. In addition, log any of the terms from this section, "Building Your Vocabulary." Consider logging the following terms: *pedestrian, glaucoma, hemorrhaged, patriarchal* or *patriarchy,* and *matrilineal.*

Writing this information will help you learn new words *if* you review and study them. Also, you must *practice using your new words* if they are to become a part of your expanding vocabulary. Try using these new words as you answer questions or respond in journal assignments. In the chapters to come, plan to include them in your essays.

## ▲▼▲ Practicing the Reading Process

So far in this chapter you've studied the PARTS of the reading process and have explored some strategies for using the dictionary and building your vocabulary. You're ready now to begin practicing what you've learned. In the reading assignments that follow, you'll encounter many of the writing structures you explored in Chapter 2. In addition, you'll have the opportunity to practice and develop your reading-writing-critical thinking connection as you explore people's roles in society.

## ▲▼▲ Reading the Personal Narrative

In "The Struggle to Be an All-American Girl" earlier in the chapter, you encountered a type of writing called the personal narrative. In a **personal narrative**, an individual recounts an event or series of events from his or her own life, usually to make a point or to help the reader better understand an issue. In Wong's case, she retold her story about wanting to be "an all-American girl" so that she could tell what she had learned from her experience—that it's important to remember your own cultural heritage. In the essay that follows, writer Jim Bobryk shares his personal experience.

### *Reading Assignment #1*

### *"Navigating My Eerie Landscape Alone"*

***Preview*** This is a personal narrative that appeared in a popular magazine. You can assume that it will follow journalistic format, with shorter paragraphs and few topic sentences. Review the title, the quotation underneath the title, and the first two paragraphs.

*Anticipate*   What do you think this personal narrative will be about? Use the "Notes" column to record your answer.

*Read*   Now read the entire article quickly and continue to anticipate as you read. Highlight unfamiliar terms and jot down any questions in the margins. (Remember, because you're reading quickly, it's all right not to understand everything the first time through.)

*Notes*

### Navigating My Eerie Landscape Alone

*"Unless I ask for help, strangers are so afraid of doing the wrong thing that they do nothing at all."*

*by Jim Bobryk*

This *Newsweek* article, by writer and executive Jim Bobryk, appeared on March 18, 1999.

1   Now, as I stroll down the street, my right forefinger extends five feet in front of me, feeling the ground where my feet will walk.

2   Before, my right hand would have been on a steering wheel as I went down the street. I drove to work, found shortcuts in strange cities, picked up my two daughters after school. Those were the days when I ran my finger down a phone-book page and never dialed Information. When I read novels and couldn't sleep until I had finished the last page. Those were the nights when I could point out a shooting star before it finished scraping across the dark sky. And when I could go to the movies and it didn't matter if it was a foreign film or not.

3   But all this changed about seven years ago. I was driving home for lunch on what seemed to be an increasingly foggy day, although the perky radio deejay said it was clear and sunny. After I finished my lunch, I realized that I couldn't see across the room to my front door. I had battled glaucoma for 20 years. Suddenly, without warning, my eyes had hemorrhaged.

4   I will never regain any of my lost sight. I see things through a porthole covered in wax paper. I now have no vision in my left eye and only slight vision in my right. A minefield of blind spots make people and cars suddenly appear and vanish. I have no depth perception. Objects are not closer and farther; they're larger and smaller. Steps, curbs and floors

*Notes*

all flow on the same flat plane. My world has shapes but no features. Friends are mannequins in the fog until I recognize their voices. Printed words look like ants writhing on the pages. Doorways are unlit mine shafts. This is not a place for the fainthearted.

5   My cane is my navigator in this eerie landscape. It is a hollow fiberglass stick with white reflector paint and a broad red band at the tip. It folds up tightly into four 15-inch sections, which can then be slipped into a black holster that attaches to my belt with Velcro.

6   Adults—unless they're preoccupied or in a hurry—will step aside without comment when they see me coming. Small children will either be scooped up apologetically or steered away by their parents. Only teenagers sometimes try to play chicken, threatening to collide with me and then veering out of the way at the last moment.

7   While I'm wielding my stick, strangers are often afraid to communicate with me. I don't take this personally—anymore. Certainly they can't be afraid that I'll lash at them with my rod. (Take *that,* you hapless sighted person! Whack!) No, they're probably more afraid *for* me. Don't startle the sword swallower. Don't tickle the baton twirler.

8   The trick for the sighted person is to balance courtesy with concern. Should he go out of his way or should he get out of the way? Will his friendliness be misconstrued by the disabled as pity? Will an offer of help sound patronizing? These anxieties are exaggerated by not knowing the etiquette in dealing with the disabled. A sighted person will do nothing rather than take the risk of offending the blind. Still, I refuse to take a dim view of all this.

9   When I peer over my cane and ask for help, no one ever cowers in fear. In fact, I think people are waiting for me to give them the green light to help. It makes us feel good to help.

10   When I ask for a small favor, I often get more assistance than I ever expect. Clerks will find my required forms and fill them out for me. A group of people will parade me across a dangerous intersection. A salesclerk will read the price tag for me and then hunt for the item on sale. I'm no Don Juan, but strange (and possibly exotic) women will take my hand and walk me through dark rooms, mysterious train stations and foreign airports. Cabbies wait and make sure I make it safely into lobbies.

11   It's not like it's inconvenient for friends to help me get around. Hey, have disabled parking placard—will travel. Christmas shopping? Take me to the mall and I'll get us front-row parking. Late for the game? *No problema.* We'll be parking by the stadium entrance. And if some inconsiderate interloper does park in the blue zone without a permit, he'll either be running after a fleeing tow truck or paying a big fine.

Notes

12. Worried about those age lines showing? Not with me looking. Put down that industrial-strength Oil of Olay. To me, your skin looks as clean and smooth as it was back in the days when you thought suntanning was a good idea.
13. So you see, I'm a good guy to know. I just carry a cane, that's all.
14. None of this is to make light of going blind. Being blind is dark and depressing. When you see me walking with my cane you may think I'm lost as I ricochet down the street. But you'll find more things in life if you don't travel in a straight line.

*Reread*   Once you've completed a first reading, read Bobryk's narrative a second time. Slow down to answer your own questions and look up the meanings of any words you don't know or can't figure out. Add these to the vocabulary section of your notebook.

Here is a list of words to get you started. Be sure to include any other unfamiliar terms and definitions. (You may skip any of the terms that you're familiar with already.)

par. 3: glaucoma; hemorrhaged

par. 4: porthole; minefield; mannequins

par. 5: eerie

par. 7: wielding

par. 8: misconstrued; etiquette

par. 11: interloper

par. 14: ricochet

*Think Critically, Summarize, and Respond*   The questions and activities that follow will help you develop your reading skills as you complete the reading process.

## ▼ Questions for Critical Thought

### "Navigating My Eerie Landscape Alone"

1. What caused Jim Bobryk to lose his sight?
2. Bobryk explains that his cane is now his "navigator." What does he mean by this?
3. In what ways has Bobryk's life changed as a result of his losing his eyesight?

**Notes**

4. Bobryk explains that "strangers are often afraid to communicate" with him, but when he asks for assistance, he finds that people are more than willing to help. How does he account for these different forms of treatment?

5. Identify two places in the article where Bobryk uses humor to make his point. Why would a writer use humor to make a serious point?

6. Bobryk states, "I'm a good guy to know. I just carry a cane, that's all." What does he want his audience to understand from this statement?

7. Bobryk's article appeared in *Time* magazine. Who would most likely be included in his audience? What overall point or message do you believe Bobryk conveys in this article?

### ▼ Activity

#### Summarize "Navigating My Eerie Landscape Alone"

After making a list of the main points and most important supporting points, write a summary of Bobryk's article. Be sure to include author, title of article, and where it was published. Also include a general statement telling what the article is about, followed by its main points. When you've finished a draft of your summary, return to the article to check for accuracy and revise as necessary.

---

#### Journal Assignment

##### Respond to "Navigating My Eerie Landscape Alone"

Take ten to fifteen minutes to respond to Bobryk's article. You might comment on Bobryk's use of humor in the piece. (Look back at paragraphs 7, 9, 10, and 11.) You could write about a similar experience of your own or of someone you know. You might also write about what you have learned from Bobryk's article.

---

### ▲▼▲ Reading Textbook Chapters

In Chapter 2 you studied the structure of textbook chapters. You know that this type of writing follows basic essay format and contains an introduction and clear thesis that leads the reader through the chapter. A textbook chapter's body paragraphs usually consist of topic sentences followed by supporting detail and explanation. Most end with at least a concluding remark. In this section, there are two textbook chapters, one from a history text and the other from a sociology text. Both explore people's roles in our society, but at different times in history.

## Reading Assignment #2

"Seventeenth Century Roles for Puritan Men, Women, and Children"

*Preview* This segment comes from a history textbook, so you know that it will follow the expected format of a clear introduction, body paragraphs, and concluding remarks. Review the title, author, and introductory information. Then read the opening paragraphs as well as the topic sentences throughout the piece.

*Anticipate* After reviewing the introduction and topic sentences, what do you believe this textbook selection will be about? Use the "Notes" column to record your answer.

*Read* Quickly read through the excerpt. Anticipate what information will appear next as you read. Be sure to highlight unfamiliar terms and write any questions you may have in the margins.

### Seventeenth Century Roles for Puritan Men, Women, and Children

*by James Kirby Martin et al.**

This selection appeared in the history textbook, *America and Its People*.

1     The early Puritans looked at their mission as a family undertaking, and they referred to families as "little commonwealths." Not only were families to "be fruitful and multiply," but they also served as agencies of education and religious instruction as well as centers of vocational training and social welfare. Families cared for the destitute and elderly; they took in orphans; and they housed servants and apprentices—all under one roof and subject to the authority of the father.

---

*Note: This selection was written by more than one author. The first author's name is followed by "et al.," a Latin phrase which means "and others."

### Notes

COMMONWEALTH:
① The people of a state or nation
② A state or nation governed by the people.

FRUITFUL & MULTIPY
HAVE A LOT OF CHILDREN

Section I  Establishing the Connections

**Notes**

*coverture:*

*prenuptial agreements:*

*Bigamy:* Entry into marriage with one person while still legally married to another.

*Dowries:* Money or property brought by a bride to her husband at marriage

2   The Puritans carried *patriarchal* values across the Atlantic and planted them in America. New England law, reflecting its English base, subscribed to the doctrine of *coverture,* or subordinating the legal identity of women in their husbands, who were the undisputed heads of households. Unless there were prenuptial agreements, all property brought by women to marriages belonged to their mates. Husbands, who by custom and law directed their families in prayer and scripture reading, were responsible for assuring decency and good order in family life. They also represented their families in all community political, economic, and religious activities.

3   Wives also had major family responsibilities. "For though the husband be the head of the wife," the Reverend Samuel Willard explained, "Yet she is the head of the family." It was the particular calling of mothers to nurture their children in godly living, as well as to perform many other tasks—tending gardens, brewing beer, raising chickens, cooking, spinning, and sewing—when not helping in the planting and harvesting of crops.

4   Most Puritan marriages functioned in at least outward harmony. If serious problems arose, local churches and courts intervened to end the turmoil. Puritan law, again reflecting English precedent, made divorce quite difficult. The process required the petitioning of assemblies for bills of separation, and the only legal grounds were bigamy, desertion, and adultery. A handful of women, most likely battered or abandoned wives, effected their own divorces by setting up separate residences. On occasion the courts brought unruly husbands under control, for example, a Maine husband who brutally clubbed his wife for refusing to feed the family pig. There were instances when wives defied patriarchalism, including one case involving a Massachusetts woman who faced community censure for beating her husband and even "egging her children to help her, bidding them knock him in the head."

5   Family friction arose from other sources as well, some of which stemmed from the absolute control that fathers exercised over property and inheritances. If sons wanted to marry and establish separate households, they had to conform to the will of their fathers, who controlled the land. Family patriarchs normally delayed the passing of property until sons had reached their mid-twenties and selected mates acceptable to parents. Delayed inheritances help to explain why so many New Englanders did not marry until several years after puberty. Since parents also bestowed *dowries* on daughters as their contributions to new family units, romantic love had less to do with mate selection than parental desires to unite particular family names and estates.

6   Puritans expected brides and grooms to learn to love one another as they went about their duty of conceiving and raising the next generation of children. In most cases spouses did develop lasting affection for one another, as captured by the gifted Puritan poetess Anne Bradstreet in 1666 when she wrote to her "dear and loving Husband":

> If ever two were one, then surely we.
> If ever man were lov'd by wife, then thee;
> If ever wife was happy in a man,
> Compare with me the women if you can.

7   Young adults who openly defied patriarchal authority were rare. Those who did could expect to hear what one angry Bay Colony father told his unwanted son-in-law: "As you married her without my consent, you shall keep her without my help." Also unusual were instances of illegitimate children, despite the lengthy gap between puberty and marriage. As measured by illegitimate births, premarital sex could not have been that common in early New England, not a surprising finding among people living in closely controlled communities and seeking to honor the Almighty by reforming human society.

*Reread*  Complete a second, slower reading of the textbook excerpt. Respond to questions you wrote in the margins during your first reading. Look up terms and record their definitions in your notebook.

Consider adding the following terms to your vocabulary list. Remember to try to figure out the word in its context. Then use the dictionary to verify meaning.

par. 1: "little commonwealths"; apprentices

par. 2: patriarchal; coverture; prenuptial agreement

par. 5: dowries

*Think Critically, Summarize, and Respond*  Continue the reading process as you think critically, summarize, and respond to what you've read.

### ▼ Questions for Critical Thought

*"Seventeenth Century Roles . . ."*

1. The reader is told that Puritan society was a patriarchal society. Explain how this society operated.

*Notes*

2. Look up the word "commonwealth." Write out the meaning. Explain how Puritan families operated as "little commonwealths."

3. What does the command "be fruitful and multiply" mean? Where might this command have come from? Why did the Puritans believe and obey it?

4. According to the selection, what were the husband's responsibilities or duties in the early Puritan household? What were the wife's?

5. Look back at the term *coverture* and its definition in paragraph 2. How were Puritan women affected by the doctrine of *coverture*?

6. Describe what early Puritan marriages were like. Did they seem to work? What happened if trouble developed in a Puritan marriage?

7. Did romantic love play a large part in the selection of a mate in those days? Why? Why not?

8. What might have happened to a son or daughter who rebelled against his or her father's wishes in marriage?

9. Was premarital sex a common occurrence in early Puritan New England? Why? Why not?

10. In what ways has the family changed since early Puritan times?

11. Who would be the audience for this piece? What is the authors' purpose in presenting this reading to this particular audience?

### ▼ Activity

**Summarize "Seventeenth Century Roles . . ."**

Write a summary of this excerpt. Because it follows essay form, you can check for a thesis in the introduction and main ideas in the topic sentences. Begin by listing the most important points. Open your summary with the excerpt's main idea. Follow with the most important points. Look back at the excerpt to check main ideas. Don't forget to identify author, title, and the textbook.

### Journal Assignment

**Respond to "Seventeenth Century Roles"**

Spend ten to fifteen minutes responding to this excerpt. Consider the positive and negative aspects of love and marriage past and present.

> Think about how modern views compare to Puritan views. You might write about what you believe to be the ideal approach to love and/or marriage. You might write about a time when love and marriage worked best, or respond to something else in the text that interests you.

*Notes*

## Reading Assignment #3

*"Feminism: The Struggle for Gender Equality"*

*Preview*   This excerpt is from a sociology textbook, so you should expect it to follow basic essay form. Consider the title, authors, and introductory information. Next, read the introduction and topic sentences to get a sense of what this segment is about.

*Anticipate*   What do you anticipate this segment will be about? Use the "Notes" column to record your answer.

*Read*   Now read through the excerpt quickly, using your anticipation skills to guess what's coming next. Highlight unknown terms and write your own questions in the "Notes" column.

### Feminism: The Struggle for Gender Equality
*by William E. Thompson and Joseph V. Hickey*

This textbook excerpt from *Society in Focus: The Essentials* comes from the chapter titled, "Sex, Gender, and Age."

1   The struggle for women's rights has been a long and hard-fought battle in the United States. The first major wave of **feminism,** *an ideology aimed at eliminating patriarchy in support of equality between the sexes,* was linked to the pre–Civil War abolitionist movement. When it became clear that emancipation leaders were not seeking the same rights for women as for black men, however, Elizabeth Cady Stanton, Susan B. Anthony, and Lucretia Mott organized a convention on women's rights at Seneca Falls, New York, in 1848. The main thrust of the early feminist movement was women's suffrage (the right to vote) and with the passage of the Nineteenth Amendment in 1920, much of the movement's fervor dissipated.

2   The second wave of feminism arose in the 1960s, and again it was initially linked to the struggle for civil rights for blacks and other minorities. Social activism of the times provided the milieu for contemporary feminism, and Betty Friedan's book *The Feminine Mystique* (1963) ignited public consciousness. Friedan described the relative isolation, dis-

content, and alienation of American women trapped in the stereotypical roles of housewife and mother. Many American women identified with the plight Friedan described, and in 1966 the National Organization for Women (NOW) was formed. This organization and the women's movement attracted large numbers of women and men into their ranks.

3. Although the feminist agenda is diverse and feminists disagree about how best to accomplish its goals, there is consensus that laws, policies, regulations, and programs that discriminate against women should be abolished. A major goal of the contemporary feminist movement was the passage of the Equal Rights Amendment (ERA) to the U.S. Constitution. Initially proposed in 1923, the ERA simply states that equality under the law cannot be denied or abridged on the basis of sex. The amendment passed both houses of Congress in 1972, but despite widespread support from both men and women, it fell three states short of the 38 needed for ratification, with feminists' only consolation being that women are protected by the Fourteenth Amendment.

4. Within the feminist movement, a more radical faction emerged that not only endorsed all reforms proposed by more moderate elements but also sought revolutionary social change. The ideological basis for radical feminism was spawned by Kate Millett's book *Sexual Politics* (1970) and Germaine Greer's work *The Female Eunuch* (1972), which concluded that the goals of feminism could not be accomplished without abandoning the institution of the family.

5. The feminist movement, especially in its more radical forms, has met with social resistance. In the early 1970s, Phyllis Schlafly became identified as the leader of the antifeminist movement, arguing that passage of the Equal Rights Amendment and the rest of the feminist agenda would destroy the American family. She and other antifeminists not only fear change but also believe that feminist ideas are "unnatural" because they violate traditional sex roles. In her book *Backlash,* Susan Faludi (1991:x) asserted that virtually every positive stride women have made toward achieving equality has met a social backlash from those who want to maintain the status quo; folk wisdom has it that "women are unhappy precisely *because* they are free." This, Faludi asserted, amounts to no less than an "undeclared war against women."

6. Despite resistance, feminism persists, and feminist scholarship is making an important contribution to virtually all fields of study, especially sociology. Feminists argue that gender, like social class, is one of the most important dimensions of social organization. Thus gender refers not only to the ways that sex differences become socially significant but also to social relationships between men and women and the differential allocation of social power based on sex. Simply put, from the

feminist perspective, power is a central aspect of gender relations; women have less access to most types of power than men, and most stereotypical gender differences are a result of this imbalance of power (Laslett and Brenner, 1989; Vance and Pollis, 1990; Lips, 1991, 1993; Andersen, 1993; Wood, 1994).*

*Reread* Complete a thorough second reading. Answer any questions you wrote in the "Notes" column. Look up new words and write definitions in your notebook.

Consider adding these words to your vocabulary notebook. Use context clues to try to figure out what they mean. Then check their meanings by looking them up in the dictionary.

par. 1: feminism; patriarchy; abolitionist; emancipation; women's suffrage; fervor; dissipated

par. 2: milieu; discontent; alienation

par. 3: consensus; abolished; abridged; ratification

par. 4: faction; endorsed

par. 5: antifeminist movement

par. 6: differential

*Think Critically, Summarize, and Respond* Follow through with your reading process by answering questions for critical thought and completing the activities.

## ▼ Questions for Critical Thought

*"Feminism: The Struggle for Gender Equality"*

1. What is feminism? What was the main focus of the early feminist movement in America?
2. What caused a "second wave of feminism" in the 1960s?
3. What does ERA stand for? Who was in favor of the ERA? Who was against it?
4. According to authors Thompson and Hickey, the antifeminist movement arose in opposition to the feminist movement. Who led the antifeminist movement? What were the basic beliefs of this group?

---

*The names and dates in parentheses refer to specific research studies.

Notes

5. From the feminist perspective, who has the most power in our society, males or females? Do you believe that an "imbalance of power" exists in America today? Explain your position.
6. Who is the audience for this piece? What is the authors' purpose in presenting this reading to this particular audience?

## ▼ Activity

### Summarize "Feminism: The Struggle for Gender Equality"

Now that you've read and discussed the excerpt, make a list of the main points. (Remember, in a summary your job is to include all the main points of the original and to leave out your opinion.) Then write a summary of the article. Identify author and title first as well as the overall main idea of the excerpt. Relay the main points from your list. Once you've written your summary, return to the original and check to see that you've included all the main points and have stated them correctly. Revise as necessary.

---

### Journal Assignment

#### "Feminism: The Struggle for Gender Equality"

Now that you've gone through the stages of an effective reading process, take the time to respond to what you've read. Think about feminism and how it affects our lives. You might share a personal belief about feminism. You could share a personal insight or talk about your own experience. Write for ten to fifteen minutes about what interests you most.

---

## ▲▼▲ Reading Magazine and Newspaper Articles

Back in Chapter 2 you examined the feature story and a newspaper column. In this chapter, you will read two feature stories, one from a magazine and the other from a newspaper. Keep in mind that these types of articles contain shorter paragraphs and fewer topic sentences than the textbook excerpts you have just read.

### Reading Assignment #4

#### "In India, Men Challenge a Matrilineal Society"

*Preview*  This article appeared in a magazine, so you should expect shorter paragraphs and fewer topic sentences. Review the title, author, and publication information. What do you know about this magazine? Who would most likely be the audience for this particular article? Read the first two paragraphs.

*Anticipate* What do you think this magazine article will be about? Use the "Notes" column to record your answer.

*Read* Now quickly read the article through the first time. Practice your anticipation skills as you read. Highlight terms and write questions in the "Notes" column.

### In India, Men Challenge a Matrilineal Society
*by Kavita Menon*

Kavita Menon wrote this article for the September/October 1998 issue of *Ms.* magazine.

1   Meghalaya, a district tucked away in the remote northeastern corner of India, is home to the Khasi, one of the largest surviving matrilineal societies in the world. In this hill tribe of nearly 650,000, descent is traced through the mother's line and women have an honored place in the society. Here, baby girls are quite welcome, and, some argue, even more highly prized than boys. Since the woman's family holds the cards when arranging a marriage, the question of dowry—paying a man's family for accepting the "burden" of a wife—would never even arise. No social stigma is attached to women, whether they choose to divorce, remarry, or stay single.

2   Anthropologists say the Khasi matriliny developed as a practical measure: the men were often away fighting in wars, so it made sense for the women to hold all that was precious to a family. Money, land, and lineage were passed from youngest daughter to youngest daughter, since it was expected she would be the last to marry.

3   But a growing number of Khasi men are not interested in the logic of the old system. They say the matriliny has empowered women at the expense of men and the community as a whole. The epicenter of this dissent is a tiny office in a pleasant residential neighborhood in Shillong, Meghalaya's capital city. This is where the Syngkhong Rympei Thymmai (SRT)—which means "organization for the restructuring of Khasi society"—has its headquarters. The SRT, which was formed eight years ago and has a membership of about 400, including a handful of women, aims to dismantle the matriliny. It wants property to be equally divided among all the children in a family, and children to carry their father's surname. . . .

**Notes**

4   Many SRT members, like Lyngdoh, believe it is both a biological and a divine imperative for a man to be the head of the family. They argue that it is the man who plants the seed that becomes the child and that for this reason almost all children resemble their fathers. For many, passing on their titles—or establishing ownership of their children and their wives—is even more important than the matter of inheritance.

5   SRT members believe the Khasi matriliny has favored the development of Khasi women to the detriment of the men. "Women have all the inheritance and therefore all the power," says SRT vice president Pilgrim Lakiang. "They are making more progress than the men and boys."

6   Women are indeed prominent in Khasi life. There are more Khasi women doctors than men, more Khasi women graduating from colleges, more Khasi women conducting business in the market places. Women are now even seen in the traditional governing bodies, or durbars, which were once off-limits to them.

7   In contrast, Khasi men are said to be drinking too much, and are increasingly worried about losing their jobs, their land, and their women to migrants from West Bengal and Bangladesh. "Well-to-do families give their daughters to nontribals instead of to Khasi boys, and property and other assets that belong to the Khasi society pass to them," bemoans the writer of an article in one SRT booklet. . . .

8   Donakor Shanpru is a single woman in her late forties whose family home is situated on the same block as the SRT headquarters. She lives in the home of her youngest aunt, who is also unmarried, with other members of the extended family including her father, a widower; a brother, who has left his wife and child; and two sisters (whose husbands have both left them, then tried to return, only to be turned away) and their children.

9   Shanpru, who teaches Khasi literature at one of Shillong's four women's colleges, has no patience with the SRT or its views. As far as she's concerned, it is a minority group expressing a minority position, and she's happy to let you know that its president has been kicked out of her house three times for "talking nonsense." For all the SRT's huffing and puffing, Shanpru says, Khasi men have been invested with important duties, as husbands, fathers, and maternal uncles in the clan. Maternal uncles in particular exercise a lot of clout—though the youngest daughter holds the purse strings and her opinions matter, it is typically the oldest maternal uncle who decides when and how to spend the clan's money.

10   But while the SRT positions are seen as extremist by some, they do fit into a larger debate within the society and attract some unexpected

sympathizers. Patricia Mukhim, a journalist from Shillong, agrees to some extent with what the SRT is saying. She believes that giving boys an equal share of the family property will boost their self-esteem and encourage them to be more responsible, industrious husbands and citizens. Mukhim also blames the matriliny for making Khasi marriages "very brittle." Divorce has become too easy, she says, because husbands and wives can always return to their respective clans.

11   Where Mukhim disagrees with the SRT is in the speed of change. "We can't turn the system inside out so suddenly," she says. But change must come, she feels, since the problems that the men are facing affect everybody in the end.

12   A traditional society is being pressured to adjust to a modern world that is increasingly urban, and one in which families are smaller and more distant. Although the men's movement and the anxiety it expresses are city-based—men's roles are less of an issue in the villages where the traditional system still serves people's needs—the debate is widespread. . . .

13   Even though the matriliny has been the norm in Khasi society, that doesn't mean there are no gendered roles. In one traditional Khasi dance, for instance, the women are required to creep slowly forward by wriggling their toes like inchworms. They move in large groups, chins upturned and eyes downcast, looking very regal in their elaborate headdresses and long gowns. The role of the men is to "protect" the women—and they look like they're having great fun galloping, skipping, and spinning in circles around the women, while madly waving long, feathered whisks.

14   In the dance, the women are locked into the lines and circles assigned them, a reminder that in addition to being doctors and teachers and shopkeepers, they are still expected to be dutiful daughters, good mothers, and patient wives. And, for all the SRT members' talk of being downtrodden, men in a traditional Khasi home are still served the top of the rice bowl as a blessing on the family—and they very rarely cook or clean.

**Reread**   Read Menon's article a second time. Take your time as you read, stopping to look up definitions and to answer your questions.

Add these new terms to the vocabulary section of your notebook. Use context clues and your dictionary to find word meanings.

par. 1: matrilineal; dowry; stigma

par. 2: matriliny; lineage

par. 3: epicenter; dissent; dismantle; surname

**Notes**

par. 4: divine imperative
par. 5: detriment
par. 6: durbars
par. 7: assets
par. 9: clout
par. 14: downtrodden

*Think Critically, Summarize, and Respond* Complete your reading process as you work through the following activities and questions.

### ▼ Questions for Critical Thought

**"In India, Men Challenge a Matrilineal Society"**

1. What is a matrilineal society? How has the Khasi clan developed into a matriliny, according to anthropologists?

2. Who is most concerned about the system being dominated by women? Why?

3. What have been some of the positive results of such a system? What have been the negative results? Does this system seem fair? Why? Why not?

4. What does SRT stand for? What does this group propose?

5. Writer Kavita Menon includes a variety of perspectives on whether or not the Khasi system is fair. List two of the people interviewed and explain their perspectives.

6. According to Menon, in what instances do women still take on traditional roles?

7. This article appeared in *Ms.*, a magazine that supports women's rights. Knowing this, who would most likely be the audience for this article? Do you think this audience would be sympathetic to the men of the Khasi clan? Why? Why not?

### ▼ Activity

**Summarize "In India, Men Challenge a Matrilineal Society"**

Now that you've read the article at least twice, list the main ideas from the article and write a summary. Be sure to include the author, title, and publication. Begin with a general introductory statement and follow with the main points of the piece. Return to the article to make sure you've relayed the main ideas accurately. Make any necessary revisions.

*Notes*

> ### Journal Assignment
>
> *Respond to "In India, Men Challenge a Matrilineal Society"*
>
> Write a ten to fifteen minute response to Menon's article. What do you think of the Khasi's matrilineal system? How does their system compare to our American system today? What do you think of the viewpoints expressed in the article? Write about what interests you most.

### Reading Assignment #5

"Not a Two-Bit Problem"

*Preview*  This feature story appeared in a newspaper, so you should expect an opening statement (the lead), short paragraphs, and few topic sentences. Begin by reviewing the title, author, publication information, and opening paragraphs.

*Anticipate*  What do you believe this article will be about? Use the "Notes" column to record your thoughts.

*Read*  Quickly read the article. As you read, highlight unfamiliar words and write your questions in the "Notes" column.

### Not a Two-Bit Problem

*Women earn about 75 cents for every dollar men receive. Here are several reasons.*

*by Dave Murphy*

This feature story was written for the *San Francisco Examiner* newspaper, April 11, 1999.

1      The typical full-time female worker earns about 75 cents for every dollar that the typical man earns. Is that a misleading statistic—or an indicator that women still are a long way from workplace equality, 36 years after the federal Equal Pay Act was passed?

2      Yes, on both counts.

Notes

3. The federal government statistic is misleading because it simply compares the median earnings of all full-time workers of both sexes, not taking into account experience, education, ability or even the type of job involved. Women were at 74 cents per men's dollar in 1997, the last year that figures are available. In the first quarter of 1998, the figure rose to 76 cents, mainly because of increases in the minimum wage.

4. "We would not say that all of that is pure discrimination," says Susan Bianchi-Sand, executive director of the National Committee on Pay Equity in Washington, D.C.

5. According to figures from the committee's Web site (feminist.com/fairpay.htm), women were at only 60 percent of men's earnings until 1980, but increased to 72 percent by 1990.

6. "The reason the gap has actually closed is that men's wages have stagnated," Bianchi-Sand says. "You don't close the gap by holding men's wages down. No one is interested in that."

7. The Economic Policy Institute in Washington says that through 1997, the inflation-adjusted median wages for women had grown just 0.8 percent during the 1990s. Men's wages had fallen 6.7 percent.

8. Although the wage gap is a flawed statistic, experts say women still are being underpaid for several reasons—including discrimination. In the late 1980s, the President's Council of Economic Advisors found that 12 cents of the wage gap could not be explained, says Kelly Jenkins-Pultz, policy advisor to the director of the Department of Labor's Women's Bureau.

9. The AFL-CIO's Web site for working women (aflcio.org/women) points to wage gaps in a variety of jobs. It says, for example, that female attorneys earn nearly $300 a week less than male attorneys, and female professors are paid $170 a week less than male professors.

10. Bianchi-Sand says much of the gap is because many jobs traditionally held by women don't pay as well as jobs traditionally held by men.

11. "It's a lot about attitude, which in some cases translates into overt discrimination," she says. "Attitudes are harder to change than laws, it appears."

12. Sometimes discrimination laws are of little help because they apply only to jobs that have workers of both sexes, Bianchi-Sand says. She explains that social workers (typically female) have many of the same duties as probation officers (typically male), but are paid substantially less. That is not discrimination under the law because they are different jobs.

13. Among jobs available to people without a college degree, many of the highest paying involve danger or physical labor. Those jobs are traditionally held by men—in some cases because few women want them.

14   Jenkins-Pultz agrees that many women are in low-wage jobs like cashiers and secretaries, or in low-wage industries like service and child care. Still, she is encouraged because more women are ending up in managerial and administrative jobs, or in high-paying professional jobs like doctors and lawyers.

15   "They're not nontraditional jobs for women anymore," she says.

16   Jenkins-Pultz also is encouraged because more bachelor's degrees now are being awarded to women than men, and more women are developing the kind of work experience that can get them better jobs. She says women traditionally have had less education and less work experience than men, two legitimate reasons for part of the wage gap.

17   Three other factors can contribute to the gap; perception, pricing, and parenthood. Here's how:

18   **Perception:** Sometimes even those who agree that women are discriminated against don't recognize that they're part of the problem.

19   A 1997 Romac International survey of human resources executives found that 52 percent believed that women were being paid less than men for comparable work, but only 21 percent thought it was happening in their own companies.

20   **Pricing:** Sometimes female workers don't negotiate as hard or as well for a high salary as their male counterparts do. Or they may find other aspects of the job that are worth more to them than money.

21   Leon A. Farley, a San Francisco executive search consultant for 27 years, says men and women earning more than $500,000 a year tend to emphasize compensation equally. For those whose compensation is $150,000 to $500,000, however, he sees men pushing harder for the extra pay than women do.

22   Some of it is because of family, Farley says. More of the women in that category have spouses who also work, so they may be more concerned with a good opportunity or other benefits than with bringing in extra money.

23   Age can be a factor as well. Although he acknowledges there are plenty of exceptions, Farley says younger women—who grew up playing sports and being encouraged to compete more than their mothers had been—are more likely to push for equal wages. . . .

24   **Parenthood:** When families have children, mothers are far more likely than fathers to leave the work force for several years to raise the kids. When people leave the work force for several years, their skills get rusty and their careers suffer.

25   But the problem goes deeper than that, Bianchi-Sand says.

26   It's a vicious circle. Because of the fear that female employees will have children and leave, she says, some employers won't give women

*Notes*

the same training or opportunities that men receive. So the women don't do as well and don't earn as much money.

27   So when married couples have to decide which parent should stay home to raise the children, it makes perfect sense for the spouse with the lower income to stay home—and for the spouse who stays employed to emphasize money more than before.

***Reread*** Take the time to read Murphy's article again. Read slowly and think about the issues Murphy has raised. As you read carefully, be sure to answer your questions in the "Notes" column and take the time to define any unknown words.

Here are words to consider adding to the vocabulary section of your notebook. Be sure to consider context clues, then verify meaning by looking up unfamiliar words in your dictionary.

title: two-bit
par. 6: stagnated
par. 11: overt
par. 16: legitimate
par. 21: compensation

***Think Critically, Summarize, and Respond*** Continue to move through the reading process as you complete the activities and questions for critical thought.

### ▼ Questions for Critical Thought

*"Not a Two-Bit Problem"*

1. Why does Murphy pose a question in the opening paragraph? Is this an effective strategy for beginning an article? Why? Why not?
2. Government statistics show that a female worker earns approximately 75 cents for every dollar that a male worker makes. Why, according to Murphy, is this figure misleading?
3. What are some of the reasons given to explain why women are still underpaid?
4. How does perception contribute to the gap in wages? How does pricing? How does parenthood?
5. What, if anything, should be done about this difference in wages?

6. Who is the audience for this article? In your opinion, what is the writer's reason for having written this article?

▼ **Activity**

*Summarize "Not a Two-Bit Problem"*

Now that you've discussed the article, summarize the main points. Begin by listing them. Then write your summary from this list. Be sure to include a general opening statement about the article and include author, title, and publication information. Return to the article to check your facts. Make any necessary revisions.

> **Journal Assignment**
>
> *Respond to "Not a Two-Bit Problem"*
>
> Take ten to fifteen minutes to respond to Murphy's article. Consider the current difference in wages. Think about the explanations given for this difference and who suffers as a result. You may write about something from the article that you find interesting. You may also write about your personal experience or the experiences of others you know.

▲▼▲ **Time to Reflect**

> **Journal Assignment**
>
> *Your Progress as a Writer, Reader, and Critical Thinker*
>
> Think about the chapter and the skills you have developed, then respond in your journal by discussing
> - new reading skills you have begun to develop,
> - how using the reading process will help you become a better reader and writer,
> - the kinds of writing activities you found most helpful, and
> - new reading and writing goals.

▲▼▲ **Summary of Chapter 3**

In Chapter 3, you have examined the strategies used by effective readers and the PARTS of an effective reading process:

Preview

Anticipate

**Notes**

Read and Reread
Think Critically
Summarize

You have also
- contemplated and responded to a variety of challenging readings about people's roles in society,
- learned to use your dictionary and search for context clues to discover meanings of unknown words and phrases,
- learned the importance of retaining new words to build your vocabulary, and
- started logging definitions in a section of your notebook for easy review.

As you continue to practice the stages of the reading process and become a more experienced reader, you'll not only see your reading skills improve, but your writing and critical thinking skills as well.

## ▲▼▲ Identifying Verbs

*Action Verbs*
*Linking Verbs*
*Helping Verbs*
*Revising Your Definition of Verbs*

In Chapter 2 you practiced identifying verbs and got a sense of what a verb is and how it works within the sentence. Now you're ready to look at several specific types: action, linking, and helping verbs. You'll also learn some strategies for identifying verbs as well as words "posing" as verbs in your sentences.

### Action Verbs

One type of verb is called the **action verb**. An action verb expresses activity or movement. Rewrite and complete sentences 1–4, and you'll begin to see how action verbs work. Be sure to underline the verb.

*"Male and Female Roles"*
*Some would say that men and women should have clear, defined roles in the household.*

1. Women ____*make*____ the food.
2. Men _____ the lawns.
3. Daughters _____ the dirty clothes.
4. Sons _____ the car when it breaks down.

The words you supplied are **action verbs**: they represent movement, work, or someone doing something.

### Linking Verbs

Another kind of verb is called a **linking verb**. These verbs, as you'll see, don't show action. They connect (or link) parts of the sentence.

A chart of the linking verbs follows.

**Identifying Verbs**

Section I   Establishing the Connections

Notes

| |
|---|
| *All forms of "to be"*<br>　is<br>　am<br>　are<br>　was<br>　were |
| *(words associated with our five senses)*<br>　look<br>　sound<br>　smell<br>　feel<br>　taste |
| *(a few others)*<br>　appear<br>　seem<br>　become<br>　grow<br>　turn<br>　prove<br>　remain |

These verbs must be followed by descriptive information or a noun that renames a subject when they are acting as linking verbs.

Rewrite and complete sentences 1–8 using a different linking verb for each sentence. (The first one is done for you.) Be sure all the linking verbs you choose would make sense if the eight sentences were written as one paragraph. (You may want to refer to the previous chart when searching for the best linking verb.)

**"Traditional Values"**
*Traditional values have changed for some people.*

1. He ___*is*___ happy in the kitchen.
2. He thinks the kitchen _____ wonderful when bread is baking.
3. She _____ eager to work in the yard.
4. She _____ anxious if she must stay in the house all day.

5. The young woman _____ exhilarated working as a stockbroker.
6. The young father _____ happy caring for the children all day.
7. He _____ content to be a house-husband.
8. She _____ fulfilled to be the breadwinner.

As you can see from these exercises, linking verbs often help you express feelings or describe things. They don't show action. (They link the subject to a description or feeling.)

*Using Action Verbs*
Write five sentences of your own that use *only* action verbs. Be sure to underline these verbs and check your work with a neighbor.

Hint: Try to describe activities. It's okay to write about five unrelated activities.

*Using Linking Verbs*
Now write five sentences of your own that use *only* linking verbs. Be sure to underline these verbs and check your work with a neighbor.

*Hint:* You may want to write about feelings or descriptions. These sentences don't need to connect to one another.

*Working on Style and Control*
Both action verbs and linking verbs are important to your writing. However, keep in mind that action verbs often create a more vivid and interesting picture for your reader.

Read this student's paragraph. She did her best to use only action verbs.

> I sat on the roof; the splintery brown shingles scratched my legs. The house was on a cliff by the coast. The sky above me, bright blue and clear, provided the playground for the white seagulls that dipped and soared. The pelicans cried out their warnings and then fell into the water to snatch fish up and carry them away. I peered through the binoculars at the beach that lay below me. A group of sandpipers landed at the water's edge. When the ocean drew her tide back, the sandpipers scampered out towards the waves and stuck their long skinny beaks into the sand, searching for sandcrabs. The water raced back in the hope of encircling them, but the birds were

*Notes*

> too quick and flew out of the reach of the ocean. Out beyond all others, there was a small white sailboat that swam on the edge of the world. It coasted back and forth against the bright blue screen, until the blue turned to orange and red. The little white boat changed its favorite path and floated slowly in towards the dock.
>
> —*Christine Smith*

1. Underline all of the action verbs Christine uses in her paragraph. Then circle the linking verbs. (*Hint:* There are three linking verbs.) Suggest action verbs that could be used instead.

2. Now, here's your chance to flex your verb muscles: write a coherent paragraph that uses only action verbs. (All sentences should relate to one another and flow.) This will probably be easier if you write about some sort of activity—a day at the park, a scene from your favorite sport. Any activity will do. To be successful at this, you should follow the directions below carefully.

   a. List at least three *specific* topics you might write about. Then circle the one that seems most promising.

   b. Draft a paragraph using mainly action verbs. Write at least five sentences that fit together. Then underline all verbs. (Don't try to use only action verbs at this point.)

   c. Go back and check all your verbs. Circle any linking verbs you may have used.

   d. Change the sentences with linking verbs so that you can use action verbs instead. Then rewrite your paragraph.

   e. The final version of your paragraph should be neatly written with no spelling errors.

   f. Underline all verbs.

### Helping Verbs

The **helping verbs** include: do, does, did, can, could, may, might, will, would, shall, should, must, is, am, are, was, were.

Some of these verbs can work alone as regular verbs, or they can work with others as helping verbs. They are called *helping verbs* when they work with another word to create a verb. (Note: *is, am, are, was,* and *were* can be linking verbs or helping verbs, depending on how they are used in a sentence.)

*Examples* (the complete verb is underlined):

Identifying verbs <u>is</u> important.

She <u>is working</u> on her English homework.

He <u>did discuss</u> his ideas with his classmates.

He <u>might finish</u> his essay tonight.

The instructor <u>has canceled</u> class.

The students <u>had been hoping</u> for a break.
[Sometimes a complete verb consists of two helping verbs *plus* another verb.]

They <u>do</u> not <u>mind</u> missing one class.
"Not" and "never" sometimes come between the parts of the verb.]

<u>Will</u> we <u>meet</u> next week?
[In a question, the parts of the verb are often separated, with the subject in between.]

*Notes*

In the sentences below, identify the verbs by underlining them. After you have checked your work with a classmate and feel that you have identified all the verbs, highlight the complete verbs that are made up of a helping verb *plus* another verb.

Jenkins-Pultz also is encouraged because more bachelor's degrees now are being awarded to women than men, and more women are developing the kind of work experience that can get them better jobs. She says women traditionally have had less education and less work experience than men, two legitimate reasons for part of the wage gap.

—Dave Murphy from "Not a Two-Bit Problem"

Next you'll read six more paragraphs from Dave Murphy's article. After you've read, underline the verbs in each sentence. Then highlight those verbs that are made up of a helping verb *plus* another verb. The first paragraph is done for you.

3     The federal government statistic <u>is</u> misleading because it simply <u>compares</u> the median earnings of all full-time workers of both sexes, not taking into account experience, education, ability or even the type of job involved. Women <u>were</u> at 74 cents per men's dollar in 1997, the last year that figures <u>are</u> available. In the first quarter of 1998, the figure <u>rose</u> to 76 cents, mainly because of increases in the minimum wage.

Notes

4   "We would not say that all of that is pure discrimination," says Susan Bianchi-Sand, executive director of the National Committee on Pay Equity in Washington, D.C.

5   According to figures from the committee's Web site (feminist.com/fairpay.htm), women were at only 60 percent of men's earnings until 1980, but increased to 72 percent by 1990.

6   "The reason the gap has actually closed is that men's wages have stagnated," Bianchi-Sand says. "You don't close the gap by holding men's wages down. No one is interested in that."

7   The Economic Policy Institute in Washington says that through 1997, the inflation-adjusted median wages for women had grown just 0.8 percent during the 1990s. Men's wages had fallen 6.7 percent.

8   Although the wage gap is a flawed statistic, experts say women still are being underpaid for several reasons—including discrimination. In the late 1980s, the President's Council of Economic Advisors found that 12 cents of the wage gap could not be explained, says Kelly Jenkins-Pultz, policy advisor to the director of the Department of Labor's Women's Bureau.

***Your Own Work***   Copy two paragraphs from your own writing (an essay or journal perhaps) and underline the verbs. Then *circle* those verbs that are made up of a helping verb *plus* another verb.

### Revising Your Definition of Verbs

Take a look at the definition you wrote of verbs in Chapter 2. Rewrite that definition making it clearer and adding any new information. Share your new information with your classmates or work as a whole class to develop a class definition.

### ▲▼▲ More about Verbs

### Verbs Tell Time
### Reviewing and Defining Verbs

Thus far in your sentence work, you've practiced identifying verbs, and you've considered the differences between action verbs, linking verbs, and helping verbs. In this section, you'll learn about a unique characteristic verbs possess which makes them easy to identify.

## Verbs Tell Time

Verbs possess a unique characteristic: they tell time. That is, verbs change **tenses** based on when the action takes place. The most common verb tenses are the past, present, and future tenses. You should know, too, that the verb is the only part of the sentence that changes when the tense changes.

Here are some examples of how verbs change when the tense changes.

Today I <u>walk</u>.              Today I <u>sing</u>.
Yesterday I <u>walked</u>.       Yesterday I <u>sang</u>.
Tomorrow I <u>will walk</u>.     Tomorrow I <u>will sing</u>.

Consider this paragraph:

> Today, there is a twenty-five cent per hour gap between women's and men's wages in America. Some people claim there are reasons for this gap. They say that unlike male employees, female workers don't compete for higher salaries. They also say women leave the job market to raise their children while men stay in it. But even when we take such factors into consideration, we still can't account for such a difference in earnings.

1. When did this take place? (Today? In the past? In the future?)
2. How do you know? Write down specific words from the paragraph that help you understand when the story occurs.
3. Did you find all of them? Check with a classmate.
4. Are the verbs in the present tense, past tense, or future tense?

### Manipulating Verb Tense

1. Now rewrite the paragraph as though the events happened in the *past*. Use the word *yesterday* at the beginning of each sentence.
2. Underline the verbs.
3. What tense are the verbs in now?

**The Future Tense**   To make verbs tell *future* time, all you have to do is add "will" before the base (plain) form of the verb.

   *Example:*   She <u>understands</u> physics. (present tense)
                She *<u>will</u> <u>understand</u>* physics. (future tense)

**Identifying Verbs**

Notes

1. Read the following paragraph, then rewrite it in the future tense. Add the word *tomorrow* at the beginning of sentence one.

   Today many mothers work out of their homes. This allows them to conduct business while remaining close to their children. Some make calls and answer e-mail during children's nap time. Others carry laptops to their kids' soccer practice and portable phones to the pizza parlor following the game.

2. Now go back through your rewrite of the paragraph and underline all the verbs. Be sure to underline the entire verb (*will* + _____).

### Reviewing and Defining Verbs

Remember
- All verbs can change tense.
- Only verbs can change tense.

To figure out if a word is a verb, use the **test of time**. This means that you place the word *today, yesterday,* or *tomorrow* at the beginning of a sentence and see which word (or words) can or must change. The word that changes is the verb. (Don't be fooled by words that *look* like verbs. Use the test of time.)

Use the test of time to figure out the verb of this sentence:

   A dramatic wage gap exists in America.

- *Yesterday,* a dramatic wage gap *existed* in America.
- *Today,* a dramatic wage gap *exists* in America.
- *Tomorrow,* a dramatic wage gap *will exist* in America.

Revise your definition of a verb to include the new information in this chapter. Use as many sentences as necessary to express your definition of a verb.

### ▲▼▲ Imposters

#### Imposter #1: -ing Words
#### Imposter #2: to + Verb Combinations

Using the *test of time* can really help when searching for the verb (and knowing which words are verbs can help you avoid subject-verb agreement errors.) Besides using the *test of time* to identify verbs, you should also be aware of two kinds of **imposters**—words that might look like verbs but really aren't.

### *Imposter #1: -ing Words*

Words ending in *–ing* (snow<u>ing</u> or talk<u>ing</u>) cannot change tenses, so they cannot be verbs all by themselves. However, *–ing* words can work as verbs *if* they get some help.

*Example:* (complete verbs are underlined)
a. Earning equal pay for equal work <u>is</u> important.
b. The female worker <u>is earning</u> less than the male worker.

In sentence (a) *Earning* cannot change tense and still make sense in the sentence. Therefore, it isn't a verb. It does not make sense to say: [Yesterday] earned equal pay for equal work <u>is</u> important.

In sentence (b) *is earning* can change tense to *was earning* or *will earn* when we use the test of time. It does make sense to say: The female worker <u>was earning</u> less than the male worker. Or the female worker <u>will earn</u> less than the male worker. Thus, *is earning* acts as a verb in sentence (b).

*Note:* When you have a helper verb and another word, only the helper verb will change *tense* although the other word may change *form*. (For example, compare *was earning* to *will earn*.)

Circle the *-ing* imposters in the paragraph below. Then underline the verbs.

Many men are choosing the role of "househusband" today. Dusting, vacuuming, and cooking are just some of the daily chores the househusband is responsible for. On weekdays, he rises at 6:00 A.M. to cook breakfast and carpool the children to and from school. Then he spends his afternoons running errands and driving the children to after-school activities. He devotes his evenings to helping the children with their homework and then tucking them into bed. Around midnight he finds himself ready to fall into bed. Although he considers it exhausting, he finds his chosen profession rewarding at the same time.

*Notes*

Notes

### Imposter #2: to + Verb Combinations

*to* + verb combinations (**infinitives**) cannot change tenses, so they cannot be verbs.

*Example:* (complete verbs are underlined)
Some women <u>choose</u> to enter traditional career fields.
Others <u>break</u> gender barriers to become firefighters or police officers.
Notice that in each of the two examples, there is an infinitive.

1. Circle these infinitives now.

2. Rewrite these two sentences and change the tense of these sentences to future tense. (Begin each of your sentences with *tomorrow*. Notice that the infinitives don't change. They cannot change tense. Therefore, they cannot be verbs.)

## Prepositional Phrases

You now know that you must ignore imposters when looking for the verb. A **prepositional phrase**, which consists of a preposition and its object, is another group of words that you can eliminate when searching for verbs.

Sometimes words in a prepositional phrase may look like verbs. However words in a prepositional phrase cannot be the verb(s) for the sentence.

Consider this sentence from Dave Murphy's article:

> Among jobs available to people without a college degree, many of the highest-paying involve danger or physical labor.

Finding the verb in this sentence can be a little tricky. But if you place brackets around any prepositional phrases, you'll find the verb is easier to identify. You can put brackets around *among jobs available, to people, without a college degree, of the highest-paying* because these are prepositional phrases. Only *many* and *involve danger or physical labor* remain. The only word here that will change tenses when you use the test of time is *involve*. So *involve* must be the verb.

How can you spot prepositional phrases? There are so many prepositions that you cannot memorize them, but you can learn to recognize them. They usually suggest location, time, or belonging.

*Examples:* (the preposition is in italics and the object follows)

| location | time | belonging |
|---|---|---|
| *in* the dark woods | *at* four o'clock | *by* William Shakespeare |
| *at* the old farm | *before* noon | *of* my family |
| *on* the table | *after* dark | |

The *object* of the preposition follows the preposition and may be long, or it may be just one little word.

1. As a class or in small groups circle *–ing* and infinitive imposters, and bracket the prepositional phrases in the paragraph that follows. Underline the verbs. The first two sentences have been done for you.

   Most Puritan marriages <u>functioned</u> [in at least outward harmony]. If serious problems <u>arose</u>, local churches and courts <u>intervened</u> (to end) the turmoil. Puritan law, again reflecting English precedent, made divorce quite difficult. The process required the petitioning of assemblies for bills of separation, and the only legal grounds were bigamy, desertion, and adultery. A handful of women, most likely battered or abandoned wives, effected their own divorces by setting up separate residences. On occasion the courts brought unruly husbands under control, for example, a Maine husband who brutally clubbed his wife for refusing to feed the family pig. There were instances when wives defied patriarchalism, including one case involving a Massachusetts woman who faced community censure for beating her husband and even "egging her children to help her, bidding them knock him in the head."

   —*James Kirby Martin et al. from "Seventeenth Century Roles for Puritan Men, Women, and Children"*

2. Two paragraphs from a different reading follow. Underline the verbs, circle the imposters, and bracket the prepositional phrases. The first two sentences have been done for you. Be careful to include helping verbs and exclude imposters. (Use the test of time to identify verbs when you are in doubt.)

   . . . [In this hill tribe] [of nearly 650,000], descent <u>is traced</u> [through the mother's line] and women <u>have</u> an honored place [in the society]. Here, baby girls <u>are</u> quite welcome, and, some <u>argue</u>, even more highly prized [than boys]. Since the woman's family holds the cards when arranging a marriage, the ques-

*Notes*

tion of dowry—paying a man's family for accepting the "burden" of a wife—would never even arise. No social stigma is attached to women, whether they choose to divorce, remarry, or stay single.

Anthropologists say the Khasi matriliny developed as a practical measure: the men were often away fighting in wars, so it made sense for the women to hold all that was precious to a family. Money, land, and lineage were passed from youngest daughter to youngest daughter, since it was expected she would be the last to marry.

—Kavita Menon from "In India, Men Challenge a Matrilineal Society"

## Manipulating Verb Tense

1. Write a paragraph of your own (at least 5–7 sentences) in which you explain what you think about either the Khasi's matriarchy or the Puritans' patriarchy. This paragraph should be written in the present tense. (Imagine the word *today* before any sentence when you want to check that you are using the present tense.) Underline *complete* verbs, circle imposters, and bracket prepositional phrases.

2. Now rewrite your paragraph as if you are writing about what you used to believe or think in the past. (You may want to start with *A few years ago, I . . . .*) Underline *complete* verbs, circle imposters, and bracket prepositional phrases.

# Examining the Writing Process

**CHAPTER 4**

### Main Topics

- Examining the writing process
- Communicating your ideas about advertisements and evil characters
- Identifying subjects in your sentences
- Creating sentences with consistent subject-verb agreement

Washington Post Writer's Group, 1997

**Notes**

In the past, people often assumed that good writing was a matter of genetics—either you were born a Hemingway, or you weren't. Fortunately, good writing is not a result of special writing genes, nor is it a matter of "tricks." Good writing is largely the result of taking the right steps, of using an effective writing process.

You can think of this process as being similar to what you might do if you were preparing a presentation at work. The presentation doesn't simply appear. You must research your topic, gather information and props, plan the sequence of information, and perhaps write out a script.

Similarly, each writer must (and can) develop an effective writing process in order to produce effective essays. The assignments in this chapter will help you develop a writing process that works well for you.

## ▲▼▲ The Stages of an Effective Writing Process

The writing process can be broken into stages that you'll begin using in this chapter.

### Discuss and Engage

You'll talk about the general topic and begin to get involved in the topic.

### Read, Discuss, Think Critically

You'll read, discuss the readings, and think critically about the readings and how they relate to the writing assignment.

### Explore the Writing Assignment

You'll carefully review the actual writing assignment and explore what kind of information should go into your essay. You may also take the time at this stage to outline and plan your essay.

### Draft

You'll write a complete essay. The essay might be a little rough, so you'll have to work on the draft and improve it.

### Revise

You'll change and improve the draft. You might add information, delete information, and move ideas around.

### Edit

You'll work on sentence structure, usage, punctuation, and spelling. This is the "polishing" stage.

## Points to Remember about the Writing Process

- The writing process stages will not always happen in this exact order. They may overlap, and some stages may need to be repeated.
- Approaching an essay assignment as a series of steps will actually make your task easier. You will be able to take your essay assignment one step at a time.
- All writers have some kind of writing process. Some processes are more effective than others and make writing easier, so it's important to refine your process until it works well for you.

---

### Journal Assignment

**Your Writing Process, Past and Future**

In a sense, Snoopy, on page 119, uses some of the steps in the writing process. He rereads his work, and he revises (although perhaps not very effectively).

In your notebook, describe the writing process you have used up to now. Consider some of the following questions:
- What do you do before you begin to write?
- Do you talk to anyone about your assignment?
- Do you handwrite your ideas on a notepad first?
- Do you compose on a word processor or computer?
- Do you usually write more than one draft?
- Are there certain steps that you must improve or add to your process? Explain.

---

## Developing an Effective Writing Process

Analyzing your past writing process and thinking about how to improve your writing process are important activities. Of course, the next step is to begin *practicing* an effective writing process.

In this chapter you will be offered three writing assignments. These assignments will help you begin to sharpen and refine your reading,

*Notes*

writing, and critical thinking processes as you analyze some challenging subjects: advertising and the human character.

## ▲▽▲ Writing Assignment #1: Analyzing Advertisements

In this assignment, you'll sharpen your critical thinking skills as you analyze a selection of advertisements. This analysis will require you to study the details of the ads so that you can draw conclusions about the ads and the motives of the advertisers.

Here, in brief, is the writing assignment that you are preparing for:

*Write an essay in which you analyze one advertisement by discussing the strategies the advertiser is using to make the product "appeal" to buyers. Comment on how successful you think the advertisement is.*

Keep this assignment in mind as you dig deeper into the issue of advertisements and prepare to write.

Keep all the writing you do in preparation of your writing assignments. This writing will become your **process package,** a collection of work—including class notes, a brainstorm, an outline, a draft, and more. This process package will represent the writing process that takes you from initial ideas to a finished essay.

### Discuss and Engage

Research shows that this is one of the stages of the writing process that some writers skip. These people jump into writing their papers before they discuss and think about the topic even though they would never consider purchasing a new car without discussing their options with experts, friends, or family members. They would take the time to discuss the various makes and models (1995 Ford Explorer vs. 1997 Jeep Grand Cherokee), extras (CD player, air conditioning, passenger air bags), and price before purchasing their vehicles. Otherwise, they might end up dissatisfied or even with a "lemon."

Discussion, planning, and critical thinking are also important when writers are given essay topics. Writers who discuss their topics with classmates, their instructor, a tutor, friends, or family members before writing are more satisfied with their papers than those who do not. In addition, these writers save time in the long run, because they have taken time at the beginning to get to know the topic before they start to write.

## Non Sequitur

*Notes*

Washington Post Writer's Group, 1997

### ▼ Activities

#### Discuss Advertisements

Discuss with your class advertisements that you remember and why you remember them.

- How did the advertisements appeal to you?
- Do you remember some advertisements because they didn't appeal to you?
- Do you sometimes buy products because of the advertisements you've seen?
- Are advertisers always straightforward and honest in the way that they advertise?

Review the Non Sequitur cartoon.

- What product are the characters looking to sell?
- What tricks will they use?
- Why is this funny?
- Why does the second man say, "We?"

*Notes*

> ### Journal Assignment
> 
> **Review Discussion**
> 
> Think about your class discussion and write your thoughts about advertisements. This is an opportunity to express your thoughts privately and freely. (Refer back to your journal when you're ready to begin drafting your essay.)

### Read, Discuss, Think Critically

In this stage, you gather information by reading material related to the topic. Inexperienced writers often worry that they do not have anything to say about an assigned topic. These writers need to realize (through discussions and journal writing) that they already know *something* about an assignment although they probably need more information on the subject (often gained through reading).

    Returning to our analogy of buying a car, it would be wise to "read up" on the car you intend to buy before following through with the purchase. You may want to know, for example, what *Consumer Reports* or *Car and Driver* has to say about the car's performance, value, or gas mileage. Once you become knowledgeable on the subject, you will be better prepared to make a purchase. In the same way, the more you know about your writing topic, the better prepared you are to write about it.

### Reading Assignment

#### The Advertisements

*(The questions and suggestions that follow will help you continue to use the PARTS of the reading process.)*

***Preview***   Note where each advertisement came from (the place of publication, the magazine.)

***Anticipate***   Each magazine attracts a certain audience, and in each magazine you'll find advertisements that are targeted for that specific audience. Look at each ad again and and think about where the ad came from. What kinds of ads do you think each magazine usually carries? What type of an audience are the advertisers speaking to? (Make notes about your anticipation ideas next to each advertisement.)

***Read and Reread***   As you read, pay attention to the words, knowing that they were carefully chosen by the advertiser. Also note the objects, the placement of these objects, and the people (their clothes, their postures, the expressions on their faces). Mark interesting parts or words in the advertisements and make notes.

# Chapter 4  Examining the Writing Process

## Notes

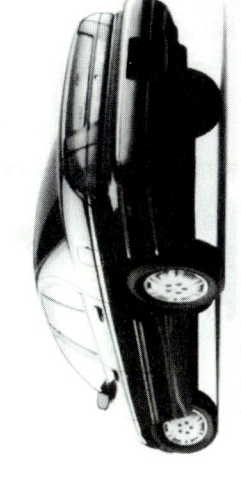

*Better Homes and Gardens* (4/98)

**126** Section I  Establishing the Connections

Notes

*Self* (6/98)

*Sports Illustrated* (1/26/98)

*Sports Illustrated* (2/23/98)

*Living Fit* (3/98)

**Notes**

*Rolling Stone* (8/7/97)

Chapter 4 Examining the Writing Process 129

Notes

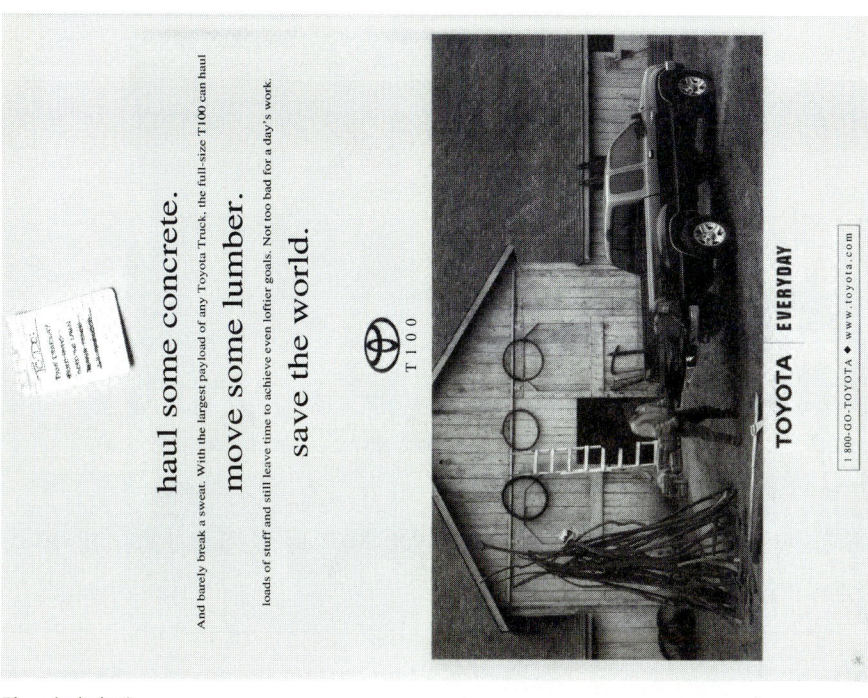

Time (2/2/98)

Copyright © 2001 by Addison Wesley Longman, Inc.

Time (2/9/98)

**130** Section I   Establishing the Connections

*Notes*

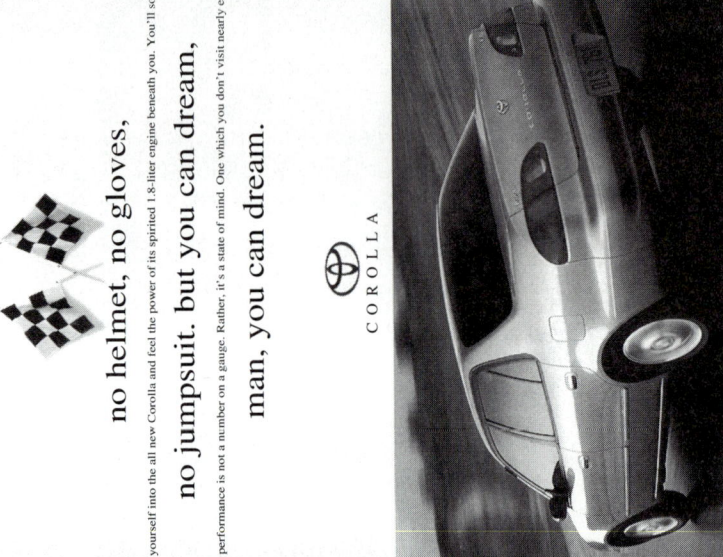

Sports Illustrated (2/8/97)

Time (12/29/97)

▼ **Activity**  Notes

### Discuss Selected Advertisements

In groups, discuss what you see in each advertisement. What sorts of words are used? What colors? What is (or is not) in the picture? If there are people, what do they look like? What sort of expressions and clothes do they wear? How are the advertisers manipulating you? What kind of audience will respond best to the advertisement and want to buy the product? (Think about gender, age, ethnicity, economic status, and so on.) Are the advertisers relying on stereotypes? Explain. (Be sure to take notes during your class discussion.)

---

#### Journal Assignment

*Review Discussion*

Think about your group discussion and review your notes and the advertisements. Now write down your thoughts. (Answer as many of the previous questions as you can, and add any other thoughts.) Exchange this journal with one or more classmates. When you read someone else's, simply say "Thank you" when you return the journal to the author. Don't criticize or discuss.

---

## Explore the Writing Assignment

At this stage, you and your classmates will carefully study the writing assignment. (No one wants to finish an assignment only to find out he or she wrote "off topic.") It is at this point that you and your classmates can discuss how you might respond to the essay topic. What is the assignment asking? What kind of main point do you want to focus on? How will you prove your main point? Are you unclear about any facts? Talk with other people to help you think through the topic and help you make good choices as you begin writing.

▼ **Activities**

### Review the Writing Assignment

Here, again, is your writing assignment. Review it carefully before continuing. Underline the important terms in the assignment.

*Write an essay in which you analyze one advertisement by discussing the strategies the advertiser is using to make the product "appeal" to buyers and comment on how successful you think the advertisement is.*

*Notes*

### Choose an Advertisement

Choose an advertisement you would like to write about. Note: it is acceptable to change your mind later about which advertisement to write about, but you will save yourself some time if you first carefully consider your choices. Choose an advertisement that you find interesting and that has a number of features you want to think about and study.

### Explore the Advertising Assignment

Explore the topic: Review and discuss the assignment with your classmates and consider these critical thinking questions. What advertisement do you want to focus on? Why? What sort of information needs to be in your essay? What doesn't? What will you say? In what order will you state your points? What kinds of details and explanations will you give? (Make notes as you do this.)

### Analyze an Advertisement

To further analyze your advertisement, fill in the following chart.

| Advertiser's Strategies | How does the strategy work? | How effective is it? |
|---|---|---|
| 1. | | |
| 2. | | |

| Advertiser's Strategies | How does the strategy work? | How effective is it? |
|---|---|---|
| 3. | | |
| 4. | | |

***Brainstorm*** When you have read and thought about the topic and made notes and discussed your ideas with classmates, you may want to let your thoughts flow freely on paper in a **brainstorm.** Let yourself write freely with no interruptions or worries about corrections. This can help you discover what points most interest you about a certain topic. The key is to let yourself write freely for as long as you can, even repeating ideas, because the ideas you repeat may be the ideas that most intrigue you. These are the ideas that might become the focus of your essay.

▼ *Activity*

### Brainstorming

Focusing on the current writing assignment and the advertisements you have been studying, write freely for as long as you can. Let your mind wander, but periodically look back at the assignment to remind yourself of what you will be writing an essay about. If you run out of ideas, look back at your class notes and reread what you've already written. Remember, it's okay to repeat yourself when you're brainstorming.

*Create Your Thesis Statement*   The thesis is the sentence at the end of your introduction that expresses the main idea of your essay. This important sentence should directly respond to the **essay assignment** (also known as the **essay prompt**.) It may take a few attempts before you are able to create a sentence that clearly states your main point. In fact, you may even return to this step later in your writing process. When you are drafting or revising, you may decide to change your thesis so that it clearly communicates what you will prove or explain in your essay. Writing a good thesis statement requires using your critical thinking skills as you decide what your essay will focus on.

### ▼ Activity

#### Creating a Thesis

Sometimes it's helpful to change the essay assignment, or prompt, into a question, if it isn't already a question. For example, your current essay topic is

> *Write an essay in which you analyze one advertisement by discussing the strategies the advertiser is using to make the product "appeal" to buyers and comment on how successful you think the advertisement is.*

If you turned this into a question, it might read like this:

> *What strategies is the advertiser using to make the product appeal to buyers, and how successful is the advertisement?*

Your answer to this question could become your thesis statement.

Now, focusing on the advertisement you have chosen, write down some possible answers to this question. Share your responses with classmates or a tutor. Work on polishing the sentence so that it clearly communicates your main idea. Remember, it's okay to come back later and improve your thesis statement.

*Outline*   Another helpful tool for writers is the **outline**. An outline can be a formal and thorough list of all the major and supporting points in an essay, or it can be a quick list of just the major points to be covered. The benefit in creating an outline is to make a plan for yourself so that you stay focused on your main idea, and on ideas that directly support it. When creating an outline, think about what your major points will be and what order these points should be in. You'll need to use your critical thinking skills as you choose what to include in and what to leave out of your essay.

Some writers spend a lot of time perfecting their outlines—listing major points, supporting points, and details. These writers revise and perfect their outlines until the entire essay is just about written. Other writers start with a rough, quick outline—listing the thesis and topic sentences—and then jump into drafting the essay, looking at the outline just to see if they are staying on track. These writers may drift away from their outline and decide that drifting away is okay because the outline wasn't quite right for what they have decided to say. Some of these writers take the time to revise their outlines as a way of checking their draft.

The goal with outlines is to make a plan first before diving into an essay. If you think about your thesis and what your major supporting points should be, you are more likely to stay on track and not get lost in many other related topics. Also, you can use an outline as a tool for sharing your ideas. That is, before writing an entire draft, you can test out your ideas by simply showing your outline to a reader and getting feedback.

▼ **Activity**

### Outline

Write down your thesis statement at the top of a page. Then make a list of supporting ideas. Again, you'll have to experiment and use your critical thinking skills as you decide what your major points should be. If you want to, add some notes under each major supporting point to remind yourself of the details you will use from the advertisement.

Share this outline with a classmate or tutor to see if you are responding clearly and directly to the writing assignment.

### Draft

When you have discussed a topic, read about it, discussed related readings, thought critically about the topic and readings, and written an outline, it's time to begin drafting your essay.

Write a draft that you'll want to share with your classmates, a tutor, or your instructor. It should be complete—with an introduction, body, and conclusion. (This complete draft will naturally be imperfect.

Notes

*Notes*

You'll have opportunities later in your writing process to rearrange ideas, add ideas, or even take out some ideas if they don't fit.) Keep your audience in mind as you write your draft and repeat any earlier steps of your writing process as necessary. (For example, if you feel that midway through your essay you have run out of things to say, go back and look at the advertisement again, review your class notes, or talk to a classmate or tutor.)

Consider completing your draft on a computer so that you don't have to retype the entire essay after each improvement.

## ▼ Activities

### Draft Your Advertisement Essay

Draft your essay about the advertisement you selected. (Be sure to use the notes, charts, and the outline you've made so far.) Remember, you're writing an essay to a reader who has never seen your advertisement before, so in your introduction summarize what you see in your advertisement and what you believe the advertiser is trying to accomplish. In the body of your essay, support what you have said in your introduction by exposing the strategies the advertiser uses. Be specific. In your conclusion, comment on the effectiveness of the advertisement.

### Study a Student Sample

The following is the introductory paragraph from a student's essay about a milk advertisement. Read it carefully and mark what you think is good about this introduction. Then answer the questions that follow.

> The advertisement I chose to analyze is advertising the dairy product milk. It appeared in *Rolling Stone* magazine. The person who is promoting the product is the late-night talk show host Conan O'Brien. Conan is sitting at a desk in a classroom wearing blue jeans that are cuffed way up, high tops and a striped t-shirt. He looks like he is portraying a little kid. He has a little kid innocent look on his face, and he is also wearing a milk mustache which goes along with the caption that reads under the picture, "Where's your mustache?" Next to the picture of Conan is a little paragraph that states why Conan likes to drink milk and how drinking milk can benefit a person. To convince people to buy milk in this advertisement, the advertiser successfully uses such tricks as colors, words, an eye-catching setting, and a celebrity.
>
> —Jennifer Arch

There are many ways to introduce an essay, and Jennifer found a way that worked well for her. Respond to the following questions in your notebook and be prepared to discuss your responses with classmates.

1. What do you particularly like about this introduction? What good decisions did Jennifer make?

2. An introduction to an essay should tell you *what* the topic of the essay is and *why* the reader should read. (What will the reader learn from reading the essay?) Can you find the *what* and *why* in this introduction? Underline the parts that you find and then discuss them with your class.

3. An introduction usually has a thesis (a sentence that states the main idea.) Do you see Jennifer's thesis? Where?

## Revise

**Revising** means *reseeing* what you have written and then *rewriting* it to make it better. It involves using your critical thinking skills to make choices and rearrange parts of your essay to help "make sense" of the topic. As you revise, you may need to add more information to help the reader see your point. Or you may need to delete information that does not fit. The revising stage overlaps with the previous stage because each time you revise (or rewrite), you'll end up with a new draft.

### Points to Remember about Revision

- All writers need to revise. Revision is a normal and healthy part of the writing process.
- Effective revising requires the writer to think about audience and to use his or her critical thinking skills to decide what necessary changes need to be made.
- All writers need feedback on their work. Even professional writers have editors and friends comment on their work before publishing it. Be sure to share your writing with classmates and other readers.
- Effective writers take pride in their work, making it their own. This means that while they consider others' advice, they do not let others take over their work.

Notes

▼ **Activity**

*Share Your Writing*

Find a classmate to work with. Read each other's essays and discuss the following questions in relation to each essay.

- Does your introduction tell *what* your essay is about and *why* your reader should read?
- Have you given your reader enough details? Will he or she be able to "see" the advertisement in his or her mind?
- Have you told your reader what strategies the advertiser is using?
- Do you support your statements about the strategies with proof from the advertisements? (words? images?)
- Have you clearly expressed how successful you feel the advertiser was in making the product appealing?
- Make a list of things you want to change in your essay. Start with the most important.

Begin rewriting your essay. Focus on one problem area at a time. Write more than one new draft. (Each time you rewrite, your essay will probably get better.)

## Edit

When you have revised your paper to the point that you feel confident about its organization and development of ideas, then it's time to begin editing your essay. This is the stage where writers work on spelling, punctuation, and grammar to make sure their sentences are grammatically correct.

▼ **Activity**

*Edit Your Advertising Essay*

When you feel your essay says everything you want it to (or when your deadline is nearing), then begin "polishing" it. (Note: many writers feel that they could go on improving an essay forever—that's normal.) It's a good idea to have your teacher or tutor show you one area you need to work on (for example, subject-verb agreement). Have that person explain that type of error, and then focus your editing work on just that area. Remember to check your spelling.

*Notes*

## Writing Assignment #2: Creating an Advertisement

In this assignment, you'll create your own advertisement and analyze it. You'll exercise your critical thinking skills and practice your reading and writing processes as you consider your audience and your goals as an advertiser.

Here, in brief, is the writing assignment that you are preparing for:

*Create an advertisement to promote a product of your choice. Then, write an essay in which you analyze your own advertisement.*

Keep this assignment in mind as you dig deeper into the issue and prepare to write.

## Discuss and Engage

Notes

▼ *Activity*

### Discuss Creating an Advertisement

Discuss with your classmates products you might want to sell and the types of people who would be interested in buying these products. (Think about selling your favorite cereal, perfume, shampoo, or car, for example.) Be specific. Also, discuss the ways to get the attention of different groups of people.

---

*Journal Assignment*

### Products, Buyers, and Hooks

Think about products, buyers, and ways to grab consumer attention. Write down some possible products you'd like to advertise. Describe the people you would be trying to attract with each product and how you might do that. Think about the people, props, colors, and words you might use. Write about more than one advertisement you could create. (This journal is for your eyes only.)

---

## Read, Discuss, Think Critically

Remember, at this stage of your writing process you should gather more information and consider other people's thoughts on your subject.

## *Reading Assignment*

### "When Advertising Offends"

*(The questions and suggestions that follow will help you continue to use the PARTS of the reading process.)*

***Preview*** Before you read, note when and where this essay was published. Read the title and introduction. Highlight the topic sentences.

***Anticipate*** What do you anticipate this essay will be about? Use the "Notes" column to record your thoughts.

***Read and Reread*** Read the essay quickly and mark unfamiliar words. Then reread the essay more slowly, interacting with the text by making comments in the "Notes" column and highlighting important points. Define unknown words.

## When Advertising Offends: Another Look at Aunt Jemima
*Based on Westerman (1989) and Simpson (1992)*
*by John J. Macionis*

This essay comes from a college sociology textbook, *Sociology*.

1. Commercial advertisers want to sell products. However, some old ad campaigns are becoming counterproductive because they offend their audience by portraying categories of people in inaccurate and unfair ways.

2. A century ago, the vast majority of consumers in the United States were white people, and many were uneasy with growing racial and cultural diversity. Businesses commonly exploited this discomfort, depicting various categories of people in ways that were clearly condescending. In 1889, for example, a pancake mix first appeared featuring a servant mammy named "Aunt Jemima." Although somewhat modernized, this logo is widely used in the mass media, and the product continues to hold a commanding share of its market. Likewise, the hot cereal "Cream of Wheat" is still symbolized by the African-American chef Rastus, and "Uncle Ben" is familiar to millions of households as a brand name for rice. But to many people, use of such caricatures—which, after all, originally depicted the black slaves or servants of white people—is racially insensitive at best.

3. Changes in advertising have occurred in recent decades in all the mass media. The stereotypical Frito Bandito, long familiar to older television viewers, was abandoned in 1971 by Frito-Lay (a company, ironically, whose first product was a corn chip invented by a Latino living in San Antonio). The characterization of Latinos as bandits or outlaws, embodied in the bumbling cartoon figure of Frito Bandito, discredited an entire segment of the population. A host of other such images have also disappeared as businesses in the United States confront a new reality: the growing voice and financial power of minorities, who represent a market worth one-half trillion dollars a year. Taken together, Americans of African, Latino, and Asian descent represent 20 percent of the population and may constitute a national majority by the end of the next century. And, just as important, the share of the minority population that is affluent is steadily increasing.

4. Businesses are responding to the growing financial power of minorities. In the last ten years businesses have doubled their spending on advertising aimed at African Americans to about $1 billion annually. The results of this policy shift have been encouraging for the businesses involved—far higher sales—and pleasing to people who have historically found little to like in commercial advertising.

Notes

### ▼ Questions for Critical Thought

#### "When Advertising Offends"

1. Find the thesis statement in this essay and underline it. What is the main point of this essay? Write it down in your own words.

2. What stereotypes are discussed in this essay?

3. It could be argued that advertisers must rely on stereotypes to some degree. Usually these stereotypes are harmless although, obviously, some stereotypes can be hurtful. Respond to this idea of "harmless" vs. "hurtful" stereotypes.

4. When you write your advertisement, will you be relying on any stereotypes? Is this okay? Explain.

5. One of the stylistic strengths of this essay is the use of **transitions,** words that add **coherence** to the essay. *(In a coherent essay, all the ideas fit together and support the thesis.)* In paragraphs 1 and 2, you can find the following words that help the different ideas flow and fit together: *however, for example, although, likewise, but.* Explain how the author used each transition to show how all the ideas fit together. (For example, how does *however* in the first paragraph help us move from the first sentence to the second? What does *however* tell us?) Discuss each of the five transitions mentioned above.

---

### *Journal Assignment*

#### *Ideas about Writing an Ad*

Write your thoughts about writing an advertisement. What is the hardest part about creating a good advertisement? What is the easiest part? What products are you considering advertising, and how is the audience different for each one? If the audience is large, how might you create your ad for an audience of a specific magazine? What will attract each different audience? (After you write this journal, exchange journals with a classmate, and say "Thank you.")

---

### Explore the Writing Assignment

Here is a more detailed description of your writing assignment.

*Create an advertisement to promote a product of your choice, and write an essay in which you analyze your advertisement. You may* sketch the ad yourself or put together pictures from other advertisements. Be sure to make it clear in your sketch (or collage) what colors you would use, what the people would look like (expressions, clothes, posture, gender, ethnicity, age), what props you would use. And, of course, write some interesting text to sell your product. Then, in your essay, describe the ad you have created, and explain what audience you are trying to attract and how you are trying to attract them. What strategies are you using?

Notes

## ▼ Activities

### Explore the Assignment

Discuss the following questions with your classmates.

1. What product will you sell?
2. What audience will you try to attract?
3. What strategies will you use?

### Create Your Advertisement

Be thoughtful and creative as you design your advertisement. After you have created your advertisement, show it to friends and classmates and ask them what strategies they see you using. Are these effective strategies? Are your friends and classmates right? Do you need to change your advertisement at all?

*Brainstorm*   With your advertisement completed, it's time to begin the second part of your assignment. Focus now on the part that says "... analyze your own advertisement." You may want to think of the prompt topic as a series of questions: How would you analyze your advertisement? What strategies are you using, and are your strategies effective? Who is in your audience? Write freely and answer these questions, but don't feel limited to them. Remember when brainstorming, you want to let your thoughts wander a bit.

*Create Your Thesis*   Use your brainstorm, readings, journal, and class notes to begin to experiment with thesis statements. You want to find a sentence that clearly explains what your essay will focus on and what you'll be explaining in your essay.

Notes

**Outline** When you've created a thesis statement you're satisfied with, begin listing ideas that will support your thesis statement. Decide what your main supporting points should be and create topics sentences that express these points. Consider the best way to organize your topic sentences. Can you use any transitions to help with coherence *(however, for example, likewise)*?

## Draft

As you begin to draft your essay, refer to your outline, but feel free to vary from it if you need to. In the introduction, describe your advertisement, giving enough detail so that your audience will "see" your ad. Also, explain who your intended audience is and what you hope to accomplish with this advertisement. (Remember to give your reader a sense of what is coming and why your essay is worth reading.) In the body of your essay, support your introduction by explaining the strategies you have used in the ad. In your conclusion, explain what you hope the reader has learned from your essay.

## Revise

Enter this stage with an open mind. Assume that you will find some weaknesses in your draft *and* that you will find ways to improve and strengthen your essay.

### ▼ Activity

**Share Your Writing**

Work with a classmate and discuss the following questions as they relate to your essays.

- Do you have a thesis? Does your introduction tell *what* your essay is about and *why* your reader should read?
- Have you given your reader enough detail? Will he or she be able to "see" the advertisement in his or her mind?
- Have you told your reader what strategies you are using? Have you explained why you are using these particular strategies? Who is in your audience?
- Have you used any transitions to help your ideas flow? *(However, for example, likewise)*

Make a list of things you want to improve in your essay. Start with the most important.

### Edit

Now begin "polishing" your essay. Are there any errors that you tend to repeat? Focus on one type of error at a time. (If you can only focus on one when editing this essay, that's okay. Sometimes it's better to focus on just one area at a time.)

### Writing Assignment #3: The Most Evil Character

In this assignment, you'll examine the decisions people make and the values reflected by those decisions. You'll exercise your critical thinking skills and practice your reading and writing processes as you analyze the story that follows.

Here, in brief, is the writing assignment that you are preparing for:

*Write an essay in which you analyze the story "The Most Evil Character" and determine who is the most evil of all the characters.*

Keep this assignment in mind as you dig deeper into the topic and prepare to write.

### Discuss and Engage

▼ **Activity**

**Making Decisions**

Discuss with your classmates some decisions you've had to make recently. What were easy decisions? What were hard ones? Did any of these choices reflect your values? What do you value in people? What are important characteristics that you think people should have?

### Journal Assignment

**Review Class Discussion**

Write down your answers to these questions: What do you value in people? What are important characteristics that you think people should

*Notes*

> have? You may also want to write down what your classmates said and what you thought about their comments. (This journal is for your eyes only. Refer back to this journal when you are getting ready to write your essay.)

## Read, Discuss, Think Critically

### Reading Assignment

"The Most Evil Character"

***Preview*** Note that this selection is not an essay. It is a fictional story used by teachers and students as a way to discuss people's values and decision making skills. (The style of the writing here is, of course, different than academic essays.) Read the title and the first few sentences.

***Anticipate*** What do you anticipate this story will be about? Use the "Notes" column to record your thoughts.

***Read and Reread*** Read the story quickly and mark unfamiliar words. Then reread the story more slowly, interacting with the text by making comments in the "Notes" column and highlighting important points. Define unknown words.

### The Most Evil Character

*(author unknown)*

Jack is in his third year of college and doing passing but below-average work. His mother has been insisting that he plan to enroll in law school and become an attorney, like his father. Angry at him for not receiving better grades, she has told him that under no circumstances will he get the car or the trip that he has been promised unless his average goes up one full grade. Although Jack has done slightly better work this term, he has been having trouble with his psychology course, especially with the term paper. Twice he has asked for a conference (not during office hours, the time of which conflicts with another class he cannot miss) with his teacher, but Professor Brown has told him that he is not being paid to run a private tutoring service. So Jack postpones writing the paper and finally puts it together hastily the night before it is due. Then Professor Brown calls him in and tells him that the paper is disgraceful and that he has no chance of getting a passing grade or even an incomplete unless he submits a more acceptable essay by 9 a.m. the next day. Jack tries to explain his situation and his mother's demands, and he asks for some more time to revise the paper, but his teacher is inflexible and says, "You probably don't belong in college anyway." Since there is no way that Jack is going to be able to produce the revised essay on time, he decides to salvage the car and the trip by getting somebody to write it for him. He has heard about Victor, a recent graduate who always needs money. Victor agrees and, after some haggling about the fee, he writes an acceptable paper overnight. A few days after Professor Brown has accepted the paper and given Jack his grade, Jack gets a call from Victor, who says that, unless he gets double the original fee, he will reveal the entire transaction to Professor Brown and the Dean. Jack does not have the money and cannot tell his parents.

## ▼ Activities

### Summarize the Story

Write a summary of "The Most Evil Character." What are the main points, the facts, and the names that you need to remember?

### Who Is the Worst?

Discuss the reading with your classmates. First, review the facts about what happened. (Refer to your summary.) Then begin discussing how the characters in the story rank. Who is the worst character and why? Who is the most innocent/best character and why? What does all of this suggest about your values?

### Journal Assignment

#### Review Class Discussion

Immediately after your class discussion, write down your thoughts. How do you feel about the characters in the story? Why? How do your classmates feel? Why? Did any of your classmates change your opinions? Did any of your classmates disagree with you? How did your values influence your rating of the characters?

(Be sure to exchange your journal with a classmate and say "Thank you.")

Notes

## Explore the Writing Assignment

Here is a more detailed description of your writing assignment.

*Write an essay to a reader who has never read "The Most Evil Character." You will briefly summarize for the reader what happens in the story. Then you will tell the reader what your judgment of the characters is. Who do you think is the most evil character and who is the least evil? Where do the other characters rank? You will also explain why you have made these judgments.*

### ▼ Activities

#### Explore the Assignment

Discuss with your classmates what kind of information you think you need to put in your essay. Perhaps you want to make a list. What will your judgments be? How will you explain your judgments? What will come first in your essay? Second?

#### Charting Your Thoughts

As a way of organizing your thoughts, fill in the chart that follows. Compare your chart with your classmates'. (Keep in mind that it's not necessary for your charts to agree.)

| Character | Deed | Judgment (Why?) |
|---|---|---|
| 1. | | |
| 2. | | |
| 3. | | |

| Character | Deed | Judgment (Why?) |
|---|---|---|
| 4. | | |
| 5. | | |
| 6. | | |

***Create Your Thesis*** When you begin to work on your thesis for this assignment, review the writing assignment carefully and then ask yourself these questions: What do I want my audience to know after they have read my essay? What main point should stick in the reader's mind? You may want to summarize the assignment (in writing or out loud to a tutor) and explain what it is asking for. Summarizing and explaining will help you clarify what you must focus on with your thesis (and in your essay.) Then experiment with sentences until you find one that would function well as a thesis statement.

***Outline*** Write your thesis statement at the top of a blank page and review, again, your writing assignment, notes, and chart. What major points should you cover in your essay to support your thesis? Make a list of possible points to cover. Use your critical thinking skills to decide which of these points should be made into topic sentences. Take your time in creating thoughtful topic sentences.

**Notes**

## Draft

Refer to your outline as you begin drafting. In your introduction, you'll need to summarize the story for the reader and establish your position as to who is the most evil character. In the body of your paper, you'll want to explain and prove why that person is the most evil. You'll also want to show how the other characters rank and why. In your conclusion, discuss the values that you are supporting. Your goal is to complete an essay with an introduction, body paragraphs, and conclusion.

### ▼ Activities

#### Study a Student Sample

The following is an introductory paragraph from a student's essay. Read it carefully and underline what you think works well, then answer the questions that follow.

> "The Most Evil Character" is a story about a college student named Jack with mediocre grades who tries to live up to both his mother's and Professor Brown's expectations. With the help of Victor, a graduate student who is constantly in need of money, Jack achieves his goal by less than honest means. We will now examine the characters from the most to the least evil.
>
> —Miguel Viera

1. What do you think Miguel did particularly well?
2. If a reader had never read "The Most Evil Character," would this introduction be clear? Why or why not?
3. Does this writer have a clear thesis? If so, where?

#### Study a Student Sample

In the next student sample, you'll read the first body paragraph from another student's essay. (This student's thesis was: "I intend to prove that Victor is 'The Most Evil Character' in this story." This thesis was the last sentence in the introduction.) Then answer the questions that follow.

First body paragraph:

Notes

> Jack's mom wanted him to become a lawyer, like his father. *Setting Limits,* by Robert J. MacKenzie, Ed.D., says that "the exploration is the most important part . . . Teens need to try out new roles, new values and beliefs, new relationships and commitments." She did not give him that chance. Instead, she promised him a car and a trip to pursue the career of her choice. Because his grades were not commendable, she warned him that if he did not bring his average up one grade he would not receive the offering, and this became his first ultimatum.
>
> —*Keisha Harris*

1. This paragraph has a number of strengths. What do you think Keisha did well?
2. Study Keisha's paragraph. What is Keisha proving in this paragraph? Write your own topic sentence for this paragraph. (Remember, your topic sentence should show how this first body paragraph connects to the idea expressed in the thesis.)

### Study a Student Sample

In the next student sample, you'll read a concluding paragraph from yet another student's essay. As you read it, think about what a conclusion should do and mark the parts of the conclusion that you like best. Then answer the questions that follow.

> To wrap it all up, Jack by far is the evil person, in my opinion. He has created his own mess. He needs to stop and take a long look at his life, also his situation and fix it no matter what the outcome may be. Mom and Victor need to get real lives and stop the blackmail games. Professor Brown maybe could be a bit less open in his own personal opinion of his student's life outside of his classroom. As for dad and the Dean they are just names thrown into a situation that they were not directly a part of.
>
> —*Ruth Hathaway*

Notes

1. From reading this conclusion paragraph, can you tell what Ruth's thesis probably was? If yes, write a thesis for her essay.
2. From this conclusion paragraph, can you tell what Ruth's main supporting points might have been? Write topic sentences (in your own words) for body paragraphs that might work in her essay.
3. Will the conclusion in your essay be anything like Ruth's? Explain.

## Revise

Use your critical thinking skills and find strengths and weaknesses in your own writing *before* you hear what others think. This will help you become an independent writer.

Then, when you do have a classmate or a tutor look at your essay, listen carefully. But *you* make the decisions about what to change and what not to change. You are in control of your own writing.

### ▼ Activity

**Share Your Writing**

Find a classmate to work with. Read each other's essays and discuss the following questions as they relate to your essays.

- What concerns do you have about your essay?
- Have you summarized the events of the story?
- Have you ranked the characters in order to show who is the *most* evil?
- Is it clear who the *least* evil character is?
- Do you support and explain your ideas?
- Do your ideas flow from one sentence to the next and from one paragraph to the next? Does each point clearly connect to the thesis?
- Does the essay contain an introduction, body paragraphs, and conclusion?

Make a list of things you want to change in your essay. Start with the most important. Are there certain things that your instructor wants you to focus on when you revise?

Begin revising your essay. Focus on one problem area at a time. Write more than one new draft.

## Edit

Now begin "polishing" your essay. Carefully check your essay for typing errors, spelling errors, and subject-verb agreement errors.

## ▲▼▲ Time to Reflect

> ### Journal Assignment
> *Your Progress as a Writer, Reader, and Critical Thinker*
>
> Reflect on the skills you have strengthened in this chapter. Write a journal entry in which you discuss
>
> - what you have learned in this chapter,
> - the skills you are improving,
> - the skills you feel need more work,
> - changes in your reading process, and
> - changes in your writing process.

## ▲▼▲ Summary of Chapter 4

This chapter has focused on understanding and effectively using the stages of the writing process.

Discuss and Engage

Read, Discuss, and Think Critically

Explore the Writing Assignment

Draft

Revise

Edit

As you have studied advertisements, advertising strategies, and evil characters, you have

- used your reading, writing, and critical thinking skills and
- seen the advantages of using an effective writing process.

Your tasks as a writer are easier when you approach writing as a process. In addition, your writing will be clearer, better organized, and more developed. Using the writing process effectively is key to writing well.

Notes

 **Subjects**

*Identifying Subjects*
*More about Subjects*
*The Implied Subject*

Now that you have learned the importance of verbs and how to identify them in your sentences, it's time to turn to the next major ingredient of a sentence: the **subject**. The subject of a sentence is the person or thing the sentence is about. The subject performs the action expressed by the verb, or it is linked to other information by the verb. Learning to identify the subject and discovering how it works within the sentence will help you create clearer sentences.

## Identifying Subjects

To identify the subject of a sentence, ask, "Who?" or "What?" about each verb. Underline the verb twice.

*Example:*

a. I like funny advertisements.

Question: Who *likes*?

*Answer*: I

The answer to your question is the subject of that sentence. Underline the subject once.

a. I like funny advertisements.

*Hints:* One verb can have more than one subject, and one subject can have more than one verb.

b. Magazines and newspapers have a lot of advertisements.

c. People respond to the ads and buy the products.

(Sentences with multiple subjects and verbs will be covered in more detail in Chapter 5.)

Sometimes it is easier to find the subject if you ask "Who?" or "What?" after the entire predicate. The **predicate** of a sentence is the verb and all the words that are not part of the subject.

In sentence (a) you could ask, "Who or what like funny advertisements?"

In sentences (b) and (c), the predicate is underlined twice and the subject is underlined once

   b. <u>Magazines and newspapers</u> <u><u>have a lot of advertisements.</u></u>

   c. <u>People</u> <u><u>respond to the ads and buy the products.</u></u>

In the following sentences, identify the verbs and underline them twice. (Remember not to let "imposters" fool you—be sure to underline the whole verb.) Then, after you ask the "who?" or "what?" question, identify the subjects and underline them once.

1. Advertisers create advertisements, or ads, in order to sell products.
2. To be successful at this, advertisers must use a number of tools.
3. Color is one important tool.
4. Models, props, and special photography are other tools they use.
5. And, of course, words in an advertisement can do more than just give us information.
6. Writers choose special words to make the product attractive to us.
7. For example, when describing a car, an advertiser might use words like "sexy," "timeless," "defiant," and "independent."
8. We don't usually associate words like these with cars.
9. But advertisers know how to manipulate us.

## More about Subjects

A. Think about sentences 1–9 and answer the following questions.
   1. Does each sentence have at least one verb?
   2. Can you have a sentence with no verbs?
   3. Can you have a sentence with no subjects?
   4. Does every verb have a subject?

B. Complete this sentence:

   A complete sentence must have _____.

## The Implied Subject

Look at the following sentences. (These are directions that you might receive some day if you work for an advertising firm. Note that the directions are quite similar to the directions for the second writing assignment in this chapter.) Underline the verbs twice.

Notes

*Study this product. Write an advertisement for a magazine. Then carefully choose the colors, props, people, and words to use. Think about your audience. Create an appealing advertisement.*

In the paragraph above, who is supposed to do all the work?

The sentences in the paragraph are called **command sentences.** They give someone work to do. They give directions. Command sentences do not have stated subjects: they have **implied subjects.** The implied subject is "you."

*[You] study this product. [You] write an advertisement for a magazine. [You] then carefully choose the colors, props, people, and words to use. [You] think about your audience. [You] create an appealing advertisement.*

**Testing Your Understanding of Subjects and Verbs**

1. Choose a paragraph from one of your essays—preferably one you are currently working on. Copy the paragraph down on a sheet of paper. Then underline all the verbs twice. After asking the "who" or "what" questions, underline the subjects once.

2. After you've completed this part, show your work to a classmate and see if he or she thinks you've underlined all the subjects and verbs correctly. Show any questionable sentences to your instructor or tutor.

## ▲▼▲ Subject-Verb Agreement: Keeping Your Meaning Clear

### Subject-Verb Agreement
### Prepositional Phrases Cannot Be Subjects

In standard American English, readers will expect your subjects and verbs to agree in number. **Subject-verb agreement** errors can cause confusion for your readers and will make your work seem less professional. This section of sentence work will draw on your ability to identify subjects and verbs, and will teach you what subject-verb agreement means and how to correct subject-verb agreement errors.

### *Subject-Verb Agreement*

It is important to be able to identify subjects correctly so that you can figure out if you need a singular or plural verb. Underline the verbs twice and the subjects once in the two examples that follow.

1. Example (singular subject and singular verb):
    (a) Instructor Smith works with students after class.
2. Example (plural subject and plural verb):
    (b) Students work in groups in the library.

Readers get confused if your subjects and verbs don't agree in number. Underline verbs twice and subjects once in the next two examples.

3. Examples of sentences that confuse readers because subjects and verbs don't agree in number:
    (c) Students is under a lot of pressure.
    (d) My teacher listen to our problems.

If you identified the verb in sentence 3 (c) as *is*, you were right. This is a **singular verb**: it works with *one* person or *one* thing. For example: *The student is under a lot of pressure. Students*, on the other hand, is **plural** (meaning, there are more than one). When a reader sees a plural subject and a singular verb, he or she will stop and reread, wondering if he or she read the sentence incorrectly or missed something the first time around.

Look at sentence (d). What is wrong with sentence (d)?

Remember, in the present tense, when the subject is *he, she, it,* or another word that could be replaced by *he, she,* or *it,* the verb has an -s on the end. Refer to the following chart, which illustrates when present tense verbs need -s on the end.

### Present Tense Verbs

| Singular | Plural |
| --- | --- |
| I eat | we eat |
| you eat | you eat |
| he, she, it eats | they eat |
| (or the man eats, Susie eats) | |

4. Write a sentence that begins with *I*. Underline the verb twice. Underline your subject once. Now rewrite that sentence and begin with *he, she,* or *it.* See how your verb changes. Underline your verb twice and your subject once.

5. Repeat this process with two more sentences that start with I.

**Subject-Verb Agreement Rule:** Subjects and verbs must agree in number. This means that single subjects must have single verbs. Plural subjects must have plural verbs.

Notes

**Prepositional Phrases Cannot Be Subjects**

There are some sentences where subject and verb agreement becomes less clear. This usually happens when finding the subject is more difficult. See a, b, and c below.

> a. Grading standards at their school are tough.
>
> b. Computers in the classroom are an asset to writing students.
>
> c. A tutor from one of the learning centers helps dedicated students.

With a classmate, underline the verb in each sentence twice and then ask the "who" or "what" question to find the subject. Underline the subjects once. Do the verbs and subjects agree in each sentence?

In sentences a, b, and c it's hard to pick the right subject. If you accidentally picked *school* in sentence a since it is right next to the verb *are*, then *are* does not agree in number. However, the subject is actually *grading standards,* and *are* is correct. Prepositional phrases in all three sentences tend to confuse things.

The prepositional phrases in sentences a, b, and c are:

> at that school
> in the classroom (to writing students)
> from one (of the learning centers)

**Preposition Rule:** Prepositional phrases, or anything in the prepositional phrase, cannot be the subject or the verb of the sentence.

Prepositional phrases usually suggest, location, time, or belonging. *Examples:* (the preposition is in italics and the object follows)

| location | time | belonging |
|---|---|---|
| *in* the street | *before* noon | *of* the community |
| *on* the roof | *after* breakfast | *by* Amy Tan |

The object of the preposition follows the preposition and may be long, or it may be just one small word.

In the sentences which follow

1. Underline the verb twice.
2. Put brackets around the prepositional phrases.
3. Ask your "who" or "what" question, and, when you find the subject, underline it once.
4. Double check to see if all the subjects and verbs agree in number.

5. Mark any sentences with subject/verb errors. (Note: "Who" can be a subject.)

The first sentence is done for you.

<u>It</u> <u>is</u> important [for employees] to have good decision making skills. Employers of all kinds look for people who can make independent decisions. A good employee in a business office can answer some of his own questions. And he can judge the actions of others. Such an employee can become a manager some day. And on a hiring committee, managers decide who gets the job and who doesn't. Managers, in another kind of situation, determine whether or not to fire a troublesome employee. In those kinds of situations, managers decide how serious the problems with the employee is. Keep strengthening your decision making skills. They will come in handy.

***Your Own Work*** Copy a paragraph from your current writing assignment. (It would be especially useful to choose a paragraph that you suspect has a subject-verb agreement error in it, so you can fix it.) Underline all the verbs twice and the subjects once. Bracket prepositional phrases. Do the subjects and verbs agree in number? You may want to use some of the following steps to help you with this task.

  a. To see if you have selected verbs correctly, check to see if your verbs would change if you changed the tense of the sentence by using *today, tomorrow,* or *yesterday* at the beginning.

  b. To see if you have selected subjects correctly, ask the "who" or "what" question before each verb.

Are there any confusing sentences in your paragraph? Discuss these with your tutor/classmate/instructor.

## ▲▼▲ *Revisiting Those -ing Words*

*-ing Words as Nouns, Subjects*
*-ing Words Can Describe*

In Chapter 3 you learned that *-ing* words cannot be verbs unless they have helper verbs. So what are *-ing* words when they don't have helper verbs? Well, they can act as nouns and in some of those cases they can be subjects (gerunds). They can also act as adjectives (participles). Be-

**Notes**

ing able to identify *-ing* subjects will help you when you want to make sure your subjects and verbs agree in your essays, and using *-ing* subjects and *-ing* adjectives in your own writing is one step toward adding variety to your writing.

### -ing *Words as Nouns, Subjects*

First consider how *-ing* words can function as nouns and subjects.

    Definition: **Nouns** name people, places, things, or ideas.
*Examples: tree, book, happiness, mom, Fred, fighting*

1. Put a box around the nouns in sentences a–d.

    a. The class discusses the topic.

    b. The student writes in her journal.

    c. The instructor assigns a reading.

    d. The student reads the essay and answers the discussion questions.

2. Some of the nouns you boxed in sentences a–d are also the subjects of those sentences. Underline the verbs in those sentences twice, and then ask your "who" or "what" questions to find the subjects. Underline the subjects once.

3. Underline the verbs in sentences e–h twice, and then ask your "who" or "what" questions to find the subjects. Underline the subjects once. You may want to discuss these sentences with your class.

    e. Writing takes a lot of time.

    f. Expressing your thoughts is not always easy.

    g. However, communicating with the written word gives you power.

    h. Reading is another key to power.

4. Copy two sentences from your essays or paragraphs or journals where there are *-ing* words that work as the subjects of each sentence. Identify the subject and verb in each sentence. (Before you have anyone look over your work in 4, 5, and 6, you should complete the next section about *-ing* words that describe to make sure you haven't accidentally marked *-ing* words that are actually adjectives—and not subjects.)

5. Look at one of your readings from this class or from another class and find two more sentences that have *-ing* words as the subjects. Identify the subject and verb in each of those sentences. Write these sentences down.

6. Write two sentences that use *-ing* words as subjects. Identify the subjects and verbs in those sentences.

### *-ing* Words Can Describe

Next, consider how an *-ing* word can act as an adjective. An **adjective** is a word that describes nouns. The adjectives are highlighted in the sentences below. Draw an arrow to the nouns they describe.

That talented writer had a great year.

He wrote powerful essays.

And his novels got terrific reviews

He should receive some prestigious awards.

When an *-ing* word is *neither* a subject *nor* a verb, it may be working as an adjective. Below are examples of *-ing* words working as adjectives.

  a. The man yelling is the editor of the paper.
  b. The woman laughing at my poem is my sister.

1. In sentences a and b identify the verbs (underline twice), subjects (underline once), and the *-ing* words that work as adjectives (highlight). What words are the *-ing* words describing? (Draw arrows.)

2. In sentences c–f, identify the verbs (underline twice), the subjects (underline once), and *-ing* adjectives (highlight). (Some *-ing* words are working as verbs.)

  c. I am writing an essay.
  d. And, I am listening to music at an ear-shattering level.
  e. Also, I am drinking some scorching coffee.
  f. My words, flowing like water, are brilliant.

3. Look at some of your own writing and find a sentence in which you use an *-ing* word as an adjective. Write that sentence down. Underline the verb once, underline the subject twice, and highlight the *-ing* adjective.

Notes

4. Look at one of your textbooks and find a sentence with an *-ing* word working as an adjective. Write that sentence down. Underline the verb twice, underline the subject once, and highlight the *-ing* adjective.

5. Create a sentence with an *-ing* word working as an adjective. Underline the verb twice, underline the subject once, and highlight the *-ing* adjective.

Remember: You can test for verbs by using the "test of time," and you can ask the "who" or "what" question to find subjects.

***Your Own Work*** You have studied *-ing* words (as subjects and as adjectives) in this section so that you will have an easier time making sure your subjects and verbs agree. You also should recognize that you can use *-ing* words to add detail and description to your essays. You will practice using *-ing* words as adjectives more in the future. For now, write down a paragraph from an essay you are working on. (It's okay to make improvements on the paragraph as you copy it down.) Then do the following.

Underline all verbs twice.

Underline all subjects once.

Highlight any *-ing* words used as adjectives.

Make sure that your subjects and verbs agree in number.

## ▲▼▲ Subjects and the There Sentence

As we study subjects we learn more about the dynamics of sentences, and we learn how to avoid errors like subject-verb disagreement. Here is another type of sentence that can sometimes lead to subject-verb agreement errors.

### The There Sentence

a. There are many ways to write an essay.

b. There are, however, a few key steps.

c. There is the planning stage.

d. There is the crucial step of rewriting, too.

e. There are tutors, instructors, and books to help you.

Notes

1. Find the verbs in sentences a–e. (You may want to cross out the infinitives first.) (To review infinitives see Chapter 3.)
2. All of the sentences start with *there*, but some of the sentences have plural verbs and some have singular verbs. Why? How can you explain that? (There aren't any subject-verb agreement errors here.)
3. Very carefully ask the "who" or "what" questions and find the subject of each verb. (Watch out for prepositional phrases!)
4. Discuss your answers to 1, 2, and 3 with classmates (or a tutor).
5. Summarize what you know about *there* sentences.

Read sentences a–e aloud. You'll notice how boring they sound. Part of the reason they sound boring is that they all begin in the same way (with *there*). Keep this in mind when writing your own essays; avoid starting all your sentences the same way. As practice, revise sentences a–e so that they don't start with *there*.

Here is (a) done for you:
There are many ways to write an essay.
*Revision:* I know many ways to write an essay.
   or
Essays can be written many different ways.
(Note: There are usually many ways to revise a *there* sentence.)

**Your Own Work**

1. Write five *there* sentences of your own and underline verbs twice and subjects once. (Do your subjects and verbs agree in number?)
2. Now revise these sentences so that they don't start with *there*. (This is important to practice because an occasional *there* sentence is acceptable, but you want to avoid overusing them in your own writing.)

# SECTION II

# Employing the Connections

*This section offers you four chapters, each devoted to a different contemporary theme. In each chapter, you'll read about the topic and be guided through productive reading, writing, and critical thinking processes as you create essays that communicate your thoughts on these themes.*

**CHAPTER 5**
Writing about Heroes

**CHAPTER 6**
Writing about Technology

**CHAPTER 7**
Writing about Television

**CHAPTER 8**
Writing about Music and Poetry

# Writing about Heroes

**CHAPTER 5**

### Main Topics

- Focusing your writing
- Communicating your ideas about heroes
- Using pronouns effectively
- Utilizing outside sources
- Shaping sentences

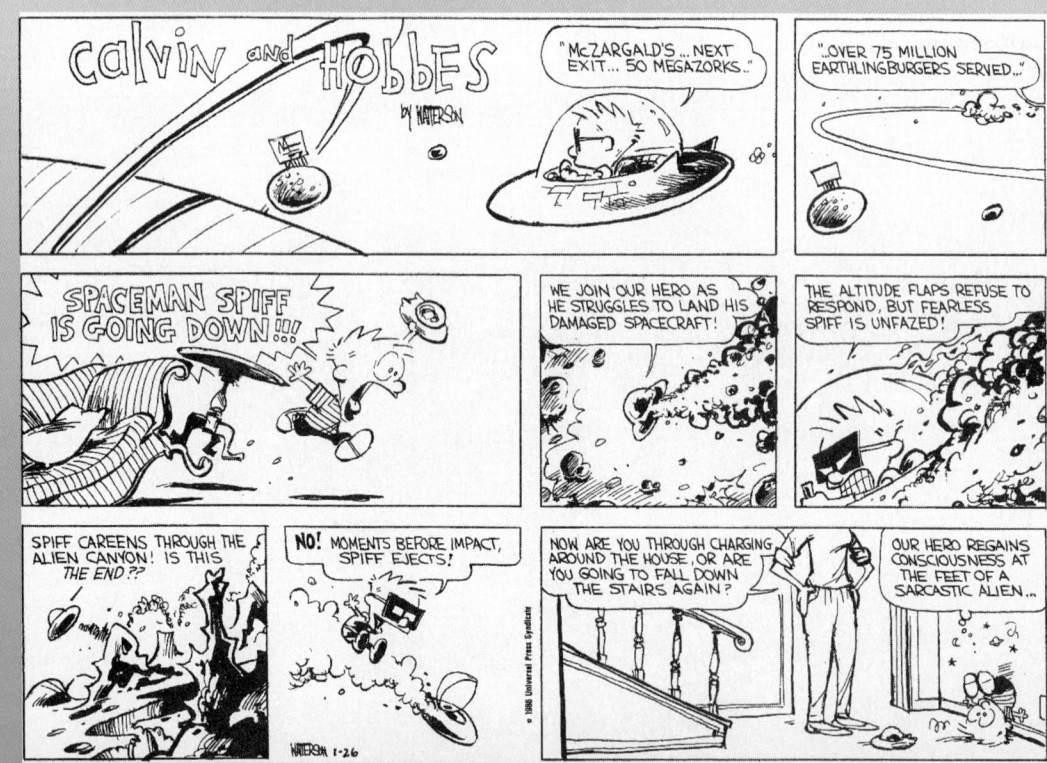

The Essential Calvin & Hobbes Treasury, Andrews & McMeel (Universal)

One of the first things readers expect from academic paragraphs and essays is for the writing to be **focused**. When we speak, we often wander from one topic to another. That's acceptable in speech. (Consider the stand-up comedian who can begin talking about his mother-in-law and end up talking about car repair.) However, in academic writing, your audience expects you to choose a subject and stay focused on it. This requires you to think critically about your topic and your own writing. Writers must make choices about what to say and how to say it so that their audience doesn't get distracted from the main message. In this chapter, you'll explore the topic of heroes and then write a focused definition and essay about a hero. You'll get practice focusing your writing as you write an essay on the heroic qualities of the person you choose.

## ▲▼▲ Focusing Your Writing

Imagine that your photography instructor asks you to photograph one person in a crowd of people. He wants you to study a crowd and choose one face that interests you. You go downtown during the weekday lunch hour and watch people as they go to lunch, do their shopping, and so on. Then, after you make your choice, you take a close-up photograph, making sure that this person's face is in perfect focus. Everyone around this person is blurry.

photo courtesy of Milenko Vlaisvljevic

*Notes*

Writing an essay is similar to this type of photography. You are given a topic (a crowd), you explore your options (the many faces), and then, using your critical thinking skills, you choose one manageable, interesting point to make (the best face). Finally, you write your essay about that point only, leaving out all distracting information. (One person is in focus and all the rest are blurry.) This kind of focus helps your reader stay interested and understand what you want to explain or prove.

## Focusing the Paragraph

A **focused paragraph** will have a clear, informative topic sentence that tells the reader what the main idea of the paragraph is. This sentence should not be too broad or too narrow. That is, it must be broad enough to express an idea worth developing in a paragraph, but it shouldn't be so broad that the reader has a hard time telling where your writing is going next.

The sentences that follow the topic sentence are called the body of the paragraph, and these sentences will clearly support the topic sentence. This support can be in the form of examples, statistics, details, explanations, comparisons, or other forms of evidence. In addition, paragraphs sometimes have a wrap-up sentence that closes the paragraph by summarizing points made or restating the main idea.

All of the sentences in the well-focused paragraph must stick to and support the main idea in the topic sentence. To achieve this clear focus, good writers use the writing process: they brainstorm, draft, and revise. Throughout the process, they make choices.

For example, if a student who has been reading about and discussing heroes in class wants to write a paragraph on why a particular athlete is a hero, he may need to write down a list of ideas and many trial topic sentences before finding a main idea he is comfortable with. After he has a topic sentence (a main idea), he drafts the paragraph and makes choices about which ideas support his topic sentence the best. When he adds information that strengthens the paragraph and takes out information that doesn't, he is revising effectively, and improving the focus of the paragraph.

## ▼ Activity

### Miguel's Focused Paragraph

Read the following paragraph.

(This is the third paragraph in an essay about Roberto Clemente. The second paragraph focused on how well Clemente played baseball and on his dedication to the sport.)

> In the same manner that Roberto played baseball with all his heart and soul, he also gave to all those who were less fortunate than him. In Puerto Rico he had a baseball clinic where he donated all of the equipment and spent much of his off time teaching children the fundamentals of baseball. Roberto also donated large amounts of money to children's charity. He understood how much he meant to children and people in general and took his role as a leader of youth very seriously and always held himself to a higher standard.
>
> —Miguel Viera

1. Write *T.S.* next to the topic sentence. Highlight the part of the sentence that announces what this paragraph will focus on.

2. Write *S* next to specific pieces of support in the body of the paragraph that stay focused on the topic sentence. Note how the topic sentence and specific pieces of support work together to create a focused paragraph.

3. Why would the following topic sentence be *less* effective for Miguel's paragraph?

*Roberto Clemente had other good qualities.*

## Focusing the Essay

A **focused essay** relies on a thoughtful thesis statement: the sentence at the end of the introduction that announces the main idea of the essay. Writers must read, discuss, think, brainstorm, draft, and revise to find the thesis statement that expresses a focused idea worth developing. Sometimes writers must return to earlier steps in the writing process to find a good, focused thesis. For example, a writer might be in the middle of writing an essay when she realizes that part of her essay doesn't seem to support her thesis. If this happens, the writer must use

*Notes*

her critical thinking skills and make some choices. Should the thesis be changed? Should certain ideas she has written down be left out of the essay? Perhaps she needs to go back and take another look at her brainstorm and outline. The writer must stay sensitive to the reader's need for focus.

Of course, the thesis isn't the only part of the essay that is important to focus. The topic sentence of each body paragraph and each piece of support should clearly relate to the thesis. Good topic sentences in a focused essay often repeat key terms from the thesis, and always announce a major point that directly supports the thesis.

## ▼ Activities

### A Focused Outline, Malcolm X

Consider this outline for a well-focused essay on a hero.

*Thesis:* Malcolm X is a hero to me because of the strength he showed in his fight to improve his life and the lives of others.

*Topic sentence for body paragraph #1:* First of all, he had the strength to turn away from the life of street crime he knew so well and become a respectable citizen.

> supporting information—explain:
>> he had been involved in crime for a long time
>> his friends were all criminals
>> he had to turn his back on everything he knew well
>> he reached out to family and religion

*Topic sentence for body paragraph #2:* Malcolm X also drew on great inner strength when he taught himself to read and write in prison.

> supporting information—explain:
>> read and copied the entire dictionary
>> read many, many books
>> studied late at night (broke curfew)

*Topic sentence for body paragraph #3:* After deepening his understanding of his Muslim religion, Malcolm X showed great strength as he moved away from separatist beliefs and fought to create a peaceful, multiracial community.

> supporting information—explain:
>> he traveled to Mecca

he learned the truth about his religion
he courageously changed his views about separating blacks and whites

*Topic sentence for body paragraph #4:* Finally, I admire Malcolm X's strength and determination to help the black race.

supporting information—explain:
his life revolved around politics
he didn't work to get rich
he spoke honestly

*Topic sentence for conclusion:* Overall, I see Malcolm X as a hero because he showed such strength as he evolved from a poor, uneducated criminal to a leader of people.

1. Highlight the key words in the thesis statement that tell the reader what the essay will be about.

2. Highlight the words in each topic sentence that show that the topic sentence connects directly to the thesis.

### Checking the Focus, "My Dad"

Study the thesis and notes that follow.

*Thesis:* My father is a hero in our neighborhood.

The thief who stole my friend's car was caught by an alert neighbor.

My uncle, who lives down the street, had his house broken into three times before the neighborhood watch program. Since we started the program, he hasn't had a single problem.

My father became an important man in our neighborhood when he organized a neighborhood watch program and helped reduce crime in the neighborhood.

He helped clean up all the broken glass, old newspapers, and tires that littered the neighborhood.

He took charge because my brother got hurt playing in the empty lot next door.

We walked door to door and talked to people about the way our neighborhood looks and organized a clean-up day.

Also, my father made our neighborhood a more attractive place to live.

My dad is an outstanding golfer, and he plays basketball too.

1. Which of the sentences here might make good topic sentences for an essay that focuses on the thesis statement the student wrote?

**Notes**

2. Which sentences might act as support to which topic sentences?
3. Which of the ideas don't connect clearly to the thesis?
4. Rewrite the sentences showing how you might group them to create an outline for an essay.

### Points to Remember about Focus

As you work through this chapter and think about focusing your writing, remember these points:

- When you first start the writing process, let your mind wander and explore many different ideas.
- Spend plenty of time brainstorming, reviewing readings, and talking to classmates before you choose a focus for your essay.
- Allow yourself to change the focus of your essay if your thesis isn't working for you.
- When you revise, think critically about what you've written. Do your words communicate a focused idea to the reader?

## ▲▼▲ Investigating Heroes

This section of the chapter is the beginning of your writing process. You'll discuss heroes; then you'll read about heroes and discuss the readings. Toward the middle of the chapter, you'll find two writing assignments and some support and advice as you complete the writing process.

### Discuss and Engage

We've all heard about Superheroes—Batman, Superman, Wonderwoman, Spiderman, the Power Rangers, even Underdog. These characters have certain human qualities that we admire and think of as heroic. However, they also have superhuman abilities, such as x-ray vision, which help them perform heroic feats. Film heroes also have extraordinary qualities—sometimes to the point of being superhuman. Think about, for example, a film hero's ability to fight off five attackers, dodge hundreds of bullets, and jump out a window just before a bomb explodes (and look good while doing it). Although you'll be writing about real-life heroes in this chapter, let's consider for a moment what we love about superheroes and film heroes.

> ### Journal Assignment
> #### Calvin and Hobbes
> In the *Calvin and Hobbes* comic strip on page 166, Calvin pretends to be a superhero named Spiff. Study the comic strip and think about the qualities Spiff seems to have. What heroic qualities has Calvin's imagination created?

## ▼ Activities

### Superheroes

Discuss with your classmates what you admire about various superheroes. Create a chart similar to the one below to record your class discussion notes. Then answer the class discussion questions.

| Superhero | Admirable Qualities | Superhuman Abilities |
|---|---|---|
| Superman | | |

1. What heroic or admirable qualities do these heroes share?
2. How do their superhuman abilities differ from their heroic qualities?
3. In your opinion, why do we enjoy our superheroes?

(Remember to take notes during class discussion.)

*Notes*

### Film Heroes

Before we move on to "real-life" heroes, think about film heroes. Most people love to watch men and women in films who act, look, and live like heroes. Take a few minutes to consider this kind of hero.

Discuss with your classmates some of your favorite film heroes. Who are they? In what films do they perform? What makes them heroes? Do film heroes look and act a certain way? How are film heroes different from real-life heroes? Explain. (Be sure to take notes.)

***Real-Life Heroes*** Studying superheroes and film heroes helps us begin thinking about heroes and what makes a hero, but what about "real-life" heroes? Do they have certain qualities? Do they look and act in certain ways?

As you begin to define heroes, consider what these students had to say about them.

> A hero is a person who has shared or done some good deeds in a country or in the world. Heroes may risk their lives and some even die for their own fellow men. They're often written about and remembered through history.
> —*Diony Fernandez*

> A hero can be any person on this planet, who, without ever thinking about it, goes to the rescue of his fellow man. I'd like to think that each of us has been a hero at one time or another in our lives, and didn't even realize it. A hero is a person who is sensitive to the feelings of others, and receives the pleasurable satisfaction of being able to help as their reward. A hero is that one person who wasn't noticed, recognized or sometimes even thanked. The real hero receives his or her rewards within because they don't want to be known as a hero.
> —*Maria Gonzales*

> A hero is a person that goes above and beyond what any normal person can do. It's a person that works for what he or she believes in and helps others to be better people in society.
> —*Doris Maysonet*

▼ **Activity**

Notes

*Defining Real-Life Heroes*

If you ask a group of people to list their heroes, certain names keep showing up. Consider the names that follow.*

Maya Angelou
Cesar Chavez
Hillary Clinton
Marie Curie
Albert Einstein
Mahatma Gandhi
Michael Jordan
Martin Luther King, Jr.

Wilma Mankiller
Mother Theresa
Rosa Parks
Eleanor Roosevelt
Harriet Tubman
George Washington
Tiger Woods

Now, discuss with your classmates what you admire about some of these real-life heroes. Create a chart similar to the one below and list some names and admirable qualities.* Then respond in your notebook to the questions after the chart.

| Real-Life Heroes | Admirable Qualities |
|---|---|
|  |  |

1. What qualities do these real-life heroes have in common?
2. What kinds of heroic acts have these real-life heroes performed?
3. What are the differences between a hero and a "normal" person?

---

*The reading "Who Is Great?" in Section III offers information about many "great" people, some of whom might also be considered heroes.

*Notes*

4. Are there less obvious heroes among us in society, people who don't perform dramatic acts of bravery, but who could still be considered heroes? Explain.

5. How would you define the term *hero?*

> ### Journal Assignment
> *Reviewing Your Hero Discussions*
>
> Write about your class discussions. Were there any important heroes left out of your discussions? Write about the heroes and qualities that interest you most. Also, you may want to write about any heroes in your own life or in your community.

### ▼ Activity

#### Definition Paragraph

Write a focused paragraph in which you define a hero. Your topic sentence should announce the focus of your paragraph, and all of your body sentences should support this topic sentence. Remember to use the writing process (brainstorm, make choices, plan, draft, revise, edit). Keep this paragraph. You might want to include all or part of it in your essay.

### Read, Discuss, Think Critically

This section of the chapter offers you five readings about heroes. The author of the first essay looks at many different kinds of heroes and discusses the role of heroes in our lives. The authors of the later essays discuss specific heroes and the qualities and actions that made these people heroes.

### Reading Assignment

#### "Move Over, Barney"

*Preview* This is a long essay. Begin previewing and reading when you have enough time to read the entire essay without being interrupted. Read the title and the first two paragraphs. Read and highlight topic sentences.

*Anticipate* What do you think this essay will be about? Use the "Notes" column to record your response.

*Read and Reread*  Read the entire essay, marking unknown terms and interesting points. Then reread more slowly and use the "Notes" column to interact with the essay. Use your dictionary to define unknown words.

Notes

## Move Over, Barney:  Make Way for Some Real Heroes
### by Dennis Denenberg

This essay was published in the *American Educator*, a magazine published by the American Federation of Teachers, a labor union. Dennis Denenberg is a full professor of education at Millersville University of Pennsylvania. He and Lorraine Roscoe are the authors of *Hooray for Heroes* (The Scarecrow Press, 1994), an annotated guide to children's books and activities about outstanding men and women, and are currently working on a new book, *50 American Heroes Every Kid Should Meet!*

1   William Penn was an obsession for Elaine Peden, the *Philadelphia Inquirer Magazine* reported in 1991. Peden had devoted enormous time and energy to promoting recognition of Pennsylvania's founder. In 1984, she had persuaded Congress to extend honorary United States citizenship to both Penn and his wife, Hannah. But her successes in bringing Penn into the consciousness of Americans had been soured for her by disappointments. When she visited the restored William Penn statue on top of Philadelphia's City Hall, she expected to see again in the waiting areas the seventy-five paintings of events in the life of the Penns done by high school students. Instead she found a blowup of the Phillie Phanatic, the cartoonish mascot of the city's professional baseball team. The city's founder was out: The city's newest fantasy figure was in.

2   The situation is not much better at our country's official museum. Recently, the Smithsonian Institution's National Museum of American History published a new brochure to guide kids through the museum. It is written around the Charles Schulz figures, with their pictures everywhere. So there's Snoopy leading our kids around our national history museum—instead of Sacagawea who led Lewis and Clark across our nation!

3   We continually think we have to "dumb down" things to amuse kids. Well, we don't have to. We can challenge them to think, and most of them will love it and rise to the occasion. Our national history museum exists to teach us about our history, and while pop culture is a part of it, it should not dominate the turf. Harriet Tubman risked her life to lead more than 300 slaves to freedom—imagine the exciting trail she could lead kids on through the museum. Instead, there's Lucy entertaining the kids, and probably boring them, too.

Notes

4   Classrooms and homes around the United States resemble that Smithsonian brochure and the Philadelphia City Hall waiting area. Pictures of great people have given way to fantasy creatures. At one time many—if not most—public school classrooms in America displayed portraits of George Washington and Abraham Lincoln. Today, if such portraits appear at all, it is usually for a two-week period in February, during Presidents Day commemorations. In their place, Garfield (the cat, not the president), Michelangelo and Leonardo (the turtles, not the artists), and of course, Walt Disney's Mickey Mouse and his numerous compatriots hold prominent positions. They, not great women and men, are the figures young people see repeatedly—and come to think of as "heroes."

5   I have visited hundreds of classrooms over the past twenty years. I have talked with teachers, observed displays, and examined curriculum materials, and I have become aware of how fantasy figures compete with real-life heroes for students' attention. Often, the fantasy ones are winning.

6   Cartoon and other fantasy characters pervade children's lives. Little Mermaids and big Beasts adorn the clothing kids wear and the lunch pails they carry. Think of kids in the world today. A little girl gets up in the morning. Her head probably rested on an Aladdin pillowcase. She goes down to breakfast and eats cereal from a box with a cartoon character on it, then gets dressed in a T-shirt with Bugs Bunny on it, picks up her Garfield lunch pail, and heads off to school where there is a bulletin board with cartoon figures on it.

7   Teachers and parents choose such materials so frequently, they tell me, because they believe these figures have motivational value. Cartoon mice and ducks are familiar. "They can be comforting to kids," parents and teachers say.

8   Perhaps fantasy characters motivate and comfort. But junk food motivates and comforts, too. Like junk food, popular fantasy and cartoon characters are sweet, enticing to the eye—and empty of real value. Like junk food, they displace what is more important. They fill kids up. The kids no longer hunger for the nourishment they need to become healthy, fully mature adults.

9   Is it any wonder that teenagers become hooked on the next level of fad fantasy figures—the super-rich athletes and popular culture rock and entertainment stars. Their presence in the media is everywhere, with entire cable channels devoted to the icons of music and athletics. So the Barney T-shirts eventually become Smashing Pumpkins shirts, Power Ranger backpacks become Dennis Rodman gym bags, and the very in-

nocent Little Mermaid poster in a child's bedroom is replaced by a nearly life-sized one of Madonna (and not the religious one!). Think about it: It's an easy transition from the fantasy world of Spiderman for kids to the unreal world of Michael Jackson for teenagers.

10   The over-presence of fantasy characters in our culture and in our schools and homes contributes, I am convinced, to a confusion for our children and adolescents about the value of real-life human accomplishments. It is not surprising, I think, that when in 1991, a Harrisburg-area school district asked its fifth to twelfth graders to name people they most admired, the teenagers chose rock stars, athletes, and television personalities, people who often seem to be larger than life. Other than Nelson Mandela, no famous people from any other field of endeavor were mentioned. No great artists, inventors, humanitarians, political leaders, composers, scientists, doctors—none were mentioned by the 1,150 students.

11   Likewise, when the Scripps-Howard newspaper chain asked a representative sample of twenty-five- to forty-five-year-olds to write a two-page essay about their favorite hero, there were a lot of blank pages; 60 percent of the group said they have no personal heroes.

12   I frequently am asked to give presentations on why heroes are important for children. I sometimes begin by putting on the familiar Mickey Mouse ears, and I lead my adult audience in a rousing rendition of the "Mickey Mouse club" song. Almost everyone knows the words. Then I switch to a colonial hat and recite a portion of the Patrick Henry speech that ends with a very famous line (or at least what once was a very famous line). I leave it to the audience to finish the speech, but few can. The comparison with the Mickey Mouse song leads to a spirited discussion of what has happened to real heroes in our culture.

13   "Look around," I say to my audiences. "You're surrounded by people. Count thirty people, yourself among them. One of that thirty would probably have polio if it weren't for Jonas Salk. That's how prevalent polio was. But when Salk died two years ago, we as a nation hardly took notice. Certainly, few young people have any sense of how that great doctor saved their generation from a crippling disease."

14   Have we lost a generation of people who don't have heroes, who don't know what a hero is or don't understand what a positive influence a hero can be in a person's life?

15   A hero is an individual who can serve as an example. He or she has the ability to persevere, to overcome the hurdles that impede others' lives. While this intangible quality of greatness appears almost magical,

*Notes*

*Notes*

it is indeed most human. And it is precisely because of that humanness that some individuals attain heroic stature. They are of us, but are clearly different.

16   We look to heroes and heroines for inspiration. Through their achievements, we see humankind more positively. They make us feel good. They make us feel proud. For some of us they become definite role models, and our lives follow a different direction because of their influence. For others, while the effect may be less dramatic, it is of no less import, for these heroes make us think in new ways. Their successes and failures lead us to ponder our own actions and inactions. By learning about *their* lives, *our* lives become enriched.

17   Molly Pitcher saw what had to be done and did it. Women had a defined role in the war; they were a vital support to the fighting colonials. But when her husband was wounded, and the cannon needed to be fired, she knew what she had to do. Molly Pitcher was, and is, a heroine, and her story deserves to be told and retold. Neither a great statesman or soldier, she was an ordinary person who performed an extraordinary deed.

18   Michelangelo spent a lifetime at his craft, leaving the world a legacy of magnificent paintings and sculptures. His hard work was a daily reaffirmation of his belief in a human's creative potential. Through toil, he produced artistic monuments that have continued to inspire generations.

19   This world has had (and still has) many Molly Pitchers and Michelangeloes, people who set examples that inspire others. Some had only a fleeting moment of glory in a rather normal life, but oh, what a moment. Others led a life of longer-lasting glory and had a more sustained impact on humankind. All were individuals who, through their achievements, made positive contributions.

20   Where are the heroines and heroes for children today? They are everywhere! They are the figures from our past, some in the historical limelight, others still in the shadows. They are the men and women of the present, struggling to overcome personal and societal problems to build a better world.

21   Indeed they are everywhere, but most children know so very few of them. Quite simply, in our schools and in our homes, we have removed these great people from our focus. They have become "persona non grata" instead of persons of importance. The greats are still around; they have merely been removed from everyone's view.

22   "Once upon a time . . ." kids had heroes, and lots of them. Some of these great individuals were real (Lincoln, et al.); others were legendary

(such as Paul Bunyan and Casey Jones); still others, like Hercules, were of a different realm altogether. Most of them were male and white, as if heroics somehow knew gender and racial lines of distinction. Frequently, kids pretended to be these heroes or at the very least their followers. Since not every boy could be King Arthur, the others could be Knights of the Round Table. Yes, it was clearly better to be the King, but even as a knight, one got to slay a dragon now and then. All—kings and knights—were capable of great deeds!

23    These heroes seemed to be everywhere. They were part of the curriculum, so textbooks and other reading materials (even the classic comic books) provided details of their adventures. The movies portrayed details of their adventures. The movies portrayed them in action, adding an exciting visual dimension. Heroes truly came alive for kids, who not only learned about them but, often, learned values from them.

24    Whether or not "the Father of Our Country" ever did chop down a cherry tree is not a question of significant historical importance. What is telling is that for generations the story helped children understand the meaning of honesty. Even heroes had faults, but they were moral enough to admit their errors.

25    The inclusion of heroes in schools served dual purposes. In addition to learning about specific great individuals, students also were exposed to the ethical nature of those persons. The presence of heroes provided a focus for children's dreams and wishes, and those heroes were cloaked in mantles of virtuous behavior.

26    As the advertising industry grew, however, heroes became displaced persons and virtually disappeared from children's views. Through the wonders of the mass media, a whole new array of characters became a daily part of American culture. Cartoon creatures and company advertising mascots existed for many decades, but not until the advent of megacommunications did they intrude into everyone's lives in a seemingly unending manner. Billboards, print ads, television and radio programs, commercials, videotapes, and many other avenues provide ads "ad infinitum." Even while relaxing on the beach, one's attention is pulled skyward to read the fly-by advertisements.

27    The issue is not so much that they have joined the ranks of known figures, it is rather that they have totally replaced real heroes for children. Today the role models are often whatever the latest commercial fad creatures happen to be. Once the new character catches the public's attention, the merchandising machine marches on. The T-shirts, buttons, books, book bags, greeting cards, games and toys, trading cards, movies, and, of course, television series all follow in rapid succes-

sion.* The presence of the latest sensation dominates the child's world. Consciousness leads to demands for the newest marketable item bearing the creature's image. And everywhere—in the child's mind, in the home, and in the classroom—the character assumes a new status of heroic proportions. It's out with Ben Franklin entirely; here comes the Mouse!

28   I think parents and teachers should replace many of these fantasy characters with *real* heroes, real-life women and men. We should "de-mouse" (to start with the most successful cartoon character of all time) not only the classroom, but our homes, as well. We should offer people of significance equal space and time.

29   For what I like to call a "De-mousing Starter's List," I would choose people whom I think American children should know. We need to show our children that heroes come from both sexes, every race, every ethnic background, and every field of human endeavor. Young people need to encounter images of Thomas Edison, Jane Addams, George C. Marshall, and Cal Ripken, Jr. They need to come in contact with Lech Walesa and Mother Theresa, with Stephen Hawking and Rosa Parks. They should learn about the real Michelangelo instead of knowing only his modern-day amphibian namesake. . . .

30   Let me emphasize that in the efforts to bring great people to the attention of children, balance and focus must be watchwords. Flooding the classroom, school, or home with dozens of pictures of famous people may have little effect. I would be selective and concentrate on a few people at a time, so that a genuine understanding and appreciation can be established. And I would focus on the essence of the individual's contribution to humanity, not the minutia that so often ends up obscuring a hero's greatness.

31   Balanced, focused attention to significant people may mean that even Walt Disney becomes a hero. We should, perhaps, give time and space to the cartoonist whose studio has helped create such an unbalanced attention to fantasy creatures.

---

*One individual who has resisted the commercialization of his creation is Bill Watterson, famous for his brilliant Calvin and Hobbes strip. Now retired from drawing the strip (because he felt his ideas were becoming redundant), Mr. Watterson did something unheard of in the fad business. How many stuffed Hobbes tigers do you see in the store? How many Calvin and Hobbes backpacks? T-shirts? bed sheets? juice glasses? and so on and so on . . . . None! Because Mr. Watterson believes fantasy figures belong on the comic page, not in every aspect of our children's lives. Hooray for a real hero—Bill Watterson, to whom principles are more important than money. [Denenberg's note.]

32. No doubt many parents and teachers have already taken up the cause. It is time for the rest of us to return great individuals to the pedestals they deserve. Young people need to see that humans can and do make a difference. Children can learn that they too are capable of re-shaping life in a positive way. By reintroducing heroes to children, parents and teachers can show them that there are real people worthy of recognition and emulation.

## ▼ Questions for Critical Thought

### "Move Over, Barney"

1. a. Denenberg says cartoon figures are taking over and replacing real-life heroes. What examples does he give that cartoon figures are everywhere in children's lives?

   b. How does having a lot of examples help a writer prove his or her point?

2. a. In paragraph 8, Denenberg chooses to make a comparison between cartoon figures and junk food. Explain what he is saying here. Do you agree?

   b. Think about the comparison between cartoon figures and junk food. How do comparisons help a writer explain ideas?

3. In paragraph 9, Denenberg says that as children get older, they trade in their childish heroes for other pop heroes. What doesn't Denenberg like about kids having Dennis Rodman or Madonna (or other popular figures) as their heroes?

4. Why is it important for kids to know about the other kinds of heroes Denenberg mentions at the end of paragraph 10 (artists, inventors, humanitarians, political leaders, composers, scientists, doctors)?

5. In paragraph 16, Denenberg says, "We look to heroes and heroines for inspiration." He also says, "For some of us they become definite role models, and our lives follow a different direction because of their influence." Can you think of a hero who has influenced you or anyone you know? How has that hero been an influence?

6. Does Denenberg want to completely get rid of cartoon heroes? Give proof from the essay to support your answer.

Notes

7. The last word in this essay is "emulation." What does this word mean? (If you are unsure of the meaning, first try to figure out the meaning by using context clues. Then use a dictionary. See "Building Your Vocabulary" in Section IV to review "context clues.")

8. "Emulation" and "emulate" are key words when discussing heroes. Put each word into a sentence of your own. (Consider using these words in your essay about heroes.)

9. a. Who is Denenberg's audience?

   b. What is his purpose? (What does he hope his audience will learn from his essay?)

   c. Denenberg's essay is well-focused even though it doesn't have a stated thesis. Create a thesis that expresses Denenberg's main idea.

## Reading Assignment

*"Rosa Parks Joins Children's Wall of Heroes"*

***Preview*** Read the title, the information about the author, and where the essay was published. Read the first few paragraphs.

***Anticipate*** What do you anticipate this essay will be about? Record your response in the "Notes" column.

***Read and Reread*** Because this essay is written by a journalist and was published in a newspaper, we can guess that it will be written in journalistic style. This style and the relatively short length of the essay suggest that you will be able to read this essay fairly quickly and easily. (Consider reading it all the way through once before marking anything.) When rereading, define terms and use the "Notes" column.

### Rosa Parks Joins Children's Wall of Heroes
*by Sandy Banks*

Sandy Banks is a *Los Angeles Times* columnist. This essay was published in the editorial section of the *Sacramento Bee* on 4/23/98.

1   You would have thought I'd announced a meeting with one of the Spice Girls, from the reaction I got at home.

2   "I can't believe you get to meet her, in person."

3   "Please, please, Mom, can I go with you?"

4   And, to a friend, "You won't believe who my mom is taking us to meet."

5   The object of their excitement wasn't a rock diva or movie star. It was an elderly woman—hardly bigger than my oldest child—who rolled toward us in a wheelchair, climbed out carefully and adjusted her pillbox hat before extending a soft brown hand to each of my daughters.

6   "So pleased to meet you," she said, asking each girl her name, gazing straight into their shining eyes. "I'm Mrs. Rosa Parks."

7   I don't recall that I even knew her name as a child, although she's known the world over now as the mother of the civil rights movement.

8   The Rev. Martin Luther King Jr. was the reigning hero of the movement-in-progress when I was growing up in the 1950s and 1960s. But it is Rosa Parks who ignited the indignation of the masses 43 years ago with her simple act of defiance aboard a Montgomery, Ala., bus.

9   Then a middle-age seamstress, Parks was tired from eight hours on her feet when she boarded the bus that would take her home from work. Blacks were banned from the first four rows, so she settled in the middle section, which could be occupied by either whites or blacks. But segregationist Jim Crow laws dictated that if a white passenger needed a seat, all the black people seated in those middle rows had to get up and move, so that no white person would have to sit next to a black passenger.

10  That day, though, as whites filled the bus, Parks merely sighed, slid closer to the window to make room on her seat and told the driver, "I am not going to move."

11  Police were called, and Parks was arrested. She was bailed out of jail by a local civil rights activist, who then enlisted a young minister—26-year-old King—to help organize a boycott of the city's bus line.

12  The yearlong boycott—which ended when the U.S. Supreme Court ruled that Montgomery's bus segregation laws were unconstitutional—garnered Parks a place in history but cost her her job and forced her and her husband Raymond, to move north to Detroit to rebuild their lives.

13  It also made her an international symbol of courage, whose influence reaches to the children of today.

14  I suppose we were too close to the moment when I was growing up to appreciate the import of what she did. History only becomes historic when you can stand back and view it through the prism of time.

15  It is different for my daughters—who learn about our struggle for civil rights as they celebrate Martin Luther King's birthday and study Black History Month in their mostly white schools.

Notes

16. And it is Rosa Parks who represents to them all that was good about that tumultuous period of our country's history—with an act so straightforward that even my first-grader can understand: A tired woman on a bus, who simply decided not to get pushed around anymore; whose refusal to stand struck a blow for fairness and freedom, and spoke volumes about courage and righteousness and faith.

17. There is a majesty in that looming larger for my children than all they have learned about marches on Washington and Supreme Court decisions—mighty events, but beyond their grasp.

18. It's an overly simplistic view of history, I know—reducing it to one moment, one woman. But I don't mind.

19. It is enough to see my daughters glowing with pride, as I snap their photo standing next to this small, brave, 85-year-old woman from their history books.

20. And to know that Puff Daddy, Leonardo DiCaprio and the Spice Girls have to move over. They're about to be bumped by a new face on the bedroom wall.

### ▼ Questions for Critical Thought

#### "Rosa Parks Joins . . ."

1. Try to put yourself in Rosa Parks' place on that bus. Think about how she was feeling as she sat down and the many different emotions she must have gone through as she decided to stay in her seat and deal with the consequences. Describe how you think she might have felt as she sat down, as she spoke to the bus driver, as she was arrested. Describe how you think she felt when she lost her job and had to move.

2. In what ways is Rosa Parks a hero?

3. Banks seems to think like Denenberg: they're both glad to see popular figures "move over" to make room for other heroes. Why would Banks rather have a poster of Rosa Parks on the wall than, say, a poster of the Spice Girls or Leonardo DiCaprio?

4. Because Banks' essay is not written in academic form, she doesn't have an introductory paragraph with a thesis statement at the end. Review her essay and find sentences that come close to expressing the main idea of the essay. Can you find a sentence that expresses the overall focus of the essay? Explain.

## Reading Assignment

### "How One Woman Became the Voice of Her People"

*Preview*   This is a long essay. Begin previewing and reading when you have time to read the entire essay without being interrupted. Read the introductory information in italics, the title, and the first four paragraphs. Read and highlight topic sentences.

*Anticipate*   What do you anticipate this essay will be about? Write your thoughts in the "Notes" column.

*Read and Reread*   Read the essay quickly and mark unknown terms. Reread more slowly, using the "Notes" column and a highlighter to record and mark important ideas. Define unknown terms.

### How One Woman Became the Voice of Her People
*by David Wallechinsky*

This article was first published in *Parade Magazine*, January 19, 1997.

> *Aung San Suu Kyi was forty-three and living outside her native Burma in England, as a housewife and mother of two. Then, almost overnight, she became the heart of her people's struggle for freedom and democracy.*

1   In the exotic southeast Asian nation of Burma, a country of forty-six million people, a battle of wills of heroic proportions is taking place. On one side is a brutal military dictatorship known as SLORC (State Law and Order Restoration Council). On the other is a slim, fifty-one-year-old mother of two named Aung San Suu Kyi, who is leading her people in a nonviolent struggle for democracy.

2   For six years, from 1989 to 1995, Aung San Suu Kyi (pronounced Awng-Sahn-Soo-Chee) was kept in isolation under house arrest for speaking out against the government, which has used torture and forced labor and which refuses to hand over power, even though it lost a national election. In 1991, still under house arrest, Aung San Suu Kyi was awarded the Nobel Peace Prize.

3   Following her release in 1995, she continued to challenge the junta, every weekend addressing the thousands of followers who congregated in front of the gate to her house and across the street. It had become the only forum for free speech in the country. But since September the government has cracked down on these gatherings. It has arrested

## Notes

more than 1000 people—usually in the middle of the night. And Aung San Suu Kyi is again restricted to her home.

4. Aung San Suu Kyi has been an inspiration, but the personal cost has been great: Since her struggle began, she has been allowed to see her husband and children only infrequently. While under house arrest, she did not see her children for two and one-half years.

5. Aung San Suu Kyi comes from a politically prominent Burmese family, but until the age of forty-three she had been leading a quiet life in England as a housewife and academic. How did she transform herself into the leading speaker for democracy and a symbol of freedom? And what gave this woman, by all accounts a devoted mother, the strength to sacrifice the satisfactions of marriage and motherhood, as well as the courage to risk her life again and again?

6. For the Burmese people, much of Aung San Suu Kyi's power comes from her being a living link to history. She is the daughter of Burma's greatest modern hero, Aung San, who founded the Burmese Army in 1941 and is considered the father of his nation. At the end of World War II, Aung San, like George Washington, made a successful transition from military leader to political leader. He negotiated with the British and arranged for national independence to be proclaimed by Jan. 4, 1948. But before that day arrived, Aung San was assassinated by political rivals. He was thirty-two. His daughter was barely two years old.

7. Besides his wife and daughter, Aung San left two sons: One died while still a child; the other is now an American citizen, an engineer living in San Diego. "Although I was too young to retain a direct memory of my father," Aung San Suu Kyi told me, "my mother taught me about his life and his principles, as did his old friends." (As an adult, she wrote a biography of Aung San.)

8. At fifteen, Aung San Suu Kyi moved to New Delhi when her mother, Khin Kyi, was appointed ambassador to India. Later, she studied at Oxford University in England. After graduating with a degree in philosophy, politics and economics, she worked for almost three years at the United Nations in New York City. It was a time of political and social turmoil in the U.S. "The young people were for love and not for war," she recalled. "There was a feeling of tremendous vigor. I had been moved by Martin Luther King's 'I Have a Dream' speech and how he tried to better the lot of the black people without fostering feelings of hate. It's hate that is the problem, not violence. Violence is simply the symptom of hate."

9. In 1972, Aung San Suu Kyi married Michael Aris, a British scholar specializing in Tibetan studies. He is now a don at Oxford. Prior to their marriage, she wrote these words to him: "I only ask one thing, that

should my people need me, you would help me to do my duty by them."

10  In the meantime, she lived a reasonably normal life. She gave birth to two sons, Alexander in 1973 and Kim in 1977. For several years, she devoted herself to raising her family and continuing her studies. Then her life changed dramatically.

11  In April 1988, she received word from Burma that her mother was gravely ill. She returned to Rangoon to care for her. This visit coincided with unusual political activity in Burma. In March, riot police had shot to death 200 demonstrators, most of them students, who had protested government policies and repression. Despite the shootings, the demonstrations grew. Increasingly, protesters demanded free multiparty elections.

12  "Government leaders are amazing," Aung San Suu Kyi said. "So they are the last to know what the people want." Many demonstrations were staged in front of the U.S. embassy, because the U.S. was seen as a symbol of democracy. Between Aug. 8 and 13, 1988, the police killed nearly 3000 people.

13  Aung San Suu Kyi watched these developments with growing concern. Many of the pro-democracy demonstrators carried signs with pictures of her father. On Aug. 26, a general strike was called and several hundred thousand attended a rally in front of Rangoon's Shwedagon pagoda. Here, for the first time, Aung San Suu Kyi spoke to the crowd.

14  Recalling her father's assassination, she said, "People have been saying I know nothing of Burmese politics. The trouble is, I know too much." As the crowd warmed to her, she concluded, "I could not, as my father's daughter, remain indifferent to all that is going on. The national crisis could, in fact, be called the second struggle for independence."

15  Overnight, Aung San Suu Kyi became the leading representative of the movement for freedom and democracy. In September, the military seized control of the government, declared martial law and killed 1000 demonstrators. Aung San Suu Kyi joined with other anti-government leaders to form the National League for Democracy (NLD). She traveled the country, giving more than 1000 speeches.

16  During this period she was involved in a dramatic incident. On the evening of April 5, 1989, as they were returning home, she and a group of pro-democracy organizers were stopped and ordered off the road by government soldiers. Aung San Suu Kyi waved the others away and kept walking toward the soldiers. "It seemed so much simpler," she later explained, "to provide them with a single target." A captain ordered his troops to raise their rifles and shoot. She continued advancing. At the last second, a major ran forward and overruled the captain.

*Notes*

Notes

17  Three and a half months later, exasperated by her growing popularity, the Burmese dictators placed Aung San Suu Kyi under house arrest. She was not allowed to see her children for more than two and one-half years.

18  "I felt very guilty about not looking after them," she said. "The antidote to such feelings was knowing that others had it much worse. I knew that my children were safe with my husband in England, whereas a lot of my colleagues were in the terrible position of being in prison themselves and not knowing how safe their children were going to be."

19  She described seeing her younger son for the first time in almost three years: "I would not have recognized him if I had seen him on the street."

20  Later, in England, her husband told me that he supports his wife fully but could not talk on the record for fear that the Burmese government will accuse him of being a foreigner interfering in their affairs. I also met in London with Burmese women who had been arrested by SLORC and kept apart from their families. They confirmed what Aung San Suu Kyi had told me. One woman I met, who had been jailed for three years, gave birth in prison and immediately had the baby taken away from her.

21  In 1990, SLORC agreed to hold an election—an attempt to satisfy potential foreign investors. Only the military leaders were surprised by the results: Aung San Suu Kyi herself was not allowed to run for office, but her party, the NLD, won eighty percent of the vote and seats. The party of the military won only ten seats out of 485 contested.

22  SLORC announced that the election didn't count. Since then, it has followed "the Chinese model": liberalize the economy while keeping a tight lid on political dissent. Unfortunately, only a small percentage of the population has become richer, while most Burmese, suffering from spiraling inflation, actually have seen their lives become harder.

23  But even if the economy were to improve, Aung San Suu Kyi stressed that there is more to life than material success. "This is something you Americans would be in a better position to talk about," she told me, "because there is certainly material prosperity in the United States. And yet material prosperity has not insured happiness and harmony or even contentment. I do believe in the spiritual nature of human beings. To some it's a strange or outdated idea, but I do believe there is such a thing as a human spirit. There is a spiritual dimension to man which should be nurtured."

24  Aung San Suu Kyi is adamant about sticking to her policy of nonviolence. "There are those," she explained, "who believe the only way we can remove the authoritarian regime and replace it with a democratic one is through violent means. But then, in the future, those who do not

25     approve of a democratic government would be encouraged to try violent means of toppling it, because we would have set a precedent that you bring about political change through violence. I would like to set strongly the precedent that you bring about political change through political settlement and *not* through violence."

25     The government, meanwhile, is trying to persuade foreign investors to bring their business to Burma. They also have declared 1996–97 "Visit Myanmar* Year" for tourists. Aung San Suu Kyi's advice: "Tourists should wait until Burma is a freer and happier country." Foreign investors, she said, "will get better returns for their money if they invest in a country that is stable and which has a strong framework of just laws."

26     I asked what Americans can do. Although Aung San Suu Kyi stressed that it is up to the people of Burma to solve their own problems, it *is* possible for others to help. "Don't support businesses which are supporting injustice in Burma," she said. In the U.S., support for Aung San Suu Kyi has united liberals and conservatives. Groups promoting democracy in Burma have been formed on more than 100 American college campuses.

27     The day before I left Burma, I talked in Aung San Suu Kyi's garden with her cousin Aye Win, who served as her press secretary. (He has since been sentenced to twenty years in prison.) I was concerned that customs officials might confiscate my photos and tapes of Aung San Suu Kyi. "You have nothing to worry about," he reassured me, "because you have the power of the U.S. government behind you. It is we Burmese who have to worry." He nodded in the direction of Aung San Suu Kyi, who was walking toward us. "All we have," he added, "is Aung San's daughter."†

## ▼ Questions for Critical Thought

### "How One Woman..."

1. How did Aung San Suu Kyi become a hero to the people of Burma? List her specific actions/beliefs.

2. In what ways does she fit the profile of the traditional hero?

---

*Burma was renamed Union of Myanmar in 1989, but is still frequently referred to as Burma.

† As of April 1999, Aung San Suu Kyi continues to live in Burma and fight for a democratic government. Her husband, Michael Aris, died in England in March of 1999. The Burmese government would not allow Aris to visit Kyi before his death. Kyi refused a visa to attend her husband's funeral in England because she feared the military government in Burma would not allow her to return.

**Notes**

3. Does everyone in Burma think of her as a hero? If not, who doesn't and why?

4. Do you believe (as she does) that it's her duty to help her people?

5. The writer of this article, David Wallechinsky, composed some wonderful paragraphs that mirror the paragraph structure you've been studying. Select one of the following paragraphs, copy it in your notebook and discuss Wallechinsky's use of topic sentence, detail, and wrap-up sentence. Describe how Wallechinsky stays focused on one idea in the paragraph you selected. (Choose paragraph 6, 17, 23, or 24.)

## Reading Assignment

"A Hero in My Family"

*Preview*   Read the title and the first two paragraphs, which serve as the introduction. Read and highlight topic sentences.

*Anticipate*   What do you anticipate this essay will be about? Use the "Notes" column to record your thoughts.

*Read and reread*   Read the essay once quickly, marking unknown terms. Reread the essay, responding to ideas in the "Notes" column and highlighting important points. Define unknown words.

### A Hero in My Family
*by Megan Burroughs*
(with permission from Elaine Roberts and Geoffrey Burroughs)

Megan Burroughs is a college English instructor and writer. This essay was written specifically for this textbook.

1    My girls, ages two, two, and five, love Mulan, the lead character in Disney's film *Mulan*. A young Chinese girl, Mulan pretends to be a boy and, to the horror of her family, dresses as a soldier and runs off to fight the Huns in her father's place. To bring honor to her family, Mulan is supposed to be a traditional Chinese young lady—feminine, quiet, beautiful, and skilled in womanly tasks like serving tea and cooking. Mulan, however, is outspoken, athletic, and headstrong. She has her own ideas, and she pursues them against many odds. Compared to some of the other "heroes" my girls have taken a liking to—Batgirl, Snow White, and Sleeping Beauty—I like Mulan quite a bit. I consider her to be a positive role model.

2   Yet, the girls know (especially my five-year-old) that Mulan is "pretend," and as Dennis Denenberg, a professor of education at Millersville University of Pennsylvania points out, children need real heroes—people, not fictional characters. My girls should learn about other heroes, people who have lived, accomplished great deeds, and made our world a better place. My girls need human footsteps to follow in. I have found a soldier in our own family whom I will tell the girls about someday when they put down their Mulan weapons (wrapping paper tubes) long enough to listen. I can't swear that I have a complete picture of this hero. I can't swear that the early parts of the story haven't been embellished over the years. He is a legend in my family, and as such, he has reached a level of perfection in my memory. And yet all the early pieces of the story seem to lead so naturally to the end of the story (which I know is true) that I will confidently tell my girls this story of Uncle Spencer, a real hero in our family.

3   Early signs that Uncle Spencer might have the characteristics of a hero began to show when Spencer was just a boy. Spencer was a handsome, athletic leader among the boys in the neighborhood. He, sixteen years older than my father, organized games for the boys to play—from soldiers to football. He was charismatic and the other kids loved him; they accepted him as a leader. As he grew older, he continued to shine as he completed college and pursued a law degree. My father once wrote in a poem about Spencer: "He was the first born son, / The scion of a family of lawyers, / Soon to graduate from Hastings . . . He had the power to help us."

4   However, beyond having the personality and the intelligence to lead and succeed, Uncle Spencer had the integrity and sensitivity of a hero. As well-liked as he was, as busy as he was, he was also kind and thoughtful. My father also wrote: "He was also the brother ever there, / Who sensed a child's confusion. / A brother who could stop for "soldiers" / On the Sunday of his wedding to Elaine." I know this meant a lot to my dad. His brother was going to leave home to fight in World War II within a few weeks, and it was the day of his wedding. But Uncle Spencer put all that aside to share some time with his little brother and play "soldiers." My father wrote: "He had room for me. / It was never, 'I'm sorry, not right now.' / What I said was heard. / What I was told I understood." This is a man my father looked up to. This is a person my girls could look up to.

5   His integrity, leadership skills, and selflessness formed the foundation to Spencer's character, and in his final minutes he became a bona fide hero not only to my family but to other families and the nation as well. I cannot tell the story of his end any better than his commanding officer

did in a letter to Spencer's wife. So, to you, reader, I submit the letter that tells how Uncle Spencer died a hero at age twenty-five.

June 9, 1945

Dear Mrs. Burroughs:

6     It is with a heavy and saddened heart that I undertake to tell you of the death of your husband in action aboard this vessel last May twenty-seven. You have my utmost and sincerest sympathy in your bereavement. We who are left to serve on are doing so with saddened spirits and a real feeling of loss. Every officer and man of this vessel is with me in the knowledge that we have lost a very dear friend and comrade, that you have lost a loving and devoted husband, and that our country has lost an admirable, able, and brave officer.

7     Sunday, May twenty-seven, had begun as a fine day for us, though we knew that enemy action might come at any moment. During the afternoon we received our mail, including packages of books and phonograph records for Spencer. After having admired the books and listened to the records we were called to general quarters as enemy planes were sighted.

8     Spencer was at his battle station supervising the firing of our after guns when an enemy plane loaded with explosives dived at us in a suicide dive. Though it was a dark night the guns gave a good account of themselves and the plane was forced to change its course and approach from astern. This put the whole burden of our defense on Spencer's gun. The men on the gun, inspired and encouraged by your husband, courageously kept up a heavy and effective fire despite the fact that the enemy plane was diving upon them at utmost speed.

9     When the plane was almost upon us their fire succeeded in detonating the bombs it carried, thus destroying the plane. The courage of your husband in facing this attack saved the lives of many, many of his shipmates, but cost him his own. He was struck in the temple by shrapnel from the exploding plane and was killed instantly. The Medical Officer and I were at his side almost immediately, but he passed away quietly and without suffering. A great sense of loss descended upon us at that moment, and will remain with us whose lives he saved until the time we can no longer feel loss or pain.

10     Spencer was buried with military honors on an Eastward slope of the military cemetery in this area. Close by is the grave of one of our men who perished with him. Had it not been for the unflinching courage of your husband in the performance of his duty those two graves might well have been twenty.

11     With this letter I send my prayer for the Divine to ease your grief and grant peace to your heart.

Sincerely,
John O. Harper

## ▼ Questions for Critical Thought

### "A Hero in My Family"

1. Burroughs doesn't come right out and list the qualities of a hero, but she does mention a number of specific qualities she considers

to be heroic. Review the entire essay carefully and identify the heroic qualities Burroughs mentions. Do you think her Uncle Spencer is a hero? Why or why not?

2. In this chapter, you've studied how thesis statements and topic sentences can help focus an essay. Write down Burroughs' thesis and topic sentences. Do they work well as tools for focus? Would you change or improve any of these sentences? If so, explain what you might change and why.

3. Identify any signs you can find that Burroughs is aware of her audience.

4. Burroughs includes interesting details in this essay that help her support her ideas. Choose two details that help you understand and enjoy her essay. (**Detail** is specific information that helps you understand ideas and perhaps paints a picture in your head.)

5. In your own words, what is Burroughs' purpose in writing this essay? Who is her audience?

## Reading Assignment

### "Florence Rena Sabin"

*Preview*   Read the title and the first paragraph. Read and highlight the topic sentences.

*Anticipate*   What do you anticipate this essay will be about? Record your thoughts in the "Notes" column.

*Read and Reread*   Read the essay quickly and mark unfamiliar words. Then reread the essay more slowly, interacting with the text by making comments in the "Notes" column and highlighting important points. Define unknown words.

### Florence Rena Sabin, 1871–1953

*by Darlene R. Stille*

This essay comes from a collection of essays entitled *Extraordinary Women Scientists*.

1   At the U.S. Capitol Building in Washington, D.C., every state in the Union is allowed to display the statues of two of its most distinguished citizens in Statuary Hall. The state of Colorado chose for one of its statues the likeness of Florence Sabin, an outstanding medical scientist who

## Notes

achieved an impressive number of "firsts" for women. She was the first woman on the Johns Hopkins Medical School faculty in Baltimore, Maryland; the first woman member of the Rockefeller Institute; and the first woman elected to the National Academy of Sciences. Sabin had not one, but three distinguished careers, first as a researcher and teacher at Johns Hopkins, then as a researcher of tuberculosis at the Rockefeller Institute. Her third career began after she retired. She overhauled the state public health system of Colorado and, at age seventy-six, became head of Denver's new city health department.

2   Florence Rena Sabin was born in Central City, Colorado, on November 9, 1871, the youngest of two daughters born to Serina and George Sabin. At that time, mining was a booming business in Colorado, where Florence's father worked as a mining engineer. After his wife's death, George could not cope with raising two daughters, so he sent Florence, then four years old, and her sister Mary, to Wolfe Hall boarding school in Denver. A short time later, George's brother, Albert Sabin, brought the girls to Chicago, Illinois, where they could be part of a family. These were four of the most happy and intellectually stimulating years for Florence. When she was twelve years old, she went to live with her grandparents on their farm in Vermont and eventually enrolled at Smith College in 1889.

3   While at Smith College, Sabin developed two great interests—medicine and women's rights. She actively worked for passage of laws giving women the right to vote and decided to go to medical school to become a doctor. After graduating in 1893, Sabin taught two years at Wolfe Hall in Denver and a year in the zoology department at Smith. With the money she had saved, she applied to Johns Hopkins Medical School. This was her best bet, because the school had been funded by a group of women who insisted that women be admitted on the same basis as men. She was admitted and began making lasting contributions even while she was a student. Her abilities and enthusiasm so impressed anatomy professor Franklin P. Mall that he encouraged her to create a model of the brain. This work, which she undertook as a student, was published in 1901 as *An Atlas of the Medulla and Midbrain*, and became a popular text for medical students.

4   After earning her M.D. in 1900, Sabin served a one-year internship and then began a research and teaching career at Johns Hopkins that eventually spanned twenty-five years. Beginning with a fellowship, Sabin became an assistant in anatomy, an associate professor in 1905, and a full professor in 1917. When Franklin Mall, chairman of the anatomy department, retired, Sabin expected to replace him, but a man was appointed instead. When colleagues asked whether she would re-

sign in protest, Sabin replied, "Of course I'll stay. I have research in progress."

5   Her particular interest was the development of the blood cells and the lymphatic system. In the early 1900s, scientists were just beginning to learn how organs, tissues, and systems develop in the body. Sabin spent untold hours peering into a microscope at blood cells and blood vessels. By injecting the vessels in pig embryos with India ink and tracing them, she learned that the lymph vessels grow from veins in the early stages of development. Lymph vessels are similar to blood vessels, but they collect fluid that seeps out of tiny blood vessels and return the fluid to the bloodstream.

6   In 1925, she went to work as a scientist at the Rockefeller Institute, now Rockefeller University. She took on the study of tuberculosis, a major public health scourge at the time. Now, tuberculosis is treated with antibiotics, but in the 1920's these drugs did not exist. Sabin headed a team that studied how the body's disease-fighting immune system reacts to the bacterium that causes TB. After a long and distinguished research career, Sabin retired in 1938. She had accumulated many awards and honors. In addition to being elected to the National Academy of Sciences in 1925, she had served as the first woman president of the American Association of Anatomists from 1924–1926 and in 1921 had been selected to represent women scientists by welcoming the great French physicist Marie Curie when she visited the United States. So Sabin had behind her a lifetime of achievements of which she could be proud when she returned to Denver to live quietly with her sister.

7   But that was just the beginning of the Florence Sabin story. Sabin became interested in public health matters during World War II (1939–1945). In 1944, the governor of Colorado invited Sabin to serve on a postwar planning committee for reintegrating servicemen into civilian life and to head a subcommittee on public health. The governor apparently appointed Sabin not so much because of her reputation as a researcher but because he had been assured that she was a nice old lady with her hair in a bun who knew little of life outside the laboratory. How wrong that assessment proved to be.

8   Florence Rena Sabin found that Colorado's public health system was inefficient, corrupt, and hampered by untrained staff and insufficient funding. She publicized these shocking findings and campaigned across the state for laws and other reforms to control infectious disease, ensure the purity of milk, and allow for sanitary sewage disposal. Her committee drafted new health laws known as the Sabin Program and worked successfully for their adoption by the state legislature.

Notes

Notes

9    In 1947, the mayor of Denver appointed Sabin manager of the city's Board of Health and Hospitals, a post she held until 1951. That year she was honored with the Lasker Award, the most prestigious honor in medical science. She finally retired for good at the age of eighty and died of a heart attack two years later on October 3, 1953.

### ▼ Questions for Critical Thought
#### "Florence Rena Sabin"

1. Do you find any heroic qualities in Florence Rena Sabin in this biographical essay? Do you consider Sabin a hero? Why or why not? How is she different from the other heroes you have discussed in class?
2. In the introductory paragraph, how does Stille help you focus and anticipate what will come in the essay?
3. Choose one paragraph that you feel has a particularly strong focus: a good topic sentence and effective, focused support. Write down the topic sentence and explain why you think the paragraph is well focused.

---

### Journal Assignment
#### Heroes

Write down your thoughts about heroes in general. Then write about one or two heroes in a bit more detail. Why do they interest you? What impresses you about them? Exchange your journal with classmates, and simply say, "Thank you."

---

### Writing Assignment #1: Defining Heroes

Here, in brief, is the writing assignment that you are preparing for.

> *Write an essay in which you define what a hero is and then prove that a person you have chosen is indeed a hero. Focus on only one person, and focus on only those qualities that make him or her a hero. Consider including information you find through research.*

Keep this assignment in mind as you proceed to dig deeper into the issue of heroes and prepare to write.

## Explore the Writing Assignment

It's important to explore your options before planning or drafting. The first topic you think of for an essay may not be the best. If you take the time to explore your options, you may find a topic that is even more interesting or worthwhile than the first one that popped into your head. You'll be putting considerable time into writing this essay, so give yourself the chance to find a hero to write about who truly interests you.

*Brainstorm* Spend ten to twenty minutes and write freely about many heroes. Refer to the list on page 175 to help you get started. Also, refer to your class notes and the readings. Write as much as you can about each hero. If there is a person you are interested in, but don't know much about, write down questions you have about that person. When you have finished brainstorming, write down the name of the person you think you will write about and why you have chosen this person.

*Gather Information about Heroes* Find some information on the person you have chosen. You may already have information (from essays in this book, materials at home, or from readings from your instructor). Study the information you have and take some notes. If you don't have enough information, go to the library (or the Internet) and research this person. Find out the basic facts (date of birth, place of birth, education, accomplishments, date of death—if applicable). Then identify the admirable qualities and actions that make you consider this person a hero. Take notes and record your source information. Use your own words; do not copy your research sources. If you find a sentence or two in an outside source that is worth quoting, practice your quoting skills.

*Think Critically about Your Choice of a Hero* Do you still want to write your essay about the first person you chose? Why or why not? Why is the person you researched considered a hero? If you have decided *not* to write about the person you researched, you should go back and look at your brainstorm. You may want to talk to your instructor or a tutor. Think about why your first choice turned out to be unsatisfactory. Then make a new choice and find information on this new person.

Notes

Notes

***Narrow Your Brainstorm*** Once you have chosen a hero and gathered some basic information, you should brainstorm again, focusing just on your chosen hero. Write freely for approximately thirty minutes about anything connected to this person. Don't use your critical thinking skills at this point. Let your mind wander and don't worry about what you write. A good brainstorm is long and full of many different ideas. Some of the ideas will prove useful and others will not, but now is not the time to make those choices.

When you have finished your brainstorm, go back, use your critical thinking skills, and highlight the ideas that seem most promising to you.

***Consider Your Audience*** Before you actually begin thinking about your thesis or outline, you should consider who is in your audience and what they want to know. Thinking about your audience will help you begin to focus your thoughts and determine what must be included in your essay.

## ▼ Activities

### Audience

In small groups, ask each other the following questions.

1. What do you know about my hero?
2. What would you like to know about my hero?
3. Do you think the person I have chosen is a hero?

When you have answers to these questions, write down your own description of a larger audience. Who is in your audience? What do they know and not know about the hero you have chosen? Will you have to persuade your readers that your hero is, indeed, a hero? Assume that your audience extends beyond your classroom. What kinds of information about heroes in general do you want to share with this larger audience? What specific information about your hero seems important?

### Speak Your Mind

Share your responses to the following prompts with a classmate. (Be sure to make notes so that you can use them when you outline and draft your essay.)

1. My definition of a hero is:

2. The person I have chosen as a hero has the following characteristics (he or she doesn't have to have all the characteristics in the hero definition):

3. The main points I should cover in my essay are:

4. I probably don't need to mention the following information in my essay:

*Create Your Thesis* Remember that a thesis statement is the sentence that expresses the main idea of your essay. It usually comes at the end of your introduction, and everything else in the essay should connect to and support this thesis. Obviously, it is an important element in your essay. You'll want to experiment with different ways of expressing your main idea. While you are experimenting with the thesis statement, you'll find that you are thinking critically about exactly what you want to prove in your essay.

Review the writing assignment, your brainstorm, activities, and class notes and write a thesis statement for your essay. You may need to write a few thesis statements before you create one that expresses your ideas well. Share your thesis statement with your classmates, tutor, and instructor. Ask them what they expect your essay to be about. Think critically about what they say and about your own reaction to your thesis statement. Is it too broad? Too narrow? Your thesis should give your reader a clear sense of where your essay is going and why.

*Outline* After revising and polishing your thesis statement, copy it down on a clean piece of paper and experiment with possible topic sentences for your essay. (Note: For a well-focused essay, your topic sentences must clearly support your thesis.) Be careful of topic sentences that give facts rather than state the main idea of a paragraph. For example, a topic sentence that says, "He was born in 1852," does not give the reader a good sense of what that paragraph will be about. Such a sentence also does not show how the paragraph will support the idea that "he" is a hero. Your topic sentences will probably focus on different heroic qualities you see in your hero.

*Notes*

Revise your topic sentences until they seem clear and effective. List them beneath your thesis statement. You may also want to list a few pieces of support under each topic sentence to remind yourself of the type of information that will go into the body of each paragraph. Share this outline with classmates, a tutor, or your instructor. Can your reader(s) tell what your essay will be about? Does everything connect to your thesis?

Feel free to change and revise your outline at any time during your writing process. The outline should be a guide, not something that forces you to state something you are no longer satisfied with.

## Draft

At this stage of the writing process, you want to create a complete essay (introduction, body, conclusion). However, remember that this is a work in progress, and you should not try to make the draft perfect. Striving for perfection at this stage will probably just make you worry about every word you put on paper. You will have the chance to revise later. In fact, you, like many writers, may write many drafts—each one better than the previous one.

When you are ready to draft your essay, remember, you should assume that your reading audience doesn't know very much, if anything, about the hero you are focusing on, so it's your job to provide important information about this person and why he or she is a hero. Your introduction should define heroes and generally explain why the person you selected is considered a hero. In your body paragraphs, describe in more detail the different heroic qualities your hero possesses. In your conclusion, tell your reader what you've learned from writing this essay and what you want the reader to learn from it.

## Revise

This is the stage in the writing process in which you change and improve your draft. As you complete this stage, you may find that you actually produce a number of drafts. It is important to have someone review your work and respond to your ideas. Don't worry about sentence corrections yet. Put your energy into improving the *focus, development,* and *organization* of your essay.

▼ **Activity**  *Notes*

**Share Your Writing**

Find a classmate to work with. Discuss the following questions as they relate to your essays.

- Do you have a clear definition of what a traditional hero is?
- Do you focus on just one person in your essay?
- Do you focus on only those qualities that make your person a hero? (For example, George Washington may have been an excellent card player, but you wouldn't mention that in the essay because it doesn't explain why he is a hero.)
- Is there enough specific evidence that this person is a hero? Do you have enough facts? Do you need to do more research? Do you cite your sources?
- Check the coherence of your essay. Will your reader see how each piece of information connects to your point that this person is a hero?

## Edit

Now is the time to work on polishing your sentences. The goal is to make your ideas clear and to project a professional image so that your reader will respect your work.

Read your essay aloud and look (and listen) for awkward spots and typographical errors.

Review your essay again, slowly, sentence by sentence, and consider the following:

- Are there any errors that you tend to repeat? Focus on them one at a time.
- Is there a certain area your instructor wants you to focus on?
- Are you using pronouns effectively? (Are you using them to improve the flow and coherence of your essay without overusing them? Do your pronouns agree in number with their antecedents?)
- Are you using outside sources correctly and effectively?
- Should you combine any sentences?

*Notes*

- Are there any misspelled words? Use spell check on your computer, or get out your dictionary and look up any words you are uncertain about. Do this early enough so that if you need it, you can get help from a tutor or instructor. Specific words to be aware of in this assignment include the following:
  - hero/heroes (notice that the singular form doesn't have an *e* on the end),
  - the name of your hero, and
  - the names of places/events (like your hero's birthplace, and so on).

## Writing Assignment #2: Analyzing a Film, "Hero"

In the next assignment, you'll study a film called *Hero,* which does not offer you the typical Hollywood hero. The realistic story in this film will challenge you as you analyze the characters. Here, in brief, is the writing assignment that you are preparing for:

> *Write an essay in which you argue that Bernie LaPlante is a hero, or write an essay in which you argue that John Bubber is a hero. Focus on only one of these men and only on those events in the film that connect to the issue of heroism.*

Keep this assignment in mind as you dig deeper into the film and prepare to write.

## View, Discuss, Think Critically

As you view the film, take notes. You may want to see the film more than once, and you'll want to share your notes with classmates.

View the film *Hero,* directed by Stephen Frears, 1992, with
- Dustin Hoffman as Bernie LaPlante,
- Geena Davis as Gale Gayley, and
- Andy Garcia as John Bubber

### ▼ Questions for Critical Thought

**Hero**

1. Which of the two main characters (LaPlante or Bubber) looks more like a typical hero? Do heroes look a certain way?

2. Does a hero have to want to perform a heroic task in order to be called a hero? What if he or she does it by accident, or unwillingly?

3. Was John Bubber a hero? What heroic acts did he perform? Why? When? How? In what ways was John Bubber not a hero? What unheroic acts did he perform? Why? When? How?

4. Was Bernie LaPlante a hero? What heroic acts did he perform? Why? When? How? In what ways was Bernie LaPlante not a hero? What unheroic acts did he perform? Why? When? How?

5. Discuss the following quotes from the movie. Do you agree or disagree with them? Why?

   John Bubber (when he first hears Bernie LaPlante's story): "A lot of people would say that's what heroism is—stupidity. Doing something that if you thought about it, you wouldn't do it if it's not in your interest."

   John Bubber (near the end of the movie): "I think we're all heroes if you catch us at the right moment. We all have something noble and decent in us trying to get out, and we're all less than heroic at other times."

### Journal Assignment

**The Hero(es) in Hero**

Review *Activity—Film Heroes* on page 174, and your notes about heroes. You may also want to look again at the readings earlier in this chapter. Write your thoughts about this film. Specifically, think about LaPlante and Bubber and their heroic and nonheroic qualities. Exchange your journal with classmates, and simply say, "Thank you."

## Explore the Writing Assignment

Take a moment to review Writing Assignment #2.

*Write an essay in which you argue that Bernie LaPlante is a hero, or write an essay in which you argue that John Bubber is a hero. Focus on only one of these men and only on those events in the film that connect to the issue of heroism.*

To make a good choice between the two writing topics, take time to explore where each topic might lead you.

Notes

▼ **Activity**

*Explore the Topics*

Discuss the following questions with your classmates.

1. What is your definition of a hero?

2. Which of these qualities does LaPlante have? What proof do you have from the film?

3. Which of these qualities does Bubber have? What proof do you have from the film?

4. What nonheroic qualities does each character appear to have? Can each character still be considered a hero?

5. Whom do you think you'll write about and why?

6. What main points will you include in your essay? (Remember, it's okay to admit that your hero is not perfect. He can still be a hero.)

*Brainstorm* Drawing on your notes from class discussions and the film, write freely and explore your thoughts on each character. Write down all the ideas that come to your mind. Don't censor your thoughts.

*Consider Your Audience* With this assignment, you can assume that your audience has seen the film *Hero*, but probably doesn't remember it well. Before you begin planning or drafting your essay, think about your audience's needs. Write down a list of basic information that will remind your audience of the **plot line** of the film. (The plot line is a concise summary that tells the reader about the major events/actions in a film).

Also, write down what you think your audience might expect in an essay about a film hero. Will you surprise your audience in any way? Will you have to *persuade* your audience to believe in any of your ideas?

*Create Your Thesis* Remember, the thesis statement is the sentence that comes last in your introductory paragraph. It tells your readers what you'll be explaining, discussing, or proving in your essay. It is important for you to shape this sentence carefully.

Review the writing assignment, your brainstorm, activities, and class notes, and begin experimenting with possible thesis statements. Write several thesis statements as you search for one that expresses your idea well. Share your thesis statement with a reader and ask him or her what he or she expects you to discuss in your essay. Think critically about what your reader says and about your own reaction to your thesis statement. Is it too broad? Too narrow? (A thesis statement that is too broad might not get the reader focused specifically on your chosen hero, or it might not get the reader focused on the idea that this character is a hero. A thesis statement that is too narrow might focus on just one heroic quality rather than on the larger point that the character you have chosen is indeed a hero.)

*Outline* After revising and polishing your thesis statement, copy it on a clean piece of paper, and experiment with possible topic sentences for your essay. Create topic sentences that focus on separate heroic qualities.

Work on your topic sentences until they seem clear and effective. List them beneath your thesis statement. You may also want to list a few pieces of support under each topic sentence to remind yourself of the type of information that will go into the body of each paragraph. Share this outline with classmates, a tutor, or your instructor. Can your reader(s) tell what your essay will be about? Does everything connect to your thesis?

Feel free to alter your outline at any time during the writing process. The outline should be a guide, not something that forces you to state something you are no longer satisfied with.

## Draft

At this stage of the writing process, you want to create a complete essay (introduction, body, conclusion). Remember that you must allow yourself to write without too many interruptions. Accept that this first draft may not be perfect. Relax and focus on ideas. Review all of your notes and the readings. Remind yourself that the first goal is to get a complete draft done. Then you can go back and improve and polish.

Your introduction should introduce the basic plot line of the movie and your definition of a hero. Your thesis should give your reader a clear sense of what you will prove in your essay and why the reader should read it. In your body paragraphs, offer the most interesting de-

*Notes*

tailed information you can from the film that shows why your character from the film is indeed a hero. Remember, each paragraph should focus on one point at a time: use topic sentences to help you with this. In your conclusion, tell your reader what you've learned from writing this essay and what you want the reader to learn. (Note: You don't have to actually say, "I have learned . . . and you should have learned. . . ." Find other ways to state your message.)

## Revise

This is your opportunity to look objectively at your essay and consider its strengths and weaknesses. This is also a time to get another reader's response to your work. When you have identified some areas that you think need work, approach revising one step at a time. Make a list of revision tasks and prioritize it.

### ▼ Activity

#### Share Your Writing

Work with one or two classmates. Read each other's essays and discuss the following questions as they relate to your essays.

- Do you have a clear definition of a hero?

- Have you clearly and quickly summarized the plot of the movie? (Too much information will bore the reader, too little will leave the reader confused.)

- Do you focus on just one hero?

- Do you focus on the most important information from the film?

- How is the coherence of your essay? Do all the paragraphs clearly connect back to your thesis? Check your topic sentences.

## Edit

After revising, work on polishing your sentences. Make your ideas clear and project a professional image so that your reader will respect your work.

Read your essay aloud and look (and listen) for awkward spots and typographical errors.

Review your essay again, slowly, sentence by sentence and consider the following:

Notes

- Are there any errors that you tend to repeat? Focus on one at a time.
- Is there a certain area your instructor wants you to focus on?
- Are you using pronouns effectively? (Are you using them to improve the flow/coherence of your essay without overusing them? Do your pronouns agree in number with their antecedents?)
- Are you using outside sources correctly and effectively?
- Should you combine any sentences?
- Use spell check or get out your dictionary and look up any words you are uncertain about. Specific words to be aware of in this assignment include the following:
  - hero/heroes (notice the singular form doesn't have an *e* on the end),
  - the name of your hero, and
  - the names of places/events (like your hero's birthplace, and so on).

## ▲▼▲ Time to Reflect

> ### Journal Assignment
> ### *Your Progress as a Writer, Reader, and Critical Thinker*
> Write in your journal your reflection on any or all of the following:
> - Have your reading and writing processes continued to change and improve?
> - What reading and writing skills do you feel really good about?
> - What skills are you most concerned about?
> - Are you using any of the tutoring resources on campus?

## ▲▼▲ Summary of Chapter 5

In this chapter you have studied the role of *focus* in effective writing. You have

- considered how topic sentences and thesis statements help writers focus their writing,
- seen how important critical thinking is in creating a focused piece of writing, and
- practiced your ability to focus your thoughts on paper while you communicated your own ideas about what makes a hero and who is a hero.

Section II    Employing the Connections

Notes             **Pronouns**

### Identifying Pronouns
### Using the Right Pronoun

A **pronoun** is a word that can be used instead of a noun in a sentence. Knowing about pronouns gives you more options when you write. You don't always have to use a noun. Sometimes, you'll want to use a pronoun to add variety and cohesion (glue) to your writing. Consequently, you need to learn to identify pronouns and to use them correctly.

### Identifying Pronouns

| Subject form | I, he, she, it, they, we, you |
|---|---|
| Object form | me, him, her, it, them, us, you |
| Possessive form | my/mine, his, her/hers, its, their/theirs, our/ours, your/yours |
| Relative/Interrogative form | who, that, which |
| Indefinite form | someone, everybody, each, neither, anybody, anyone |

Read the following passage aloud. Then, reread the passage and put boxes around the pronouns you find. (The paragraph comes from "Move Over, Barney.")

> Molly Pitcher saw what had to be done and did it. Women had a defined role in the war; they were a vital support to the fighting colonials. But when her husband was wounded, and the cannon needed to be fired, she knew what she had to do. Molly Pitcher was, and is, a heroine, and her story deserves to be told and retold. Neither a great statesman or soldier, she was an ordinary person who performed an extraordinary deed.

1. Cross out every *she* in the passage that refers to Molly Pitcher and write in *Molly Pitcher*. Also cross out every *her* and write in *Molly Pitcher's*.
2. Select a member in your class or in a small group to read the paragraph aloud the way you have rewritten it. How does the paragraph sound without using *she* or *her*?

   As you can see (hear), pronouns are important so that writing doesn't become repetitive. Also, pronouns act as glue—showing that sentences are connected by their ideas.

*Pronoun Reference Rule:* A pronoun must always have a noun to refer to. The noun the pronoun refers to is called the *antecedent*. (Otherwise your reader will become confused, wondering who *he, she, it* might be.)

Notes

Think of an "antecedent" as an "ancestor" (someone who came before you). Pronouns must have "antecedents." People must have "ancestors."

In the paragraph that follows, the pronouns are boxed and there are arrows going from the pronouns to the antecedent. (The paragraph comes from "Move Over, Barney.")

Michelangelo spent a lifetime at his craft, leaving the world a legacy of magnificent paintings and sculptures. His hard work was a daily reaffirmation of his belief in a human's creative potential. Through toil, he produced artistic monuments that have continued to inspire generations.

3. In the sentences below, put boxes around the pronouns and draw arrows to the antecedents. Notice how the pronoun/antecedent relationship helps us see the connection between different sentences. This improves the flow and coherence of the writing. (The sentences come from "Move Over, Barney" and "Rosa Parks Joins Children's Wall of Heroes.")

   a. Where are the heroines and heroes for children today? They are everywhere! They are the figures from our past, some in the historical limelight, others still in the shadows. They are the men and women of the present, struggling to overcome personal and societal problems to build a better world.

   b. Police were called, and Parks was arrested. She was bailed out of jail by a local civil rights activist, who then enlisted a young minister—26-year-old King—to help organize a boycott of the city's bus line.

Notes

**Using the Right Pronoun**

Earlier you learned that your subjects and verbs have to agree in number so that your reader doesn't get confused. Your pronouns and nouns must also agree in number.

Fill in the blanks in the following sentences with the correct pronouns. You will need to pay close attention to the meaning of the sentences.

1. I consider Harriet Tubman a hero. _____ took great risks to help other people.

2. The underground railroad Tubman created was not really underground. _____ was really just a series of complex routes and "safe houses" that brought the slaves to freedom.

3. All the slaves that took the underground railroad were successful. _____ made it to the North, and from there _____ could go to Canada.

*Pronoun Agreement Rule* If an antecedent is singular, you must use a singular pronoun. If an antecedent is plural, you must use a plural pronoun. (Remember, indefinite pronouns such as *someone, everybody,* and *anybody* are singular.)

*Example:* Heroic *people* have many different qualities. But *they* also have certain qualities in common: courage, selflessness, integrity.

An easy error to make is using *they* when the antecedent is *singular. Example of such an error:* A *person* doesn't have to be perfect to be a hero. *They* are human.

The antecedent to *they* in the example is *person. Person* is singular; *they* doesn't work because *they* is plural. Instead, you should use *he, she,* or *he or she.* Traditionally, writers have used *he,* but modern style says that it's okay to use *she* if you choose to. Many female writers choose to use *she*—as you will see the authors of this book do at times. (Some writers find *he or she* awkward.) The key here is to be consistent. If you switch back and forth between *he* and *she,* your reader may become confused.

Rewrite the following paragraph, providing appropriate pronouns.

Many heroes go unnoticed. _____ do wonderful things that don't make headlines, so people often ignore _____. For example, you may know a person who has helped change your neighborhood. _____ may have started a neighborhood watch program, or perhaps _____ looks out for the kids in the neighborhood who have parents who work all day. This type of person may sacrifice many hours of _____ own time in order to keep your neighborhood happy and safe. Anybody could be a hero. All _____ has to do is think of others first and be brave and committed.

Notes

1. Write a sentence that has an antecedent and *he* to refer to that antecedent. (Draw an arrow from *he* to the antecedent.)
2. Write a sentence that has an antecedent and *she* to refer to that antecedent. (Draw an arrow from *she* to the antecedent.)
3. Write a sentence that uses "a person" as the antecedent and has a pronoun that refers to "a person." (Draw an arrow from the pronoun to the antecedent.)
4. Write a sentence that has an antecedent and *they* to refer to that antecedent. (Draw an arrow from *they* to the antecedent.)
5. Copy down some of your notes about heroes (perhaps a journal or an answer to a reading question). Underline all the pronouns that you use. Check your use of pronouns.

## ▲▼▲ Using Outside Sources

### Introduction to Outside Sources
### Using Outside Information

The guidelines here will help you use outside information for this class. Other classes may require you to learn more about citing sources; ask your instructor about the appropriate handbook for you to refer to. Citing sources can get very complicated and must be done with precision.

### Introduction to Outside Sources

An **outside source** is a person or publication that supplies you with information.

**Outside information** is any fact or idea that someone other than you came up with.

## Using Outside Sources

Section II  Employing the Connections

*Notes*

A writer often uses information from other sources when writing her own essay, book, or article. Sometimes a writer will use something she heard on television or in a speech. Sometimes a writer will use something she read in an encyclopedia, a newspaper, a textbook, or a magazine. There are many places to get useful information.

Guidelines A–E will help you get started on using outside sources.

### A. *Why Writers Use Outside Sources*

- A writer may hear or read something interesting and want to discuss it in more detail.
- A writer may come across an idea she disagrees with and want to argue against it.
- A writer may find information that supports something she already wants to discuss.

### B. *Source of the Source*

Of course, a writer can't use information from just anywhere. The source of the information must be one that readers will respect. For example, a writer should use information from a reputable publication or a recognized expert. Readers might not believe information that comes from a gossip magazine, and they might not be too interested in what your neighbor down the street once dreamt about aliens from outer space. Choose your sources carefully. When doing research, keep careful notes on where you get your information from. Write down the following source information whenever possible:

author

title (of essay or article and the title of the magazine or newspaper it was published in) or (of book)

date

page number

volume number (when the source is a journal or encyclopedia)

### C. *Quantity of Outside Sources*

You can use a little outside information or a lot of outside information, depending on what you are writing. In a cover letter for your resumé, you probably wouldn't use many (if any) outside sources. In a scientific report, you'd probably use many outside sources. Most of the college essays you write will call for *some* outside information. Here's a good general rule: outside information should play a supporting role to what you have to say. That is, your ideas should come first and take center stage. (If you are ever worried about having too many pieces of outside information in your writing, highlight all information that you borrowed from an outside source. If you highlight more than a third of your essay, you probably have too much outside information and too few of your own original ideas.)

**D.  *Where to Use Your Outside Sources***

Generally, you want to use the quotes and borrowed information in the body of a paragraph. Sometimes you can start a paragraph with a quote, but usually you need your own topic sentence. Rarely, you can put outside information at the end of a paragraph. Usually, you, as the writer, must interpret outside information. You must explain it and analyze it for the reader. Otherwise, your reader might interpret the information in ways you don't expect.

**E.  *The Most Important Thing to Remember about Outside Sources***

Interpret, explain, and analyze your outside information. Readers don't want a bunch of quotes. They want your well-supported ideas.

Read the following paragraph.

> I think it is important to introduce my son to real life heroes. My son cannot learn all he needs to from the Power Rangers. Dennis Denenberg, a professor of education at Millersville University of Pennsylvania, explained this very well: "Like junk food, popular fantasy and cartoon characters are sweet, enticing to the eye—and empty of real value. Like junk food, they displace what is more important." I think it is more important for my son to learn about the courage of Harriet Tubman, the dedication of Albert Einstein, and the spirit of Mother Theresa. My son needs to feast on the nutrients that these real life heroes can offer.

1. Review guidelines A–E. Explain if this writer follows each of these guidelines. Discuss each guideline and how it is or is not followed.

## Using Outside Information

When you use ideas and information that belong to someone else, you must give that person credit. If you do not do this, you'll be guilty of **plagiarism.** In some cultures, it is common practice to copy the words of an expert without mentioning the expert. Such a practice stems from the idea that copying these words is the writer's way of saying, "These are better words/ideas than I could ever come up with." However, in American colleges and businesses, writers are expected to give credit to the person who first came up with the idea/information. Plagiarism can

*Notes*

be grounds for being dismissed from a college or job, so it is important that you know how to use outside information and give credit to the person who first stated the information. Giving credit to the original sources is called **citing your sources**. (The information that follows focuses mainly on how to use quotations. However, even if you put someone else's ideas into your own words and you don't use quotation marks, you must still say where you got these ideas from.)

First, you should know that information that is considered "general knowledge" doesn't have to be cited. For example, if you are writing an essay about George Washington, and you find his birth date in an encyclopedia, you do not have to cite this encyclopedia. Washington's birth date can be found in many different sources: it is considered general knowledge.

However, if you want to use a piece of information that cannot be found in many different places, you must say where you got the information from.

There are many ways of incorporating a quote into your essay. Here are five common patterns. (Note: when you introduce a quotation, put a comma after the introductory phrase and capitalize the first word in the quotation. Pattern #5 is different because of the word *that*.)

Pattern #1 (from the earlier paragraph): *Dennis Denenberg, a professor of education at Millersville University of Pennsylvania, explained this very well: "Like junk food, popular. . . ."*

[Author's name], [author information], explained:

Pattern #2: *In "Move Over, Barney" Dennis Denenberg, a professor of education, explained this very well: "Like junk food, popular . . . ."*

In [name of the article] [author's name], [author's info.], explained:*

Pattern #3: *According to Dennis Denenberg, a professor at Millersville University of Pennsylvania, "Like junk food, popular . . . ."*

According to [author's name], [author's info.],

---

*Remember from your prepositional phrase work that nothing in a prepositional phrase can be the subject of a sentence. So, if you begin a sentence with "in" as shown in Pattern #2, you must supply a subject after that introductory prepositional phrase. In Pattern #2, the subject is Dennis Denenberg.

> or
>
> According to [name of article],

Notes

If the writer had already introduced Dennis Denenberg and explained his status as an expert, the writer could have just said the following:

> Pattern #4: *Denenberg noted, "Like junk food, popular...."*
>     [Author's last name] noted,

> Pattern #5: *Denenberg said that "like junk food, popular...."*
>     [Author's name] said that [no capital letters at the beginning of the quote]

Note: The first time you use a source, it is a good idea to explain who/what your source is. If your source is a person and the person is an expert, what is this person's job title? Where does he or she work? If the source is a journalist, for what magazine or newspaper does the journalist write? If you are using statistics, from what government agency or private company did you get the statistics? Your reader is more likely to trust your information with these kinds of details.

1. Choose some interesting quotes from Denenberg's essay. Write five sentences showing that you can use each of the five different quoting patterns. Be very careful that you punctuate correctly and use capital letters when necessary.
2. Review other readings and find some other patterns for using quotes. (Look in the newspaper, textbooks, magazines, and so on.) Write down three quotes you find that have slightly different patterns than the five mentioned here.

## ▲▼▲ Shaping Sentences

So far in this book, we've been mainly focusing on parts of sentences. Now it is time to bring together your knowledge of those parts and look at whole sentences.

The rest of your sentence work in this book will focus largely on shaping sentences so that you can clearly express your thoughts in interesting ways. Your goals will be to add variety to your writing style and to avoid common errors. It is not important for you to memorize sentence patterns or shapes. The most important thing for you to do is prac-

**Notes**

tice writing well-shaped sentences. Consequently, you'll need to write out the sentences you create (not just fill in blanks or insert words). Writing sentences with different patterns helps students write sophisticated sentences in their own essays without even thinking about it.

Although some of what follows is a review, you will be putting "old" knowledge to new uses.

### Every Sentence Has a Subject

Some sentences may have an implied subject (*you*), and some sentences may have more than one subject.

*Examples:*

a. Albert Einstein is a hero to some people.

b. Michael Jordan and Tiger Woods are heroes to other people.

c. Choose a hero you are interested in.

1. Write sentences a–c in your notebook. Underline the verbs twice and underline the subjects once.
2. Write three sentences of your own that follow the patterns in a, b, c.

### Every Sentence Has a Verb

A sentence can have more than one verb.

*Examples:*

d. Michael Jordan plays basketball and works with kids.

e. Mother Theresa visits the poor and comforts them.

f. Hillary Clinton writes books and speaks on the behalf of children.

3. Write sentences d–f in your notebook. Underline the verbs twice and underline the subjects once.
4. Write three sentences of your own that have one subject each but also have two verbs each. (Be careful—don't create anything too complicated. Don't use *who*, *that*, or *which*.)

### A Sentence Can Have Multiple Verbs and Multiple Subjects

*Examples:*

g. A hero may save a single life, or a hero may improve an entire community.

Chapter 5  Writing about Heroes

Notes

h. Old people and young people can affect the lives of others and become heroes.

i. Parents and teachers should teach children about heroes and encourage children to emulate heroes.

5. Write sentences g, h, and i in your notebook. Underline the verbs twice and underline the subjects once.

6. Write three sentences of your own that have multiple verbs and multiple subjects.

Writing sentences with more than one subject and/or verb can help you say things more clearly and make your writing more interesting. (The following sentences are based on the article "I Just Reacted—I Don't Know How" by Lyric Wallwork Winic. Nora Chapman was caught in her car in flood waters near the Vela house and was rescued by the Vela brothers.)

*Example*:

j. Eddie Vela risked his life to save Nora Chapman.

k. Jose Vela risked his life to save Nora Chapman.

l. Marco Vela risked his life to save Nora Chapman.

Combination: Eddie, Jose, and Marco Vela risked their lives to save Nora Chapman. (Note how *his life* changed to *their lives*.)

**Punctuation Rule #1:**  Put commas between items in a series. See how commas were inserted between the names Eddie, Jose, and Marco above. Another example: I bought eggs, milk, and cheese at the store. (The comma before the *and* is optional with a list like this.)

Combine the sentences that follow. Remember Punctuation Rule #1.

7. m. The Vela brothers tied a rope to a parked car.

n. The Vela brothers held onto the rope.

o. The Vela brothers waded out to Chapman.

Combination:
_____

8. p. They reached her.

q. They pulled her out of her car.

Combination:
_____

*Notes*

9. r. The car filled with water.
   s. The car was swept away.

Combination: _____

10. t. Jose is a hero.
    u. Eddie is a hero.
    v. Marco is a hero.

Combination: _____

**Certain Verbs Require a Completer**

A **completer** is a word or phrase that completes the meaning of the sentence. Without the completer, the sentence is a fragment—a partial sentence. Notice how "sentences" 11–13 sound incomplete.

11. The Vela brothers saved.

12. Nora Chapman thanked.

13. To show her appreciation, she bought.

They aren't really sentences; they are only fragments. Complete the sentences—write out the new sentences. Underline the verbs twice, the subjects once, and highlight the part that becomes the completer.

As you learned in the last chapter, *-ing* words need helper verbs if they want to function as verbs. Without the helper verb, you may end up with a **fragment** (an incomplete sentence). Look at the fragments below. (The technical term for the fragments below is *verbal phrases*. You will learn later in your studies how to use verbal phrases to add variety to sentences that are already complete.)

14. Running for help.

15. Calling 911.

16. Explaining what happened.

17. Recovering in the hospital.

Add subjects and helping verbs to sentences 14–17 to create complete sentences.

# Writing about Technology

**CHAPTER 6**

### Main Topics

- Organizing your writing

- Communicating your ideas about technology

- Avoiding fragments, run-ons, comma splices

- Using transitions and concessions to improve coherence and flow

*Big Things Are Coming My Way Soon,* by S. Adams, 1995 United Features

*Notes*

At work and in college you may find yourself swimming in data, facts, observations, and ideas. As a writer, reader, and critical thinker you'll need strategies to organize this information so that you can make sense of it and utilize it. In this chapter, you'll concentrate on understanding and using different methods of *organizing* all the data, facts, observations, and ideas that you choose to communicate.

## ▲▼▲ Organizing Your Writing

One way to think about organization is to remember that as a writer you are similar to a guide leading someone who (temporarily) doesn't see well. You want to make your reader's journey as smooth as possible (no bumps, cliffs, or wrong turns—unless carefully planned for dramatic effect), so you must *organize* what you say. Of course, you already organize ideas every day: when you explain to someone how to get to a specific file on your computer, when you summarize last night's great movie plot, or when you explain to your child why dishwashing detergent doesn't work in the clothes washer, you organize. In each case, you organize your thoughts to communicate clearly and quickly.

In this chapter, the organizing and communicating will not happen quite so quickly because you will be creating more formal responses to the complex topics about technology and the Internet. You will be presented with many ideas and opinions about the advantages and disadvantages of technology in general and the advantages and disadvantages of the Internet more specifically. It will be your job to use your critical thinking skills, to carefully consider and sort through the ideas and opinions, to form your own opinion, and to focus and organize your ideas as you create a clearly written essay.

### Organizing the Paragraph

In an organized paragraph, the writer states the main idea in the topic sentence. Then the writer offers detail and support that usually grows more specific and/or more important. A writer must also include an explanation of the details and supporting ideas. Paragraphs sometimes end with a wrap-up sentence that reminds the reader of the main point of the paragraph. Most paragraphs follow this general pattern:

main idea, increasingly specific and/or increasingly important details and support, followed by explanation.

For example, consider the following body paragraph from a student's essay on the advantages of having Internet access in high school. The topic sentence announces the paragraph's main idea. The second sentence emphasizes the importance of the main idea. The writer then gives a specific example and explains the significance of this example. Finally, the writer wraps up the paragraph with a note of explanation that also emphasizes the importance of the main idea.

> Obtaining other people's views may be limited in a small city or town, but with the Internet, students can communicate with other students from all over the world. This can lead to the understanding of others' views and opinions. For example, students who take French can enhance their skills by talking with someone in France. A student is not only learning the language but can learn about the culture from someone with first hand experience, instead of what may be in an outdated book. All of this knowledge will lead our children to a better understanding of the world.
>
> —Stacy Michel

*main idea and explanation*

*specific example and explanation*

*concluding explanation that emphasizes importance of point*

However, some paragraphs have other, distinct patterns. Here are some other **patterns of organization** that you use every day for speaking, thinking, and writing:

- least important ideas first, most important ideas last
- least interesting ideas first, most interesting ideas last
- (time) first idea/event that occurred, second, third, and so on.

Occasionally these patterns overlap. That is, a writer might organize his ideas by a time pattern (telling what happened first, second, and so on), *and* he might have in mind that he is organizing his ideas according to importance. (The first event was least important to him and the last event was most important to him.)

When revising a paragraph, a writer needs to think critically about organization and perhaps experiment with the order a bit. The writer must also make sure that the reader can see the logical organization of ideas. The writer can help the reader by using transition words and phrases that show the relationships between ideas. For example, if the

Notes

writer wants to show that the ideas in her paragraph go from the least important idea to the most important idea, she might use any of these transition phrases:
- significantly
- more importantly
- of most importance

If the writer wants to show that the ideas in her paragraph move from the first thing that happened to the second thing that happened and so on, she might use any of these transition words:
- first
- second
- next
- then
- last

There are many different words and phrases writers can use to organize their thoughts and keep the reader on track. Consider how the following words help to explain the relationships between ideas.

To show a similar idea follows
- also
- in addition
- similarly
- furthermore
- in fact (also adds emphasis)

To show an example follows
- for example
- for instance

To show an opposite idea follows
- in contrast
- otherwise
- however

To show that one idea has "caused" another
- consequently
- as a result

Chapter 6   Writing about Technology

▼ *Activities*    Notes

### Study an Organized Paragraph

Carefully read the paragraph that follows.

> I am concerned that entertainment technology—television, CD players, Nintendo, computers—has led families to spend less quality time together. I don't know any families who spend time together creatively: dancing, singing, painting or drawing. Similarly, I don't know any families who regularly play Monopoly or other board games. In fact, I can only think of one family I know that sits down together for dinner everyday with no television blaring in the background. Quality time together is crucial so that adults can teach children social and communication skills. Perhaps more importantly, this time together shows that the parents care for the children and want to spend time with the children. Children gain much of their self-esteem from time spent with their families. I think that we need to watch our use of technology more carefully. What good is technology if it destroys the fabric of our families?

1. In the margins, mark the topic sentence (TS), the support (S), and explanations (E).

2. Highlight or circle any transition words you find, and think about what relationships these words are expressing

3. What organizational pattern (or patterns) is the writer using?

### Organize These Thoughts

Read the following topic sentence and list of supporting ideas for a single paragraph. The sentences have been mixed up and are in no order. Study the information and then decide what order the sentences should be in. (You may want to review the patterns of organization.) Referring to the earlier list of transitions, find transition words and phrases that would help build bridges between the ideas in the paragraph and rewrite the sentences so that you have an organized paragraph with transition words that help the reader understand how all the ideas fit together.

Hint: There may be more than one way to organize the sentences logically. There are many different transition words to choose from.

*Topic Sentence:* I rely on modern technology to maintain my family ties.

> Since she and I both have fax machines at work, sometimes I'll fax Mom a letter I received from someone else in the family.

*Notes*

My company has set up the daycare rooms with cameras that are linked to our computers at work so that I can look in on my kids any time during the day.

That way we can keep up on family news.

I am in regular e-mail contact with two cousins, an aunt and uncle, and all three of my sisters.

I rely on the computer even more.

The phone is important to me so that I can call my mom in Alaska once a month.

I use the computer to check in on my kids at the daycare center.

E-mail saves me a lot of money on long distance bills, and it's so quick!

Now I can check to see if my kids are having fun and if they are being treated well.

I love technology.

---

## Organizing the Essay

The same principles for organizing a paragraph apply to organizing an essay. That is, the ideas in an essay, like the ideas in a paragraph, must be in a thoughtful, logical order. In addition, essays rely on transitions just as paragraphs do.

The organized essay has a clear thesis and topic sentences that relate to that thesis. Often the topic sentences will begin with transition words that explain to the reader why the paragraphs have been organized in a certain pattern. The patterns listed for paragraphs also work with essays. Here, again, are those patterns and some additional patterns:

- least important ideas first, most important ideas last
- least interesting ideas first, most interesting ideas last
- (time) first idea/event that occurred, second, third, and so on
- (alternating pro/con ideas) pro argument, con argument, pro argument, con argument, and so on*
- all pro arguments (divided into different paragraphs) and then all con arguments (divided into different paragraphs)*

---

*A **pro argument** is an argument in *favor* of something. A **con argument** is an argument *against* something.

▼ **Activity**  Notes

### Study an Organized Essay

The following essay comes from *Sociology,* a textbook. Read the essay carefully once, marking any unknown words.

### Modernization and Women: A Report from Rural Bangladesh
*by John J. Macionis*

1. In global perspective, gender inequality is greatest where people are poorest. Economic development, then, weakens traditional male domination and gives women opportunities to work outside the home. Birth control emancipates women from a continual routine of childbearing, allowing them to benefit from schooling and to earn more in the paid work force.

2. Even as living standards rise, however, economic development has drawbacks for women. Investigating a poor, rural district of Bangladesh, Sultana Alam (1985) reports that women confront several new problems as a result of modernization.

3. First, economic opportunity draws men from rural areas to cities in search of work, leaving women and children to fend for themselves. Men sometimes sell their land and simply abandon their wives, who are left with nothing but their children.

4. Second, the eroding strength of the family and neighborhood leaves women who are deserted in this way with few sources of assistance. The same holds true for women who become single through divorce or the death of a spouse. In the past, Alam reports, kin or neighbors readily took in a Bangladeshi woman who found herself alone. Today, as Bangladesh struggles to advance economically, the number of poor households headed by women is increasing. Rather than enhancing women's autonomy, Alam argues, this spirit of individualism has actually reduced the social standing of women.

5. Third, economic development—as well as the growing influence of Western movies and mass media—undermine women's traditional roles as wives, sisters, and mothers while redefining women as objects of men's sexual attention. The cultural emphasis on sexuality that is familiar to us now encourages men in poor societies to desert aging spouses for women who are younger and more physically attractive. The same emphasis contributes to the world's rising tide of prostitution. . . .

6. Modernization, then, does not affect men and women in the same ways. In the long run, the evidence suggests, modernization does give

**Notes**

the sexes more equal standing. In the short run, however, the economic position of many women actually declines, and women are also forced to contend with new problems that were virtually unknown in traditional societies.

1. Reread the essay more carefully. Mark the thesis and topic sentences. Define any unknown terms. Note that the first *two* paragraphs act as the introduction to the essay.

2. Mark all transition words and phrases you find (at the beginning of paragraphs and within paragraphs).

3. Note in the margins the organizational pattern the author has used to put his paragraphs in order. Note also how individual sentences relate to one another. For example, look for transitional words or phrases that tell you the author is connecting opposite ideas.

4. In your own words, what is the writer's main point in this essay?

## One Approach to Organization

Just as there are many different ways that writers brainstorm, gather information, and draft essays, there are also many different ways to organize information for an essay. In this chapter, you will practice one approach that utilizes notecards. When you reach the point in your writing process when you are ready to outline the ideas of your essay, you'll write down one point per index card, label the card, and perhaps even color code the card. Then you'll be able to arrange the cards in different orders until you find an organizational pattern that fits with what you want to say. Here are some examples of how you can create the cards for an essay about the advantages and disadvantages of technology.

(front of card)

Label the card as *Advantage* or *Disadvantage.* State one point on the front of the card.

> *Advantage*
>
> Television can be used by teachers to teach classes to people who can't get to the college or training center in person.

## Notes

(back of card)

> personal experience

On the back of each card, explain where you got your idea.

(front of card)

> *Disadvantage*
>
> Television has encouraged the idea that women are sex objects.

(back of card)

> personal experience and Macionis, "Modernization and Women: A Report from Rural Bangladesh," paragraph 5.

    Cards for the work in this chapter should be labeled as *Advantage* or *Disadvantage,* since every writing assignment in the chapter deals with advantages and disadvantages of either technology or the Internet. You may even want to color code your cards—one color for advantage cards and another color for disadvantage cards. Use your own words when making these notes. On the front of each card, you'll have just one idea. On the back of the card, you'll write down where you got the information. If the information comes from a reading, you'll have to write down the author's name, the title of the reading, and the paragraph number. Then you'll be able to go back and read more

*Notes*

about an idea if you need to, and you'll have your source information ready when you begin writing your essay.

You may find that some cards have ideas that will become topic sentences. Other cards will have ideas that belong in the bodies of paragraphs. The key is to write just one idea per card. Then you can easily move the ideas around until you have found the best way to group them and organize them.

Feel free to make many cards because this way you'll have many ideas to choose from as you prepare to write your essay, and it's easy to set aside a card that you decide doesn't fit. (Keep all the cards you make in this chapter. If you are assigned a second essay from this chapter, some of your cards may be needed again.)

### Points to Remember about Organization

- Although only five organizational patterns have been described so far, there are more than just five ways to organize ideas in an essay, and some of the patterns mentioned here can be combined. (You'll be introduced to more patterns later in the chapter.)
- Use a pattern that makes sense to you, that seems to fit with what you want to say.
- Stick to your pattern. Your reader will have an easier time understanding your ideas if you have a clear pattern of organization and if you stick to your pattern. Your reader will enjoy the smooth path you create.
- Use transition words to help guide your reader.

### ▲▼▲ Investigating Technology

Now that you have begun to think about the skill of organizing, you'll begin your writing process. You'll discuss technology, the Internet, and the many ways our lives have been affected. You'll have quite a bit of information to consider and sort through. Toward the middle of the chapter, you will find three writing assignments and some guidance as you complete your writing process.

### Discuss and Engage

**Technology** is a broad term encompassing anything that science has created, usually relating to industry and commercial items. In other words, technological advances include the creation of the telephone, the microwave oven, the home computer, and compact disc players. Technology is also responsible for changing how we shower, store food, and travel from place to place. With so many items to consider, it's no wonder that people find much to praise about technology and much to criticize.

> ### Journal Assignment
> **Dilbert in the Office**
>
> Reread the cartoon on the preview page of this chapter. What does the woman mean when she says, "Goodbye 'Paperless,' hello 'Clueless'"? What is the author of this cartoon saying about technological advances in the office? Has technology affected your work? Explain.

### ▼ Activity

#### Technology Inventory

1. Working with a classmate, make an inventory of how technology affects your daily life. That is, make a list of mechanical devices that you use to get through your day. You may want to begin your list by thinking about how you start your day. For example, do you rely on an alarm clock to get up in the morning? (You won't be able to list <u>every</u> technological device that touches you. Concentrate on creating a thoughtful list.)

2. After you have listed many items technology has produced, highlight those items on your list that are the most technologically advanced. (Which items have been created most recently and seem to be the most sophisticated?)

3. Which of the highlighted items do you most value? Which seem to clearly make your life better? Are there any items that seem to negatively affect your quality of life? Can an item both increase and decrease your quality of life? Explain.

***The Internet*** Take some time now to think specifically about the Internet as a technological advancement that affects the lives of many people. Some of you may be familiar with the Internet. Some of you may feel a bit uncomfortable when you hear the word "Internet." What is it? How do you use it?

*Notes*

Basically, the Internet is a network of computers that can communicate with each other. By "logging on" to the Internet, you can use your computer to access information on any other computer that is part of the network—anywhere in the world. You can think of this computer network as being similar to the network of phone lines you use when you use your telephone. In fact, computers on a network use *modems* and the telephone lines to communicate with other computers.

Some people use this network—the Internet—for research, and they visit libraries, museums, or government offices. Other people use the Internet for entertainment: they listen to music, play games, or meet new people. And, you've probably heard of e-mail—a method of sending letters over the Internet. There are also specific discussion groups and chat rooms where people can discuss their ideas about a particular interest—parenting, surviving cancer, fixing cars, watching birds, just about any topic. In addition, businesses use the Internet to advertise their products: there is a Pepsi home page, a Gap clothing home page, and many more.

### ▼ Activity

**Discussing the Internet**

Discuss with your class your knowledge of and/or your questions about the Internet.

### ▼ Questions to Consider

1. Who in the class has used the Internet? For what reasons? Where did you use the Internet? (at home?) (at the library?)
2. Can anyone with experience with the Internet describe what it is?
3. How do you "log on" to the Internet?
4. What kinds of things have you learned about or done on the Internet?

### ▼ Activities

**Exploring the Internet**

Find a partner in class and set a time to explore the Internet. Decide when and where you will meet. Plan on spending no more than one hour on the

Internet. Your goals are to get on the Internet, explore a few Web sites, and record your experience in a journal entry. (Your teacher may give you a specific Internet address to visit.) In your journal entry, write about where, when and how you got on the Internet. How much time did you spend? What did you see or learn about? What difficulties did you have? (Be prepared to come to class and share some of your thoughts from your journal.)

Helpful Hints: Don't try to get on the Internet during the peak evening hours (7:00 pm–10:00 pm). If neither you nor your partner has ever been on the Internet, go to a library and get a librarian to help you. A librarian can save you significant time. Stick to the one hour time limit!

### Your Internet Experiences

Share your research experiences with classmates.

1. Did you enjoy the experience? Did you have any difficulties or frustrations?

2. As a class, create a description of the Internet for someone who has absolutely no experience with it.

3. What do you see as some of the best uses for the Internet?

4. Do you think there are any negative aspects to the Internet?

### Journal Assignment

#### Advantages and Disadvantages of Technology/the Internet

Review your class notes on technology and the Internet. Consider, too, your Internet experiences. Write freely about technology, and the Internet specifically. What do you find most promising about current technological advances (including the Internet)? What worries you the most about technology (and the Internet)? Have your classmates said anything in class discussions that surprised you or that you disagreed with? Explain. (This journal is for your eyes only. Refer back to this journal when you are getting ready to write your essay.)

### Writing Assignment #1: Discussing Technology in Our Lives

Here, in brief, is the writing assignment you are preparing for.

*Write an essay in which you discuss some of the advantages and disadvantages of technology in your life.*

Notes

## Read, Discuss, Think Critically

This section of the chapter offers you two readings about the advantages, disadvantages, and limitations of technology and the Internet. The first reading is a college student's essay that was published in a magazine. The second reading is a newspaper column.

## Reading Assignment

"Stop the Clock"

*Preview*   Read the first two paragraphs.

*Anticipate*   What do you anticipate this essay will be about? Use the "Notes" column to record your response.

*Read and Reread*   Read the entire essay, marking unknown terms and interesting points. Then reread more slowly and use the "Notes" column to interact with the essay. Mark important points and define unknown terms.

### Stop the Clock
*by Amy Wu*

This article first appeared in *Newsweek* magazine, January 22, 1996.

1   My aunt tends to her house as if it were her child. The rooms are spotless, the windows squeak, the kitchen counter is so shiny that I can see my reflection and the floors are so finely waxed that my sister and I sometimes slide across in socks and pretend that we are skating.

2   Smells of soy sauce, scallions and red bean soup drift from the kitchen whenever I visit. The hum of the washing machine lulls me to sleep. In season, there are roses in the garden, and vases hold flowers arranged like those in a painting. My aunt enjoys keeping house, although she's wealthy enough to hire someone to do it. I'm a failure at housework. I've chosen to be inept and unlearn what my aunt has spent so much time perfecting. At 13, I avoided domestic chores as my contribution to the women's movement. Up to now, I've thought there were more important things to do. I am a member of a generation that is very concerned with saving time but often unaware of why we're doing it. Like many, I'm nervous and jittery without a wristwatch and a daily planner. I am one of a growing number of students who are completing college in three years instead of four—cramming credits in the summer. We're living life on fast-forward without a pause button.

*Notes*

3   In my freshman year, my roommates and I survived on Chinese take-out, express pizzas and taco take-home dinners. We ate lunch while walking to class. Every day seemed an endless picnic as we ate with plastic utensils and paper plates. It was fast and easy—no washing up. My girlfriends and I talked about our mothers and grandmothers, models of domesticity, and pitied them. We didn't see the benefits of staying at home, ironing clothes and making spaghetti sauce when canned sauces were almost as good and cleaning services were so convenient. A nearby store even sold throwaway underwear. "Save time," the package read. "No laundry."

4   We baked brownies in ten minutes in the microwave and ate the frosting from the can because we were too impatient to wait for the brownies to cool. For a while we thought about chipping in and buying a funky contraption that makes toast, coffee and eggs. All you had to do was put in the raw ingredients the night before and wake up to the smell of sizzling eggs, crispy toast and rich coffee. My aunt was silent when I told her about plastic utensils, microwave meals and disposable underwear. "It's a waste of money," she finally said. I was angry as I stared at her perfect garden, freshly ironed laundry and handmade curtains. "Well, you're wasting your time," I said defensively. But I wasn't so sure.

5   It seems that all the kids I know are timesaving addicts. Everyone on campus prefers e-mail to snail mail. The art of letter writing is long gone. I know classmates who have forgotten how to write in script, and print like five-year-olds. More of us are listening to books instead of reading them. My roommate last year jogged while plugged in. She told me she'd listened to John Grisham's "The Client." "You mean read," I corrected. "I didn't read a word," she said with pride.

6   My nearsighted friends opt for throwaway contacts and think the usual lenses are tedious. A roommate prefers a sleeping bag so she doesn't have to make her bed. Instead of going to the library to do research we cruise the Internet and log on to the Library of Congress.

7   Schoolkids take trips to the White House via Internet and Mosaic. I heard that one school even considered canceling the eighth-grade Washington trip, a traditional rite of passage, because it's so easy to visit the capital on the Information Highway. I remember how excited my eighth-grade classmates and I were about being away from home for the first time. We stayed up late, ate Oreos in bed and roamed around the Lincoln Memorial, unsupervised by adults.

8   It isn't as if we're using the time we save for worthwhile pursuits like volunteering at a soup kitchen. Most of my friends spend the extra minutes watching TV, listening to stereos, shopping, hanging out, chatting on the phone or snoozing.

Notes

9   When I visited my aunt last summer, I saw how happy she was after baking bread or a cake, how proud she seemed whenever she made a salad with her homegrown tomatoes and cucumbers. Why bother when there are ready-made salads, ready-peeled and -cut fruit and five-minute frosting?

10  Once, when I went shopping with her, she bought ingredients to make a birthday cake for her daughter. I pointed to a lavish-looking cake covered with pink roses. "Why don't you just buy one," I asked. "A cake is more than a cake," she replied. "It's the giving of energy, the thought behind it. You'll grow to understand."

11  Slowly, I am beginning to appreciate why my aunt takes pleasure in cooking for her family, why the woman down the street made her daughter's wedding gown instead of opting for Vera Wang, why the old man next door spends so much time tending his garden. He offered me a bag of his fresh-grown tomatoes. "They're good," he said. "Not like the ones at the supermarket." He was right.

12  Not long ago, I spent a day making a meal for my family. As the pasta boiled and the red peppers sizzled, I wrote a letter to my cousin in Canada. At first the pen felt strange, then reassuring. I hand-washed my favorite skirt and made chocolate cake for my younger sister's 13th birthday. It took great self-control not to slather on the icing before the cake cooled.

13  That night I grinned as my father and sister dug into the pasta, then the cake, licking their lips in appreciation. It had been a long time since I'd felt so proud. A week later my cousin called and thanked me for my letter, the first handwritten correspondence she'd received in two years.

14  Sure, my generation has all the technological advances at our fingertips. We're computer-savvy, and we have more time. But what are we really saving it for? In the end, we may lose more than we've gained by forgetting the important things in life.

## ▼ Questions for Critical Thought

### "Stop the Clock"

1. Wu's personal essay doesn't follow traditional academic essay style. For example, she doesn't have a thesis statement at the end of the introduction. Review her entire essay and, in your own words, write down Wu's main point, her implied thesis.

2. What does Wu mean in paragraph 2 when she says she was making her "contribution to the women's movement"?

3. Study how Wu has organized her essay. In the margins, note the place where she mentions timesaving conveniences in a positive, or

at least neutral, light. Now note in the margins the places where she hints that she is no longer satisfied with her fast-paced life. Where does the essay begin to really focus on the positive aspects of living more slowly?

4. One of the strengths of Wu's essay is the number of interesting and vivid pieces of detail. Select a few of your favorite pieces of detail from her essay and explain why these details are so effective.

5. Wu mentions a number of timesaving devices that she and her friends have relied on. List those devices and highlight the ones that most clearly connect to recent technology.

6. What timesaving devices do you use? How do you spend the time you "save"? (Review Wu's paragraph #8.)

7. Review paragraphs 10 and 14. Do you have any old-fashioned domestic interests (like baking or gardening)? What do you think are the important things in life? How should you spend your time? Can technology help you do this? Explain.

## Reading Assignment

### "Resistance to Internet Grows Weak"

*Preview*  Note that this personal essay is from a newspaper and will be written in journalistic style. Read the title and first paragraph.

*Anticipate*  What do you anticipate this essay will be about? Use the "Notes" column to record your response.

*Read and Reread*  Read the entire essay, marking unknown terms and interesting points. Then reread more slowly and use the "Notes" column to interact with the essay. Mark important points and define unknown terms.

### Resistance to Internet Grows Weak
*by Peter H. King*

This article first appeared in the *Sacramento Bee* newspaper, April 26, 1998.

1   Berkeley—It's getting lonelier out here in the offline wilderness. One by one my compadres have slipped away in the night, vanishing into that ethereal world known as the Internet. The will to resist grows weaker. Promoters of a computer paradise keep piling on the temptations.

Notes

2    Go online and buy a book. Go online and beat the taxman. Go online and improve your jumpshot, whiten your teeth, chat with like-minded strangers, learn the chord changes to every Bob Dylan song ever recorded, and more. Go online and get . . . empowered.

3    For a long time I've held out, hopeful that the Internet would turn out to be a wrong fork in the technological road, a replay of the eight-track cassette. Now it seems virtually inescapable. My new newspaper home, for instance, prints the computer addresses of its columnists, and so I have begun to receive e-mail from readers. With mounting shame, I've yet to respond to these communiqués—not out of rudeness, but simply because I don't know how.

4    I can learn easily enough, I know; it's not rocket science. Still, something holds me back, makes me wary about plunging into the world that waits behind that pale green screen. And so last Thursday, seeking counsel and reinforcement, I hooked up with Cliff Stoll, a voice of hope for us dinosaurs still clumping about in a Webless world.

5    A Berkeley astronomer and self-described "computerjock," Stoll was a pioneer of the Internet. He's also a skeptic. A few years back he wrote a provocative book entitled "Silicon Snake Oil (Second Thoughts on the Information Highway)," in which he declared: "I've listened to plenty of spoken and implied promises about computer networks. . . . I claim these promises are myths, grounded in dreams of an information Shangri-la that can never be realized. And were it to happen, many of us would prefer to remain behind."

6    Now three years and 100,000 sold copies later, I wondered if Stoll still was hanging tough, if he had any third thoughts on the Information Highway. I asked one question, and away he went:

7    "Over and over I hear people say that the Internet is an empowering experience. Well, after spending five hours browsing Web sites, I don't feel empowered. I feel enfeebled. I feel as if my night has just dribbled out a modem. . . ."

8    And, "Information isn't power. Who has the most information in my neighborhood? Librarians, and they are famous for having no power. Who has the most power? Politicians, and they are notorious for being poorly informed."

9    And, "Only a goose believes that technology brings benefits without a cost. Every other widespread invention has had a price to pay. Superhighways caused suburban sprawl. The automobile created a massive dependence on foreign oil. Television caused us to become a society of strangers. Well, we only hear the good things that the Internet will deliver. I ask, what are the costs—to the nation, to the individual, to our souls?"

10   And, "What does the Internet most resemble? Television. And so I ask, to what extent does our society really need more TV?"

11   Stoll said his main emphasis these days is education. His next book will be entitled, "Why Computers Don't Belong In Schools." He considers the rush to wire-up classrooms a tragic fad, one that mistakes the skill of snagging facts, information, for true learning and puts a machine in the way between teachers and their pupils:

12   "Lack of information is not a problem in any classroom. Encyclopedias are filled with information. Most teachers I know say, 'I got way too much information to teach. What I need more of is time.' Sticking a kid's face in front of a computer cuts down on the amount of time left for teaching."

13   In short, Stoll's views have not changed much, although he has softened his stance a bit, here and there. He has learned, for example, to stress that he is not a critic of computer technology, but rather of the hyperbole that surrounds it. Pointing to my dog-eared copy of his book, he volunteered that "some of the stuff I wrote in there now seems silly."

14   Like what? I asked.

15   "Oh," he said, "like the criticisms of e-mail. There's nothing wrong with answering your e-mail."

16   Sigh. I suppose I can get trained this week.

## ▼ Questions for Critical Thought

*"Resistance to Internet . . ."*

1. Explain King's attitude and experiences with the Internet at the beginning of the article.

2. What does King mean in paragraph 2 when he says that he had hoped the Internet would take the same path as the eight-track tape? (What is the eight-track tape?)

3. In paragraph 5, Eric Stoll is described as a "skeptic." What is a skeptic?

4. What is the most common myth about the Internet, according to astronomer Eric Stoll?

5. Look up the word "hyperbole." Then give examples of the "hyperbole" surrounding the Internet.

6. The Internet is most like what other information technology? According to Stoll, what effect did that technology have on society?

Notes

What other types of technology does Stoll mention and what were the negative sides to these pieces of technology?

7. According to Stoll, why don't computers belong in the classroom? Do you agree or disagree?

8. Is the writer's purpose to discourage readers from using the Internet? If so, why? If not, what is the writer's purpose?

> ### Journal Assignment
> **Technology in Modern Life**
>
> Reflect on the essays "Stop the Clock" and "Resistance to Internet Grows Weak," and your class discussions so far. Then consider this quotation: "By his very success in inventing labor-saving devices, modern man has manufactured an abyss of boredom that only the privileged class in earlier civilizations have ever fathomed" (Lewis Mumford, *The Conduct of Life*, 1951). What ideas in the readings, class discussions, and this quotation do you most strongly support? What ideas do you want to argue with? Share this journal with a classmate. When you read your classmate's journal, just say "Thank you" in response.

## Explore the Writing Assignment

Here, again, is your writing assignment. Review it carefully before continuing. Underline the important terms in the assignment.

> *Write an essay in which you discuss some of the advantages and disadvantages of technology in your life.*

***Brainstorm*** Write freely in response to the writing assignment. Explore the many different advantages and disadvantages of technology that you read about and discussed in class. Let your mind wander, and let yourself repeat ideas that keep coming to your mind.

When you have completed a lengthy, thoughtful brainstorm, go back and highlight any promising ideas for your essay. Pay attention to ideas that you repeatedly came back to.

***Consider Your Audience*** Your audience will be familiar with most technological advances, but if you are interested in discussing lesser-known technological devices, think about what kind of background information you should give your audience. Also, do you expect your audience to agree with everything you say? Do you expect some disagreement? What will your audience expect from an interesting, thoughtful essay? Make a list of things to keep in mind when writing for your audience.

*Create Your Thesis*   Review the writing assignment. Note that the assignment uses the word "some." This means that you are not expected to write about every technological advance you can think of. Choose advantages and disadvantages that most interest you and that connect logically to one another. For example, you may want to focus on technological advances in the area of entertainment, or in the areas of housekeeping or work. Your thesis should show that you have carefully narrowed the scope of your essay. Also note that the writing assignment asks for both advantages *and* disadvantages. You should cover both in your thesis and essay. Experiment with thesis statements until you find one that expresses what you want to focus on in your essay.

*Outline*   Keeping your thesis in mind, carefully review your notes and readings. Write down on index cards the technological advantages and disadvantages you think you should cover in your essay. You may want to review the section on notecards at the beginning of the chapter. When you have all your cards filled out, decide how you might want to organize your essay. Review the five patterns from the beginning of the chapter.

As you review your cards and think about how you might organize your ideas, you'll probably find cards that you don't know what to do with or cards that you simply aren't interested in. Get rid of these cards—or at least set them aside. You should only work with the cards that are most interesting to you and that fit your general message. (You are working on your focus skills when you do this.)

Experiment with different ways to organize your cards. Note: Plan on discussing only one technological advantage or disadvantage per paragraph. Of course, it is possible that you'll have more than one index card per advantage or disadvantage. For example, you might have two or three index cards dealing with the advantages of e-mail. In that case, you'd want to group these cards together as one paragraph and experiment with how the ideas in that paragraph should be organized. You'd also want to experiment with where you'll place that paragraph in your essay.

*Notes*

When you think you have a pretty good idea of which index cards you'll use and the order you'll put them in, get together with a small group of classmates and show them what you've decided. Explain your choices. You may find that you need to make some changes, and you may get some new ideas from listening to how your classmates are organizing their cards.

## Draft

Using your notecards as a guideline, draft your essay. In your introduction, prepare your audience to read about technology and the advantages and disadvantages you have been thinking about. In the body of your essay, discuss one advantage or disadvantage in each paragraph. In your conclusion, discuss what you and your reader should have learned from your essay.

## Revise

 **Activity**

### Share Your Writing

Find a classmate to work with. Read each other's essays. Then discuss the following questions as they apply to each essay.

- Have you chosen a reasonable number of points to cover?
- Do you cover just one advantage or disadvantage per paragraph?
- Do you offer interesting support and explanations in each paragraph?
- Is the organization of your points logical?
- Do you use transitions to help your reader? Do you need more? Fewer?

## Edit

You may want to review earlier, graded essays to see what, if any, sentence errors you tend to repeat. Then carefully review your technology essay and look for any of these errors.

Read your essay aloud, listening for awkward spots and looking for typographical errors. You may want to have a friend read your essay aloud to you. Sometimes it's easier to find mistakes this way.

Additional ideas for editing:

- Carefully review your essay for spelling errors.
- Note that *Internet* is always capitalized. (*World Wide Web* is capitalized also.)
- Check your essay for fragments, comma splices, and run-ons. Some students find it helpful to cover the essay with a sheet of paper and look at only one sentence at a time. This helps you concentrate on finding any errors—one sentence at a time. Another approach is to ask a tutor to check your essay for fragments, comma splices, and run-ons. Have the tutor tell you how many (if any) of each kind of error you have. Then find the errors yourself and correct them. Finally, review your work with the tutor.

## Writing Assignment #2: Arguing about Internet Access in High School

Here, in brief, is the writing assignment you are preparing for.

> Write an essay in which you argue *for* or *against* Internet access in your local high school.

## Read, Discuss, Think Critically

This section of the chapter offers you four readings about the advantages and disadvantages of letting high school students have access to the Internet at school. All four of the readings, found on the Internet, come from the *New York Times*, a respected newspaper, and are written in journalistic style.

## Reading Assignment

### "Internet Access Puts Burden of Control on Schools"

*Preview*   Read the title, the first three paragraphs and the topic sentences for all other paragraphs.

*Anticipate*   What do you think the article will be about? Use the "Notes" column to record your response.

*Read and Reread*   Read the entire essay quickly, marking unknown terms. Then reread more slowly and use the "Notes" column to interact with the essay. Mark important points and define unknown terms.

Notes

# Internet Access Puts Burden of Control on Schools
*by Abby Goodnough*

This article first appeared in the *New York Times*, April 19, 1997.

1. More than half the nation's public schools have access to the Internet and hundreds more could join them in the coming weeks, as volunteers lay the wiring through a month long project known as Net Day.

2. But experts say the schools should temper their headlong rush to the Internet with this question: How can they keep students—who are often more technologically savvy than their teachers—from abusing their computer privileges?

3. The question is not theoretical. Educators whose schools are already hooked up say the possibility of students glimpsing scabrous material on the World Wide Web is by no means the only concern. They note other problems they have seen, from chain letters that jam school networks to the pilfering of one student's computer files by another.

4. In Stamford, Conn., a high school student sent a prank death threat to President Clinton from a school computer last October, prompting a Secret Service investigation.

5. In Ames, Iowa, a federal laboratory that had allowed a local high school to use its computer network revoked the privileges last March because so many students were attempting to steal one another's passwords and get into confidential files. And in Athol, Mass., a high school student was suspended in February for creating a Web site that listed his school's "most hated" teachers.

6. In response, some school districts, like the one in Hazlet, N.J., have bought filtering software, which blocks access to Internet chat rooms and Web sites they consider offensive. Other schools, like Hunterdon Central High School in Flemington, N.J., use monitoring devices to track students' every move on the Internet—raising questions from civil libertarians about the students' right to privacy.

7. Thomas O'Neill, the coordinator of Net Day in New Jersey, said that while the project has wired several hundred schools so far, including several dozen in Trenton and other cities this month, volunteers have not kept track of each school's approach to the Internet.

8. "It's like a dad teaching his kid to ride a bike," said O'Neill, who added that more than 100 additional schools in New Jersey would be wired this month. "You get them up and running, but you can't tell what they're doing once they go around the block."

9. Education officials say that almost every school district with Internet access is hurriedly drafting a policy that spells out what is forbidden.

10   "You need a policy in place before you set the first kid loose," said Dr. Roland Pare, director of information systems for Hunterdon Central, which was among the first public schools in the country to connect to the Internet. "You can't stop them altogether from making trouble, but you need to let them know what is expected of them."

11   In a three-page contract that all students and parents are asked to sign, Hunterdon Central prohibits students from using vulgarities, destroying files and revealing their home addresses on the Internet. It also warns that administrators may read students' electronic mail and computer files.

12   Elsewhere, Internet policies are even more restrictive. In Neptune, N.J., students may not send chain letters or use the Internet for political lobbying. And in North Providence, R.I., students must promise not to meet with anyone they talk to on line or visit Web sites that contain "racial, ethnic or minority disparagement" or "advocation of violence."

13   But experts say that many school officials, still naive about the Internet, have not thought seriously about appropriate-use policies, as they are commonly known. And they complain that wiring projects like Net Day—which is planning to send volunteers into thousands of additional schools to lay cable on Saturday—give schools the technology without teaching them how to use it.

14   "It does provide some initial wiring solutions," said Lynn Reuss, who oversees technology programs for the New York state Department of Education. "But what's missing is sound instructional training to tell them why, where, and what for."

15   Although most school officials say that Internet policies are crucial, they have mixed feelings about filtering software that limits student access.

16   Many, like Superintendent Timothy Nogueira of the Hazlet, N.J., school system, say they could not function without it. "It saves us a great deal of trouble," said Nogueira, whose district pays an Internet service provider to block out chat rooms and thousands of Web sites. But others say that no amount of monitoring can block out every objectionable site, and that besides, students should know such sites exist.

17   "We don't want to shield kids from everything in the world," said Kieran O'Connor, the systems consultant for the Cortland, N.Y., school district. "The idea is to teach them what is appropriate rather than try to filter everything out."

18   Some educators say that filtering software is problematic because it often blocks potentially informative sites. Censoring sites that contain

*Notes*

Notes

the word "breast," for example, would block information about breast cancer, they say.

19   "You do a block like that and there go half the sites related to science," said Pare of Hunterdon Central, which does not use filtering software. "If a student wants to go to a white power site because they're studying the Ku Klux Klan in social studies, maybe that is appropriate. They need to know these attitudes exist."

20   Pare said that students at Hunterdon Central tapped into obscene Web sites almost daily, but he and others said that serious mischief-making—hacking into school administrative files, for example, or downloading illegal files onto school computers—was far more common at the college level.

21   "Breaking into computer files and e-mailing child molesters, these are things that tend to happen from homes," said Dr. Edward Friedman, a professor at Stevens Institute of Technology in Hoboken, N.J. "Schools are a much more supervised environment."

22   Still, some schools are erring on the side of caution. Pare said Hunterdon Central keeps track of every Web site students access throughout the school network. Since students can log onto the school network from home computers, a systems engineer sometimes checks in at night to see which students are using the system.

23   "We have ways kids haven't even dreamt of to track where they have gone on the Net," Pare said.

24   Some of the most highly publicized cases of alleged misuse have involved students who have used home computers to create Web sites that lampoon their schools. But the American Civil Liberties Union has defended students in such incidents, and in most cases, schools have apologized for punishing them.

25   Ann Beeson, an ACLU lawyer specializing in the Internet, said that parents are starting to protest school Internet policies that prohibit students from visiting "objectionable" sites without being more specific. Policies that ban political discussions on the Internet are also under scrutiny, she said.

26   As more students get school-sponsored e-mail accounts, civil libertarians are also questioning whether school officials have the right to monitor their correspondence, Ms. Beeson said. But so far, schools are focusing on simpler questions, like whether to allow students to write e-mail during school hours.

27   "There are real concerns about order and discipline, but a kid sending his father e-mail during the school day is not a problem in my

mind," said Cheryl Williams, the director of technology programs for the National School Boards Association. "It's bridging distances and, let's face it, it's helping the kid's writing skills."

### ▼ Questions for Critical Thought

#### "Internet Access Puts . . ."

1. What words in this reading are new to you? Create a list and use context clues to try and figure out the meanings. Then check the definitions in a dictionary. Add these words to your vocabulary notebook.

2. What are some of the negative things the author, Goodnough, mentions in this article that students could do when on the Internet?

3. What are some of the things schools/parents might do to make sure the Internet is used in an appropriate way? Does everyone like these "controls" or "safety measures"?

4. In paragraph 8, Thomas O'Neill makes a comparison between bike riding and using the Internet. Is this a helpful comparison? Do you use comparisons when you are trying to explain something? Do you use comparisons when you write? Make a comparison between your first time on the Internet and something else.

5. In paragraph 10 Goodnough gives source information. What do we learn here? Why is this source information useful?

### Reading Assignment

#### "On Web, New Threats to Young Are Seen"

*Preview*   Read the title and paragraphs 1–5. Then read the topic sentences for the rest of the paragraphs.

*Anticipate*   What do you anticipate this article will be about? Use the "Notes" column to record your thoughts.

*Read and Reread*   Read the entire article, marking unknown terms. Then reread more slowly and use the "Notes" column to interact with the essay. Mark important and interesting points and define unknown terms.

Notes

**On Web, New Threats to Young Are Seen**
*by Seth Schiesel*

This article first appeared in the *New York Times*, March 7, 1997.

1   If cyberspace has become an after-school playground, parents may be surprised at some of the characters lurking there.

2   Take J.C. Roadhog, the cartoonish rodent star of an online game who races through a desert littered with empty tequila bottles bearing the label of Cuervo Especial, the sponsor of the game on the brand's World Wide Web site.

3   Visitors to an Anheuser-Busch Inc. Web site called "The Pad" meet the three frogs from Budweiser's television commercials, including Budbrew J. Budfrog, whose biography reveals that he was elected president of his college fraternity and that he "likes to hang on the beach with a hot babe, a cold Bud and a folio edition of the Kama Sutra in its original Sanskrit."

4   Absolut vodka's home page on the Web features video clips of the Absolut bottle in witty disguises. The print versions of Absolut ads have recently become collector's items among some children.

5   Since the advent of the Internet, concerns about children in cyberspace have focused on pornography accessible with the push of a button. Now, children's advocates and public health officials are becoming increasingly concerned that liquor and beer companies and, to a lesser extent, tobacco companies are turning their marketing muscle to cyberspace.

6   Not only do some of the sites ask users to provide their identity and other personal information, which can be used in other marketing efforts. But youth under the legal drinking age, critics say, are especially vulnerable to slick Internet pitches that combine games, online chat forums and other sorts of entertainment with messages touting drinking and smoking.

7   "The marketers of alcohol and tobacco see the Internet and the World Wide Web as a powerful way to market their products and reach youth," said Kathryn C. Montgomery, president of the Center for Media Education, a Washington-based nonprofit group that released a report Thursday detailing the online efforts of alcohol and tobacco companies.

8   "A lot of what we see has been happening under the radar of most parents," she said. "They have created Web sites that are really more like playgrounds. They are really very, very appealing to youth."

9   The critics include the National Parent Teachers Association, the American Psychiatric Association, the Center for Science in the Public Interest and the Campaign for Tobacco-Free Kids. These groups argue

that the government should declare that the entertaining Web sites violate the liquor and beer industries' promise not to market to children, and that cigarette Web sites are an unfair way around a quarter-century-old prohibition of tobacco advertising on radio and television.

10   The new report, which was sponsored by the Robert Wood Johnson Foundation and the Carnegie Corporation of New York, appears to be the first comprehensive look at how alcohol and tobacco companies are marketing in cyberspace. The authors say that at least 35 alcohol brands have full-blown Web sites and that most of them include elements meant to appeal to children.

11   Some executives of alcohol companies say the criticisms are unfounded.

12   "We don't think there is anything on the site that has inherent appeal to youth," said John A. Shea, a spokesman for Heublein Inc., the unit of Grand Metropolitan PLC that imports and bottles the Jose Cuervo family of tequilas. "We strive to insure that our Internet sites are responsible and do not in any way target underage drinking."

13   Anheuser-Busch's vice president for consumer awareness, Francine I. Katz, said: "The pages attract exactly the visitor we want: male beer drinkers age 21 to 34. There's nothing on this site that a family will not see on an Anheuser-Busch brewery tour."

14   Bevin Gove, a spokeswoman for the unit of Seagram Co. Ltd. that imports Absolut, said: "Our sites are in no way intended for those under the legal drinking age. We strongly believe that our Web sites meet with our commitment of using responsible and tasteful messages aimed solely at adult audiences."

15   A representative of the Tobacco Institute, which represents the industry, declined to be interviewed about the new study.

16   Among the examples of tobacco-industry Web sites mentioned in that study is one operated by Brown & Williamson, a unit of BAT Industries, as part of its new Lucky Strike cigarette campaign. Though the Web site, called Circuit Breaker, does not mention Lucky Strike, it does offer entertainment information for people in the San Francisco area and free Lucky Strike and Circuit Breaker T-shirts to visitors who identify themselves as smokers.

17   In its report, the Center for Media Education urged liquor and beer companies to make their Internet sites less appealing to children. But it hopes to ban tobacco marketing from the Internet altogether. The center asserted in its report that the Public Health Cigarette Smoking Act of 1969, which keeps cigarette advertisements off radio and television, would allow the Federal Communications Commission to ban cigarette marketing from the Internet.

*Notes*

*Notes*

18   But top officials of the American Civil Liberties Union, which is fighting the government's proposed regulation of indecency on the Internet, disagreed strongly.

19   "The Internet is not a broadcast medium," said Barry S. Steinhardt, the union's associate director. "It is not subject to FCC regulation any more so than newspapers. For the FCC to get involved in regulating the content of the Internet would kill the Internet."

### ▼ Questions for Critical Thought

*"On Web, New Threats . . ."*

1. Review the first five paragraphs of the reading. What is the purpose of each paragraph? (What does the author, Schiesel, want you to learn from each paragraph?)

2. What do the alcohol and tobacco companies say in response to the criticism of their Web sites?

3. How does Schiesel organize his ideas? Make a quick outline of the article—noting what each of the nineteen paragraphs is about. Consider using a similar pattern in one of your future essays.

### Reading Assignment

*"School District Organizes Itself around Internet"*

***Preview***   Read the title and the first two paragraphs. Read the topic sentences for all the other paragraphs.

***Anticipate***   What do you anticipate this article will be about? Use the "Notes" column to record your thoughts.

***Read and Reread***   Quickly read the entire article, marking unknown terms. Then reread more slowly and use the "Notes" column to interact with the essay. Mark important points and define unknown terms.

### School District Organizes Itself around Internet
*by Tina Kelley*

This article first appeared in the *New York Times*, April 23, 1997.

1   KENT, Wash.—Teachers in the Kent School District, just south of Seattle, used to post excellent student work on hallway bulletin boards.

Now they post the work on the district's Web page for all the world—and especially parents and grandparents—to see.

2   Kent is among the school districts leading the way to a new realm of computer use in the classroom in which not only details of a student's schoolwork are put online, but also many details about the school system itself.

3   The district has 25,000 students, 38 schools and a full-time Web master. Its computer system keeps track of the district's $160 million annual revenues, right down to every 50-cent towel fee for high school students.

4   Its Web page, now three years old, won top honors from the National School Public Relations Association last year, and includes a teacher's toolbox of lesson plans, reference materials, annual performance reports for each school and links to the state education laws. Lightspan, a large educational software company, and other companies have bought the district's "Go Dog Go" software, which automatically sends parents or staff members e-mail on topics they choose—lunch menus, teacher training sessions, band concerts and whenever a particular child is absent.

5   Student artwork can be viewed online, accompanied by descriptions like this one by a 10-year-old from Springbrook Elementary School here: "I modeled the picture after the style of Georgia O'Keefe. Georgia lived in Arizona and collected bones and flowers to paint."

6   Those connected to the district's online efforts say there are tangible benefits to putting children on such a visible stage.

7   When it comes to writing, "they know they're going to be on the Web, that makes them spell better," said Kent Keel, the director of information technology for the district.

8   When it comes to encouragement, "I think there's a direct correlation with the number of refrigerator magnets they go home to, and the work they do," said Rick Feutz, manager of training for the district's computer program. "This is just a huge refrigerator magnet, posting their work around the world."

9   Such access does raise concerns. Wary of cases of criminals finding young victims through the Internet, the district identifies a student only by classroom and first name. The district may start posting attendance records, but would require a parent to have a password to have access to them. Other records, like test scores, are broken down by school, not individually.

10   One teacher, Darlene Bishop, has put her ninth grade social studies curriculum on ancient Egypt on the district's page and even used slides from a recent trip. Ms. Bishop said teachers from Canada and the East Coast had written to her about the information, which can be downloaded, printed out or projected on large screens in other classrooms.

*Notes*

Notes

11     "It starts taking the place of books," Keel said, noting that many of the district's textbooks are outdated, still covering the former Yugoslavia, for instance.

12     The Web site, its programming, hardware and related teacher training cost the district $4 million over three years.

13     "It was costing us big bucks not to do it," Keel said, recalling the time and trouble it took to produce class schedules and report cards without computers.

14     But how many people are able to tap into all this information? Keel estimates 15 percent to 20 percent of the homes in the district have personal computers.

15     About 2,000 school districts have Web pages, though few have used the Internet to the extent that Kent has. In Orange County, Calif., the schools have elaborate plans to broaden their computer use. By the fall, the county department of education hopes to have a $2.5 million to $3 million program in place for its 450,000 students.

16     Bill Habermehl, the associate superintendent of the Orange County schools, said about 40 percent of the county's homes had personal computers, and Habermehl said he expected that figure to double when Internet access became available through cable television, for about $300 plus a monthly charge. But only 20 percent to 25 percent of poorer families in the district have cable television, and still fewer have personal computers.

17     "Shouldn't they be the ones who you most want to be involved?" Habermehl asked.

18     One solution, he said, would be to insure that computers and access to school Web sites were available at parents' workplaces or even, eventually, in grocery stores.

19     But exposure to computers has to happen in school, said Gwen Davis, educational technology coordinator with the Orange County unified school district, "because some kids will never get it at home."

20     Ms. Davis envisioned high school students taking their laptops to the library, sending e-mail to teachers and meeting once a week for dinner and Socratic teachings. The school building, she said, could become obsolete.

21     The Orange County system intends to use the same encoding procedures that keep credit cards safe, and will limit parents to viewing their own child's work and progress reports. Testing of the software should begin by the end of this year, Habermehl said.

22     "The value to the parents will be just overwhelming, compared to the cost," he said. "Having 24-hour-a-day, 7-days-a-week access to your son or daughter's files, you can be more actively involved in their education from Day 1. Now as a parent you often don't find out if they're not doing well until nine weeks into the semester."

23  Some teachers give mixed reviews to the new technology, because increased parental involvement usually results in higher student performance, but more work for teachers.
24  "It's a dilemma, but a manageable dilemma," Habermehl said.
25  Keel acknowledged that the Internet alone would not solve all of the problems that schools face.
26  "The magic is still between students and teachers talking together to learn something," he said. "This is just another tool."

## ▼ Questions for Critical Thought

### "School District Organizes..."

According to this article, what are all the advantages and disadvantages to having Internet access at school? List the advantages and disadvantages for parents, teachers, students on index cards (one advantage/disadvantage per card). When necessary, explain why something is an advantage or disadvantage. You may also want to jot down your own examples or details on these cards. (Write down the paragraph number of where you found each item.)

*Hint:* Use your own words as much as possible.

sample card (front)

---

*Advantage (for parents)*

Parents can see their child's work posted on the Web page. This is a neat way for busy parents to know what students are doing.

---

sample card (back)

---

"School District Organizes...," paragraph 1

---

Notes

## Reading Assignment

"Class Acts: How Three Schools Use New Technology to Empower Students"

*Preview*  Read the title and the first paragraph. Read the bold subtitles and then the topic sentences for the rest of the paragraphs.

*Anticipate*  What do you anticipate this article will be about? Record your thoughts in the "Notes" column.

*Read and Reread*  Quickly read the entire article, marking unknown terms. Then reread more slowly and use the "Notes" column to interact with the essay. Mark important points and define unknown terms.

### Class Acts: How Three Schools Use New Technology to Empower Students
*by Marie Faust Evitt and Joanne Cleaver*

Joanne Cleaver is a freelance writer who specializes in technology and small home-based business. This article appeared on the World Wide Web, http://www.connect-time.com, August 1997.

[Note: Information on one of the schools has been deleted because it did not directly relate to the Internet.]

1   Across America computers are changing the way students learn.... Students are improving their research skills, learning firsthand from experts, sharing experiences with others around the world and gaining access to information as never before. The stories here typify what's happening in a growing number of classrooms everyday: In California, computers are bringing together scientists and students for research projects; in rural Kentucky, they're eliminating the isolation faced by students....

**Forging global connections**

2   It's 11:15 a.m. and three sophomores from Peggy Foletta's biology class in Kingsburg, California, are outside at their homemade weather station. On this hot, cloudless day, there's no water in the rain gauge. But the students diligently record on a clipboard the clear sky, zero precipitation, the high and low temperature for the last 24 hours, as well as the current temperature (30° C, 86° F) and soil moisture levels. Later, their classmates will enter the data on a Web site as part of Global Learning and Observations to Benefit the Environment (GLOBE), a government-sponsored program that teams students with scientists online to research the world climate.

3   Kingsburg High School is among 3,500 schools in more than 50 countries that participate in GLOBE. The program lets Kingsburg students collect weather data, compare weather notes by e-mail with other schools from Finland to Australia and pose questions about soil and water quality in online chats with program scientists.

4   One of the first schools to join GLOBE in 1995, Kingsburg High has contributed some 5,000 measurements in the past two years, more data than any other school. In addition to recording daily weather readings (even during weekends, holidays, and summer vacation), students twice a month monitor the temperature, water chemistry and surrounding habitat of the Kings River, about two miles from the school. All these measurements are available for program scientists and students around the world to study, demonstrating in a practical way the power of the Internet.

5   Scientists expect to use the student measurements to look for shifts in temperature and rainfall patterns. "Students are providing scientists with data which is sometimes hard to get," says Elissa Levine, a soil scientist at the Goddard Space Flight Center in Maryland. "The range of questions the students ask is enormous. I'm really impressed."

6   Only about five percent of the 950 students at Kingsburg High are online at home, estimates Foletta, the lead teacher on the project. Her classes participate in this program with just two Power Macintoshes and a laptop that can be hooked up to a television monitor.

7   GLOBE has turned Jason Terry, 17, into an Internet expert. "At first I had no idea what I was doing, but I learned to input data last year, and soon I was learning how to surf the Net and find things for school projects," he says. "Now I'm designing Web pages and teaching teachers how to use the Internet."

8   Because the students know their measurements are used by scientists, they take the work seriously, Foletta notes. "They are learning that you have to collect data correctly or it's not scientifically OK. Some kids who don't normally work very hard are really putting in effort."

9   The students' Internet use through GLOBE has also spilled over into other subjects at Kingsburg High. "Now that they are familiar with Internet capabilities, they are eager to use it," Foletta says. Kids come in during lunch or after school to search for information on Native American tribes for English papers. English teachers are also instructing students in recording scientific observations, and the art teacher is giving lessons on nature sketching. Chemistry and physics classes have also gotten into the act, taking measurements and analyzing data.

10   "I'm much more aware of the environment now," says sophomore Crystal Mero. "I never thought about soil moisture or cloud cover be-

fore. I really love the hands-on science. Plus I've learned how to get online."

—Marie Faust Evitt

## Leveling the playing field

11  Eastern Kentucky is rippled with ridges and valleys—the famed "hills and hollers" of Appalachia. Two-story rhododendrons are a flowering tower along roadsides in spring, and in autumn, the sharp slopes are misted with yellow and orange. In many ways, it's a world unto its own.

12  That was just the problem, at least for the students at Deming School. It has 350 students, from kindergarten through 12th grade, in Robertson County, where most area residents farm tobacco for a living. Lexington, just forty miles away, is another world, never mind someplace like France.

13  But then, thanks to an Internet connection, the world—and France—got closer. So close, in fact, that freshman Amanda Ison and two classmates found themselves talking face-to-face with a patron at a Paris café while learning to operate the school's new CU-See Me video conferencing technology. "I've never talked to anybody in any other language," Ison recalls. "I didn't know I knew French that well to actually talk to anybody."

14  In 1995, the Kentucky Board of Education decreed that all of the state's schools would be fully wired for Internet connections by 1998. Ever since, Deming has been leading the state in integration of the Web into everyday curriculum topics.

15  Every classroom has a Net-connected computer so teachers can quickly click to a screen and have the kids gather 'round. In consumer science class, students produce brochures from material they've gleaned from the Web: nutritional information from food manufacturers, trade groups and government sources; clip art from graphics sites; and ideas for desktop publishing from online publications.

16  Freshman Sara Lynn Sellers says that she wouldn't have been able to even track down, let alone interpret and use, statistics on interracial marriages for a report on segregation last year had she not mastered the basics of Internet searching. Along the way, she also found "a lot of first-person comments" on sites and message boards that she says deepened her understanding of the emotional impact of racism.

17  The school's rapid adoption of the Internet into as many classroom activities as possible has leveled the playing field between Deming and more resource-rich schools, says Patti Price, the school's curriculum coordinator. For the first time, her students not only have access to extensive research materials, but also ask questions directly of scientists, artists and writers.

Notes

18. Students near universities and major museums take field trips and classroom visits by experts for granted. At Deming, virtual interaction is the only first-person contact that many students probably will have.

18. This year, Deming students will observe, via the Internet, several on-going scientific projects. (Last year, they followed oceanographic research conducted at a national institute.)

19. Price also wants to greatly expand the school's Web site. For example, the junior high students will electronically inventory, sort, research and display the exhibits and artifacts owned by a local historic museum.

20. Use of the Web in the classroom is gradually shifting the teacher-student dynamic, Price says. "The teachers are now taking more of a facilitator role than just spilling out information to students," she says. "They're pointing students in the right direction and letting them look for themselves."

21. The students' growing sense of ownership of the process—from asking a question to finding the answer—is visibly instilling confidence in their ability to tackle real-life problems as well. When a group of students ran into a problem setting up new video equipment, Price suggested they check the Web. Within minutes, they had accessed the manufacturer's site, received help and been able to e-mail the company for more information. More important, they were reminded that the Web is more than just a glorified library; it's a place where students can empower themselves—no matter where they live.

—Joanne Cleaver

## ▼ Questions for Critical Thought

### "Class Acts..."

1. According to this article, what are the advantages to having students use the Internet? Writing one advantage per index card, make as many *Advantage* cards as you can.

2. Which of these advantages are most important? (You and your classmates may disagree here, but it is important to hear what your classmates think.)

3. Which of the advantages that you have considered so far seem unimportant or minor? (You might leave these out of your essay.)

4. Study one of the following paragraphs: 9, 17, or 21. Explain how these paragraphs follow good academic style. (You may want to review paragraph structure in Chapter 5.)

*Notes*

5. Reread paragraphs 11, 12, and 13. How do the words "That" at the beginning of paragraph 12 and "But then" at the beginning of paragraph 13 act as glue and connect these paragraphs, improving the coherence of the article? What could you replace "That" with to make the transition even clearer?

> ### Journal Assignment
> **The Internet in Schools**
>
> Think about the articles you have read so far in this chapter and the class discussions you have had. Write down your thoughts about students and the Internet. What particular advantages do you see to students using the Internet? What concerns do you have about students using the Internet? Exchange your journal with a classmate and simply say, "Thank you."

## Explore the Writing Assignment

Here, again, is your writing assignment. Review it carefully before continuing. Underline the important terms in the assignment.

> *Write an essay in which you argue **for** or **against** Internet access in your local high school.*

## ▼ Activities

### Visit Some Web Sites

Because it is helpful to have firsthand experience about your writing topic, you'll now gain a little more experience with the Internet. Choose one topic from the following list and use the Internet to visit one of the Web sites.*

(Be sure to follow the instructions below very carefully.) If you do not have a computer at home and Internet access, consider using a computer at your college library, your public library, or a learning center on your campus. There may also be other public places in your town that offer free Internet access. See your instructor for more information.

1. Choose *one* topic from this list and then *one* Web site

---

*You may find that the Web sites created by alcohol manufacturers require you to be 21 years old to visit the site. If you visit a Web site and don't find any written directions on the screen, try clicking on a picture.

*Topic:* Alcohol, Tobacco and Youth  *Notes*

| | |
|---|---|
| Jose Cuervo Home Page: | //www.cuervo.com/main.shtml |
| Budweiser Online: | //www.budweiser.com/ |
| Absolut Vodka: | //www.absolutvodka.com/ |
| R. J. Reynolds: | //www.rjrt.com/ |

*Topic:* Educational Sites and Schools Using the Internet

| | |
|---|---|
| Kent School District: | //www.kent.wednet.edu |
| Springbrook Elementary School: | //www.kent.wednet.edu/cgi-bin/info.cgi?SB |
| Globe: | //www.globe.gov/ |
| Deming School District: | //www.robertson.k12.ky.us |

2. Visit your chosen Web site.

3. Make notes during your research. Make notes about where you went to log on to the Internet, your experience getting to the Web site, and what you saw at the Web site.

4. Prepare a short oral report in which you will tell your classmates about your Internet experience. Tell them about your difficulties and successes in getting to the Web site. If you visited one of the alcohol or tobacco Web sites, do you think they might be harmful to high school students? If you visited one of the Web sites about schools using the Internet, what did you see/learn?

### Debate the Issues

As a way of exploring both sides of this issue, you will debate the pros and cons of letting high school students have Internet access. You probably have not chosen a side to argue in your essay yet, for you are still in the planning stage and should keep an open mind. However, for the sake of this exploratory activity, your instructor will assign you to a "pro" or "con" team and ask you for the time being to argue for one side or the other. (You will learn not only about your side but the other side as well, as you anticipate and then actually hear the other side's arguments.)

1. Work with your team members to create a list of points that support your position. You will want to review the readings carefully and discuss personal experiences. Find details, quotes, and specific examples to support your ideas (note your source information). Since you are preparing for a debate, you'll want to find out from your instructor if

*Notes*

you will have a time limit or if you should count on making a certain number of arguments. This information will help you decide how many points to discuss in detail with your team members and in what order you should plan on presenting your points.

2. Discuss with your team members the points you think your opponents might bring up. Which of these points is valid? Do you have any counter-arguments? It's OK to admit that the other side has some good points that you can't argue against. The key is to make counter-arguments when possible and to show that your position has better, more persuasive points.

3. Formulate a closing argument if this will be part of your debate format.

4. Debate the advantages and disadvantages of having Internet access in the high schools. Each side should make an argument and then let the other side respond. Continue taking turns stating arguments and responding in the time allowed by your instructor.

5. Keep notes about the best points made during the debate. These notes will help you write your essay.

***Brainstorm*** Write freely about Internet access in the high schools. Don't worry about choosing a side right now. Use this as an opportunity to explore both sides. Review readings, class notes, and debate notes when you run out of things to write about. Also, you may want to imagine yourself as a high school student working alone at home on the Internet. What is that experience like? What might it be like to be a student in a computer-assisted class at school? What is it like to be in a high school class that focuses on reading, small group discussions, and large class discussions? Keep writing for as long as you can.

When you are done writing, review your brainstorm and decide which side you want to take on this issue. Highlight the parts of your brainstorm you think might be useful when writing your essay.

***Consider Your Audience*** You may choose to write to a very general audience—all people in your community. Or you may want to write to a more select audience—the students at the high school or perhaps the PTA of the high school or the state school board. When you have selected an audience, write down what your audience knows about the issue and what different people in the audience are likely to believe about the issue. When writers write argumentative essays, they don't try to persuade people who are in complete disagreement. Instead, they focus on the people who are undecided or perhaps just leaning in the pro or con direction. These people will be interested in what you have to say and may respond by supporting your position.

*Create Your Thesis* In your own words, what must you do in your essay? Review the writing assignment, if necessary. Experiment with thesis statements until you find one that will explain your position clearly to your reader.

*Outline* Keeping your thesis in mind, carefully review your notes and readings. Although you completed some index cards following two of your readings, you will now need to create a complete set of cards that represents the ideas to cover in your essay. You may want to review the section on notecards on pages 228 and 229. When you have all your cards filled out, begin thinking about how you might want to organize your essay. Review the five patterns from the beginning of the chapter.

As you review your cards and think about how to organize your ideas, you'll probably find cards that you don't know what to do with or cards that you simply aren't interested in. Get rid of these cards—or at least set them aside. You should only work with the cards that are most important to your argument and that fit with your general message. (You are working on your focus skills when you do this.)

Experiment with different ways to organize your cards. (Note: One index card does not necessarily equal one paragraph. A paragraph can be built around one or more index cards.)

Here are some additional pointers about organizing a successful argumentative essay.

To show your audience that you are well-educated and fair, you should mention that you are aware of what your opponents believe. You may even admit that your opponents have some legitimate points. However, you will want to point out that your points are more important, more persuasive, and probably more in number. How do you address *the opposition* without weakening your own argument?

Here are a few methods:

- Mention fewer of your opponents' ideas compared to the number of your ideas.
- Mention your opponents' ideas early and then focus the rest of your essay on your ideas.

Notes

- Mention your opponents' ideas and then carefully and fairly explain why these ideas are not strong and/or why your ideas are better.

(The section in this chapter on *concessions* will help you form sentences that you can use when arguing and addressing the opposition.)

When you have a pretty good idea of which index cards you'll use and the order you'll put them in, get together with a small group of classmates and show them what you've decided. Explain your choices. You may find that you need to make some changes, and you may get some new ideas from listening to how your classmates are organizing their cards.

## Draft

Using your cards as a guide, begin drafting your essay. Your introduction should explain what your topic is and why it's important. (Remember that your audience includes people who want the Internet in the high schools and people who do not. If you're writing to a specific group of people (like high school students) make it clear in your introduction that this is who you are writing to. In your body paragraphs, discuss the points you have selected. Concentrate on being persuasive. In your conclusion, tell your reader what you intended to accomplish by writing this essay.

## Revise

### ▼ Activities

**Study a Student Sample**

Here is an introductory paragraph from a student's essay on Internet access in high schools. Read it carefully and mark the parts you like best.

> The technological changes that this century has seen are fantastic. In today's world, it is no longer good enough to know how to use a typewriter or to go to the library and spend hours doing research. In this fast paced world it is very necessary to keep up with all the technological changes if one plans to be successful. The Internet is the perfect tool to success. There is no better place to teach students the Internet than in high school.
>
> —*Aura Northy*

- Aura decided to begin her introduction on a general note with a comment about "technological changes." In her introduction, she gradually becomes more specific until she comes right down to her well-focused thesis. Highlight words in her second sentence that represent "old" approaches to studying.

- Notice in her third sentence she again mentions "technological changes." In her fourth sentence, she actually names the technological change she wants to focus on. Highlight the technological advancement she mentions.

- Her last sentence, her thesis, is even more specific. What words show she has further narrowed the main point of her essay? What will she be arguing in her essay?

### Study a Student Sample

Here is the introductory paragraph from another student's essay. Read it carefully and mark the parts you like best.

> How will I know that my son or daughter is using the Internet for educational purposes and not for something that he or she should not be accessing? What about the protection of my child from dangerous people, and the confidentiality of personal information? Most importantly, isn't the Internet going to cost us parents a lot of money? These are just a few of the most frequently asked questions that parents may have about bringing the Internet into classrooms. As a parent, I believe that our children should be granted access to the Internet. Children are the key to our future, and we must let them expand their horizons through the use of the Internet.
>
> —*Paul Gregorio*

1. As you can see, Paul chose to start his essay with a series of questions. Which organizational pattern did Paul use to organize these questions?

2. What audience is Paul writing to? How can you tell?

3. Is Paul's position clear? Which sentence most clearly expresses his main point?

Notes

**Share Your Writing**

Find a classmate to work with. Read each other's essays, and discuss the following questions as they relate to both essays.

- Is your position clear?
- Are you being fair in your essay?
- Have you mentioned the opposition?
- Are you being persuasive? Is there enough information/detail so that your reader will believe what you believe? Have you used quotes from the readings in the textbook that help support your ideas?
- Have you mentioned where you got your information? (Cite your sources.)
- Can your classmate understand and describe your organizational pattern? Can you make any improvements? Have you used transitions and concessions?
- What has your instructor been telling you to work on? Do you have any questions about this essay and the skills your instructor wants you to work on?
- What questions do you have about your essay? What are your greatest concerns?

## Edit

Pay special attention to errors that you tend to repeat and focus on one at a time. Also, does your instructor have a certain area he or she wants you to focus on?

Additional ideas for editing:

- Note that *Internet* is always capitalized. (*World Wide Web* is capitalized also.)
- Note that *high school* is two words.
- Check your essay for fragments, comma splices, and run-ons. Some students find it helpful to cover the essay with a sheet of paper and look at only one sentence at a time. This helps you concentrate on finding any errors—one sentence at a time. Another approach is to ask a tutor to check your essay for fragments, comma splices, and run-ons. Have the tutor tell you how many (if any) of each kind of

error you have. Then find the errors yourself and correct them. Finally, review your work with the tutor.

## Writing Assignment #3: Internet Research vs. Traditional Research

Here, in brief, is the writing assignment you are preparing for.

*Write an essay in which you offer advice to other students on how to research interesting occupations. Compare the advantages of using the Internet to the advantages of using the traditional methods of observation and interviews.*

## Read, Discuss, Think Critically

This section of the chapter offers you a personal essay from a newspaper and a quotation from an experienced writer. Each reading discusses the type of information writers need to write stories and articles.

## Reading Assignment

"Reality Writes—Web Is but a Tool"

*Preview*   Read the first four paragraphs of the article and the topic sentences of all the other paragraphs.

*Anticipate*   What do you anticipate this article will be about? Record your thoughts in the "Notes" column.

*Read and Reread*   Quickly read the entire article, marking unknown terms. Then reread more slowly and use the "Notes" column to interact with the essay. Mark important points and define unknown terms.

### Reality Writes—Web Is but a Tool
*Susan Swartz*

Susan Swartz is a columnist for the *Press Democrat* in Santa Rosa, California. This essay appeared in the *Sacramento Bee* newspaper, January 8, 1998.

1   The finest place to gather words is in the home of the story teller. In a room with pictures on the wall and food smells.

Notes

2     This is not to take away from the Internet, which provides virtual visits that can deliver everything from instant family news to RSVPs and keep the dialogue going with new and old correspondents.

3     And certainly when it comes to words, the computer is a wizard. When we are writing a story, we can dip into an encyclopedia and thesaurus and find the ultimate word without waiting, the ideal quote from famous people living or dead. The computer is full of appropriate, vibrant and lyrical choices, containing more words than what's in all our bookshelves put together.

4     But the words that tell a story must first come from the source and that requires being there. These words count most—the ones a person gives directly to a writer, sometimes whispered, sometimes shouted, words carefully sought through squeezed-shut eyes to define a life.

5     They may be as drab as a person's yellow wallpaper or as flip as the pink camellia bush scraping across their window. The writer, recording the words and the moment, makes sure they stay in context with the life.

6     The writer will be there to note that when the businessman talks about his father he rubs his knee hard. The oldest daughter of the flooded family twists her ring. The feminist leader wears fuchsia-colored lipstick.

7     The writer must be actually, not virtually, present in order to wrap smells and noises around the words so that, later, the reader will be able to imagine the subject in a kitchen that smells like sage and intuit something about a man who keeps pictures of his dead sister on the piano.

8     As reporters, we make our livings off other people's words. We start out with nothing to report and find someone to tell us something. We are constantly listening for words to tell a story, solve the crime, remember the victim, describe the rescue. We think if we look in a subject's eyes we'll know if they're telling the truth. They think if they look in our eyes they'll know if they can trust us.

9     Then we hope for a "bingo" quote that will end up in the first paragraph of the story or the clincher line in a column and even screamed in large type in a headline.

10     The computer, it is true, is a wonderful tool, but writers get our best stuff away from our desks. Once we get the information, the computer can make us sound better and smarter than we did before. It can analyze our data, find the numbers we need to prop up a story, search out expert commentary to lend strength to the story. With a few keystrokes it can change our words around and spell them right.

11     But we still need to go out and get the words, which to me is the most seductive and satisfying part about being a writer.

12	In search of someone's story, I have spent time in living rooms and kitchens that I would never have stumbled upon or been invited into without a notebook.

13	I have sat at the bed of a dying woman, perched on a pillow with a pagan priestess, discussed menopause with a prize-winning poet.

14	If you're going to write about people, you have to walk in, in the middle of their lives, sometimes before they have time to clean up the dishes or get the dog off the only good chair.

15	People give us entree to ask our questions and we get to stay for small talk. We scrape our feet on the mud mat outside and enter the farmhouse through the kitchen door and talk about lemonade. Or sometimes we sip tea from china cups and talk about men and roses.

16	Sometimes when I'm being the reporter I ask something unnecessary just to gain time to scribble down not their answer but the extra details—their hair color, the magazine on the coffee table, the political cartoon on the refrigerator.

17	The storyteller's words are unique to them and the moment. If they had a spokesman, most people's words might end up prettier or stronger, but they wouldn't be sincere or intimate.

18	As much as I now rely on the Internet to provide research and the word processor to groom my sentences, I will always prefer word gathering by foot and notebook.

19	The computer delivers the world, but it's not as real as what you find down a street you've never driven talking to people you've never met.

20	I get to say, "Can I ask you a few questions?" and sometimes they say "sure" and sometimes they say "why?" but seldom do they say "no."

21	And the story begins.

## ▼ Questions for Critical Thought

### "Reality Writes..."

1. What is Swartz's main point in this essay? Where does she express this idea most clearly?

2. What does Swartz use the Internet and the word processor for?

3. Swartz enjoys using detail to make her ideas come alive. An example of this is the sentence "The feminist leader wears Fuchsia-colored lipstick" (paragraph 6). What image comes to your mind when you read this sentence? Why does Swartz find this image interesting?

Notes

4. List some other examples of when Swartz uses detail to paint an image in our minds. (Consider doing this in your own essays.)

## Reading Assignment

### Quotation

The following is a quote from a Kenyan author who is discussing his ideas about writing fiction. Read the quotation and answer the questions that follow.

> A writer needs people around him. He needs live struggles of active life. Contrary to popular mythology, a novel is not a product of the imaginative feats of a single individual but the work of many hands and tongues. A writer just takes down notes dictated to him by life among the people . . . I love to hear the voices of the people working on the land, forging metal in a factory, telling anecdotes in crowded matatus and buses, gyrating their hips in a crowded bar before a jukebox or a live band . . . I need the vibrant voices of beautiful women: their touch, their sighs, their tears, their laughter. I like the presence of children prancing about, fighting, laughing, crying. I need life to write about.
>
> Ngugi wa Thiong'o (b. 1936) Kenyan writer, *Detained*

## ▼ Questions for Critical Thought

### Quote by Thiong'o

1. Thiong'o is discussing writing fiction. How are his ideas similar to Swartz's ideas about writing journalistic articles?

2. How do the opinions voiced by Swartz or Thiong'o relate to you and your education? Explain.

---

### Journal Assignment

#### Researching

Reflect on the last two readings and your class discussions. How do you feel about researching using the Internet? Using traditional methods? How much experience have you had with each? Exchange your journal with a classmate and say "Thank you."

---

## Explore the Writing Assignment

Here, again, is your writing assignment. Review it carefully before continuing. Underline the important terms in the assignment.

*Write an essay in which you offer advice to other students on how to research interesting occupations. Compare the advantages of using the Internet to the advantages of using the traditional methods of observation and interviews.*

Notes

## ▼ Activities

### Testing the Research Approaches

This activity will help you further familiarize yourself with the different types of research (Internet vs. observations/interviews). After completing the following steps, you'll be better prepared to offer advice to other students when you write your essay.

- Make a list of occupations that you might be interested in pursuing as a career choice for yourself. Here are a few suggestions: librarian, chef, doctor, nurse, lawyer, grocery store manager, retail/department store manager, firefighter, police officer, college instructor, daycare provider.

- Rank your list according to your level of interest.

- Cross out occupations that you could not easily research. (For example, if you want to be an astronaut, visiting NASA during this school term might be too difficult.)

- Choose an occupation to investigate and have your instructor approve your choice. (You may want to have one or two back-up choices in case you have difficulty finding information on the Internet.)

### The Internet Approach:

The goal with this part of the assignment is for you to see what it's like to research occupations on the Internet.

- Visit one of the following Web sites:

    http://www.bls.gov/ocohome.htm

    (This is a Web site offering you information from the Bureau of Labor Statistics, Occupational Outlook Handbook. It is an excellent site.)

    http://www.nationjob.com

    (At the nationjob site, you might want to go to "Specialty Pages" or "Custom Job Pages.")

*Notes*

- Find the occupation you are interested in, read carefully and take notes—using your own words. *In a journal entry*, record what you learned and how you felt about your research experience.

- Oral Reports: Tell your classmates what you learned and how you felt about your research experience. Prepare this presentation ahead of time so that you don't simply read your journal.

The Traditional Approach:

The goal with this part of the assignment is for you to see what it's like to research an occupation using traditional methods.

You may complete this research through silent observation, or you may combine observations with interviews. The requirements are as follows:

- Set up an observation time (and interview time if desired). (It is okay to work in pairs, but be sure to take your own notes.)

- Go to the place of employment and observe the inanimate surroundings (colors, pictures, plants, paint, and so on), people (their dress, the pace of their work, their apparent attitudes, and so on), the smells, the sounds.

- If you're going to interview someone, be sure to have a list of questions to guide your discussion, but don't be surprised if you don't follow your list exactly.

- *Immediately* following your observation/interview, *complete a journal* in which you record everything you observed and heard. (In this journal, you will be using the notes you've taken during your visit to create a more complete picture of what you saw.)

- Oral Reports: Share with your classmates where you went, what you saw, and what you learned about the occupation you chose, and how you felt about your research experience.

### *Panel Discussion on Research*

1. To prepare for this activity, think about your researching experiences and the research experiences of your classmates. Also, review the two readings in this section of the chapter.

2. Use index cards to write down the greatest advantages to the Internet approach and the greatest advantages to the traditional approach (one advantage per card). For each advantage, use other index cards to write down supporting ideas and information.

3. To have a panel discussion, sit in a circle facing your classmates and share what you believe to be the greatest advantages of each research approach.

4. If you have questions or concerns about an advantage that a classmate discusses, ask questions or express your concerns and see what the rest of the panel has to say.

5. What recommendations would this panel make to students who want to research occupations? The panel may not reach complete agreement.

*Brainstorm*   After reviewing the assignment, your notes, and readings, write freely about the issue. Picture yourself speaking to students and telling them about researching occupations. What seem to be the most significant advantages to each research approach? What would you say to students who are afraid to use the Internet? What would you say to students who feel uncomfortable researching in person?

*Consider Your Audience*   Your audience for this assignment is other students. You can assume that the students have done some research in the past, but they probably haven't thought too much about the advantages of the Internet and traditional approaches in specifically researching occupations. Make a list of things your audience needs to know.

*Create Your Thesis*   Remember that this assignment asks you to focus *only* on advantages although you may find there are more advantages to one type of research than the other. Review the work you have done so far in the writing process, and create a thesis statement that expresses what your main point will be.

*Outline*   Keeping your thesis in mind, review your readings, notes, and brainstorm. Look at the notecards you created for your panel discussion. Make additional notecards to cover other ideas you are thinking of including in your essay. You may want to review the section on notecards on pages 228 and 229. (Label your cards Advantage—Internet or Advantage—Traditional.) When you have all your cards filled out, think about how you might organize your essay. Review the five patterns from the beginning of the chapter and consider these specific patterns for comparison essays.

**Notes**

- (comparison essays) everything about Subject A,* divided into separate paragraphs, then everything about Subject B,* divided into separate paragraphs.
- (comparison essays) one point about subject A, a corresponding point about subject B, another point about subject A, a corresponding point about subject B, and so on.

As you review your cards and think about how you might organize your ideas, you'll probably find cards that you don't know what to do with or cards that you simply aren't interested in. Get rid of these cards—or at least set them aside. You should only work with the cards that are most interesting to you and that fit with your general message. (You are working on your focus skills when you do this.)

Experiment with different ways to organize your cards. (Note: One index card does not necessarily equal one paragraph. A paragraph can be built around one or more index cards.)

When you think you have a pretty good idea of which index cards you'll use and the order you'll put them in, get together with a small group of classmates and show them what you've decided. Explain your choices. You may find that you need to make some changes, and you may get some ideas about organizing from listening to your classmates.

### Draft

Using your cards as a guide, begin drafting your essay. Your introduction should explain what your topic is and why it's important. In your body paragraphs, you should discuss the most important advantages of both methods of research although there doesn't necessarily have to be an equal number of advantages for each approach. If you choose to, you may include some of the information you discovered about the occupation you studied. Details about what you found may help your reader understand the advantages to each kind of research. In your conclusion sum up your advice for the student who wants to research an occupation.

---

*For this essay, Subjects A and B each represent one of the research approaches, Internet or Traditional.

## Revise

### ▼ Activity

**Share Your Writing**

Find a classmate to work with. Read each other's essays and discuss the following questions as they relate to each essay. (You might want to read aloud. Often this helps you find weaknesses that might otherwise go unnoticed.)

- Are there signs in your essay that suggest who your audience is?

- Have you explained to your reader some of the advantages to researching occupations on the Internet? And some of the advantages to researching occupations in person? Have you focused on the most important advantages?

- Can your classmate understand and describe your organizational pattern? Can you make any improvements? Have you used transitions?

- Have you included enough specific information/detail so that your reader can clearly see the advantages?

- Have you mentioned where you got your information? (Cite your sources.)

- What has your instructor been advising you to work on? Do you have any questions about this essay and the skills your instructor wants you to work on?

- What questions do you have about your essay? What are your greatest concerns?

## Edit

Pay special attention to errors that you tend to repeat and focus on one at a time. Also, does your instructor have a certain area he or she wants you to focus on?

Additional ideas for editing:

- Note that *Internet* is always capitalized. (*World Wide Web* is capitalized also.)

- Check your essay for fragments, comma splices, and run-ons. Some students find it helpful to cover the essay with a sheet of paper and

*Notes*

check only one sentence at a time. This helps you concentrate on finding errors. Another approach is to ask a tutor to check your essay for fragments, comma splices, and run-ons. Have the tutor tell you how many (if any) of each kind of error you have. Then find the errors yourself and correct them. Finally review your work with the tutor.

## ▲▼▲ Time to Reflect

> ### Journal Assignment
>
> ### Your Progress as a Writer, Reader, and Critical Thinker
>
> As you look back over the chapter, consider carefully what you have learned about organization.
> - What should writers remember about organizing an essay well?
> - What do you think you benefited from most in this chapter? And what did you do best in your essay(s)?
> - As a reader, what skills did you sharpen in this chapter? Do these skills relate to organization?
> - How is organizing an essay a critical thinking challenge?

## ▲▼▲ Summary of Chapter 6

In Chapter 6, you have
- seen that organization is one key to keeping your readers interested and helping them understand and, perhaps, be persuaded by your ideas,
- learned that thinking critically about organization patterns, choosing a logical pattern, and sticking to that pattern is important in creating a well-written essay, and
- learned to use transitions to build bridges between ideas to help your readers see your organizational structure.

## ▲▼▲ Sentence Boundaries

*Identifying, Understanding and Correcting Fragments*
*Identifying, Understanding and Correcting Run-Ons*
*Identifying, Understanding and Correcting Comma Splices*

*Sentence boundaries* are important to clear writing: readers need to know when ideas start and when they end. There are three kinds of sentence boundary errors: fragments, run-ons, and comma splices. All three will be covered in this chapter.

### Identifying, Understanding, and Correcting Fragments

As you can probably guess from the name *fragment*, a sentence fragment is a piece of a sentence. It is part of a sentence—not a whole sentence.

*Complete sentences will have at least one subject and one verb. Some sentences need a completer, too.*

Another way of looking at sentences is to say that *a complete sentence will have a subject and predicate*. (For further review see Chapter 4.) The predicate includes the verb and everything attached to that verb (the words that act as the completer). In the following examples, the subject is underlined once and the predicate is underlined twice.

<u>Computers</u> <u><u>are important tools for work</u></u>.
<u>We</u> <u><u>use computers at school too</u></u>.
<u>I</u> <u><u>am taking a course about the Internet</u></u>.
<u>I</u> <u><u>love surfing the Web</u></u>.

A fragment, on the other hand, is missing some of these important parts. Perhaps a subject is missing. Perhaps a verb is missing, or perhaps a completer is missing. (If there is only a subject, then the whole predicate is missing.)

1. Here are five fragments. Why aren't these complete sentences? What is missing? Explain.

    a. The new computer.

    b. Works on research.

**Notes**

    c. Going to the library.

    d. The Internet offers.

    e. The student finds.

2. Revise these sentences and make them complete.

One type of fragment is a phrase (as in a, b, and c). A **phrase** is a group of words that is missing a subject or predicate or both. (In d and e, there is a subject and verb, but no completer.)

A **clause**, however, is a group of words with a subject *and* predicate. There are two types of clauses:

    the **independent clause**—can stand alone as a sentence

    the **dependent clause**—cannot stand alone as a sentence and is another type of fragment

Examples of dependent clauses:

    f. When the new computer is installed.

    g. If she does some research.

    h. Because the library offers free Internet access.

    i. Since her research partner is sick.

Read sentences f–i aloud. (See if you can read them in such a way that they "sound" like fragments.)

Even though sentences f–i have subjects and predicates, they are still fragments. The "problem" is that they begin with words called **subordinators** (*when, if, because,* and *since*). Subordinators make independent sentences turn into dependent clauses.

*To correct this type of fragment*, do one of the following.
- Get rid of the subordinator.
- Join the subordinated clause to an independent clause or sentence.

3. Write sentences f–i without the subordinators and then read them aloud.

4. Now, instead of deleting the subordinator, complete the original version of sentences f–i by putting a comma where the period is and then adding an independent sentence that completes the thought. Read the sentences aloud now. (See one way of revising f below.)

f) When the new computer is installed, I can start working.

Here is a list of common subordinators:

| | | |
|---|---|---|
| as | before | though |
| after | even though | unless |
| although | if | when |
| because | since | while |

You can add the independent clause before or after the dependent clause.

*Examples:*

j. When I got on the Internet, I found the information I needed.
k. I found the information I needed when I got on the Internet.
l. My friend got lost on the Internet when she got on for the first time.
m. When she got on for the first time, my friend got lost on the Internet.

## Punctuation Rule #2
When you *begin* a sentence with a subordinated or dependent clause, you must put a comma after the subordinated clause.

6. What is the punctuation rule if the subordinated clause comes after the independent clause? Look at sentences j and k and write Punctuation Rule #3.

## Punctuation Rule #3
_____
_____
_____
_____

Note: When preparing an essay for college or a report for work, read your work aloud slowly and carefully. Do you hear any sentences that might actually be fragments? Double check your use of subordinators in your writing. Did you accidentally create any fragments?

*Notes*

Read the following sentences from "Internet Access Puts Burden of Control on Schools."

a. In Ames, Iowa, a federal laboratory that had allowed a local high school to use its computer network revoked the privileges last March because so many students were attempting to steal one another's passwords and get into confidential files. (paragraph 5)

b. Although most school officials say that Internet policies are crucial, they have mixed feelings about filtering software that limits student access. (paragraph 15)

c. Some educators say that filtering software is problematic because it often blocks potentially informative sites. (paragraph 18)

d. As more students get school-sponsored e-mail accounts, civil libertarians are also questioning whether school officials have the right to monitor their correspondence, Ms. Beeson said. (paragraph 26)

7. There are two clauses in sentences a–d. Highlight the dependent clause in each sentence. Circle the subordinators that create the dependent clauses. Are the sentences punctuated correctly?

8. Find two sentences in any of your readings that have subordinated clauses in them. Write these sentences down and record where you got them.

**Your Own Work**

Review the essays you have already written in this class this semester. Do you have any fragments? If you do, write these fragments in your notebook (and note where they came from). Explain why these are fragments and not complete sentences. Then revise these fragments so that they are complete.

### *Identifying, Understanding, and Correcting Run-ons*

The second type of sentence boundary error is the run-on. Sometimes a run-on sentence is called a **fused sentence**. A writer creates a **run-on sentence** when she lets one sentence run into the next sentence without putting a period or other appropriate punctuation mark between the two sentences. This is confusing to the reader.

Notes

Examples of run-on sentences:

a. Child advocates worry about alcohol and tobacco Web sites they say the sites seem dangerously interesting to children.

b. The alcohol and tobacco companies don't think there is anything to worry about the Web sites are meant for adults.

c. Parents have trouble keeping track of where their kids go on the Internet schools will have the same trouble.

d. Some people want the government to police the Internet the government could check to see if these Web sites are too appealing to children.

e. Others say that the government should stay out of it the Web represents free speech.

1. Review sentences b–e and draw a slash between the two complete sentences.

    Example: a. Child advocates worry about alcohol and tobacco Web sites/they say the sites seem dangerously interesting to children.

To *fix a run-on sentence*, do one of the following.

- Put a period after the first sentence and then begin the next sentence.
    a. Child advocates worry about alcohol and tobacco Web sites. They say the sites seem dangerously interesting to children.
- Put a semicolon after the first sentence and then begin the next sentence. (A semicolon is just as strong as a period.)
    a. Child advocates worry about alcohol and tobacco Web sites; they say the sites seem dangerously interesting to children.
- Join the two complete sentences with a comma and a coordinator (*for, and, nor, but, or, yet, so*).
    a. Child advocates worry about alcohol and tobacco Web sites, *for* they say the sites seem dangerously interesting to children.
- Join the two complete sentences by adding a subordinator to one of the complete sentences.
    a. Child advocates worry about alcohol and tobacco Web sites *because* they say the sites seem dangerously interesting to children.

**Notes**

2. Revise sentences b–e and correct the run-on errors. Fix each sentence two different ways. (Refer to the four methods you've been given and create eight new sentences.) Check your punctuation.

### Punctuation Rule #4
You may use a semicolon to separate two complete sentences.

Note: Reading your work aloud and identifying subjects and verbs will help you identify any run-on sentences in your writing.

**Your Own Work**
Review the essays you have written so far this term. Do you have any run-ons in any of these essays? If you do, write them down in your notebook. Then correct each one two different ways.

### Identifying, Understanding, and Correcting Comma Splices
The final type of sentence boundary error we will look at is the comma splice. A writer creates a **comma splice** when she joins two complete sentences with a comma. A comma is not strong enough to do this.

Examples of sentences with comma splices:

a. The computer is not working, it is "down."
b. We will have to postpone our research, we'll come back later.
c. The Internet is not an option right now, however, we can use the encyclopedias.
d. Instructor Smith wants our reports today, he is expecting an oral presentation.
e. Oral reports make me nervous, they give me cold palms.

Most often, comma splices occur when a writer has two sentences that are very closely related in their meanings. One sentence seems to further explain the other. Other times, as with sentence c, the writer tries to join two sentences with a word that can't join sentences. (*However* cannot join two complete sentences with only a comma.)

*To correct comma splices,* do one of the following.
- Put a period where the comma is and create two distinct sentences.
   a. The computer is not working. It is "down."

- Join the sentences with a coordinator (for, and, nor, but, or, yet, so).
   a. The computer is not working, *so* it is "down."
- Make one of the sentences a dependent clause by using one of the subordinators.
   a. *When* the computer is not working, it is "down."
- Put a semicolon where the comma is. (A semicolon is just as strong as a period.)
   a. The computer is not working; it is "down."

Correct sentences b–e using the four methods explained here. Correct each sentence two different ways. (You will be writing eight complete sentences.)

**Your Own Work**
Review the essays you have written so far this term. Do you have any comma splices in any of these essays? If you do, write them down in your notebook. Then correct each one two different ways.

Note: When checking your own work, review every comma you use and check your subjects and verbs. Have you created any comma splices?

## ▲▼▲ Transitions and Concessions

### Transition Words
### Concession Words

In this chapter, you're faced with opposing ideas about technology— ideas that contradict one another. One of your challenges in this chapter is to discuss such *opposite* ideas in your essays without making your readers feel you're jumping around. You need to create bridges from one idea to another.

There are many ways to create these bridges. However, in this chapter you'll learn just two ways. The first method of moving from one idea to another requires that you use transition words. (The technical term is **conjunctive adverbs**.) The other method, that you'll practice later in this chapter, requires you to use special subordinators called *concessions*.

Section II    Employing the Connections

Notes

### Transition Words

Here is a list of common transition words and their meanings: (conjunctive adverbs)

To express *addition of similar ideas*: also, furthermore, next, similarly

To express *cause-effect*: consequently, therefore, thus

To express *opposites*: however, otherwise

To express *time*: then, next, finally, now

These transitions (and the transitional words and phrases mentioned at the beginning of the chapter) *do not* join sentences the way a subordinator or coordinator might (see Chapter 8). When you use a transition word to create a bridge between two complete sentences, you must use a period or semicolon.

*Example:*
Without a transition word, the following two sentences seem choppy and disconnected.

a. The Internet is a wonderful tool. It has some drawbacks.

Here is how a transition word can create a bridge.

b. The Internet is a wonderful tool. *However*, it has some drawbacks.

Here is another way to punctuate this sentence.

c. The Internet is a wonderful tool; *however*, it has some drawbacks.

### Punctuation Rule #4 (review)

A semicolon (the mark that comes after the word "tool" in the following sentence) works like a period. Use a semicolon when you want to show that two complete sentences have closely related ideas.

The Internet is a wonderful tool; *however*, it has some drawbacks.

More examples:
Some teachers think it is important for students to gain Internet skills; *similarly*, some employers look for young people who are proficient at using computers and the World Wide Web.
(Here is another way to express this idea about the Internet.)

Some employers loo\\k for young people who are proficient at using computers and the World Wide Web. *Consequently*, some teachers encourage their students to gain Internet skills.

Note: Transition words are like glue; they help the ideas in your essay fit together. (They improve the *coherence* of your essay.) But don't overuse them. Too much "glue" makes for a messy creation.

1. Review your readings and notes so far from this chapter. Create sentences about technology or the Internet that can be paired by using transitions. Your goal here is to have ten sentences, or five pairs.
2. With a tutor or classmate, check to see if your pairs make sense. Check to see if you have punctuated your sentences correctly.

You can also add a transition word to the middle of a single sentence.

*Example:* The Internet, however, is a wonderful tool.
   The students, therefore, want Internet access.

The transition words interrupt the flow of the sentence. Put a comma before and after the interrupting word.

3. Look at your notes again and write three sentences in which you could use a transition word in the middle. Check your punctuation.

### Punctuation Rule #5
Put commas around interruptive words/phrases in a sentence.

### Concession Words

In Chapter 8 we'll practice using all the subordinators mentioned earlier in this chapter. For now we'll focus on three of the subordinators that can be used for a special purpose.

When you are arguing for one idea over another, you may need to use concessions to express your ideas clearly. **Concessions** are words that, like transitions, create bridges between ideas. However, concessions do a couple of things that transition words cannot do.

*Concession words can emphasize one idea over another.*
*Concession words create a dependent clause and can, therefore, join two sentences.*

*Concession Words:*
   although         even though         though

Notes

Read these two sentences aloud.
*Some students might misuse the Internet at school.*
*Some students will gain important skills by using the Internet.*

If you wrote these two sentences in your essay, you might sound like you couldn't make up your mind about what you want to say.

Concession words can create clearer relationships between ideas. Where you put the concession word is very important. Look at the following two examples.

a. *Even though* some students might misuse the Internet at school, some students will gain important skills by using the Internet.

b. *Even though* some students will gain important skills by using the Internet, some students might misuse the Internet at school.

Note that whatever the subordinator attaches to becomes less important. Highlight the independent clauses in a and b. The independent clauses have the ideas that the writer wants to emphasize.

Review these sentences:

c. Although the tobacco companies say that they are not trying to attract young people, their ads sure seem attractive to teenagers.

d. The tobacco companies say that they are not trying to attract young people although their ads sure seem attractive to teenagers.

1. Highlight the independent clauses in sentences c and d; these are the ideas that are emphasized. The subordinated ideas are de-emphasized. Which sentence belongs in an argumentative essay defending the tobacco companies? Which sentence belongs in an argumentative essay attacking tobacco companies?

Review these sentences:

e. Though parents have some legitimate concerns about money, students have some important reasons for wanting to use the Internet.

f. Though students have some important reasons for wanting to use the Internet, parents have some legitimate concerns about money.

2. Highlight the independent clauses in sentences e and f; these are the ideas that are emphasized. The subordinated ideas are de-emphasized. Which sentence belongs in an essay that argues for Internet access? Which sentence belongs in an essay that argues against Internet access?

3. In small groups, write some sentences like sentences a–f that you can use to test other groups of classmates. Find some opposing ideas about the Internet to put into one sentence and then experiment with where you put the subordinator. Make sure that the sentences you write make sense even after you move the subordinator around. Repeat this procedure so that you end up with a similar exercise to what you did in steps 1 and 2. Exchange your exercise with another group and complete the exercise that you are given.

*Your Own Work*
When you write your own argumentative essays (in this chapter, or in Chapters 7 or 8), consider using concession sentences. They are very useful because you can mention the ideas of the opposition (a sign of a sophisticated writer) while still *emphasizing* the ideas on *your side*.

# Writing about Television

**CHAPTER 7**

### Main Topics

- Developing your writing
- Evaluating the effects of television
- Creating more expressive sentences
- Combining sentences to improve coherence

*Sacramento Bee,* March 7, 1999, E:6.

Essay assignments, like blueprints, are designed to guide students in developing their essays. An assignment outlines a basic plan for completing an essay, but it's up to the student to take that plan and build upon it. In the same way a building contractor transforms blueprints into a building, a writer focuses on the plan, organizes the development of the project, and then moves the project through different levels of development until it reaches completion.

**Development** is the process of moving from a basic idea to a fully expressive, well-supported main idea that communicates to a specific audience for a specific purpose. Although you have been practicing some forms of development through the lists, charts, journals, workshop questions, and essays you've written in earlier chapters, this chapter will teach you specific strategies for further developing your essay ideas as you write about the effects of television upon the family.

## ▲▼▲ Developing Your Writing

When writing a paper, it's possible to follow an assignment and give just enough information to prove the thesis. This kind of a paper usually leaves the reader wanting more. A developed essay, however, offers more than just the facts. It interests, persuades, enlightens, informs, or delights the reader because of the choices made by the writer, choices that enrich the writing and compel the reader to read. Such writing may contain a single, detailed, thoughtful example, or it might contain a layering of several examples, depending on the point the writer wants to make. The developed piece of writing also has a strong voice, one that says, "Listen to me. I have something important to say." In developing a piece of writing, the writer anticipates the reader's needs, supplies enough evidence to prove the main point, and expresses her opinion in a distinct voice.

As you have written your essays, you have been practicing several forms of essay development already. If you *analyzed* advertisements to explain how a particular ad worked, you practiced a form of development. Whenever you have *added examples* to support your paragraphs in your essays, you have practiced another form of development. As you began to *include your own opinion* and *explain your position* on an issue such as children's access to the Internet, you developed your essay. In *using and citing sources*, you practiced development. In fact, wherever you have added examples, made comparisons, offered re-

**Notes**

search data, or shared personal experience that related directly to your thesis, you have developed your writing.

## Examining Developed Paragraphs

In a developed paragraph, the writer includes evidence, analysis, and detail that support the topic sentence and enrich the paragraph discussion. Sometimes examples appear layered, as the writer builds upon the paragraph's main idea. This kind of paragraph communicates the main idea to the audience through precise examples, careful wording, and clear structure. In the examples that follow, you will see how three writers constructed well-developed paragraphs.

> Television is the most popular of the popular media. Indeed, if Nielsen research and other studies are correct, there are few things that Americans do more than they watch television. On average, each household has a TV on almost fifty hours a week. Forty percent of households eat dinner with the set on. Individually, Americans watch an average of thirty hours a week. We begin peering at TV through the bars of cribs and continue looking at it through the cataracts of old age.
>
> —Joshua Meyrowitz from "Television: The Shared Arena"

You may have noticed that Meyrowitz's paragraph isn't long, yet it includes enough interesting information and focused support to prove his topic sentence—"Television is the most popular of the popular media." Though a well-developed piece of writing is usually longer than an undeveloped piece, the term development doesn't necessarily suggest length. It refers more to the choices made by the writer that enrich his writing and help prove the main idea.

One choice Meyrowitz made is to follow his topic sentence with statistics that will make the reader stop and think. It's shocking, for instance, to think that in the average household, the television is on almost fifty hours a week. That means that the television runs longer than most people's work week. Before the reader has a chance to react to this fact, Meyrowitz offers a second, even more sobering, fact to reinforce the first. On the average, most individuals watch thirty hours of television per week. If statistics alone are not enough to convince you that television is the most popular form of media, the writer takes another approach, employing a creative example to make his point when he concludes that most people begin watching television as babies and continue watching into old age. If you take a moment to reflect on this idea in terms of hours of viewing over a lifetime, then you would probably have to agree with Meyrowitz that television is more popular than any other of the popular media. Indeed, Meyrowitz makes a powerful statement about television by backing his statement with statistics and a creative example.

Here is the second well-developed paragraph.

> TV is one of the things that brings us together as a nation. Thanks to television, the Super Bowl has become our greatest national spectacle, watched in at least 40 million homes. (By contrast, Ross Perot's first "town meeting," which was wildly successful compared to other political broadcasts, was watched in only 11 million homes.) Such peak moments generated mind-boggling revenues. Advertisements during the 1993 Super Bowl, which NBC sold out a month before kickoff, cost in the neighborhood of $28,000 per second. Nevertheless, because virtually the entire nation assembles to watch this single game in January, advertisers such as Pepsi, Budweiser, and Gillette gladly ante up, and others have found it a perfect showcase for major new products. It was during Super Bowl XVIII in January 1984 that Apple introduced the world to the Macintosh personal computer. (The Los Angeles Raiders beat the Washington Redskins, 38 to 9.)
>
> —Douglas Gomery from "As the Dial Turns"

Gomery, like Meyrowitz, proves his main idea by layering statistics and examples, each more powerful than the previous. For one thing, the writer has anticipated his reader's need to know who's made money off the Super Bowl (not only networks but powerful companies—Pepsi, Budweiser, Gillette, and Apple Computer). Notice, too, that Gomery has placed the score of Super Bowl '84 in parentheses. Could his point be that the game itself took a back seat to the advertising? Certainly Gomery proves that the Super Bowl generates lots of money for advertisers, but he also makes the more subtle point that such an emphasis on advertising de-emphasizes the game.

Here is the third effectively developed paragraph.

> One of the most ambitious and conclusive studies (conducted by Dr. Leonard D. Eron and others) examined a group at ages 8, 19, and 30 in a semirural county of New York State. The findings: the more frequently the participants watched TV at age 8, the more serious were the crimes they were convicted of by age 30; the more aggressive was their behavior when drinking; and the harsher was the punishment they inflicted on their own children. Essentially the same results emerged when the researchers examined another large group of youths for three years in a suburb of Chicago. And when they replicated the experiment in Australia, Finland, Israel, and Poland, the outcome was unchanged: as Dr. Eron states it, "There can no longer be any doubt that heavy

Notes

exposure to televised violence is one of the causes of aggressive behavior, crime, and violence in society. The evidence comes from both the laboratory and real-life studies. Television violence affects youngsters of all ages, of both genders, at all socioeconomic levels, and all levels of intelligence."

—Neil Hickey

from "How Much Violence," TV Guide Magazine, August 22, 1992. Reprinted with permission from TV Guide. © 1992 TV Guide Magazine Group, Inc. TV Guide is a registered trademark of TV Guide Magazine Group, Inc.

Hickey also uses the technique of layering in his paragraph on television violence. Rather than sharing just one study on violence, Hickey uses study after study to make Dr. Eron's point "that heavy exposure to televised violence is one of the causes of aggressive behavior, crime, and violence in society." You may have noticed that Hickey has inverted the typical paragraph form here as well. In this paragraph, he begins with evidence and ends with his paragraph point.

▼ *Activity*

*Examining Developed Paragraphs*

Think about the ways in which Meyrowitz, Gomery, and Hickey developed their paragraphs about television.

1. Read each paragraph a second time.

2. In the "Notes" column, label the topic sentence(s) in each as well as types of support (statistics, examples, studies) used to prove each paragraph idea.

3. Write what you have learned about development from Meyrowitz's, Gomery's, and Hickey's paragraphs. Think about their use of precise examples, careful wording, and clear structure. At this point, how would you define *development*?

## *Examining a Developed Essay*

Like the developed paragraph, the developed essay includes evidence, analysis, and detail that help support the main idea and enrich the discussion. To develop an essay, the writer must explore and focus ideas first, then think critically about which examples, studies, statistics, experiences, and other forms of evidence to use in the essay. The writer of the developed essay selects only those pieces of evidence that would help forward the thesis. This kind of writer strives to create a balance of evidence and discussion. If the writer, for instance, included a quotation by an expert to support the thesis, he would follow that quotation with a sentence or two of explanation to help the reader understand the expert's opinion *and* to reinforce the thesis. In this way, the well-developed essay contains more than just examples. It contains a balance of evidence, carefully selected detail, and discussion.

▼ **Activity**

**Study a Developed Essay**

In the essay that follows, writer Nancy Signorielli has balanced evidence and explanation in her discussion of television roles for women. Read the essay carefully once, marking unknown words.

**"Gender Role Images on Television"**
*by Nancy Signorielli*

Signorielli, a media researcher, writes frequently about television and its effects on the family. The following excerpt is from a longer essay, "Television, the Portrayal of Women, and Children's Attitudes."

1  For the past twenty years, in study after study, men have outnumbered women by two or three to one in prime-time dramatic programming. Women are likely to be younger than men; tend to be cast in traditional and stereotypical roles. . . . This is not to say that "liberated" or nontraditional women do not appear on television; it is just that these images are not found consistently. Naturally, most people can easily cite five, six, or more examples of women who are not stereotyped and most of the research examining nonstereotyped roles has focused upon a small number of programs. Consequently, it is easy to forget that the majority of female characters in prime time are found in more traditional roles.

2  Overall, occupational portrayals on television are varied but stereotyped. Women's employment possibilities are somewhat limited, with clerical work the most common job. Television does not recognize adequately that women can successfully mix marriage, homemaking, and raising children, with careers. Rather, programs in which married women work outside the home (e.g., Claire Huxtable on *Cosby*) often focus on the character's home-related role rather than her work per-

sona. Nor does the television world adequately acknowledge the importance of homemaking and raising children. As in the real world, on television the woman who stays home has less status than the one who has a career.

3. Content analyses on seventeen week-long annual samples of prime-time network dramatic programs, conducted as part of the Cultural Indicators project, sheds some light on the traditional and stereotypical ways in which characters are portrayed. Women are seen less often than men and in many respects may be considered as less important. When women do appear, they usually are younger than the men; they are also more attractive and nurturing; more often seen in the context of romantic interests, home, or family; and are more likely to be victimized. Women are somewhat more likely than men to be married, and if they are married, they usually are not employed outside the home. Only 26% of the women who are employed outside the home are also married or have been married. This schism is not perpetuated for male characters.

4. Women who are employed outside the home are usually cast in traditional female occupations—nurses, secretaries, waitresses, and teachers. Nevertheless, the world of television does not always accurately reflect women's work roles. There are a number of occupations in the U.S. labor force where women outnumber the men, but in the television world, due to the general overabundance of men, the men outnumber the women. These include teachers and restaurant workers.

5. Men, on the other hand, are presented as older. They tend to be more powerful and potent than women and proportionately fewer are presented as married. Significantly more men are employed outside the home, and they usually work in high prestige and traditionally masculine occupations such as doctors, lawyers, police, and other higher status and higher paying jobs. Moreover, among married male characters, about three quarters are employed and one quarter are either not working or their employment status is unknown. Among women, the pattern is reversed—only three out of ten married female characters are also employed, a finding quite different from the "real world," in which more than half of all married women are employed. Thus, the image conveyed by prime-time television is that women, especially if married, should stay home and leave the world of work to men. . .

1. Reread the essay more carefully. Mark the thesis and topic sentences. Define any unknown terms.

2. Move from paragraph to paragraph through the body of the essay (paragraphs 2–5). On a separate sheet of paper, in your own words write down the main idea of each paragraph. Then list instances of support Signorielli used to develop each paragraph idea.

3. In which paragraph does Signorielli offer the best balance of evidence and discussion? Explain how evidence and discussion develop the paragraph point.

4. Which paragraph contains the most effective detail? Explain how the detail helps develop the paragraph point.

5. Explain how Signorielli's choices contribute to her development of her main idea.

## ▲▼▲ Developing the Focused Essay

As you focus and develop your essays in this chapter, you will continue to engage in the same productive writing-reading-critical thinking process you have been practicing. Before you write, you'll read, discuss, think critically, brainstorm, research, and observe. You'll spend time gathering information, examining research, and analyzing studies. You'll think about personal experiences. In fact, having some of this material early in the process helps you consider your options and gives you a pool of information and research from which to draw support when developing your essay idea. Once you have determined your essay's focus, you'll begin the process of organizing and thinking critically about what information to include when developing your essay.

After focusing and organizing your thoughts, you'll begin writing your essay. As you add carefully selected examples, statistics, and other forms of evidence to prove your main ideas, and as you explain and analyze your evidence, you'll be developing your essay. Then to help make sure you are developing all aspects of a topic as you write, you should answer the questions that follow. These questions, used by writers and journalists, are called the **Questions for Development**.

WHO? Who is involved?
Who is interested?
Who believes this?
Who said this?

WHAT? What happened?
What else does my reader need to know?
What can I explain further?

WHEN? When did it happen?
When will it occur again?
When will it be resolved?

Notes

| | | |
|---|---|---|
| | WHERE? | Where did it occur? |
| | | Where were the participants? |
| | WHY? | Why is it important? |
| | | Why did it happen this way? |
| | | Why would you or I care? |
| | | Why would my audience care? |
| | HOW? | How did it happen? |
| | | How does it work? |
| | | How can it be resolved? |

Asking these questions helps you make sure you have fully explained, explored, and supported your essay and paragraph ideas. You may apply these Questions for Development at any stage of the writing process.

### ▼ Activity

**Your Favorite Television Series**

Using the Questions for Development, describe your favorite television program in a paragraph (or two). Your goal is to develop your paragraph, making it so interesting that your reader will want to watch the program. Be sure to tell when it's on, who's in it, what happens in a typical episode, where it's set (location), why you like it, how you first heard about it, and why you began to watch.

1. Rather than beginning your paragraph with the typical—"My favorite program is . . ."—spend a few minutes creating a topic sentence that will draw the reader's interest. Consider the following entries:

    - For those who love drama, [name of show] is worth watching.
    - Looking for excitement and intrigue? Then you must see [name of show] . . .
    - Consistently funny, [name of show] . . .

2. As you support your topic sentence, you should try to anticipate your reader's questions and answer them fully.

3. Ask a classmate to read your paragraph(s). Does he or she need more information? Supply any missing information.

## Points to Remember about Development

- Explore and focus your ideas before you develop them.
- Use examples, studies, statistics, experiences, and other forms of evidence to develop your thesis and topic sentences.
- Include *only* the pieces of evidence that help you develop your thesis or topic sentences.
- Create a balance between examples and discussion.
- Include your own opinion and analysis of research, ideas, and issues.
- Include creative sentences and examples that help develop ideas.
- Use the Questions for Development to help you develop ideas.

## ▲▼▲ Investigating the Effects of Television

Most Americans living today grew up with a television in the home. In fact, ninety-nine out of one hundred American families own at least one television set, and many families own two or more. As a result of cable, some Americans have access to as many as two hundred stations on a daily basis. And in most households, the television is on the better part of the day. Can so much exposure to television be good for us?

> ### Journal Assignment
> #### Who's Watching TV?
> Look at the Peanuts cartoon on page 286. Write a response explaining the job Linus has "signed up for." What message does this comic strip send about television in the home today? Should we be concerned that television is such a large part of children's lives?

Many experts are concerned over the possible negative effects of television on children and the family. Some believe that television has taken over families, stripping them of valuable time they once spent reading or interacting with each other. Others warn that children are being exposed to too much violence via the screen. However, other experts assert that television can have a positive impact if used as an educational tool or if monitored by responsible parents. Recent advances in technology have resulted in new forms of instructional television and WebTV—Internet access via the television set. And the V-chip—a

*Notes*

device that will allow parents to block objectionable programming—is now available on new televisions.

> ### Journal Assignment
> **TV Yesterday and Today**
>
> Thinking back to your childhood, you can probably remember watching a favorite program. Perhaps you grew up watching *The Brady Brunch* or *The Cosby Show*. Or, maybe as a young child you watched *Sesame Street* or *Mister Rogers' Neighborhood*.
> 1. Describe your early television viewing experiences. What programs did you watch as a child? Why? Describe your favorite program. Who starred in it? Where was it set? What happened on a typical episode?
> 2. Overall, do you believe you were influenced in a positive way by your early experiences watching television? Explain. Do you think your viewing experiences as a child had a negative effect? Explain. (If you didn't watch television as a youngster, explain what other activities took its place and their effects on you.)
> 3. Now describe your current television viewing experiences. What programs are you drawn to now? Why? Describe your favorite program.
> 4. In general, in what ways has television changed since your childhood? Are these changes positive or negative? Explain. (This journal is for your eyes only. Refer back to it when you begin to write your television essay.)

## Read, Discuss, Think Critically

This section of the chapter offers you a single reading. It's a lengthy excerpt from a book, so plan your reading time well. The reading is organized with eight subheadings that have been numbered and appear in bold.

### Reading Assignment

"The Trouble with Television"

*Preview*   Read the title, introductory material, and the eight subheadings in bold.

*Anticipate*   What do you anticipate this excerpt will be about? Use the "Notes" column to record your thoughts.

*Read and Reread*   Read the entire excerpt, being careful to highlight unknown terms and interesting points. Then reread more slowly and write your responses in the "Notes" column. Mark important points and define unknown terms.

*Notes*

### The Trouble with Television
*by Marie Winn*

Marie Winn, mother of two and author of *Unplugging the Plug-In Drug*, is known for her concern over television and its effect on the family. In this chapter from her book, she argues there are "eight significant ways" television affects children and families. She suggests that all families try a "No TV Week" to break the TV habit.

#### *Most Parents Worry about TV—But Not for the Right Reasons*

My parents don't think I should watch as much TV as I do. They think a lot of the programs I watch are meaningless.

—Fifth grader, P.S. 84, No-TV Week

1. Of all the wonders of modern technology that have transformed family life during the last century, television stands alone as a universal source of parental anxiety. Few parents worry about how the electric light or the automobile or the telephone might alter their children's development. But most parents do worry about TV.

2. Parents worry most of all about the programs their children watch. If only these weren't so violent, so sexually explicit, so cynical, so *unsuitable*, if only they were more innocent, more educational, more *worthwhile*.

3. Imagine what would happen if suddenly, by some miracle, the only programs available on all channels at all hours of day and night were delightful, worthwhile shows that children love and parents wholeheartedly approve. Would this eliminate the nagging anxiety about television that troubles so many parents today?

4. For most families, the answer is no. After all, if programs were the only problem, there would be an obvious solution: turn the set off. The fact that parents leave the sets on even when they are distressed about programs reveals that television serves a number of purposes that have nothing to do with the programs on the screen.

5. Great numbers of parents today see television as a way to make childrearing less burdensome. In the absence of Mother's Helper (a widely used nineteenth-century patent medicine that contained a hefty dose of the narcotic laudanum), there is nothing that keeps children out of trouble as reliably as "plugging them in."

Notes

6   Television serves families in other ways: as a time-filler ("You have nothing to do? Go watch TV"), a tranquilizer ("When the kids come home from school they're so keyed up that they need to watch for a while to simmer down"), a problem solver ("Kids, stop fighting. It's time for your program"), a procrastination device ("I'll just watch one more program before I do my homework"), a punishment ("If you don't stop teasing your little sister, no TV for a week"), and a reward ("If you get an A on your composition you can watch an extra hour of TV"). For parents and children alike it serves as an avoidance mechanism ("I can't discuss that now—I'm watching my program"), a substitute friend ("I need the TV on for company"), and an escape mechanism ("I'll turn on the TV and try to forget my worries").

7   Most families recognize the wonderful services that television has to offer. Few, however, are aware that there are eight significant ways television wields a negative influence on children and family life:

### 1. TV Keeps Families from Doing Other Things

> The primary danger of the television screen lies not so much in the behavior it produces—although there is danger there—as in the behavior it prevents: the talks, the games, the family festivities and arguments through which much of the child's learning takes place and through which his character is formed. Turning on the television set can turn off the process that transforms children into people.[1]

8   Urie Bronfenbrenner's words to a conference of educators almost two decades ago focus on what sociologists call the "reduction effects" of television—its power to preempt and often eliminate a whole range of other activities and experiences. While it is easy to see that for a child who watches 32 hours of television each week, the reduction effects are significant—obviously that child would be spending 32 hours doing *something* else if there were no television available—Bronfenbrenner's view remains an uncommon and even an eccentric one.

9   Today the prevailing focus remains on improving programs rather than on reducing the amount of time children view. Perhaps parents have come to depend so deeply on television that they are afraid even to contemplate the idea that something might be wrong with their use of television, not merely with the programs on the air.

---

[1] Urie Bronfenbrenner, "Who Cares for America's Children?" Address presented at the Conference of the National Association for the Education of Young Children, 1970.

## 2. TV Is a Hidden Competitor for All Other Activities

> Now that I couldn't watch TV I thought of other things to do. I read all the books that I had classified as "boring" and discovered how good they really were.
>
> —Sixth grader, Marshall, Missouri, Turn-Off

10   Almost everybody knows that there are better, more fulfilling things for a family to do than watch television. And yet, if viewing statistics are to be believed, most families spend most of their family time together in front of the flickering screen.

11   Some social critics believe that television has come to dominate family life because today's parents are too selfish and narcissistic to put in the effort that reading aloud or playing games or even just talking to each other would require. But this harsh judgment doesn't take into consideration the extraordinary power of television. In reality, many parents crave a richer family life and are eager to work at achieving this goal. The trouble is that their children seem to reject all those fine family alternatives in favor of television.

12   To be sure, the fact that children are likely to choose watching television over having a story read aloud to them, or playing with the stamp collection, or going out for a walk in the park does not mean that watching television is actually more entertaining or gratifying than any of these activities. It does mean, however, that watching television is easier.

13   In most families, television is always there as an easy and safe competitor. When another activity is proposed, it had better be really special; otherwise it is in danger of being rejected. The parents who have unsuccessfully proposed a game or a story end up feeling rejected as well. They are unaware that television is still affecting their children's enjoyment of other activities, even when the set is off.

14   Reading aloud is a good example of how this competition factor works. Virtually every child expert hails reading aloud as a delightful family pastime. Educators encourage it as an important way for parents to help their children develop a love for reading and improve their reading skills. Too often, however, the fantasy of the happy family gathered around to listen to a story is replaced by a different reality: "Hey kids, I've got a great book to read aloud. How about it?" says the parent. "Not now, Dad, we want to watch 'The Cosby Show,'" say the kids.

15   It is for this reason that one of the most important *Don'ts* suggested by Jim Trelease in his valuable guide *The Read-Aloud Handbook* is the following:

Don't try to compete with television. If you say, "Which do you want, a story or TV?" they will usually choose the latter. That is like saying to a 9-year-old, "Which do you want, vegetables or a donut?" Since *you* are the adult, *you* choose. "The television goes off at eight-thirty in this house. If you want a story before bed, that's fine. If not, that's fine too. But no television after eight-thirty." But don't let books appear to be responsible for depriving children of viewing time.[2]

### 3. TV Allows Kids to Grow Up Less Civilized

> The Turn-Off showed us parents that we can say "no" without so many objections from the kids.
> —Mother, Buffalo, New York, Great TV Turn-Off

16   It would be a mistake to assume that the basic childrearing philosophy of parents of the past was stricter than that of parents today. American parents, in fact, have always had a tendency to be more egalitarian in their family life than, say, European parents. For confirmation, one has only to read the accounts of eighteenth- or nineteenth-century European travelers who comment on the freedom and audacity of American children as compared to their European counterparts. Why then do parents today seem far less in control of their children than parents not only of the distant past but even of a mere generation ago? Television has surely played a part in the change.

17   Today's parents universally use television to keep their children occupied when they have work to do or when they need a break from child care. They can hardly imagine how parents survived before television. Yet parents did survive in the years before TV. Without television, they simply had to use different survival strategies to be able to cook dinner, talk on the telephone, clean house, or do whatever work needed to be done in peace.

18   Most of these strategies fell into the category social scientists refer to as "socialization"—the civilizing process that transforms small creatures intent upon the speedy gratification of their own instinctive needs and desires into successful members of a society in which those individual needs and desires must often be left ungratified, at least temporarily, for the good of the group.

19   What were these "socialization" strategies parents used to use? Generally, they went something like this: "Mommy's got to cook dinner now (make a phone call, talk to Mrs. Jones, etc.). Here are some blocks (some clay, a pair of blunt scissors and a magazine, etc.). Now you have to be a good girl and play by yourself for a while and not interrupt Mommy." Nothing very complicated.

---
[2] Jim Trelease, *The Read-Aloud Handbook*. Penguin, 1985.

20   But in order to succeed, a certain firmness was absolutely necessary, and parents knew it, even if asserting authority was not their preferred way of dealing with children. They knew they had to work steadily at "training" their child to behave in ways that allowed them to do those normal things that needed to be done. Actually, achieving this goal was not terribly difficult. It took a little effort to set up certain patterns—perhaps a few days or a week of patient but firm insistence that the child behave in certain ways at certain times. But parents of the past didn't agonize about whether this was going to be psychologically damaging. They simply had no choice. Certain things simply *had to be done,* and so parents stood their ground against children's natural struggle to gain attention and have their own way.

21   Obviously it is easier to get a break from child care by setting the child in front of the television set than to teach the child to play alone for certain periods of time. In the first case, the child is immediately amused (or hypnotized) by the program, and the parent has time to pursue other activities. Accustoming children to play alone, on the other hand, requires day-after-day perseverance, and neither parent nor child enjoys the process very much.

22   But there is an inevitable price to pay when a parent never has to be firm and authoritative, never has to use that "I mean business" tone of voice: socialization, that crucial process so necessary for the child's future as a successful member of a family, a school, a community, and a nation is accomplished less completely. A very different kind of relationship between parent and child is established, one in which the parent has little control over the child's behavior.

23   The consequences of a large-scale reduction in child socialization are not hard to see in contemporary society: an increased number of parents who feel helpless and out of control of their children's lives and behavior, who haven't established the parental authority that might protect their children from involvement in such dangerous activities as drug experimentation, or from the physical and emotional consequences of precocious sexual relationships.

### 4. Television Takes the Place of Play

> I always used to turn the TV on for my 2½-year-old son Alexander in the morning. Then I noticed during No-TV week that he played in a different way all morning. He seemed less irritable—in a better mood—everything was entirely different. I realized it wasn't Alexander who wanted to watch TV—it was I who needed to turn it on for him.
> —Parent, P.S. 84, New York City, No-TV Week

24   Once small children become able to concentrate on television and make some sense of it—usually around the end of their second year of

*Notes*

life—it's not hard to understand why parents eagerly set their children before the flickering screen: taking care of toddlers is hard! The desperate and tired parent can't imagine *not* taking advantage of this marvelous new way to get a break. In consequence, before they are three years old, the opportunities of active play and exploration are hugely diminished for a great number of children—to be replaced by the hypnotic gratification of television viewing.

25   Yet many parents overlook an important fact: children who are suddenly able to sustain attention for more than a few minutes on the TV screen have clearly moved into a new stage of cognitive development—their ability to concentrate on TV is a sign of it. There are therefore many other new activities, far more developmentally valuable, that the child is now ready for. These are the simple forms of play that most small children enjoyed in the pre-television era: cutting and pasting, coloring and drawing, building with blocks, playing games of make-believe with toy soldiers or animals or dolls. But the parent who begins to fill in the child's time with television at this point is unlikely to discover these other potential capabilities.

26   It requires a bit of effort to establish new play routines—more effort, certainly, than plunking a child in front of a television screen, but not really a great deal. It requires a bit of patience to get the child accustomed to a new kind of play—play on his own—but again, not a very great deal. It also demands some firmness and perseverance. And a small amount of equipment (art materials, blocks, etc.), most of it cheap, if not free, and easily available.

27   But the benefits for both parent and child of *not* taking the easiest way out at this point by using television to ease the inevitable child-care burdens will vastly outweigh the temporary difficulties parents face in filling children's time with less passive activities. For the parent, the need for a bit more firmness leads to an easier, more controlled parent-child relationship. For the child, those play routines established in early childhood will develop into lifelong interests and hobbies, while the skills acquired in the course of play lead to a sense of accomplishment that could never have been achieved if the child had spent those hours "watching" instead of "doing."

**5. TV Makes Children Less Resourceful**

> Tuesday I got home from school and didn't get to watch any of those old reruns that I've seen a hundred times before. I did my homework right after school, then I practiced my clarinet and guitar.
> —High school student, Richmond, Indiana, Turn-Off

28   Many parents who welcome the idea of turning off the TV and spending more time with the family are still worried that without TV they would constantly be on call as entertainers for their children. Though they *want* to play games and read aloud to their children, the idea of having to replace television minute-for-minute with worthwhile family activities is daunting. They remember thinking up all sorts of things to do when they were kids. But their own kids seem different, less resourceful, somehow. When there's nothing to do, these parents observe regretfully, their kids seem unable to come up with anything to do besides turning on the TV.

29   One father, for example, says, "When I was a kid, we were always thinking up things to do, projects and games. We certainly never whined to our parents, 'I have nothing to do!'" He compares this with his own children today: "They're simply lazy. If someone doesn't entertain them, they'll happily sit there watching TV all day."

30   There is one word for this father's disappointment: unfair. It is as if he were disappointed in them for not reading Greek though they have never studied the language. He deplores his children's lack of inventiveness, as if the ability to play were something innate that his children are missing. In fact, while the *tendency* to play is built into the human species, the actual *ability* to play—to imagine, to invent, to elaborate on reality in a playful way—and the ability to gain fulfillment from it, these are skills that have to be learned and developed.

31   Such disappointment, however, is not only unjust, it is also destructive. Sensing their parents' disappointment, children come to believe that they are, indeed, lacking something, and that this makes them less worthy of admiration and respect. Giving children the opportunity to develop new resources, to enlarge their horizons and discover the pleasures of doing things on their own is, on the other hand, a way to help children develop a confident feeling about themselves as capable and interesting people.

32   It is, of course, ironic that many parents avoid a TV Turn-Off out of fear that their children won't know what to do with themselves in the absence of television. It is television watching itself that has allowed them to grow up without learning how to be resourceful and television watching that keeps them from developing those skills that would enable them to fill in their empty time enjoyably.

## 6. TV Has a Negative Effect on Children's Physical Fitness

Dear Diary:
Today instead of TV I did exercises. I kicked my legs 50 times and

*Notes*

> jumped up and down 50 times. Then I took a bath. Then I cut papers and drew. Then I did knitting five times. It did not turn out so good.
> —Fifth grader, P.S. 84, No-TV Week

33   Not long ago a study that attracted wide notice in the popular press found a direct relationship between the incidence of obesity in children and time spent viewing television. For the 6–11 age group, "children who watched more television experienced a greater prevalence of obesity, or superobesity, than children watching less television. No significant differences existed between obese, superobese, and nonobese children with respect to the number of friends, their ability to get along with friends, or time spent with friends, alone, listening to the radio, reading, or in leisure time activities," wrote the researchers. As for teenagers, only ten percent of those teenagers who watched TV an hour or less a day were obese as compared to twenty percent of those who watched more than five hours daily. With most other variables eliminated, why should this be? The researchers provided a commonsense explanation: Dedicated TV watchers are fatter because they eat more and exercise less while glued to the tube.[3]

### 7. TV Has a Negative Effect on Children's School Achievement

> One day my class was getting ready to have a science test. There was nothing to do during the Turn-Off Week so I studied instead. I got S –, a good grade. My parents were proud of me.
> —Fourth grader, Marshall, Missouri, Turn-Off

34   It is difficult if not impossible to prove that excessive television viewing has a direct negative effect on young children's cognitive development, though by using cautionary phrases such as "TV will turn your brain to mush" parents often express an instinctive belief that this is true.

35   Nevertheless an impressive number of research studies demonstrate beyond any reasonable doubt that excessive television viewing has an adverse effect on children's achievement in school. One study, for instance, shows that younger children who watch more TV have lower scores in reading and overall achievement tests than those who watch less TV.[4]

36   Another large-scale study, conducted when television was first introduced as a mass medium in Japan, found that as families acquired televi-

---

[3] W. H. Dietz and S. L. Gortmaker, "Do We Fatten Our Children at the Television Set? Obesity and Television Viewing in Children and Adolescents." *Pediatrics* 75 (1985).

[4] S. G. Burton, J. M. Calonico, and D. R. McSeveney, "Effects of Preschool Watching on First-Grade Children." *Journal of Communications* 29:3 (1979).

sion sets children showed a decline in both reading skills and homework time.

37  But it does not require costly research projects to demonstrate that television viewing affects children's school work adversely. Interviews with teachers who have participated in TV Turn-Offs provide confirmation as well.

38  Almost without exception, these teachers testify that the quality of homework brought into class during the No-TV period was substantially better. As a fifth grade teacher noted: "There was a real difference in the homework I was getting during No-TV Week. Kids who usually do a good job on homework did a terrific job. Some kids who rarely hand in assignments on time now brought in surprisingly good and thorough work. When I brought this to the class's attention during discussion time they said, 'Well, there was nothing else to do!'"

## 8. Television Watching May Be a Serious Addiction

> Every time I walked through the living room I longed to sit down, relax, and watch dumb reruns on TV. I think I was suffering from TV withdrawal symptoms. After a few days, though, I was used to doing other things with my time.
> —Tenth grader, Marshall, Missouri, Turn-Off

39  A lot of people who have nothing but bad things to say about TV, calling it the "idiot box" and the "boob tube," nevertheless spend quite a lot of their free time watching television. People are often apologetic, even shamefaced about their television viewing, saying things like, "I only watch the news," or "I only turn the set on for company," or "I only watch when I'm too tired to do anything else" to explain the sizable number of hours they devote to TV.

40  In addition to anxiety about their own viewing patterns, many parents recognize that their children watch too much television and that it is having an adverse effect on their development and yet they don't take any effective action to change the situation.

41  Why is there so much confusion, ambivalence, and self-deception connected with television viewing? One explanation is that great numbers of television viewers are to some degree addicted to the *experience* of watching television. The confusion and ambivalence they reveal about television may then be recognized as typical reactions of an addict unwilling to face an addiction or unable to get rid of it.

42  Most people find it hard to consider television viewing a serious addiction. Addictions to tobacco or alcohol, after all, are known to cause life-threatening diseases—lung cancer or cirrhosis of the liver. Drug addiction leads to dangerous behavioral aberrations—violence and crime.

*Notes*

Meanwhile, the worst physiological consequences of television addiction seem to be a possible decline in overall physical fitness, and an increased incidence of obesity.

43   It is in its psychosocial consequences, especially its effects on relationships and family life, that television watching may be as damaging as chemical addiction. We all know the terrible toll alcoholism or drug addiction takes on the families of addicts. Is it possible that television watching has a similarly destructive potential for family life?

44   Most of us are at least dimly aware of the addictive power of television through our own experiences with the medium: our compulsive involvement with the tube too often keeps us from talking to each other, from doing things together, from working and learning and getting involved in community affairs. The hours we spend viewing prove to be curiously unfulfilling. We end up feeling depressed, though the program we've been watching was a comedy. And we cannot seem to turn the set off, or even not turn it on in the first place. Doesn't this sound like an addiction?

## ▼ Questions for Critical Thought

### "The Trouble with Television"

1. What main points does Winn make to support her view that television has a negative effect on the family?

2. Winn has developed each of her points over several paragraphs (except for point 6 which has been developed in a single paragraph). Which of her points appears best developed? Why? List the evidence, examples, and details she used to support this point. What other forms of support could she have used to make her point even better?

3. Which of Winn's points appears less developed or weaker than the others? What kinds of evidence might help to prove the point?

4. Which of her points do you agree with most? Explain why. What evidence does she use to help prove this point? Are there other forms of support that she could have used to strengthen her argument?

5. Which of her points do you disagree with? Explain why. What evidence does she use to help prove this point? How might you *rebut* (argue against) the point?

6. Examine Winn's use of outside sources in paragraphs 8 and 15. How did she integrate her sources in each case?

7. Identify Winn's audience. To whom is she speaking in the piece? What is her purpose for writing?

8. How does your own view of television compare to Winn's?

> ### Journal Assignment
> #### Considering Winn's View
> Think about the concerns Winn has raised regarding television and its effect on children and families. Think about your own television viewing habits as well as the habits of those in your family. Write a response in the form of a letter to Winn telling her, overall, what you think of her ideas and suggestions. Exchange your journal with a classmate or two. When you read someone else's journal, just say "Thank You" when you return it.

## Writing Assignment #1: The Effects of Television

Here, in brief, is the writing assignment you are preparing for.

> *Write an essay in which you argue **for** or **against** Winn's view of television and its effect on children and the family.*

## Explore the Writing Assignment

### ▼ Activities

#### Summary and Response

One method of exploring is to look more closely at each of Winn's arguments. In the activity that follows you'll utilize your summary and response skills as you address Winn's arguments one at a time. Complete this activity on a separate sheet.

**Summary of Introduction**

1. **TV Keeps Families from Doing Other Things**
   (list main points)

*Notes*

Do you agree or disagree that TV keeps families from doing other things? How? Why? Use examples from your own experience to develop your response.

**2. TV Is a Hidden Competitor for All Other Activities**
(list main points)

Do you agree or disagree that TV is a hidden competitor? If so, in what ways does it compete? Whom or what does TV compete with?

**3. TV Allows Kids to Grow Up Less Civilized**
(list main points)

Do you agree or disagree that kids who watch TV grow up less civilized? Offer specific examples to support your response.

**4. Television Takes the Place of Play**
(list main points)

Do you agree or disagree that TV takes the place of play? What kinds of activities does TV interfere with? Discuss specific observations you've made.

**5. TV Makes Children Less Resourceful**
(list main points)

Do you agree or disagree that children lose their resourcefulness because of TV? What evidence do you have to support your point?

**6. TV Has a Negative Effect on Children's Physical Fitness**
(list main points)

Do you agree or disagree that TV takes the place of physical activity and causes children's fitness to suffer? Offer specific examples to prove your point.

**7. TV Has a Negative Effect on Children's School Achievement**
(list main points)

Do you agree or disagree that children's achievement falls short because of television? If so, in what areas? How? Why? What evidence does Winn use to support this point?

**8. Television Watching May Be a Serious Addiction**
(list main points)

What does it mean to be addicted to something? Do you agree or disagree that people may become addicted to TV?

Discuss your views with classmates.

### Observing Children's Viewing Habits

To further explore the topic, conduct an observation and record data on the viewing habits of children and families you know.

Over a period of 3–5 days, observe a child's television habits. Apply your Questions for Development. Who is the child? What are the child's viewing habits? When does the child watch television most? Least? Where does the child sit while viewing? Does the child appear to enjoy TV? How does the child behave while viewing? Why does the child view TV? Do any of Winn's concerns appear to hold true?

### Interviewing Families

To gather additional information on families' viewing habits, conduct interviews with parents.

Using the Questions for Development, compose a set of interview questions that addresses Winn's concerns. Interview 3–5 parents from different families. Note where similarities and differences occur in their viewing habits.

Sample Questions:

- When do you watch television most? Least?
- How many hours do you (and your family) watch television daily/weekly?
- Do you monitor your children's viewing habits? When? Why? How? Which programs, if any, are off limits?
- What do you see as the positive aspects of television?
- What are the negative aspects of television?

Be careful to keep your source information, who says what, in case you want to cite any of the adults as sources in your essay.

***Brainstorm*** Write freely about Marie Winn's concerns and other possible effects of television on children and the family. Don't worry about deciding which side of the issue you are on right now. Although Winn asserts there are "eight significant ways" that television affects the family, you should not argue for or against all eight points. Instead, write on two or three of the issues that interest you most. It might help to review your summary/response sheets to see which of the arguments you found most intriguing. Also review your journals and your activities.

Notes

When you have finished writing, review your brainstorm and decide which side you want to take on the issue(s). Highlight the parts of your brainstorm you think might be useful when writing your essay.

***Consider Your Audience*** Imagine your audience as a group of concerned parents. It might help to visualize the PTA at a local elementary school. Which of Winn's concerns about television, children, and the family would you discuss with them? What might be some of their concerns? Why might they be leaning one way or the other? How would you address the concerns of those leaning away from your view? Direct your argument toward those who might be swayed by your discussion. Make a list of things to keep in mind when writing for your audience.

***Create Your Thesis*** Your thesis should reflect that you have narrowed the scope of your essay to focus on two or three of Winn's arguments. Also note that you are being asked to argue *for or against* Winn. Your position should be clearly stated in your thesis. Experiment with thesis statements until you find one that expresses what you want to focus on in your essay.

***Outline*** With your thesis in mind, list the two or three points that you intend to argue in your essay. Under each point note the kind of support you will use to develop your idea. You should also consider what your opponent (the person on the other side) might say about each point and how you would respond. At this point, you might draft a rough outline that shows how you will organize all of this information.

Here are some ways for you to consider organizing your arguments:

- offer least important ideas first, most important ideas last
- present least interesting ideas first, most interesting ideas last
- alternate your views and your opponent's views
- present all of your opponent's views (divided into different paragraphs), then all of your views (divided into different paragraphs)

## Draft

Using your summary/response sheets, your notes, the reading, your brainstorm, and your outline as a guide, begin drafting your essay. In your introduction you should introduce the two or three most important issues raised by Winn and tell whether you agree or disagree. In your body paragraphs, address these points one at a time, explaining and supporting your position with examples, personal experience, research, and discussion. Also, be sure to address your opponent's concerns. In your conclusion, remind your reader where you stand in regard to Winn.

## Revise

### ▼ Activities

**Share Your Writing**

As you work with a classmate, consider the following:

- Have you established your position in the introduction? Remember, your task is to show that you either agree or disagree with Winn. (Or, maybe you've decided to agree with some of her points, but not with them all.)
- Can your reader see your organizational pattern? Have you addressed the arguments one at a time? Is it clear which paragraphs contain pro or con arguments?

Here is an example of a topic sentence for a pro argument:

> In her article, Winn argues that television keeps families from doing things together, and I agree.
>
> —*Allison Baxter*
> *student writer*

Here is an example of topic a sentence for a con argument:

> Marie Winn said that television could become an addiction, which could be compared to a drug addiction. I strongly disagree.
>
> —*Lynita Harris*
> *student writer*

- Have you developed/supported your ideas fully? Use any of the Questions for Development that help.

*Notes*

| | | |
|---|---|---|
| | WHO? | Who is my audience? |
| | | Who is affected? |
| | | Who is interested? |
| | | Who believes this? |
| | | Who said this? |
| | WHAT? | What are the main issues? |
| | | What else does my reader need to know? |
| | | What can I explain further? |
| | WHEN? | When is it a problem? |
| | | When will it be resolved? |
| | WHERE? | Where does it occur? |
| | | Where are the participants? |
| | WHY? | Why is the issue important? |
| | | Why do you or I care? |
| | | Why will my audience care? |
| | HOW? | How does it happen? |
| | | How does it work? |
| | | How can the issue be resolved? |

- Have you included examples or personal experience to support your ideas?

Review the following paragraph to see how one student effectively used personal experience to develop a body paragraph idea.

> In her article Winn argues that television keeps families from doing things together, and I agree. Just recently, I realized that the big square box has kept me from doing things with my own children. For example, on our way home from school, my oldest son would ask me to play Monopoly with him after dinner, and of course I would agree to play. Some time after dinner, he would come to me with the board, and remind me that I had said I would play the game with him, but most of the time I would say, "Not right now. My show is on," and I would ask if we could play a little later. When he returned again with the game, I would say, "It's too late to play tonight. We will play tomorrow evening, I promise." This was very painful for my son, and I did have every intention of playing with him. I just got too involved in that mindless box.
>
> —*Allison Baxter*
> *student writer*

- Have you used transitions to move the reader smoothly from one idea to the next and to provide cohesion through your essay?

- Have you used concessions—*though, although, even though*—when you need to make one argument appear more important or stronger than another?

Example of a concession:

> Although I agree with most of Winn's article, I don't agree that TV has a negative effect on a child's academic achievement.
>
> *—Parris Ray*
> *student writer*

- Have you integrated and identified your own research findings in your essay?
- Have you included publication information for sources? Have you cited sources correctly?
- Do you have questions or concerns about your essay?

## Edit

Look carefully to catch any errors that tend to be repeated in your writing and be sure to use spell check.

Read your essay aloud. Listen for mistakes and look for typographical errors. Also consider the following issues:

- Have you used adjectives to improve your sentences?
- Have you included adverbs to improve your sentences?
- Have you combined sentences when appropriate and for variety?
- Check for fragments, comma splices, and run-ons.
- Ask the tutor to tell you how many (if any) errors and what kind so that you can correct them.

## Writing Assignment #2: Television: Good, Bad, or Tolerable?

Here, in brief, is the writing assignment you are preparing for.

> *Write an essay in which you discuss* **objectively** *the negative and positive effects of television. Come to a conclusion about what, if anything, should be done to minimize the negative effects of television and maximize the positive.*

Notes

## Read, Discuss, Think Critically

In this section, you'll read an essay in opposition to Marie Winn's, "The Trouble with Television." Reconsider the issue of television and its effects as you read the article that follows.

## Reading Assignment

*"How TV Influences Your Kids"*

*Preview*   Review the title and pay close attention to the pre-reading information after the title. Note the author's preparation for writing such an article.

*Anticipate*   What do you think this article will be about? Use the "Notes" column to record your response.

*Read and Reread*   Read the entire essay quickly, being careful to mark unknown terms. Then reread it slowly. Take your time in writing notes or reactions in the "Notes" column and highlighting or underlining important ideas. Define unknown terms.

### How TV Influences Your Kids
*by Daniel R. Anderson*

Daniel R. Anderson, "How TV Influences Your Kids," *TV Guide* Magazine, March 3, 1990. Reprinted with permission from TV Guide. © 1990 TV Guide Magazine Group, Inc. TV Guide is a registered trademark of the TV Guide Magazine Group, Inc.

Daniel R. Anderson is a Professor of Psychology at the University of Massachusetts at Amherst. Anderson and his graduate student assistant, Patricia Collins, reviewed 165 studies on the effects of TV on the development of children.

1   A few months ago, when she was twenty-three months old, Sarah started to watch TV. "She *cries* when *Mister Rogers' Neighborhood* goes off the air," her mother wrote me. "The first time she saw it, she sat quietly with me and watched the whole show. She talked about it for the rest of the day."

2   Children typically begin paying consistent attention to a few television programs at about age two. If Sarah continues to be a typical American child, she will spend about thirty percent of her waking hours in front of a TV, watching a wider range of programs as she matures. In

terms of sheer exposure, television has the potential to be a major influence on Sarah's, and most children's, development. In recent years, researchers have begun to clarify the nature of that influence. The news is both good and bad.

3   The good news is that, contrary to a widespread theory, TV doesn't transform children into mindless "vidiots." The theory first gained popularity in the 1970s when social critics began to write that television mesmerizes young children by its rapid scene changes. A consequence, so these critics believe, is that children watch TV mindlessly and passively, with little thought and reflection. And they believe the long-term effects are worse: a short attention span and a diminished intellect.

4   But the theory has a flaw. It's been based mostly on anecdotes, never convincingly proved. And more than 100 studies on TV and children's attention span, comprehension and intellectual development have largely discredited it. In other words, there is no consistent evidence that TV makes children mentally passive, shortens their attention span, reduces their interest in education or otherwise impairs their ability to think. In fact, researchers are finding that young children aren't mesmerized by TV. Children seem to pay the greatest attention when they are most mentally involved with the program. The studies also show that young children tend to ignore or reject programs that they don't understand.

5   Sarah's TV viewing illustrates this. She now enjoys watching many children's TV shows, her mother reports, but not all. When a science program directed at older kids comes on, Sarah asks her mother, "'Change? Change TV?' She doesn't just turn away," her mother wrote. "She's insistent we get rid of that program."

6   The fact that children actively think about television indicates that television can be an effective tool for education, an idea supported by a great deal of research. For twenty years PBS's *Sesame Street* has helped preschoolers learn elementary reading and arithmetic, and *Mister Rogers' Neighborhood*, also on public TV, has helped them deal with emotions and self-control. The potential of television for teaching children is beginning to be demonstrated with such science programs as *3-2-1 Contact* and the math program *Square One TV*, both on PBS.

7   Despite the lack of evidence that TV impairs intellectual development, many educators blamed TV when national achievement-test scores declined. While it is true that heavy viewers have lower achievement scores, studies suggest that heavy TV viewing is more a symptom of poor achievement than a cause. Poor achievers tend to come from

Notes

*Notes*

8   disrupted families or have parents who fail to provide intellectually stimulating activities. Such families tend to be heavy TV viewers.

Unfortunately, much of what kids watch is intended for adults and may not be limited or interpreted by their parents. When it comes to adult-oriented TV, young children take in the information but jumble up the meaning. Consider my conversation with six-year-old Sebastian. He had just seen a commercial in which a young couple sitting on the grass share a sumptuous lunch in front of their new Mercedes. When asked what the ad meant, Sebastian answered unhesitatingly, "They want you to buy picnics!"

9   Sebastian's misunderstanding was benign and amusing. Less amusing is the realization that uncontrolled TV viewing can expose a child to large doses of violence, antisocial values and sexual imagery. To the adult, this fare may have entertainment value. A given violent program may even deliver the implicit message that criminals get punished, so crime doesn't pay. The problem is that the child may see the violence of the crime and the criminal's glamorous lifestyle but not make the connection between those things and the criminal's subsequent downfall.

10   We know a lot about the effects of television violence. Studies suggest that TV has a role in producing aggressive play and real-life violence. Children who watch a lot of TV violence are described by other children as more aggressive. And some long-term studies find that viewing violent programming contributes to later aggressive behavior. Some of the most disturbing incidents occurred in 1973 after the movie "Fuzz" was aired. Apparently reenacting scenes in which youths set homeless people on fire, teenagers in Boston and Miami fatally burned two people.

11   Most researchers who study the effects of TV violence suggest that children are not equally susceptible to its influence. If parents are loving and discourage aggressive behavior, their children are unlikely to be influenced. But if parents are unavailable or permissive of violence, children are more likely to be influenced.

12   For many children from broken homes and poor neighborhoods, television may be the only window to the world outside. At its worst, television provides these children images of violence and crime associated with wealth and glamour. At its best, television provides these children with knowledge of positive alternatives in life and gives them hope.

13   Sarah, who just began watching TV, has loving parents who will monitor and limit her viewing. They will discuss programs with her and instill social values that will enable her to evaluate the things she experiences form TV. TV won't be her only entertainment and learning resource. For Sarah, TV will provide positive education and wholesome entertainment.

## ▼ Questions for Class Discussion

### "How TV Influences Your Kids"

1. Overall, what main point does Anderson make about television and its influence on children?
2. How does Anderson's view differ from Winn's? On what points does Anderson disagree with Winn?
3. What negative effects of television is Anderson concerned about? List them. Do you agree or disagree? Why?
4. What does Anderson see as the benefits of television? List them. Do you agree or disagree? Why?
5. Identify Anderson's audience. To whom is he speaking? What is his purpose for writing? How does Anderson's purpose differ from Winn's?
6. What kinds of support does Anderson use to develop his points in paragraphs 6 and 10? Are there other forms of support that he could have used to make any of his points stronger?
7. How does the story of twenty-three-month-old Sarah and her viewing habits work to provide cohesion in this article?
8. How does your own view of television compare to Anderson's?

---

### Journal Assignment

#### Considering Anderson's View

Just as you wrote to Winn earlier in the chapter, take time now to write a letter to Anderson letting him know whether you support and agree with his views or not. Consider your own viewing habits as well as what you've discovered about the viewing habits of others. Exchange your journal with a classmate. When you read someone else's journal, just say "Thank you."

---

## Explore the Writing Assignment

Here, again, is your writing assignment. Review it carefully before continuing. Underline the important terms in the assignment.

*Write an essay in which you discuss* **objectively** *the negative and positive effects of television. Come to a conclusion about what, if*

Notes

*anything, should be done to minimize the negative effects of television and maximize the positive.*

▼ **Activities**

### Charting the Negatives and Positives of Television

An effective way to generate and organize ideas is to draw charts on the negatives and positives of television. This will help you separate the arguments and reasons on both sides of the issue. Refer back to Anderson's article first, then to Marie Winn's. On the first chart, list negative effects on the left, then support, proof, and examples on the right. On the second chart, list positive effects on the left, then support, proof, and examples on the right.

| Negative Effects of TV | |
|---|---|
| **Negative Effects** | **Sources/Proof/Examples** |
| Watching violence on TV can lead to violent behavior. | In 1973 after the movie *Fuzz* was shown on TV, kids actually set some homeless people on fire. Two died. (from Anderson's article, "How TV Influences Your Kids," par. 10) |
| *Use additional pages as necessary.* | |

| Positive Effects of TV ||
|---|---|
| **Positive Points** | **Sources/Proof/Examples** |
| *Use additional pages as necessary.* | |

### Look for Information at the Library and on the Internet

To further explore the topic, look for information on the effects of television.

1. Go to the library to find books and articles on the issue of television and its effect on children and the family. Here are some titles to get you started:

    Chen, Milton. *The Smart Parent's Guide to Kids' TV.*
    Davis, Bennett. *Television and Families.*
    Gitlin, Todd. *Inside Primetime.*
    Minow, Newton N. *Making Television Safe for Kids.*
    Signorielli, Nancy. *Sourcebook on Children and Television.*
    Winn, Marie. *The Plug-In Drug.*
    Winn, Marie. *Unplugging the Plug-In Drug.*

    Note: You don't need to read the entire book to get information on the effects of television. Look in the table of contents at the beginning of the book for chapters that appear to be about the effects of television on children and the family. Also, refer to the index in the back of the text. Look up words such as *children, effects, family, education* or *violence* to find specific sections that focus on these important issues. Apply the Questions for Development to what you read.

*Notes*

    As you read sections from these books, be sure to take notes and write down source information—author, title, page numbers, publication information. Then add new information to your positive and negative effects charts.

2. Spend some time on the Internet. Look for articles on "television and violence," on "television and effects," or on "television and children." (Ask a librarian for help if you have any trouble locating sources.) Apply the Questions for Development to what you read.

    As you conduct your research, be sure to take notes and write down source information—author, title, web address. Add any new information to your positive and negative effects charts.

***Brainstorm*** Write freely about the positive and negative effects of television. Use this as an opportunity to look at both sides. Review both Anderson's and Winn's pieces. Also, go back to your lists of negative and positive effects of television and respond to the most important points on each list.

    When you are done writing, review your brainstorm. Because you'll present a balanced paper showing both the positives and negatives, focus on only the top two or three points for each side. Highlight these points for now.

***Consider Your Audience*** Imagine you are presenting an objective discussion to a group of concerned parents, teachers and other members of the community. While some would argue that television has a negative influence on children, others would point to the positive programming television has to offer. What might be some of the difficulties you'd face in fairly presenting both sides of the issue?

***Create Your Thesis*** Review the writing assignment. Note that the assignment asks that you present the negative and positive effects objectively. This means you should create a thesis that will allow you to present both sides of the issue. Your thesis should also show that you'll limit your discussion to the most important positive and negative effects.

***Outline*** Think about how you might organize the points you have highlighted in a way that will allow you to present both sides fairly. Draft an outline or make a list of the arguments you'll be presenting.

Under each point note the kind of support you'll use to develop your idea. Here are some options for organizing your essay effectively:

- Offer least important ideas first, most important ideas last.
- Present least interesting ideas first, most interesting ideas last.
- Alternate positive and negative effects.
- Present all positive effects (divided into different paragraphs), then all negative effects (divided into different paragraphs).

## Draft

Using your positive effects and negative effects lists, your notes, your own library or Internet sources, Anderson's and Winn's articles, your brainstorm, and your outline, begin writing your essay. Your introduction should explain the basic conflicts between those who believe TV is a negative influence and those who believe the opposite. In your body paragraphs, present each side's concerns, but include only one main concern per paragraph. Be sure to develop each point with support in the form of evidence, details, examples, and discussion. In your conclusion, let your reader know what you believe should be done to minimize the negative and maximize the positive effects of television.

## Revise

▼ **Activity**

**Share Your Writing**

As you work with a classmate think about the following:

- Have you presented a fair discussion with both sides represented?
- Can your reader see your organizational pattern? Have you addressed the arguments one at a time? Is it clear which paragraphs show negative effects and which ones show positive?
- Have you developed your ideas fully? Apply any of the Questions for Development that help.

    WHO?        Who is my audience?
                Who is interested in the issue?
                Who believes TV is a negative influence?
                Who believes TV is a positive influence?

*Notes*

| | | |
|---|---|---|
| | WHAT? | What are the arguments raised by Anderson? |
| | | What are the arguments raised by Winn? |
| | | What else does my reader need to know? |
| | | What can I explain further? |
| | WHEN? | When is TV a problem? |
| | | When is TV a benefit? |
| | | When will the issue be resolved? |
| | WHERE? | Where does the problem occur? |
| | | Where are the participants? |
| | WHY? | Why is the issue important? |
| | | Why should you or I care? |
| | | Why should my audience care? |
| | HOW? | How did it happen? |
| | | How does it work? |
| | | How can the issue be resolved? |

- Have you used transitions to move the reader smoothly from one idea to the next and to provide cohesion through your essay?
- Have you used concessions—*though, although, even though*—when you need to make one argument appear more important or stronger than another?
- Have you brought in your own research findings?
- Have you included publication information for sources? Have you cited sources correctly?
- Do you have questions or concerns about your essay?

## Edit

Look carefully to catch any errors that tend to be repeated in your writing and use your computer's spell check.

Read your essay aloud. Listen for mistakes and look for typographical errors.

Also consider the following issues:
- Have you used adjectives and adverbs to improve sentences?
- Have you combined sentences for variety?
- Check for fragments, comma splices, and run-ons.

- Ask the tutor to tell you how many (if any) and what type of errors exist so that you can correct them.

## Writing Assignment #3: The TV Rating System and the V-Chip

Here, in brief, is the writing assignment you are preparing for.

> Write an essay in which you argue *for* or *against* the TV rating system and V-chip.

## Read, Discuss, Think Critically

There are three articles included in this assignment. All are from the same newspaper, and all three writers discuss the same issue—monitoring what children watch on television. However, each approaches the issue from a very different perspective.

## Reading Assignment

### "V-Chip: Can It Protect Kids?"

*Preview*   Read the prereading note, the title of the article, and the first four paragraphs.

*Anticipate*   What do you believe the article will be about? Write your response in the "Notes" column.

*Read and Reread*   Read the entire article quickly, marking unknown terms. Then reread more slowly and use the "Notes" column to list ideas or responses. Highlight important points and define unfamiliar terms.

### Prereading Note

On February 8, 1996, President Clinton signed the Telecommunications Act which will, over time, affect all areas of communications technology. Regarding television, the Act calls for the development of a rating system for network and cable programming much like the one used by the MPAA (Motion Picture Association of America). In addition, it requires that a device—the V-chip—be installed in every television sold in American. The V-chip will be electronically encoded with the new television ratings and will enable parents to block out programs they don't want their children to watch. (Currently, the V-chip is in the process of being developed. Check with your local electronic/appliance store to get the most up-to-date information on this evolving technology.)

## V-Chip: Can It Protect Kids?
### by Kathryn Doré Perkins

*This news story appeared in the March 29, 1996, issue of the* Sacramento Bee *newspaper. Kathryn Doré Perkins is a staff writer for the* Bee.

1. A mountain of studies has been built from research like that of Yale researcher Leonard Eron into whether violent TV affects children.

2. After tracking 870 people since 1960, Eron concluded: "Those who had watched a lot of violent television at young ages had more criminal convictions, were more abusive towards their spouses, were more violent under the influence of alcohol and more likely to exhibit a whole host of aggressive behaviors."

3. The debate has shifted from whether violent TV affects children to who is most likely to be affected and what can be done about it.

4. Under pressure from the Clinton administration, network and cable television executives early this month reluctantly agreed to implement by January ratings similar to the G, PG-13 and R codes used for motion pictures. And by 1997 new television sets must carry a computer component—called a V-chip—that would let viewers block out programs.

5. But reviews are mixed on how effective these steps will be in protecting vulnerable children.

6. "The V-chip is a step in the right direction, but the parents who will use it already are concerned about what their children are watching," Eron said. "What concerns me are the parents who can't be with their kids because they're working, or who have no idea what TV is doing to their kids, or parents who just don't care," Eron said.

7. Almost no one really questions that there is more violence in society as a result of TV viewing, said Robert Kubey, professor of communications at Rutgers University. "If even 0.5 percent of kids are at risk, that's 200,000 people who are more violent, and that is serious."

8. As for the V-chip, Kubey said, "I wish I could be more optimistic. Potentially it's a good move, but so much depends on the coding. Will the industry's standards be acceptable and of equal quality across networks? What about news? Kids are particularly frightened by the real-world violence in news. It's hard to watch news anymore without having your finger on the mute button."

9. More effective than V-chips, Kubey said, would be media-education classes to develop kids' perspective about what they watch.

Notes

10. "Critical viewing skills are a required course in other English-speaking countries—Canada, England, New Zealand, Australia, South Africa," he said.

11. Not everyone agrees the television industry should shoulder the responsibility for what children watch on TV or carry the blame for their fears and behavior.

12. "Parents can control what children see on TV. Just turn it off," said Lynn B. Cooper, professor of social work and criminology at California State University, Sacramento.

13. "The fundamental issue is not what is on TV, but that so many parents depend on it as an electronic baby sitter . . . We're not going to accomplish much with the V-chip if we don't deal with issues of exhausted parents who don't spend enough time with their children," said Cooper.

14. "It's very, very difficult to line up the effects of violence from watching television . . . You can't isolate it from the effects of movies, economic status, where you live, the real-life violence kids face on the street and at home," Cooper said.

15. The importance of parental involvement was underscored by the findings of Joanne Cantor, a professor of communications at the University of Wisconsin, who participated in a National Television Violence Study that was released last month. For two years she investigated the reactions of 297 children, ages 5 to 14, to TV and movie ratings.

16. Children who said their parents were involved in their TV viewing were less likely to choose a program with a parent advisory, or a PG-13 or R-rated film. Kids who reported engaging in more aggression-related behaviors were more likely to choose programs with advisories.

17. "Have truth in labeling, use a word we understand, 'Violent,' not 'parental discretion advised,'" said Ron Slabey, a developmental psychologist who teaches "Television and the Developing Child" and "Preventing Violence in America" at Harvard University.

18. Under this month's agreement, television ratings will be set by a panel headed by the president of the Motion Picture Association of America. Network, cable services and syndicators will police themselves. No comment was available from the MPAA.

19. A key to making the V-chip effective, Slabey said, is unrelenting consumer pressure on networks and cable services to be responsible in their programming.

20. "Let's see the industry produce some public service programming related to preventing violence in the media," said Slabey.

21. Kids are susceptible because they don't recognize the unrealistic and glorified, he said. "In TV and the video game world, there are only two options: to be victimized or be the victimizer."

Notes

22      Children most likely to be affected are those who identify with the aggressor or victim, who judge what they see as realistic or relevant to their lives, who have been abused, or who laugh at victimization, he said.

23      Earlier this month a coalition of more than 150 groups from 58 countries launched the Cultural Environment Movement. According to founder George Gerbner, dean emeritus of the Annanberg School for Communication at the University of Pennsylvania, the movement seeks to promote diversity and less-damaging media, particularly in television.

24      "Whoever tells a culture's stories controls the ideas and laws of that culture," Gerbner said.

25      "Even though nonviolent programs get higher ratings, programs are designed with global marketing in mind: Violence travels well; second-best is sex."

### ▼ Questions for Critical Thought

#### "V-Chip: Can It Protect Kids?"

1. What are the two things the Clinton administration has proposed to help families protect their children from TV violence?

2. In paragraph 3, Perkins writes, "The debate has shifted from whether violent TV affects children to who is most likely to be affected and what can be done about it." Explain what she means.

3. Using your quoting and analyzing skills, offer two quotations from experts on the issue of children and TV violence. Do these experts believe children are adversely affected by what they view?

4. What are Professor Eron's concerns about the V-chip?

5. What are Professor Kubey's concerns? What alternative does he offer to the V-chip?

6. What did Professor Cantor discover in her study on violence?

7. What does Psychologist Slabey suggest consumers do to make the networks and cable industry more responsible (in addition to the V-chip)?

8. Perkins, the writer of this news story, has developed her discussion by including facts and examples, but mostly by including expert opinion. Do the experts agree that the V-chip will offer an effective way for monitoring programming and protecting children? If they're not in agreement, how do their views differ? How might a writer decide who is or isn't an expert?

9. Does Perkins offer her own opinion in this article? Does she present the V-chip issue from a biased or unbiased perspective? Explain.

### Reading Assignment

*"What You Can Do about Violent TV"*

*Preview*   Read the title and paragraphs 1–6.

*Anticipate*   What do you think this article will be about? Use the "Notes" column to record your thoughts.

*Read and Reread*   Read the entire article, noting unfamiliar terms. Then reread more slowly and use the "Notes" column to respond to the article. Highlight the most important points and define unknown terms.

### What You Can Do about Violent TV
*by Diana Griego Erwin*

This article, dated June 30, 1996, appeared originally in the *Sacramento Bee*. This version came from NewsBank, Inc.—off the Internet. Author Diana Griego Erwin's columns, which appear in the *Bee* three times a week, address local and national social concerns.

1   Gloria Alafonte, a Carmichael mother of three, considers herself a careful parent, especially when popular culture clashes with child-rearing concerns.

2   Her household harbors no obscene or racy videos. She and her husband, Mario, do not watch television programming with profanity or violence when the children are awake. Even the cartoons their children watch on Saturday mornings are carefully monitored; there are no Power Rangers or Ninja Turtles roughing it up on the Alafonte TV set.

3   Yet even her youngest, Carlo, four, knows who these fighting cartoon characters are. Gloria recalls the first time she saw him mimicking their tough-guy ways on the preschool playground.

4   "Sometimes I feel like everyone, all of society, is conspiring against parents who are trying to let their kids be kids," she said. "When programmers and marketing people have to choose between something good for kids and something that isn't, why not develop ideas that represent something healthy?"

5   Her concerns illustrate why many parents are looking forward to help from the V-chip, a computer chip that will be in every new televi-

sion come January. Proponents of the chip ("V" for violence) say it will help parents by enabling them to block shows depicting violence, profanity and nudity.

6   Except it won't. Or, at least not beginning next year.

7   That's the opinion of Professor Ed Donnerstein, an expert on the mass media, violence and aggression in youth at the University of California, Santa Barbara.

8   "I'm trying to remember when I last bought a new television set," he recently told a Sacramento audience. And what happens to the old one once he does? "Like most parents, we'll probably take the old one upstairs to the kids' room."

9   A separate V-chip will be available, but the kind of parent who retrofits the old set probably doesn't have a problem anyway. That parent probably already is monitoring kids' viewing habits.

10   Despite his reservations about the chip, Donnerstein believes parents should be concerned about violent media images. Every important study reports that American children have more access to violent, sexually explicit television, videos and movies than virtually any other country, he said.

11   Most at risk are children who already have a tendency toward violence. "Once you have an aggressive child, everything they see in the media will reinforce their attitude that violence is how you solve problems," he said.

12   "There is no doubt that higher levels of viewing violence are correlated to increased acceptance of aggressive attitudes and increased aggressive behavior."

13   Why Americans, specifically, possess a thirst for such images is an interesting question. The rape scene in "Showgirls" was cut in virtually every other country. Some completely banned "Natural Born Killers." Even the Mighty Morphin Power Rangers are banned in several countries, including Canada and Australia.

14   Studies show TV violence fails to acknowledge the true nature of pain and suffering. One study found that seventy-three percent of the bad guys go unpunished: fifty percent of the violence shows no pain or harm to the victim. Only four percent of all programming carries an anti-violent message.

15   Donnerstein said that exposure to such images over time results in a desensitized nation. "The more we watch, the more we can watch." His suggestions:

- Watch television together. My tip: You can say TV viewing isn't allowed when you're not there.

- Restrict viewing of violence, explaining these restrictions to your children. My tip: In time, they might even come to agree with your opinions.
- Engage in other activities with your child. My tip: Have your child make a list of the Top 10 everyday activities he or she likes to do. You'll be surprised at how far down the list TV is, if it appears at all.
- Know what your child watches. Fifty-five percent of children watch television alone, and forty-four percent watch something different when their parents aren't around.

16   It's no less important than checking out the friends a child chooses. To many children, the TV is a surrogate friend.

17   Alafonte remembers dropping in on a fourteen-year-old neighbor who was home alone, only to find him transfixed by a sensual music video. "I asked his mother about it, and she said, 'It was MTV, right? Isn't that for kids?'"

## ▼ Questions for Critical Thought

### "What You Can Do about Violent TV"

1. In the opening paragraph the reader is introduced to Gloria Alafonte, a mother of three. What are her concerns regarding TV, society, and parenting?

2. Later in the article, Professor Donnerstein offers his expert opinion on the future of television and the V-chip. Discuss Donnerstein's views on the V-chip. How do his views compare to the experts cited by Perkins in the previous article?

3. What do studies on TV violence reveal, according to Donnerstein?

4. Paraphrase Donnerstein's suggestions to parents regarding children and their viewing habits.

5. In "V-chip: Can It Protect Kids?" Perkins develops her article by citing experts. Griego Erwin uses expert opinion, too, but she relies on other kinds of support as well. What other form(s) of support does she use to develop her discussion?

6. Griego Erwin opens her column with a scenario involving a concerned mother. How does this opening differ from Perkins' news story?

**Notes**

7. Does Griego Erwin offer her own opinion in this article? From what perspective does she present the V-chip issue? Does she present a biased or unbiased view? Explain.

### Reading Assignment

*"V-Chip Will Add to Parental Chaos"*

*Preview*   Read the title and paragraphs 1–3.

*Anticipate*   What do you anticipate this article will be about? Record your response in the "Notes" column.

*Read and reread*   Read the entire article, being careful to highlight unknown terms and interesting points. Then reread more slowly and write your responses in the "Notes" column as you read. Finally, mark important points and define unknown terms.

### V-Chip Will Add to Parental Chaos
*by Michael Kilian*

Michael Kilian, writer and humorist, is a lifestyle columnist for the *Chicago Tribune*. His columns also appear in the *Sacramento Bee* and other newspapers across the country.

1   When you get suggestions from the fox about what kind of fencing to put around your chicken coop, a modicum of caution might be necessary.

2   A wrathfully righteous Congress is hellbent on ridding the nation's television screens of bullet sprays, bloody beatings, exploding bodies, Gail "NYPD Blue" O'Grady's unclothed cleavage and Dennis Franz's less than muscle-toned bare behind—replacing it all with what, "Gospel Time" and the Muppets?

3   This congressional bent for hell has already produced a pile of statutory tonnage called the Telecommunications Act of 1996, and in it a provision calling for the inclusion in television set circuitry of a magical "V-Chip" that will allow parents to program out a show rated "V" for violent with the same ease with which they now program their VCRs.

4   The television nutworks have responded to this with a great dither, from which has swiftly emerged a proposal from, yes, the Fox nutwork—to impose the same rating system on TV programs that the movie industry has long put on their movies.

5   Parents look up a show's rating, program their V-Chips accordingly, and little Junior and Sis will grow up to be Baptist ministers.

6   The "G," "PG," "PG-13," "R" and "NC-17" rating system has indeed worked well—for the movie industry. Go up to any group of shopping mall teenagers (the hard core of today's movie audiences) and ask them.

7   They'll tell you (in their own unintelligible words) that "G" to them means cuddly Disney movies for those who cannot yet talk—or walk; "PG" means movies for those who can walk and talk (sort of) that feature kids throwing up and breaking things and grown-ups looking dopey; "PG-13" means films that actual adults might possibly be willing to sit through; "R" stands for Real Movies that kids actually want to see; and "NC-17" means something even better than the Playboy magazine they've got hidden under the mattress.

8   As simple and understandable as this is for our nation's teens, I find the movie rating system wholly incomprehensible. A fine film like "Gettysburg," for example, gets a mere "PG"—one step up from "Snow White"—while Mel Gibson's equally fine "Braveheart" gets an "R." Yet they're both about precisely the same thing: mobs of patriotic men bashing one another's brains out.

9   Brilliant Shakespeare, in the form of Sir Ian McKellan's "Richard III," and compelling history, such as Steven Spielberg's "Schindler's List," get "R" ratings that keep teenagers from seeing them. Disgusting films like Sharon Stone's weirdo kinky sicko "Basic Instinct" and Linda Fiorentino's weirdo kinky sicko barfy "Jade" get "R" ratings, because though they deal almost wholly with NC-17 and X-rated subject matter, sufficient amounts of body parts have been snipped out.

10   And who stands guard over the morals of our movie-going youth? Often some teenage ticket-taker not old enough to see the films. And they're stationed at the main entrance, not at the various entrances of the individual multiplex mini-auditoriums.

11   And, anyway, like, man, who cares?

12   Who then will stand guardian at the home television V-Chips? Parents? Ho, ho and ho. Today's mommies and daddies are devoting the bulk of their time to avoiding downsizing and holding onto their jobs, so they can keep food in the cupboard and/or a second Mercedes in the garage. And when they're not off putting in ten and twelve hour days (including commuting time), they're off jogging or trying to find cyberporn on the Internet.

13   Can you see a mommy who's just collapsed in her sweats wanting to get up and reprogram the V-Chip for tonight's view of Dennis Franz's behind or the 12th broadcast this month of "Lethal Weapon III"? Fatigue is why she turned over parenting to the television set in the first place.

Notes

14    And households today don't have just one set to program. Every kid has his or her own TV—or else.

15    And, as my good friend the anti-smut-and-violence crusader Sen. Paul Simon, D-Ill., points out, a rating system would direct the kids to exactly the programs they want to see. Miss Piggy gets a "G"—or, more likely, a "PG." Avoiding that, kids can simply follow the "R" to Sharon Stone uncrossing her legs.

16    As Washington *Post* media writer Paul Farhi observes, the nutworks can feel free to load up with Sharon Stone smut and Sylvester Stallone smash bash, bang bang by hiding behind the rating system and V-Chip—saying now it's up to the parents.

### ▼ Questions for Critical Thought

#### "V-Chip Will Add to Parental Chaos"

1. In the opening paragraph Kilian states, "When you get suggestions from the fox about what kind of fencing to put around your chicken coop, a *modicum* of caution might be necessary." Tongue-in-cheek (with humor), Kilian makes a comparison between a fox guarding a chicken coop and the Fox network monitoring what's on television. What's his point in making such a comparison? Does this comparison (called an **analogy**) set the tone/attitude of the piece? If so, what is the tone?* How does the writer feel about the government's attempt to regulate television?

2. Skimming the article again, look for words or sentences that indicate the writer's attitude or sense of humor. Write down any wording that reveals his attitude or sense of humor and explain it. Does his attitude remain consistent?

3. How does Kilian view the proposed television rating system? What example(s) or comparison(s) does he use to support his view?

4. How does Kilian view the proposed V-chip? What example(s) does he use to support his view?

5. Does Kilian rely on expert opinion in the same way that Perkins and Griego Erwin do in the two earlier articles? Explain.

6. Kilian suggests that the networks like the idea of the V-chip. Why does he believe this to be so? Do you agree or disagree? Why?

---

*While Kilian's flip/humorous attitude is appropriate in this newspaper column, such an attitude might not be appropriate in an academic essay.

7. Does Kilian present a biased or unbiased view on the V-chip? Explain.

> ### Journal Assignment
> #### Responding to the V-Chip and TV Ratings
> Consider the three articles you've read on the issues of a rating system for television and the V-chip. Which of the arguments presented makes the most sense in your opinion? Why? Which makes the least sense? What have you learned about the television rating system and/or V-chip from reading the three articles? Consider your own personal views regarding children and television. In your view, whose responsibility is it to monitor what children watch? Why? Exchange your journal with a classmate or two. When you return someone else's journal, just say "Thank You."

## Explore the Writing Assignment

Here, again, is your writing assignment. Consider it carefully before continuing. Note the important words in this assignment.

*Write an essay in which you argue **for** or **against** the TV rating system and V-chip.*

## ▼ Activity

### Making Recommendations

One method of exploring the topic is to consider various views on the issue. In the activity that follows you'll hear a variety of opinions on the subject.

1. Divide the class into three groups. Each group will form a committee. One committee will represent parents, one government, and one the television industry. (Depending on which group you're in, imagine you're a member of Congress, a Ted Turner, or a PTA member.) Your committee's goal will be to make recommendations regarding television and what's best for children.

2. Define your group's responsibility in terms of children and television. What, if any, are your concerns? And why is your group concerned? Write out these concerns. Consider the negative and positive aspects of the television rating system and the V-chip. Write these down. Besides ratings and the V-chip, what other suggestions would your group make that might help curb the negative effects of television?

Notes

> Write these down. As a committee come to an agreement about which are your most important recommendations.

3. Share your concerns and suggestions with the class. Do you see overlapping areas of concern? How do the three groups' views vary on the issue of a television rating system and the V-chip? How are the views similar? What interesting and/or unique suggestions have been made regarding other ways to help curb the negative effects of television?

---

### Journal Assignment

*Evaluating the Recommendations*

Respond to the activity. Did you learn anything new from considering the views of other groups? Have you changed your mind about the television rating system or the V-chip? Write down any additional thoughts on the subject.

---

### ▼ Activities

*Considering the Experts' Views*

Another way to explore the issue would be to return to the three articles and list experts' opinions and findings. This will help you consider a variety of views as you write.

| Expert Opinions<br>The V-chip and Rating System |||
|---|---|---|
| **The Expert**<br>**(name/position)** | **Expert's Opinion**<br>**and Sources** | **Do you agree or**<br>**disagree? Why?** |
| | | |

Once you've listed the experts and their findings, look to see who's in agreement and who's not. Who do you agree with? Why? Be sure to add to this list as you find other sources. (Add more pages as necessary.) As you write, you'll draw support from this list.

### Look for Information on the Internet

Another way to explore the topic is to look for information on the Internet.

Spend an hour on the Internet to find up-to-date information. Search using any of the following words:

Telecommunications Act

V-chip

Television Rating System

Take notes as you research the topic. Consider placing information on note cards as suggested in Chapter 6.

---

*Brainstorm*   Spend five to ten minutes writing on each of the positions that follow.
- Some people believe that by using a rating system for television and the V-chip, parents will be better equipped to monitor their children's viewing habits and protect them from violent or sexually explicit material.
- Others cite problems with the rating system and V-chip and wonder how some parents will even be able to afford the technology or how overworked parents will find the time to "program" the TV set to block out offensive shows.
- Still others believe that the rating system and V-chip are merely smoke-screens for the television industry which would have more freedom to air violence and nudity since it would be left up to parents to block inappropriate programs.
- Finally there are those who suggest that the government has no business regulating what is aired. They regard the proposed restrictions as a violation of First Amendment rights (or freedom of speech).

When you are done writing on these positions, review each of your brainstorms and decide which position you want to take on this issue. Highlight the parts of the brainstorm you think might be useful when writing your essay.

Notes

***Consider Your Audience*** The audience for this paper is a general one made up of parents, educators, and other members of the community. Some are worried about the content of many television programs and children's access to these programs. Others are concerned about the government's proposal to help restrict programming. Many are unsure about how to deal with the issue of TV ratings and the V-chip. Think about how you might address a general audience with your point of view. Write down which points you could make to help persuade the undecided in the group to consider your position on the issue of TV ratings and the V-chip.

***Create Your Thesis*** Your thesis should reflect that you have narrowed the scope of your essay to take a position on the issue of TV ratings and the V-chip. Experiment with thesis statements until you find one that expresses what you want to focus on in your essay.

***Outline*** Keeping your thesis in mind, list two or three main points you'll argue in your essay. Under each point note the kind of support you'll use to develop your thesis. Also consider what your opponent (the person on the other side) might say about your position. (You may need to admit that your opponent has valid arguments. However, your arguments should outweigh your opponent's arguments.)

Here are some ways for you to consider organizing your arguments:
- Present least important ideas first, most important ideas last.
- List least interesting ideas first, most interesting ideas last.
- Alternate your views with your opponent's views.
- Present all your opponent's points (divided into different paragraphs), then all your points (divided into different paragraphs).

## Draft

Referring to your expert opinion list, your discussion notes, journals, activities, Questions for Critical Thought, and your brainstorm, begin writing your essay. Your introduction should offer an explanation of how the TV rating system and V-chip work as well as the controversy surrounding them. Your introduction should also state your position on the issue. In the body of your essay, your job is to present your view (one main idea per paragraph) and refute the opposition (show why the opposition is wrong). Your ultimate goal is to convince your reader to believe as you do about the subject. Be sure to bring in plenty of evidence to help support your view.

*Notes*

## Revise

▼

**Share Your Writing**

Working with a classmate, review the following:

- Have you established your position on the issue? Have you presented the sides fairly?
- Can your reader follow your organizational pattern? Have you presented one argument at a time? Is it clear which paragraphs are pro arguments and which are con?
- Have you developed/supported your ideas fully? Have you relied on experts' findings?
- Have you considered the Questions for Development?

    WHO?    Who is my audience?

    Who is interested in the issue?

    Who believes the TV rating system and V-chip is the answer?

    Who believes the TV rating system and V-chip won't solve the problem?

    WHAT?   What are the various arguments raised?

    What else does my reader need to know?

    What can I explain further?

    WHEN?   When is it a problem?

    When is it a benefit?

    When will the issue be resolved?

    WHERE?  Where does the problem occur?

    Where are the participants?

    WHY?    Why is the issue important?

    Why should you or I care?

    HOW?    How did the technology come about?

    How does it work?

    How can the issue be resolved?

*Notes*

- Have you used transitions effectively to move the reader smoothly from one idea to the next and to provide cohesion through your essay?

- Have you used concessions—*though, although, even though*—when you need to make one argument appear more important or stronger than another?

- Have you included evidence from the articles in the text?

- Have you brought in your own research findings?

- Have you included publication information for sources? Have you cited sources correctly?

- Do you have any questions or concerns about your essay?

## Edit

Read through your essay aloud. Reread it to catch any errors. Be sure to use spell check.

Also consider the following issues:

- Have you used adjectives and adverbs to improve sentences?
- Have you combined sentences for variety?
- Check for fragments, comma splices, and run-ons.
- Ask the tutor to tell you how many (if any) errors and what kind so that you can correct them.

## ▲▼▲ Time to Reflect

### *Journal Assignment*

### Your Progress as a Writer, Reader, and Critical Thinker

Think about what you've learned about development in this chapter. Write a journal entry explaining what you've learned. You may want to think about these questions before you write.

- What should writers keep in mind when developing their paragraph or essay ideas?
- How do the Questions for Development help writers fully develop their ideas?
- What have you learned about developing a discussion or argument?

## ▲▼▲ Summary of Chapter 7

In this chapter you have

- strengthened your development skills as you carefully selected examples, statistics, personal experience, and expert opinion to support your views on television and its effect on the family;
- learned the importance of expanding your discussion by applying the Questions for Development;
- expressed your point of view and have considered the views of others in your writing; and
- worked toward achieving a healthy balance between evidence and explanation in your writing.

Notes

Section II  Employing the Connections

Notes

### ▲▼▲ Creating Expressive Sentences

*Using Adjectives to Improve Sentences*
*Using Adverbs to Improve Sentences*
*Using Prepositional Phrases to Improve Sentences*

In this text so far, you've learned sentence terms and how to identify and avoid sentence errors. Now you'll have an opportunity to practice some of your creative skills as you experiment with sentences to make them more descriptive and expressive.

**Examining the Kernel Sentence**
First, let's look at the kernel sentence. The **kernel sentence** is the basic subject and predicate of a simple sentence.

Examples: (subjects are underlined once, predicates are underlined twice)
a) The television is on.
b) The child watches the monsters and bears.
c) The child enjoys the songs and the stories.
d) The parents watch the show, too.
e) The parents and child discuss the program.

Read sentences a–e aloud. Imagine that this is a paragraph from an essay. Most readers would find these sentences (and the essay) choppy and boring.

**Constructing More Meaningful Sentences**
So how do writers make their sentences and essays more interesting? How do writers pack in more meaning? Experienced writers do a number of different things to make their writing come alive:

- They use adjectives to describe the nouns in their sentences.
- They use adverbs to describe the action in their sentences.
- They use prepositions to add more meaning to their sentences.
- They **embed** (or insert) phrases in their sentences to include more information.
- They combine sentences to show relationships between their ideas.
  You'll begin practicing all these methods in this chapter.

## Using Adjectives to Improve Sentences

Adjectives, as you probably remember, are words that describe nouns. (Nouns are people, places, things, or ideas.)

Example (nouns are highlighted, adjectives are in color):

f) The young children want to watch their favorite television program.

g) The tired parents hope the educational program will interest the rambunctious* kids.

Draw arrows from the adjectives to the nouns they describe.

*Class Activity:* List some adjectives on the chalkboard. If you are unsure if a word is an adjective, see if you can use it before a noun in a sentence. Be sure to list some adjectives that you might use in an essay on television.

Here, again, are our kernel sentences:
a) The television is on.
b) The child watches the monsters and bears.
c) The child enjoys the songs and stories.
d) The parents watch the show, too.
e) The parents and child discuss the program.

1. Highlight the nouns you see in the kernel sentences. These are the words that you will make more interesting by using adjectives.

2. In small groups, rewrite sentences b–e, adding adjectives that make the sentences more interesting. (Do not use adverbs or prepositions yet. You'll work with those later.)

3. Share your sentences with your class.

Here is one way to improve sentence a.

The new, expensive television is on.

Note: In the new version of sentence a, there are two adjectives that describe *television*, so there must be a comma between the two adjectives. Review Punctuation Rule #1.

## Punctuation Rule #1 (review)
Separate items in a series with commas.

---

*\*rambunctious* means noisy and active.

*Notes*

Examples: The hot, delicious food is on the table.
He is tall, skinny, and handsome.
The last comma before *and* is optional.

### Sentence Combining—Using Adjectives

In the following exercises, the "K" sentence will be your kernel sentence. The sentences below this kernel sentence will have information (in this case, adjectives that are in color) that you should *add into the kernel sentence*. Of course, you'll have to write the new sentence in your notebook.

Examples:

K: I cannot watch television programs at my grandparents' house.
The television programs are violent.
The television programs are sexy.

New Sentence: I cannot watch violent, sexy television programs at my grandparents' house.

K: They watch only programs on PBS.
The programs are educational.

New Sentence: They watch only educational programs on PBS.

Combine the following sentences and use correct punctuation. (The new sentences you write in exercises 1–14 can be written as three paragraphs: 1–6, 7–10, and 11–14.)

*"Reading Winn"*

When completing #1, remember the "a/an rule." Use "a" before words that start with consonant sounds and "an" before words that start with vowel sounds.

1. K: Marie Winn wrote an essay called "The Trouble with Television."
   The essay is lengthy.
2. K: With essays that have points, it is useful to first read just the introduction, subheadings, and conclusion.
   The essays are long.
   The points are many.
3. K: Then when the experienced reader has time, she can read through the essay quickly.
   The time is ample.
   The essay is complete.
4. K: While reading, she should underline words.
   The words are unfamiliar.

5. K: Some of the words in Winn's essay are "cynical," "burdensome," and "wields."
   The words are difficult.

6. K: These are words to learn and use, but the reader doesn't have to look up their meanings when she first sees them.
   These words are important.
   The reader is efficient.

7. K: After taking these steps, the reader might want to set goals for a rereading.
   The rereading should be careful.

8. K: For example, the reader might decide to reread and take notes on just the first points.
   The points are four.

9. K: This time, she could look up words and highlight points.
   The words are unfamiliar.
   The points are significant.

10. K: Then, the next day, the reader could tackle the second points.
    The reader is smart.
    The points are four.

11. K: Additionally, the reader might write a summary about the essay.
    The summary is short.

12. K: Also, she should find an opportunity to discuss and respond to the points in Winn's essay.
    The points are key.

13. K: She might do this in class, with a study group, or with a tutor.
    The tutor is helpful.

14. K: Breaking up tasks into pieces is a study strategy.
    The tasks are long.
    The pieces are manageable.
    The study strategy is good.

### Sentence Combining—Using *-ing* Adjectives

An *-ing* word cannot be a verb without a helper, and if the *-ing* word is not working as a verb, it could be acting as either a noun or an adjective. Let's review how *-ing* words function as adjectives.

**Notes**

Examples of *-ing words* working as adjectives:

The singing dinosaur is Barney.

The dancing children are tired.

The laughing baby dinosaur is called Baby Bop.

Notice that in the sentences above, the single *-ing word* goes *before* the noun it describes.

Examples of *-ing phrases* working as adjectives.

The dinosaur singing the song is Barney.

The children dancing the tango are tired.

The baby dinosaur laughing loudly is called Baby Bop.

The parent plugging her ears is tired of Barney.

Notice that in the sentences above, the *-ing phrase* goes *after* the noun it describes.

Combine the following choppy sentences to create descriptive, sophisticated sentences. (You'll be adding regular adjectives and *-ing* adjectives into the kernel sentences.) In the first four sentences, the adjectives that you should add into the kernel sentences are in color. Remember to punctuate your sentences correctly. (The new sentences you create in exercises 1–13 can be written as a paragraph.)

*"War Time"*

It is 1944, and televisions are scarce. Kids find other ways to fill their time.

1. K: The boys are hurrying off to play in the lot.
   The boys are laughing.
   The lot is vacant.

2. K: The boys are the kids there.
   The boys are carrying the shoe boxes of toy soldiers.
   The kids are first.

3. K: The sun warms their backs as they carefully divide up the toy soldiers, cannons, and materials.
   The sun is shining down on them.
   The toy soldiers are made of lead.
   The canons are sturdy.
   The materials are for building.

4. K: The boy digs his trenches and carefully places his soldiers.
   The boy is freckled.
   The boy is working quietly.
   His soldiers are small.
   His soldiers are serious.

5. K: He thinks carefully about his strategy.
   His strategy is for war.

6. K: By lunch time a battlefield is ready.
   The battlefield is enormous.
   (Remember use "an" before words that start with a vowel.)

7. K: The boys break for lunch.
   The boys are hungry.

8. K: Then, with the sun on the men, the battle begins.
   The sun is hot.
   The sun is beating down.
   The men are young.
   The battle is raging.

9. K: The boys test their strategies.
   The boys are yelling.
   The boys are arguing.

10. K: Plans must be altered and sacrifices made.
    The sacrifices are hard.

11. K: The boy launches one attack.
    The boy is freckled.
    The attack is final.
    The attack is violent.

12. K: His planning has paid off.
    His planning was extensive.

13. K: The boy yells, "Victory!"
    The boy is freckled.
    The boy is raising his arms in triumph.

*Notes*

When completing items 4, 9, and 11, remember Punctuation Rule #1.

## Sentence Combining—Using Have Form *Adjectives*

There is another verb form that can act as an adjective: the *have form* of a verb. Usually the have form of a verb is the base form plus *-ed*. (The *base form* is the form you find listed first in the dictionary.) If the have

**Notes**

form is used with a helper verb, then the have form is being used as a verb. However, without the helper verb, the have form can be an adjective.

Examples:

| base forms | have forms |
|---|---|
| experience | experienced |
| supervise | supervised |
| walk | walked |
| look | looked |

Sometimes the have form is *irregular* (doesn't follow the normal pattern).

Examples:

| base forms | have forms |
|---|---|
| show | shown |
| see | seen |
| sing | sung |
| buy | bought |

For more examples, see the Chart of Irregular Verbs on pages 476 and 477.

If you are ever unsure about verb forms, you can look up the base form in the dictionary. After the base form, you'll find the past-tense form, the have form, and finally the *-ing* form. If the past-tense and have forms are the same, the dictionary will only list that form once. (See Using the Dictionary, page 438, for more information about how dictionaries are set up.)

Examples of the have form of verbs acting as adjectives:
The program shown late at night is meant for adults.
The violence seen on that program is graphic.

Now try some more sentence combining that uses all the types of adjectives we have discussed (regular adjectives, *-ing* adjectives, have form adjectives.) (The new sentences you write in exercises 1–9 can be written as a paragraph.)

*"Artist at Work"*

1. K: The girl's cousin sits in front of the television.
    The cousin is staring blankly at the Superman cartoon.

2. K: The girl leaves the room and sits at the kitchen table.
   The girl is bored.
   The girl is unused to watching television.
   The kitchen table is cluttered.

3. K: After moving the muffin, the coffee, and the newspaper her grandmother left behind, she takes out her paper and begins to create a spaceship.
   The muffin is half-eaten.
   The coffee is cold.
   Her paper is for drawing.

4. K: She is only seven years old, but she is an artist.
   The artist is experienced.

5. K: The girl in the kitchen draws the shell of the ship.
   The girl is concentrating.
   The kitchen is quiet.
   The shell is exterior.
   (Hint: Put "concentrating" at the beginning of the sentence and put a comma after it. You've now used an adjective as an introductory word to a sentence.)

6. K: However, she doesn't stop with the exterior.
   The exterior is simple.

7. K: She draws another view of the ship.
   The view of the ship is showing the interior control panels.
   The interior control panels are complicated.

8. K: She carefully details the buttons and switches.
   The buttons and switches are many.

9. K: She gazes up at the sky and imagines soaring away.
   She is finished.
   The sky is clear.
   (Hint: Start your sentence with the adjective "finished" and put a comma after it.)

**Your Own Work**   Create three sentences that might show up in an essay about television. Make sure that each sentence uses adjectives that help add vivid detail and meaning. Underline the adjectives in your sentences.

## Notes

### Using Adverbs to Improve Sentences

**Adverbs** are words that describe verbs, adjectives, other adverbs, and whole groups of words. Often (but not always), adverbs end in *-ly*. Adverbs usually explain *where, when, how, why,* or *to what extent.*

Examples of adverbs (the adverb is in color and the word it is describing is underlined once):

One father sadly complains about the television.

He says his child watches TV constantly.

The child listens intently to the television but not to his father.

Draw arrows from the adverbs to the words they describe.

*Class Activity:* List some adverbs on the chalkboard. If you are unsure if a word can be used as an adverb, try putting it into a sentence and discussing it with your classmates. Be sure to put some adverbs on the board that you might use in an essay on television.

In the following exercises, combine sentences using adverbs to add meaning. The words that are (or will become) adverbs are in color.

1. K: The eight-year-old boy and his dad watch a situation comedy on television.
   They watch quietly.

2. K: Although the program is funny, it does mention gangs.
   Most of the program is funny.
   (Hint: Change "most" into an adverb by adding *ly*. Put the new adverb before the adjective "funny.")

3. K: After the program, the dad listens to his son's views on gangs.
   The dad listens carefully.

4. K: The father is surprised to find out that his son learned something about gangs from television.
   The surprise is pleasant.
   (Hint: Change "pleasant" into an adverb by adding *ly*. Put the new adverb before the verb "surprised.")

### Sentence Combining—Using Adverbs and Adjectives

In the following exercises, combine sentences using adjectives and adverbs to add meaning. (You may have to change an adjective into an adverb when combining sentences.)

"A Response to Anderson's Points"

1. K: Mr. Anderson, you don't believe that Americans should throw out their television sets.
   Your beliefs are clear.
   The television sets are beloved.
   (Hint: change "clear" into an adverb and put it before "don't believe.")

2. K: You say that television doesn't mesmerize our people.
   Our people are young.

3. K: In addition, you don't believe that the television hurts a child's attention span or intellect.
   The television is mighty.

4. K: You argue that the theory about children turning into boob tube zombies is based on evidence.
   You are forceful in your arguments.
   The theory is old.
   The theory is largely based on evidence.
   The evidence is anecdotal.
   (Hint: change "forceful" into an adverb that describes "argue.")

5. K: As I understand "anecdotal evidence," you mean that people have been drawing conclusions from watching just a few kids.
   These people have been careless in drawing their conclusions.
   The conclusions are big.
   (Hint: change "careless" into an adverb and put it in front of "drawing.")

6. K: The studies, you say, suggest that children do think about and engage with their programs.
   The studies are real.
   The studies make this suggestion strongly.
   The programs are favorite.

7. K: I wish you had stated what studies you are referring to.
   You should have been clear in your statements.
   (Hint: change "clear" into an adverb that describes "stated.")

8. K: I'd like to look at these studies because I'm not convinced that changing the channel is a sign that the child is thinking in any way about the program he is watching.

Notes

These studies are important.
I'm not completely convinced.
I don't know if the way is meaningful.

9. K: However, I am persuaded by your argument that television programs can help kids learn.
The persuasion is more.
The television programs are certain.

10. K: And I also like your point that TV watching doesn't cause grades.
The TV watching is excessive.
The grades are bad.

11. K: Things cause grades.
The things are many.
The grades are bad.

12. K: And excessive TV watching might be a symptom or sign of problems at home.
The problems are serious.

Hint: Don't forget the "a/an" rule.

13. K: At the end of your essay, you point out that there should be concern about children watching television programs on a basis.
The concern is serious.
The television programs are adult.
The basis is unsupervised.

Hint: change "astute" into an adverb.

14. K: You also noted that, again, it is the parent who must be responsible for helping the child understand and benefit from what is on television.
Your notation was astute.

Hint: change "negative" into an adverb.

15. K: The child in a household where violence is acceptable might be influenced by the violence he sees on television.
The child is neglected.
The influence is negative.

16. K: I guess one of your points is that parents must be regulators and interpreters if we want television to be an influence on our children.
The point is a main one.
The regulators must be active.
The influence can be positive.

*Your Own Work*   Create three sentences that might show up in an essay about television. Use adverbs to create more meaning and detail. Underline the adverbs you have added.

## Using Prepositional Phrases to Improve Sentences

A prepositional phrase, as we studied in Chapter 3, is a phrase made up of a preposition and its object. These phrases can add significant information to sentences, making the sentences far more compelling.

Examples of sentences with prepositional phrases: (the prepositional phrases are bracketed)
[In her essay "The Trouble with Television,"] Marie Winn discusses her concerns [about television.]
She writes [about children, parents, families] and how they are all affected [by television.]
Daniel R. Anderson offers another point [of view] [in his essay] "How TV Influences Your Kids."

Class Activity: List some prepositional phrases on the chalkboard that might show up in an essay about television.

Combine the following sentences, using prepositional phrases to create more interesting sentences. The prepositional phrases that should be added to the kernel sentences are bracketed.

1. K: When I write I always research the issue.
   I write [about controversial issues].
   I research [at the library].

2. K: I go to find articles.
   I go [to the computers].
   The articles are [from magazines and newspapers].

3. K: Last week the librarian helped me find information.
   The information was [for my essay].
   My essay is [about violence and Bugs Bunny].

## Sentence Combining–Using Prepositional Phrases, Adjectives, and Adverbs

Combine the following sentences, using prepositional phrases, adjectives, and adverbs to add greater detail and meaning. (The new sentences you write in exercises 1–9 can be written as two paragraphs.)

Notes

*"Instructor Big Bird"*

1. K: The mother sang the ABC song.
   She sang happily.

2. K: The child just smiled.
   The child was small.
   The child was sweet.

3. K: The mother asked the child to sing.
   The mother was patient.
   The singing was with her.

4. K: But the child laughed and pointed and said, "You!"
   The child only laughed.
   The pointing was at her mom.
   [New paragraph]

5. K: Later, the child watched *Sesame Street*.
   It was later in the morning.

6. K: When Big Bird began to sing the ABC song and dance around, the child sang too.
   Big Bird danced happily.

7. K: The child tripped, but she was trying.
   The tripping was over the l-m-n-o-p sequence.
   The trying was at least.

8. K: The mother listened and smiled.
   The listening was to her child
   The child was struggling.
   The struggling was with the ABC song.

9. K: The child would learn.
   The learning would be easy. (Hint: change "easy" into an adverb.)
   The learning is with the help.
   The help is of Big Bird.

**Your Own Work** Write three sentences that you might use in an essay about television. Use some prepositional phrases in these practice sentences. Underline the prepositional phrases you use.

# Writing about Music and Poetry

**CHAPTER 8**

*Main Topics*

- Inferring and analyzing in your essays
- Communicating your interpretations of song lyrics and poems
- Joining sentences with coordinators and subordinators

*Sacramento Bee.* March 7, 1996, E:6.

*Notes*

On the job and in college, you'll frequently use your analysis and inference skills. These critical thinking skills require you to break down something complex into smaller pieces (**analyze**) and figure out meaning by studying these pieces (**infer**). You analyze and infer frequently throughout your day. For instance, if you ask a friend to drive you to the library, and your friend heaves a big sigh and says, "Oh, I guess I could if I have to." You automatically *analyze* the sigh and the words "guess" and "have to," and you *infer* that even though your friend said he would drive you, he doesn't really want to.

In other situations, analyzing and inferring can be more challenging. In a laboratory, for example, a scientist might analyze large bodies of data and infer information about how a particular cancer is caused, or a business person might study a product or market and infer information about how to best sell the product. In college, a history student might analyze the events leading to World War I and infer information about the cause of the war, or a literature student might analyze a novel and infer meaning from the text as part of the course work. In this chapter, you'll strengthen your analytical and inferential skills as you think about music lyrics and poetry, two forms of communication that often need to be studied in depth in order to be fully understood and appreciated.

## ▲▼▲ Analysis and Inference in Your Writing

As you may have guessed, all the essays you've been writing have required you to analyze and infer. You may have studied advertisements and inferred information about the types of audiences the ads were aimed at. You may have analyzed information about people and determined whether or not they qualified as heroes. You may have also analyzed the advantages and disadvantages of technology and television. Academic writing assignments generally require this kind of critical thinking, since studying information and discovering relationships, causes, effects, advantages, and disadvantages are at the core of college work. In this chapter, you'll take a closer look at what you've been doing in your essays and further sharpen your analytical skills.

## Analyzing and Inferring in Your Essays

When you wrote your earlier essays, you took large topics (advertising, heroes, technology, television), and broke them down into smaller pieces (one ad, one heroic person, a few advantages or disadvantages of technology or television), analyzed key facts, and inferred information. For example, if you wrote about advertising, you selected one ad to study closely and broke that down into smaller pieces to look at colors, words, people, props. In fact, if there were people in the ad, you looked even more closely and studied their age, ethnicity, expressions, clothing, posture, and so on. From this information, you inferred the advertiser's message and who the advertiser was trying to attract with the ad.

Breaking large topics down into smaller pieces is what analytical and inferential thinking is all about. The structure of an academic essay is perfect for this kind of work. The thesis allows you to state a main idea, and the paragraphs allow you to discuss pieces of that main idea one at a time. To do this well, a writer must utilize an effective writing process that allows her to explore, learn, divide things into smaller pieces, and think critically. Brainstorming, discussing, reading, outlining, drafting, revising, and editing make such exploration and learning possible.

## Analyzing and Inferring in Your Paragraphs

As you've read, academic essays are structured perfectly for analytical writing. The paragraph, in particular, offers an effective structure for analysis and inference. The topic sentence allows the writer to state one specific point that supports the thesis of the essay. Then the writer can offer detailed support gathered through reading, discussion, and critical thinking. Finally, the writer can explain her support and show how it indeed supports the topic sentence.

▼

### Study These Data and This Analytical Paragraph

Here are some statistics that were published in the *World Almanac and Book of Facts*, 1998.

*Notes*

**Sales of Recorded Music and Music Videos, by Genre and Format, 1992–96**

Source: Recording Industry Assn. of America, Washington, D.C.

**Breakdown by percentage of all recorded music sold.**

| Genre | 1992 | 1993 | 1994 | 1995 | 1996 |
|---|---|---|---|---|---|
| Rock | 31.6 | 30.2 | 35.1 | 33.5 | 32.6 |
| Country | 17.4 | 18.7 | 16.3 | 16.7 | 14.7 |
| Urban Contemp. | 9.8 | 10.6 | 9.6 | 11.3 | 12.1 |
| Pop | 11.5 | 11.9 | 10.3 | 10.1 | 9.3 |
| Rap | 8.6 | 9.2 | 7.9 | 6.7 | 8.9 |
| Gospel | 2.8 | 3.2 | 3.3 | 3.1 | 4.3 |
| Classical | 3.7 | 3.3 | 3.7 | 2.9 | 3.4 |
| Jazz | 3.8 | 3.1 | 3.0 | 3.0 | 3.3 |
| Oldies | 0.8 | 1.0 | 0.8 | 1.0 | 0.8 |
| Soundtracks | 0.7 | 0.7 | 1.0 | 0.9 | 0.8 |
| New Age | 1.2 | 1.0 | 1.0 | 0.7 | 0.7 |
| Children's | 0.5 | 0.4 | 0.4 | 0.5 | 0.7 |
| Other | 5.4 | 4.6 | 5.3 | 7.0 | 5.2 |

| Format | 1992 | 1993 | 1994 | 1995 | 1996 |
|---|---|---|---|---|---|
| Compact disc (CD) | 46.5 | 51.1 | 58.4 | 65.0 | 68.4 |
| Cassette | 43.6 | 38.0 | 32.1 | 25.1 | 19.3 |
| LP | 1.3 | 0.3 | 0.8 | 0.5 | 0.6 |
| Singles (all types) | 7.5 | 9.2 | 7.4 | 7.5 | 9.3 |
| Music video | 1.0 | 1.3 | 0.8 | 0.9 | 1.0 |

**Note:** Totals may not equal 100% because of "Don't know/no answer" responses to survey.

The following paragraph was written after careful analytical study of those statistics.

  From studying the data available, I have concluded that compact discs now outsell cassettes to such a degree that we should reduce our cassette stock considerably. I have analyzed the statistics available from the years 1992–1996 and have found that compact discs and cassettes pretty much shared the market equally in 1992, but by 1996, the market heavily favored compact discs. Specifically, in 1992, 46.5% of music products sold in music stores in this country were in the form of compact discs, and 43.6% of music products sold were in the form of cassettes. However, in 1996, 68.4% of sales were in compact discs and only 19.3% were in cassettes. Our store still carries almost as many cassettes as compact discs. These statistics show that we need to move forward with the times. We should have perhaps only 15% of our stock in the form of cassettes, and I would recommend phasing cassettes out completely within the next five years.

1. Which statistics in the almanac did this writer pay closest attention to? Highlight the statistics he used.

2. Highlight the topic sentence of this paragraph. What is this writer promising to write about? Explain his purpose in your own words.

3. Put a box around the part of the paragraph that contains the specific support for the main idea.

4. After offering specific support, this writer explains the support and then wraps up the paragraph by making a recommendation. Put E next the lines of the paragraph that *explain* the support,

and put R next to the lines that express this writer's *recommendation*.

5. Describe in your own words the different parts of this analytical paragraph.

## Analyzing Music Lyrics and Poetry

Music and poetry are both covered in this chapter because they are similar in many ways. They are both creative expressions that have the ability to go beyond the boundaries of gender, ethnicity, and class to appeal to just about everyone. While most people have favorite songs or poems, people won't always agree on how to interpret these songs or poems—which leads to interesting discussions and excellent analytical brain work.

The key difference between a song lyric and a poem is, of course, that one is set to music and the other isn't. However, many poems do have a rhythm of their own, and some poems end up being put to music. If you have never enjoyed studying poetry, but love music, you might find that many of the things you love about music—its ability to paint pictures in your mind, its ability to make you feel certain emotions, and its ability to help you escape everyday life—are also in poems.

This section of the text will offer you some basic information about lyrics and poems. You'll learn a few terms that will help you when you begin to analyze specific pieces.

*Form* The words in lyrics and poems sometimes rhyme, but often they do not. Sometimes poems will follow a specific, formal rhythmic pattern called **meter**. Other times, poems, like lyrics without their musical notes, will have an inconsistent rhythm or no rhythm.

Paragraphs in music lyrics and poems are called **stanzas**. Stanzas can be long or short, and, much like the paragraphs in journalistic writing, they generally don't have topic sentences.

*Language* Because lyricists (people who write music lyrics) and poets are interested in creating images and feelings, and because they generally don't insist on only one interpretation of their work, they don't write in complete, detailed sentences. (You'll find that capital letters and periods aren't used like they are in academic writing.) Lyricists and

**Notes**

poets choose their language very carefully, finding words that will create the message, image or feeling they are aiming for. When analyzing lyrics and poems, you'll want to pay attention to the vocabulary. Is the writer using slang? Is the language formal? Is it the language of a child? Of a parent? Of a lover? Of a sister? What types of words are being used?

Lyricists and poets also use **figurative language** to compare things—helping to paint an image in the reader's mind. "She cried like a baby," is an example of figurative language. The person, "she," is not really a baby, but the writer is saying she cried like one—painting the image of loud, constant crying in our minds. Sometimes the word "like" is left out: "The moon, a silver platter in the sky, lit our way." The moon isn't really a silver serving dish. The writer is simply saying it's similar in appearance to a "platter."

***Effect*** By choosing to use certain words and figurative language, the writer is sending a message to her audience. She is creating a specific image in the reader's mind and a certain mood in the reader's heart. For example, if a writer uses words like *unrippled water, glassy reflection, grass warm and still*, she may be trying to create images of summer at a lake. She may also be creating a quiet, calm, peaceful mood. If she adds that "the lake was a lonely child waiting for summer visitors to return," she is continuing these images by using figurative language and suggesting that the lake sits still and quiet—perhaps even sadly—like a lonely child might, waiting for the excitement and commotion of friends. The writer's message in these lines might be that there is beauty and peace in anticipating the summer. Both the quiet and the excitement can be admired.

***Responding and Interpreting*** Because lyricists and poets don't fully explain and develop their ideas the way essayists do, it's often difficult to be absolutely certain what a song or poem means. Many people find this uncertainty to be the magical part of lyrics and poetry. Each person hearing or reading the lyric or poem will create images in his own mind based on his own experiences. However, while there is usually room for more than one interpretation, your formal analytical essay must be based on a careful study of the vocabulary and the figurative language. The interpretation you offer in your essay must be something you can carefully and thoughtfully defend by offering specific support from the song or poem itself.

## Notes

*Discussing*   Discussing the lyrics and poems with classmates will help you increase your understanding of the pieces because other people will see things and make connections that you may miss. You and your classmates can help one another by listening to each other's responses and respectfully challenging each other to provide proof and support for each interpretation.

*How One Reader Analyzed and Responded to a Poem*   The handwritten notes here represent one student's personal and class notes about a poem written by Langston Hughes, a poet who lived from 1902 to 1967. A major African American voice in the field of literature, Hughes frequently wrote using vocabulary that represented southern speech and a rhythm similar to blues or jazz music. This poem, like many of his, explores the southern African American experience of migrating north. It was also put to music and can be considered both a poem and a song. Look at how one reader studied and responded to the poem by listening to class discussion and analyzing the language carefully.

*Notes from class*
*southern style vocab.*

**Evenin' Air Blues**

Folks, I come up North
Cause they told me
de North was fine.
I come up North
Cause they told me de North was fine.
Been up here six months—
I'm about to lose my mind.

*southern style vocab.*

This mornin' for breakfast
I chawed de mornin' air.
This mornin' for breakfast
Chawed de mornin' air.
But this evenin' for supper,
I got evenin' air to spare.

*He has spirit.*

Believe I'll do a little dancin'
Just to drive my blues away,
A little dancin'
To drive my blues away,

*My notes*

*suggests he used to live in the South.*

*Repeats, creates a rhythm*

*Things have not gone well.*

*Is he hungry? No Money? No job?*

*He has spirit and humor.*

*Yes. He's suffering. Things are not going well.*

*Notes*

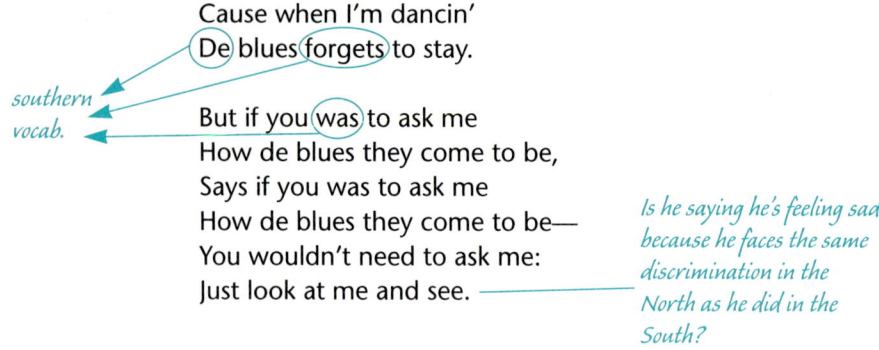

*southern vocab.*

Cause when I'm dancin'
De blues forgets to stay.

But if you was to ask me
How de blues they come to be,
Says if you was to ask me
How de blues they come to be—
You wouldn't need to ask me:
Just look at me and see.

*Is he saying he's feeling sad because he faces the same discrimination in the North as he did in the South?*

*My Informal Response to "Evenin' Air Blues"*

*I think this is a beautiful "song" about an African American man's struggle to make a life for himself after he has moved from the South to the North. It seems to me that he had high hopes when he moved: "I come up North/cause they told me de North was fine." But now he says, "I'm about to lose my mind." I don't think he has any money or job because he doesn't have anything to eat: "I chawed de mornin' air." (My instructor said that line referred to eating and was written in a southern dialect.) Oh, and one of my classmates pointed out the beauty of this poem: the speaker's spirit. Instead of crying and complaining, the speaker dances! Wow. This poem is both painful and beautiful.*

### Points to Remember about Analyzing Lyrics and Poems

- Respond honestly. Discuss lyrics and poems with others.
- Divide the lyric or poem into small pieces (lines and words), and study these pieces. Use your critical thinking skills and look carefully at vocabulary and figurative language.
- When writing an essay, have clear topic sentences that connect to the thesis and that cover one piece of the lyric or poem at a time.
- Use examples from the lyric or poem to support the points you make. Include particular vocabulary words and figurative language.
- Explain your support.

### Writing Assignment #1: Analyzing Music Lyrics

In this assignment, you'll strengthen your ability to analyze and infer as you study music lyrics. This analysis requires you to study the details of the lyrics so that you can draw conclusions about what the songs mean.

Chapter 8  Writing about Music and Poetry    361

Here, in brief, is the writing assignment you are preparing for.

Notes

*Write an essay about one of the songs in this book or a song you have chosen and reviewed with your instructor. In your essay, summarize what you think the song is about. Then choose a couple of the most interesting parts to support your point and show that you have read the lyrics carefully and have good reasons for your interpretation.*

Keep this assignment in mind as you begin to analyze music lyrics.

## Discuss and Engage

### ▼ Activities

#### Analyze the Mutts Cartoon

Analyze the cartoon on page 353 and answer the questions that follow.

1. Describe what is happening in the first frame of the cartoon. (What does the musical note represent? What does "SQUAWK KRAW EEEE" represent?)

2. In the second frame, why didn't the cartoonist write any words? What is going on between the two birds?

3. Why did the cartoonist choose the words "Man" and "digs"? What do these words mean to you?

4. Can you infer anything about the birds by the way they look?

#### Your Experiences with Music

Discuss with your classmates the types of music you like. Which songs do you like the most and why? Are there people in your class who listen carefully to lyrics in songs? What do they look for in good lyrics? Are you always sure what a song means?

#### Journal Assignment

#### Thoughts about Song Lyrics

Write about song lyrics and how you and your classmates react to them. Write down some of your favorite lyrics and explain why they are important to you. Also, write about some lyrics that you have heard/read, but haven't enjoyed. Why didn't you like these lyrics? (This is for your eyes only. Refer back to this journal when you are getting ready to write your essay on music.)

Notes

## Read, Discuss, Think Critically

This section of the chapter offers you the lyrics to five songs, in a variety of styles: classic rock (Pink Floyd), country (Randy Travis), mellow rock (Bonnie Raitt and Melissa Etheridge), and alternative rock (Alanis Morissette). Notice that the title of the song is given first, then the name of the performer and album.

### Reading Assignment

"Time"

*Preview*   Read the title and the first two stanzas.

*Anticipate*   What do you think this song will be about? What kind of mood or message do you think it has? Use the "Notes" column to record your thoughts.

*Read and reread*   Quickly read the lyrics one time, marking unknown terms. Then reread more slowly and use the "Notes" column to record images and meaning that come to mind. Also write down any questions you have. Define unknown terms. Finally, listen to the song or read it aloud.

### Time
*Pink Floyd*

*The Dark Side of the Moon*

1  Ticking away the moments that make up a dull day,
Fritter and waste the hours in an off-hand way.
Kicking around on a piece of ground in your home town.
Waiting for someone or something to show you the way.

2  Tired of lying in the sunshine, Staying home to watch the rain,
You are young and life is long And there is time to kill today.
And then one day you find Ten years have got behind you.
No one told you when to run, You missed the starting gun.

3  And you run, you run to catch up with the sun but it's sinking.
Racing around to come up behind you again.
The sun is the same in a relative way but you're older,
Shorter of breath And one day closer to death.

4  Ev'ry year is getting shorter, Never seem to find the time.

> Plans that either come to naught, Or half a page of scribbled lines.
> Hanging on in quiet desperation is the English way.
> The time is gone the song is over. Thought I'd something more to say.

*Notes*

## ▼ Questions for Critical Thought

### "Time"

1. What is your general reaction to this song? How does it make you feel? What words/images in the lyrics support your reaction?
2. Summarize what you think each stanza is about.
3. Pink Floyd uses the term "you" frequently. Using clues from the lyrics, what kind of person is this "you"? What educated guesses can you make about this person and his or her life?
4. What do you think is the general message of this song?
5. Does any particular line or image in the song remind you of yourself or your life? Explain.

## Reading Assignment

### "Old 8 x 10"

*Preview*  Read the title and the first two stanzas.

*Anticipate*  What do you think this song will be about? What kind of mood or message do you think it has? Write down your thoughts in the "Notes" column.

*Read and Reread*  Quickly read the lyrics one time, marking unknown terms. Then reread more slowly and use the "Notes" column to record images and meaning that come to mind. Also write down any questions you have. Define unknown terms. Finally, listen to the song or read it aloud.

### Old 8 x 10

*Randy Travis*

Old 8 x 10

1  Well I know it ain't much
But it's all that I have since she's gone
One black and white memory of the only love I've ever known

Notes

One moment in time when we were together
A page from the past to haunt me forever
A constant reminder that hearts heal much slower than bones
2.  Now my whole world's in one 8 x 10
With four metal walls holding it in
Through one plate-glass window
'Neath the blanket of dust
Stands an 8 x 10 picture of us
I wish I'd have told her
What I felt inside
Back when her sweet love was flowing like wine
I wish she would come back and love me again
The way that she loved me
In that old 8 x 10
3.  Now the silence is deafening
As the day turns to dark
Her presence gets stronger with each beat of my heart
I pretend that she's here and we've made a new start
And for a moment
She's back in my arms
4.  Now my whole world's in one 8 x 10
With four metal walls holding it in
Through one plate-glass window
'Neath the blanket of dust
Stands an 8 x 10 picture of us
There's an 8 x 10 picture of us

## ▼ Questions for Critical Thought

*"Old 8 x 10"*

1. What does the title tell you about the song? What does it make you think of?

2. What do the following lines refer to?

    "One black and white memory of the only love I've ever known"

    "One moment in time when we were together"

    "Now my whole world's in one 8 x 10"

    What is he singing about? (What is "black and white"? What "moment in time" is he referring to? What is the 8 x 10?) (He is using figurative language here.)

3. He also sings about "four metal walls holding it in" and "One plate-glass window." What are these walls? What is this window? (He is using figurative language here.)

4. What is the general feeling of the song? What image do you have of the speaker in the lyrics? What can you say about him, his life, his home? What details in the lyrics support your reactions?

5. Do any of the lines or images in these lyrics remind you of yourself or your life? Explain.

## Reading Assignment

*"Tangled and Dark"*

***Preview***   Read the title and the first two stanzas.

***Anticipate***   What do you think this song will be about? What kind of mood or message do you think it has? Use the "Notes" column to record your thoughts.

***Read and Reread***   Quickly read the lyrics one time, marking unknown terms. Then reread more slowly and use the "Notes" column to record images and meaning that come to mind. Also write down any questions you have. Define unknown terms. Finally, listen to the song or read it aloud.

### Tangled and Dark
*Bonnie Raitt*

*Luck of the Draw*

1   Gonna get into it
Where it's tangled and dark
Way on into it, Baby
Down where your fears are parked.
Gonna tell the truth about it
Honey that's the hardest part
When we get through it, Baby
You're gonna give up your heart

2   Gonna get into it, Baby
Gonna give them demons a call
Way on into it Baby

*Notes*

    Gonna find out once and for all
    Gonna get a little risky, Baby
    Honey that's my favorite part
    When we get through it, Baby
    We're gonna give up our hearts.
3       Well, there's no turnin back,
    No turnin back, this time
    Well there's no turnin back,
    No turnin back—
4       No use in runnin
    It's always the same
    You can count on the panic
    It's the faces that change
    We might have a chance
    To get this love off the block
    So take a deep breath
    Let's look under that rock.

## ▼ Questions for Critical Thought

*"Tangled and Dark"*

1. What does the title of the song tell you? What images come to mind?

2. What is your general reaction to the lyrics? How do they make you feel? What details in the lyrics support your reactions?

3. Throughout the song Raitt refers to *it*. Circle all the *its* you can find. What do you think some of these *its* refer to?

4. In the last line Raitt says, "Let's look under that rock." What does she mean? Explain. (She's using figurative language here.)

5. What do you think is the general message in this song?

6. Do any of the lines or images in these lyrics remind you of yourself or your life? Explain.

## Reading Assignment

*"Perfect"*

*Preview*    Read the title and the first two stanzas.

*Anticipate* What do you think this song will be about? What kind of mood or message do you think it has? Respond in the "Notes" column.

*Read and Reread* Quickly read the lyrics one time, marking unknown terms. Then reread more slowly and use the "Notes" column to record images and meaning that come to mind. Also write down any questions you have. Define unknown terms. Finally, listen to the song or read it aloud.

**Notes**

## Perfect
*Alanis Morissette*

*Jagged Little Pill*

1.  Sometimes is never quite enough
    If you're flawless, then you'll win my love
    Don't forget to win first place
    Don't forget to keep that smile on your face

2.  Be a good boy
    Try a little harder
    You've got to measure up
    And make me prouder

3.  How long before you screw it up
    How many times do I have to tell you to hurry up
    With everything I do for you
    The least you can do is keep quiet

4.  Be a good girl
    You've gotta try a little harder
    That simply wasn't good enough
    To make us proud

5.  I'll live through you
    I'll make you what I never was
    If you're the best, then maybe so am I
    Compared to him compared to her
    I'm doing this for your own damn good
    You'll make up for what I blew
    What's the problem . . . why are you crying

6.  Be a good boy
    Push a little farther now
    That wasn't fast enough
    To make us happy
    We'll love you just the way you are if you're perfect

Notes

▼ **Questions for Critical Thought**

"Perfect"

1. What is your general reaction to the lyrics? How do they make you feel? (happy? sad? relaxed? energized? mad? or?) What lines in the lyrics can you point to that make you feel this way?
2. Think about the line in stanza 3, "How many times do I have to tell you to hurry up." Who might say words like this?
3. What do you think of these lines in stanza 5: "I'll live through you/ I'll make you what I never was"? Who might say these words? How do you feel about these words?
4. Who do you think the speaker in the lyrics is? Is the speaker Morissette? Why or why not?
5. What do you think of the last line in the song?
6. What do you think the general message is in this song?
7. Do any of the lines or images in this song remind you of yourself or your life? Explain.

**Reading Assignment**

"Silent Legacy"

*Preview*   Read the title and the first two stanzas.

*Anticipate*   What do you think this song will be about? What kind of mood or message do you think it might have? Respond in the "Notes" column.

*Read and Reread*   Quickly read the lyrics one time, marking unknown terms. Then reread more slowly and use the "Notes" column to record images and meaning that come to mind. Also write down any questions you have. Define unknown terms. Finally, listen to the song or read it aloud.

### Silent Legacy
*Melissa Etheridge*

Yes I Am

1   Why did you steal the matches
From the one room motel

Notes

    Once they gave you answers
    Now they give you hell
    They will never understand
    They wonder where did they go wrong
    How could you be so selfish
    Why can't you get along
2       And as you pray in your darkness
    For wings to set you free
    You are bound to your silent legacy
3       You've seen it in the movies
    And you've heard it on the street
    Craving the affection
    Your blood is full of heat
    They don't listen to your reasons
    As original as sin
    Deny all that you feel
    And they will bring you home again
4       And as you pray in your darkness
    For wings to set you free
    You are bound to your silent legacy
5       Your body is alive
    But no one told you what you'd feel
    The empty aching hours
    Trying to conceal
    The natural progression
    Is the coming of your age
    But they cover it with shame
    And turn it into rage
6       And as you pray in your darkness
    For wings to set you free
    You are bound to your silent legacy
    You are digging for the answers
    Until your fingers bleed
    To satisfy the hunger
    To satiate the need
    They feed you on the guilt
    To keep you humble keep you low
    Some man and myth they made up
    A thousand years ago
7       And as you pray in your darkness
    For wings to set you free
    You are bound to your silent legacy

Notes

8
Mothers tell your children
Be quick you must be strong
Life is full of wonder
Love is never wrong
Remember how they taught you
How much of it was fear
Refuse to hand it down
The legacy stops here

9
Oh my child

## ▼ Questions for Critical Thought

### "Silent Legacy"

1. What does the title "Silent Legacy" mean to you?
2. What is your general reaction to the music lyrics? How do they make you feel?
3. The following lines appear in stanza 1: "They wonder where did they go wrong/How could you be so selfish/Why can't you get along." Who might say "Where did we go wrong?" or "How could you be so selfish?" or "Why can't you get along?" Look at the other times "they" is used. Who do you think "they" refers to in this song?
4. Read through the song and note where the words "sin," "shame," "guilt," show up. What do you think the person in this song is struggling with?
5. The last stanza in this song is distinctly different in tone and message. Explain.
6. What do you think the "silent legacy" is?
7. Do any of the lines or images in these lyrics remind you of yourself or your life? Explain.

### Journal Assignment

#### An Informal Response to the Songs

Write out your thoughts about two or three of the songs in this book. What do they mean? What clues do you have for the meaning? Did any of your classmates point out things you hadn't seen in the songs? Exchange your journal with one or more classmates and say, "Thank You."

## Explore the Writing Assignment

Notes

Here, again, is your writing assignment. Review it carefully before continuing. Underline the important terms in the assignment.

> *Write an essay about one of the songs in this book or a song you have chosen and reviewed with your instructor. In your essay, summarize what you think the song is about. Then choose a couple of the most interesting parts to support your point and show that you have read the lyrics carefully and have good reasons for your interpretation.*

***Brainstorm*** Review your work so far in this chapter. What song do you want to write an essay about? Write freely in response to the writing assignment and explore your reasons for choosing your selected song. What message(s), images, and emotions in this song interest you? What clues in the song support your interpretation of the song?

***Consider Your Audience*** You should not assume that your audience knows the song you'll writing about. Write a brief summary of your song that lets your audience know what the song is basically about. You may find that all or part of this summary fits into the introduction of your essay.

***Create Your Thesis*** Review your writing assignment, notes, brainstorm, and summary. Your thesis should tell the reader the general message of the song you've chosen. Experiment with several thesis statements until you find one that clearly states your conclusions about the song.

***Outline*** Consider now how you'll support your thesis statement. Remember that in an analytical essay, a writer must break the larger topic down into smaller pieces that can be studied. One approach to song lyrics is to study one stanza per paragraph. However, you may not want to cover all the stanzas. Perhaps you feel there are three or four key stanzas you want to focus on. Another approach might be to cover any or all of the following in separate paragraphs: mood, message, audience, speaker, or images.

Take time now to think critically about what your major supporting points will be, and write topic sentences that express these supporting points.

Notes

Next, think about the order of your main points. Experiment with your outline until you have found a method of organization that makes sense to you. Show your outline to a classmate, tutor, or your instructor, and see if that reader can see a focused, organized essay emerging.

## Draft

Remember, you should direct your thoughts to a reader who is unfamiliar with the song you are writing about. In your introduction, you'll need to "introduce" the song and the song writer and tell why you decided to write about this song. Then state what you intend to explain through analysis. In the body of your paper, you should go into more detail about a few parts of the song. Be sure to use vocabulary and figurative language as important parts of your explanation. As you write multiple drafts, your explanation will become clearer. In your conclusion, explain what you hope the reader learned from your essay.

## Revise

▼

### Share Your Writing

Find a classmate to work with. Read each other's essay and apply the following questions to each essay.

- Do you explain the overall message of the song?
- Do you then offer smaller pieces of the song that you study in detail? Do you have clear topic sentences?
- Are your paragraphs in a logical order? Do you have transitions where you need them?
- Do you offer the reader specific information from the song to support your major points?
- Do you explain that specific information? (What is obvious to you may not be obvious to the reader.)
- What areas of writing has your instructor suggested you work on?

After working with your classmate, make a list of improvements you want to make. Rank them from most important to least, and then tackle one task at a time.

*Edit*

Notes

Read your essay aloud and look for (and listen for) awkward spots and typographical errors.

   Review your essay again slowly and consider the following:

- Look for errors you tend to repeat, focusing on one type of error at a time.
- Does your instructor have a certain area he or she wants you to focus on?
- Put song titles in quotation marks.
- When you quote lines from a song lyric, put a slash between lines. For example, if you quoted these lines from "Time" you would use the slash like this: "Ticking away the moments that make up a dull day/You fritter and waste the hours in an offhand way."
- Have you used coordinators and subordinators to shape your sentences?

## Writing Assignment #2: Analyzing Poetry

In this assignment, you'll sharpen your analytical and inferential skills as you study poetry. This analysis requires you to study the details of the poems so that you can draw conclusions about what they mean.

   Here, in brief, is the writing assignment you are preparing for.

> Choose one of the poems in this book, or a poem you and your instructor have agreed upon, and write an essay in which you reveal the meaning of the poem to your reader. In your essay, you'll need to summarize the poem and then take the reader through the poem, stanza by stanza or line by line, in order to explain the poem's meaning.

Keep this assignment in mind as you proceed to analyze the poems presented in this chapter.

## Discuss and Engage

### Activity

### Discuss Poetry

Discuss the term *poetry* with your classmates and develop a group definition of poetry. Think about what a poem should contain or do in order to be

*Notes*

called a poem. Also talk about the kind(s) of poetry you enjoy reading or writing. Discuss any poems you remember having learned in the past.

> ### Journal Assignment
> ### Thinking about Poetry
> Write out your own definition of a what a poem is. Be sure to include what you believe to be the essential elements of a good poem. Are there similarities between music lyrics and poems? (This is for your eyes only. Refer back to this journal when you are getting ready to write your essay on poetry.)

It may help you to know one of the official definitions of *poetry*:

> A term applied to the many forms in which human beings have given rhythmic expression to their most imaginative and intense perceptions [or views] of the world, themselves, and the relation of the two.
> —C. Hugh Holman and William Harmon
> A Handbook to Literature, 5th ed.

As Holman and Harmon point out, poetry expresses humans' most creative views of themselves and the world.

Before moving on, check your definition with Holman and Harmon's. How does it compare? What are the differences? You may wish to revise your definition to include new information.

## Read, Discuss, Think Critically

This section of the chapter contains five poems. The first two poems were written by students. The last three were written by well known poets.

## Reading Assignment

"What I Saw on the Bus"

*Preview*  Read the title and the first two stanzas.

*Anticipate*  What do you think this poem will be about? What kind of mood or message do you think it has? Respond in the "Notes" column.

*Read and Reread*  Quickly read the poem one time, marking unknown terms. Then reread more slowly and use the "Notes" column to record images and meaning that come to mind. Also write down any questions you have. Define unknown terms. Finally, read the poem aloud.

### What I Saw on the Bus
*Jessicah Pratt*

student poet

1. Today I took the bus for a minute or a mile
And I saw some things that made me laugh or smile.
I watched an old dude with an attitude
Tell a boy that he would live in sin after
Disrespecting his elderly kin

2. I saw a handicapped woman get on with a fit
Because no one got up to let her sit
I saw a boy watching everyone suspiciously
As if they would all jump up and beat him viciously
Because he hadn't got his homework done on time
And that's a very serious crime.

3. I saw the people who came everyday
With their very loud and gossipy ways.

4. I saw the homeless, the drunk.
The college students and the punks.
And there was me sitting in the corner looking cool
Taking the bus so I could get to school.

Notes

▼ **Questions for Critical Thought**

*"What I Saw on the Bus"*

1. What is your general reaction to the poem? How does it make you feel? What words create this feeling?
2. Pratt uses some slang in her poetry. Underline words and phrases you consider to be slang.
3. What is the effect of using slang language? How does it affect the tone of the poem? Is the tone serious? fun? sad? happy? Can you come up with words that describe the tone more accurately? What does it reveal about the speaker and the speaker's mood? (Describe the speaker's attitude, age, perspective, and interests.)
4. What do you think Pratt would like you to learn from the poem? What would she like you to think about?

**Reading Assignment**

*"Take Wing"*

*Preview* Read the title and the first two stanzas.

*Anticipate* What do you think this poem will be about? What kind of mood or message do you think it has? Respond in the "Notes" column.

*Read and Reread* Quickly read the poem one time, marking unknown terms. Then reread more slowly and use the "Notes" column to record images and meaning that come to mind. Also write down any questions you have. Define unknown terms. Finally, read the poem aloud.

### Take Wing
*Adria Conley*

student poet

1 If the butterfly whispers
again
at daybreak
from the soft velvet
    meadow
and it's not too warm

2 I'll wait for the sun
to rise,

    then take wing and glide
    to meet her.

3   We will not speak,
    but fanned against the
        heat
    soar above the purple
        flowers,
    searching
    with black beady eyes.

4   And then we'll sit
    in the shadowy petals
        and
    sip the nectar
    of enveloping buds,
    while the long clouds
        drift
    toward the stars
    and the breezes sing
    in their fluffy bed.

5   And when twilight climbs
    the limbs
    we'll part without a
        sound,
    fulfilled, floating
    homeward as
    the warm world silences.

## ▼ Questions for Critical Thought

### "Take Wing"

1. What is your general reaction to the poem? How does it make you feel? What words create this feeling?
2. What is happening to the speaker in this poem? Which words, images tell you this?
3. What are your favorite lines in this poem? Why?

## Reading Assignment

### "Refugee Ship"

**Preview**   Read the title and the first two stanzas.

Notes

***Anticipate*** What do you think this poem will be about? What kind of mood or message do you think it has? Use the "Notes" column to record your thoughts.

***Read and Reread*** Quickly read the poem one time, marking unknown terms. Then reread more slowly and use the "Notes" column to record images and meaning that come to mind. Also write down any questions you have. Define unknown terms. Finally, read the poem aloud.

## Refugee Ship
*Lorna Dee Cervantes (b. 1954)*

Of Native American and Mexican ancestry, Cervantes is a poet, editor, and teacher.

1. like wet cornstarch
   I slide past *mi abuelita's*\* eyes
   bible placed by her side
   she removes her glasses
   the pudding thickens

2. *mama* raised me with no language
   I am orphan to my Spanish name
   the words are foreign, stumbling on my tongue
   I stare at my reflection in the mirror
   brown skin, black hair

3. I feel I am a captive
   aboard the refugee ship\*\*
   a ship that will never dock
   a ship that will never dock

### ▼ Questions for Critical Thought

"Refugee Ship"

1. What is your general reaction to this poem? How does it make you feel? What words create this feeling?

---

\**mi abuelita's* is Spanish for "my grandmother's."
\*\**refugee ship* is a boat carrying people who are fleeing to another country for safety.

2. Describe your image of the grandmother in this poem. What words make this image in your mind?

3. What do you think Cervantes means when she says "I am orphan to my Spanish name/the words are foreign, stumbling on my tongue"?

4. What do you think the speaker is saying in the last stanza?

5. Do any of the lines, images, or messages in this poem connect to your life? Explain.

*Notes*

## Reading Assignment
*"The Road Not Taken"*

*Preview*   Read the title and the first two stanzas.

*Anticipate*   What do you think this poem is about? What kind of mood or message do you think it has? Record your thoughts in the "Notes" column.

*Read and Reread*   Quickly read the poem one time, marking unknown terms. Then reread more slowly and use the "Notes" column to record images and meaning that come to mind. Also write down any questions you have. Define unknown terms. Finally, read the poem aloud.

### The Road Not Taken
*Robert Frost (1874–1963)*

American poet

1   Two roads diverged in a yellow wood,
And sorry I could not travel both
And be one traveler, long I stood
And looked down one as far as I could
to where it bent in the undergrowth.

2   Then took the other, as just as fair,
And having perhaps the better claim,
Because it was grassy and wanted wear;
Though as for that the passing there
Had worn them really about the same,

Notes

3   And both that morning equally lay
    In leaves no step had trodden black,
    Oh, I kept the first for another day!
    Yet knowing how way leads on to way,
    I doubted if I should ever come back.

4   I shall be telling this with a sigh
    Somewhere ages and ages hence:
    Two roads diverged in a wood, and I—
    I took the one less traveled by,
    And that has made all the difference.

## ▼ Questions for Critical Thought

### "The Road Not Taken"

1. What is your general reaction to this poem? How does it make you feel? What words or images in the poem promote this feeling?

2. Describe the movements of this traveler (the speaker) in the poem. Describe what the speaker sees and does in response.

3. It is possible that this "road" that the speaker did not take is an example of figurative language. Perhaps the speaker is not thinking of an actual road. What could he or she be speaking of? Do any other lines in the poem suggest that your interpretation might be right?

4. What is significant about the fact that he or she took the road "less traveled by"? If this is another example of figurative language, what does this road "less traveled by" represent?

5. Can you relate to what Frost is saying in his poem? Have you had a similar experience?

## Reading Assignment

### "A Work of Artifice"

*Preview*  Read the title and the first two stanzas.

*Anticipate*  What do you think this poem will be about? What kind of mood or message do you think it has? Record your thoughts in the "Notes" column.

*Read and Reread*  Quickly read the poem one time, marking unknown terms. Then reread more slowly and use the "Notes" column to record images and meaning that come to mind. Also write down any questions you have. Define unknown terms. Finally, read the poem aloud.

**Notes**

### A Work of Artifice
*Marge Piercy (b. 1936)*

American poet and novelist

1   The bonsai tree
    in the attractive pot
    could have grown eighty feet tall
    on the side of a mountain
    till split by lightning
6   But a gardener
    carefully pruned it.
    It is nine inches high.
    Every day as he
    whittles back the branches
11  the gardener croons,
    It is your nature
    to be small and cozy,
    domestic and weak;
    how lucky, little tree,
16  to have a pot to grow in.
    With living creatures
    one must begin very early
    to dwarf their growth:
    the bound feet,
21  the crippled brain,
    the hair in curlers,
    the hands you
    love to touch.

### ▼ Questions for Critical Thought

#### "A Work of Artifice"

1. Carefully consider the title. What does the word *artifice* mean?
2. Read the first five lines aloud. What picture do you see in your mind?

Notes

3. Read lines 6 through 8 aloud. What picture do you see now?
4. Read lines 9 through 16 aloud. What do you think of the gardener? Do you agree that the tree is lucky "to have a pot to grow in"? Explain.
5. Toward the end of the poem, the image changes, and we are no longer focusing on a tree. What do you see? What do you think this poet is saying in this poem?

> ### Journal Assignment
> *Thinking about the Poems*
>
> Write out your thoughts about two or three of the poems in this book. What does each poem reveal? What clues do you have to unlock the meaning in each poem? Did any classmates reveal an unusual interpretation of one of the poems? Which poem do you like the best? Why? Exchange your journal with classmates and say, "Thank you."

### Explore the Writing Assignment

Here, again, is your writing assignment. Review it carefully before continuing. Underline the important terms in the assignment.

> *Choose one of the poems in this book, or a poem you and your instructor have agreed upon, and write an essay in which you reveal the meaning of the poem to your reader. In your essay, you'll need to summarize the poem and then take the reader through the poem, stanza by stanza or line by line, in order to explain the poem's meaning.*

***Brainstorm*** Review your work so far for this assignment. What poem do you want to write an essay about? Write freely in response to the writing assignment and explore your reasons for choosing your selected poem. What message(s), images, or emotions in this poem interest you? What clues in the poem support your interpretation?

***Consider Your Audience*** You should not assume that your audience knows the poem you are writing about. Write a brief summary of your poem that lets your audience know what the poem is about. You may find that all or part of this summary fits into the introduction of your essay.

***Create Your Thesis*** Review your writing assignment, notes, brainstorm, and summary. Your thesis should tell the reader what the general message of the poem is. Experiment with several thesis statements until you find one that clearly states your analytical conclusions about the poem you have chosen.

***Outline*** Now think about how you'll support your thesis statement. Remember that in an analytical essay, a writer must break the larger topic down into smaller pieces that can be studied. One approach to poems is to study one stanza per paragraph. However, you may not want to cover all the stanzas. Perhaps you feel there are three or four key stanzas you want to focus on. (If you analyze "A Work of Artifice," which only has one stanza, you could select particular lines that work together to create an image or message and cover these groups of lines, each in a different paragraph.) Another approach might be to cover any or all of the following in separate paragraphs: mood, message, audience, speaker, or images.

Take time now to think critically about what your major supporting points will be and write topic sentences that express these supporting points.

Next, think about the order of your main points. Experiment with your outline until you have found a method of organization that makes sense to you. Show your outline to a classmate, tutor, or your instructor and see if that reader can see a focused, organized essay emerging.

## Draft

Remember, you should direct your thoughts to a reader who is unfamiliar with the poem you are writing about. In your introduction, you'll need to "introduce" the poem and poet and tell why you decided to write about this poem. Also, mention what you intend to explain through analysis. In the body of your paper, you should go into more detail about a few parts of the poem. Be sure to use vocabulary and figurative language as important parts of your explanation. As you write multiple drafts, your explanation will become clearer. In your conclusion, explain what you hope the reader learned from your essay.

*Notes*

Notes

▼

### Study a Student Sample

Student Sample:

Review the following introduction and conclusion from one student's essay. Mark what you like in each paragraph. Then respond to the questions/statements which follow.

(The title of the essay is "The Art of Deception")

(Introduction)
My personal interpretation of the poem "A Work of Artifice" by Marge Piercy is that the poem is about stunting growth and the deceitfulness used to accomplish it. Basically, some people often stunt other people's growth, for their own personal gains. The reason I chose this poem is because I can relate from my own personal experience. My ex-husband used the same type of deception toward me to fulfill his own idea of the person I should be. Just as the gardener stunts the growth of the bonsai tree, he determines the shape and size of the tree. The gardener even selects the tree's pot, all to his liking. I will explain as follows.

(Conclusion)
This poem in my opinion is clearly not about the tree's or creature's wants, desires or capabilities. Therefore it is about what the gardener and the person who is crippling the brain want. These people are doing the deceiving and stunting of growth, creating their own expectations of their ideals. I feel this is an injustice that happens all too often in life, far too many times, all in the name of love. I can say I have been that bonsai/creature. I speak from my own horrible experience; I have been left scarred by the treachery and deceit of such an act of love. I fell prey to the crooning and whittling until it almost cost me my life. I believed and trusted this individual, that he had my best interest at heart, only to learn that it was purely a selfish motive that drove him. Yet with every branch they whittle and prune, they still croon.

—*Ruth*

1. The writing assignment asks that you summarize the poem and your reasons for writing in the introduction. Highlight Ruth's summary and reasons for writing.

2. A conclusion should connect back to the introduction without repeating the introduction. Underline the sentences in the conclusion that connect most closely to the introduction.

3. Note in Ruth's conclusion where she borrows words from the poem. Why is this effective?

## Revise

### ▼ Activity

**Share Your Writing**

Find a classmate to work with. Read each other's essays and consider the following questions in relation to each essay.

- Do you explain the overall message of the poem?

- Do you then offer smaller pieces of the poem that you study in detail? Do you have clear topic sentences?

- Are your paragraphs in a logical order? Do you have transitions where you need them?

- Do you offer the reader specific information from the poem to support your major points?

- Do you explain that specific information? (What is obvious to you may not be obvious to the reader.)

- What areas of writing has your instructor suggested you work on?

After working with your classmate, make a list of improvements you want to make. Rank them from most important to least, and then tackle one task at a time.

## Edit

Read your essay aloud and look for (and listen for) awkward spots and typographical errors.

Review your essay again, slowly, and consider the following:

- Look for errors you tend to repeat, focusing on one type of error at a time.

Notes

- Does your instructor have a certain area he or she wants you to focus on?
- Put poem titles in quotation marks.
- Put a slash between lines of the poem. (For example, if you were to quote these lines from "The Road Not Taken," you would use a slash like this: "Two roads diverged in a yellow wood, / And sorry I could not travel both / And be one traveler, long I stood."
- Have you used coordinators and subordinators to shape your sentences?

## ▲▼▲ Summary of Chapter 8

In this chapter, you have

- strengthened your analysis and inference skills as you studied song lyrics and poetry;
- learned that analysis and inference require you to break larger subjects down into smaller pieces;
- learned that after careful study of the smaller pieces, you can infer information; and
- learned that when writing analytical essays, you must present your major point or conclusion, the pieces of proof that support the conclusion, and explanations of each piece of proof.

## ▲▼▲ Sentence Combining

*Notes*

### *Joining Sentences Using Coordinating Conjunctions*
### *Joining Sentences Using Subordinating Conjunctions*

In this chapter, you'll practice joining sentences in such a way that you are able to show your reader how different ideas relate to one another. This will improve the flow of your writing and let you express more sophisticated ideas.

### *Joining Sentences Using Coordinating Conjunctions*

**Coordinators** are special words that you can use to join independent sentences. These words help you show how the idea in one sentence relates to the idea in another sentence. So to use these words effectively, you must choose them carefully.

There are seven coordinators:

| for | and | nor | but | or | yet | so |
|-----|-----|-----|-----|----|-----|----|
| f   | a   | n   | b   | o  | y   | s  |

One way to remember these seven words is to remember the acronym *FANBOYS*.

#### Facts about the FANBOYS

- They are *coordinators*. The *co* in *coordinators* is a prefix that tells us that they create *equal* relationships between the ideas that they join. Think about the equal relationships expressed by these words: *coworkers, coauthors, coexist*. All these words suggest equality. (Neither coworker is more important. Coauthors are equal partners, and to coexist is to live together with one dominating). When you join sentences with coordinators, you will be showing how they relate to another, but you will *not* be emphasizing one idea over the other, nor will you be making either sentence a dependent clause.

- Each of the FANBOYS expresses a different relationship
  *for:* expresses a relationship of *effect-cause*. The idea in the first sentence is the effect. The idea in the second sentence is the cause.
    *example:* She chose this song, *for* it makes her feel happy.

**Notes**

**and:** expresses a relationship of *addition*. The idea in the first sentence is added to the idea in the second sentence.
  *example:* She enjoys this song, *and* she wants others to enjoy it.

**nor:** expresses a relationship of *negative addition*. The idea in the first sentence is negative, and it is added to a negative idea in the second sentence.
  *example:* I do not like her guitar playing, *nor* does he like her guitar playing. (Note: When you use *nor*, the subject and verb in the second sentence switch positions. Also, the *nor* in the second half expresses "not," so you don't need another "not.")

**but:** expresses a relationship of *opposition*. The idea in the first sentence is the opposite of the idea in the second sentence.
  *example:* I told her I didn't like her guitar playing, *but* she played anyway.

**or:** expresses a relationship of *alternatives*. The idea in the first sentence is one option. The idea in the second sentence is another option.
  *example:* She should stop playing, *or* she should go where I can't hear her.

**yet:** expresses a relationship of *opposition*. The idea in the first sentence is the opposite of the idea in the second sentence.
  *example:* She heard my opinion, *yet* she didn't stop playing.

**so:** expresses a relationship of *cause-effect*. The idea in the first sentence causes the idea in the second sentence.
  *example:* She said I hurt her feelings, *so* she stopped talking to me.

- You may use coordinators to begin sentences. Writers do this occasionally to add a little emphasis to the second sentence.
  *example:* She should stop playing. *Or* she should go where I can't hear her.

### Punctuation Rule #6
When you join two complete sentences with a coordinator (FANBOYS), you must put a comma after the first sentence.
  *example:* She said I hurt her feelings, *so* she stopped talking to me.

### Special Notes about Sentence Combining

- You'll benefit the most when doing these exercises if you write out your complete sentences. (Don't just draw arrows or insert words.) By practicing these sentence patterns and paying attention to the punctuation rules, these sophisticated patterns will eventually become second nature to you.

- Often the sentences in these exercises can be joined in more than one way. Follow the directions. (If the exercise asks you to use coordinators to join sentences, do that—even if you can think of other ways to join the ideas.)

- You and your classmates may sometimes disagree on precisely which joining word should be used. That's okay as long as you can each defend your choice.

### Sentence Combining—Warm-up

Using carefully selected coordinators, join the sentences that follow and express the relationships given to you. (Make sure that you combine two *complete* sentences.) Use each of the coordinators once.

*example*:
(express a relationship of addition)
Music is a wonderful way for people to communicate their ideas.
They can express their feelings.
*combined sentence*: Music is a wonderful way for people to communicate their ideas, and they can express their feelings.

1. (express a relationship of alternatives)
   Music can sound sad.
   It can sound happy.

2. (express a relationship of opposition)
   My favorite music sounds energetic.
   Occasionally I like to listen to mellow tunes.

3. (express a relationship of effect-cause)
   My dad is dancing.
   He hears his favorite country song.

4. (express a relationship of cause-effect)
   My sister is blaring her rap music.
   The dog hides under the carpet.

5. (express a relationship of negative addition)
   I don't like classical music.
   I don't like big band music.

6. (express a relationship of opposition)
   My mother loves rock and roll.
   My father loves country and jazz.

### Sentence Combining with Coordinators—Mozart

Using carefully chosen coordinating conjunctions, join the sentences that follow.

(Austrian composer Wolfgang Amadeus Mozart lived from 1756–1791.)

1. He was unusual.
   He began to compose music at the age of five.

2. He wrote music for the piano, violin, French horn, string quartets.
   He wrote wonderful symphonies, operas, serenades, sonatas, religious music.

3. He was quite famous during his lifetime.
   He was quite poor.

### Sentence Combining with Coordinators—Louis Armstrong a.k.a. Satchmo

Using carefully selected coordinators, join the sentences that follow. Try to use all seven FANBOYS at least once. Sentences 1–11 will create three paragraphs. The italicized sentences add extra information. You do not have to change (or join) the italicized sentences in any way. When you write your completed paragraphs, include the italicized sentences.

1. Louis Armstrong was born in 1918.
   He lived in New Orleans, Louisiana.

   *When he was seven years old, his parents separated.*

2. He and his mother needed money.
   He began singing.

3. He sang on the streets of New Orleans.
   He earned only pennies.

4. At age thirteen he was arrested.
   He was sent to a home for street children.

   *While living there, he learned to play the cornet (an instrument similar to the trumpet).*

Chapter 8  Writing about Music and Poetry

Notes

5. Two kind teachers helped him learn to play the cornet.
   They were not professional musicians.
   They accidentally taught him some bad habits.

   *One of those habits was puffing up his cheeks when he played the cornet.*

6. Later in life when he visited London as a well-known musician, the people called him Satchelmouth.
   He blew his cheeks as large as a "satchel" (a bag for carrying books or clothing).
   *That name later turned into his nickname "Satchmo."*

   (new paragraph)
   *As one of the most famous jazz trumpet players, Armstrong was a true creative artist.*

7. He was known for his ability to improvise on stage.
   He created "scat" singing where the human voice is used like an instrument.

8. Most singing relies on words.
   Instruments produce musical notes.
   Scat singing requires the singer to pronounce nonsense syllables.

   (new paragraph)
   *Finally, some remember Armstrong as a pioneer in music.*

9. He was part of the "Creole Jazz Band."
   They were the first Black jazz ensemble band to record an album.

10. Later, he had his own band.
    They performed as Louis Armstrong and His Hot Five.

    *Even though he accomplished so much in his lifetime, one private dream was left unfulfilled.*

11. He wanted to sing the national anthem at Shea stadium where his favorite team, the New York Mets, played.
    He practiced all his life.
    He was never invited to sing.

    *He died in 1971.*

**Sentence Combining with Coordinators—Selena**
Using carefully selected coordinators, join the sentences that follow. Use a variety of coordinators. Sentences 1–5 will create one paragraph.

Section II  Employing the Connections

Notes  The italicized sentences add extra information. You do not have to change (or join) the italicized sentences in any way. When you write your completed paragraph, include the italicized sentences.

1. Selena Quintanilla-Perez was born in 1971 in South Texas.
   She began performing professionally when she was only ten years old.

2. She sang Tejano music.
   She was extremely popular in the Tejano culture of the South.

3. She sang in Spanish.
   She couldn't actually read Spanish.
   She grew up speaking English in a school system that discouraged speaking Spanish.

   *When she began singing Tejano music, she had to learn the Spanish lyrics phonetically.*

4. Her band, Los Dinos, was a family band.
   Her sister Suzette played the drums.
   Her brother A.B. played bass and wrote songs.
   Her father Abraham was the manager.

   *Critics say she had a strong jubilant voice that was intoxicating in its joy and liveliness. Tragically, in 1994 she was shot and killed in a Corpus Christi motel by the president of her fan club.*

5. She did not reach her goal of breaking into the "mainstream" music scene.
   She did not see an album reach number one.

   *However, in July 1995 her posthumous album* Dreaming of You *reached number one on Billboard's album chart. She is greatly missed by her family and fans.*

**Your Own Work**  Create three sentences that might show up in an essay about one of the lyrics or poems you analyzed. (You might use sentences you wrote in response to "Questions for Critical Thought.") These sentences must have two independent clauses joined by a coordinator.

## Joining Sentences Using Subordinating Conjunctions

Notes

You may remember that a *subordinator* is a word that can attach to an independent sentence and make that sentence a dependent clause. A dependent clauses cannot stand on its own but can be joined to an independent clause, making a longer, more expressive sentence. Consider the prefix "sub." "Sub" means under or lower. Think of the words *submarine, subconscious, subfreezing, subhuman, submerge.* All these words suggest the idea of being under or lower: a *submarine* travels underwater. *Subfreezing* is below freezing. *Subhuman* means being beneath the human race in development, and *submerge* means to place underwater. So, when you use a *subordinator,* you will be lowering one idea, making it dependent.

There are many subordinators, and you don't need to memorize them. As you work through the exercises in this chapter you'll learn the important points about how to use them to combine sentences and how to punctuate these new sentences correctly.

Here are a few of the most useful subordinators:

| | |
|---|---|
| although | since |
| after | though |
| because | unless |
| even though | when |
| if | while |

Like the coordinators you just studied, these subordinators help you express specific relationships between ideas. You must choose them carefully when joining sentences.

(To review the subordinators that allow you to make concessions in your writing, see Chapter 6.)

- subordinators expressing *opposition and concession:* although, though, even though, while
- subordinators expressing *time* relationships: after, since, when, while
- subordinators expressing *effect-cause* relationships: because, since
- subordinators expressing *conditions:* if, unless

Notes

***Punctuation Rule #2 (review)***
When you *begin* a sentence with a subordinated clause, you must put a comma after the subordinated clause.
   *example: Although* the poem began with an interesting image, the rest of the poem was really quite boring.

***Punctuation Rule #3 (review)***
If the subordinated clause comes *after* the independent clause, you do not need a comma.
   *example:* The poem began with an interesting image *although* the rest of the poem was quite boring.

**Sentence Combining with Subordinators—Edgar Allan Poe**
Join the sentences that follow using subordinators that express the relationship given to you. Use as many different subordinators as possible. Your final product will be one paragraph. (Include the italicized sentences when you write out your paragraph.)

*Edgar Allan Poe was born in 1809.*

1. (express a relationship of time)
   He was very young.
   He became an orphan.

2. (express a relationship of effect-cause)
   He had nowhere to go.
   His godfather took him in, and they lived in England from 1815 to 1820.

3. (express a relationship of opposition)
   He had the opportunity to attend a number of different schools during the years 1820–1831.
   He left these schools before completing his education.

4. (express a relationship of opposition)
   He also joined the army.
   He left that too.

5. (express a relationship of opposition)
   In 1836 he married his cousin.
   She was only thirteen years old.

6. (express a relationship of time)
   His wife died at age 24.
   He wrote his famous poem "Annabel Lee."

*His other famous works include "The Raven, "The Tell-Tale Heart," and "Pit and the Pendulum." Poe had a drinking problem that seriously affected his health, and in 1849 he died at the age of forty.*

**Sentence Combining with Subordinators—Reading Poe's Poetry and Short Stories**

Join the sentences that follow using subordinators that express the relationship given to you. Use as many different subordinators as possible. Your final product will be one paragraph.

1. (express a relationship of opposition)
   I enjoy reading his poems and short stories.
   They scare me a little.

2. (express a condition)
   I won't read them.
   The lights are on.

3. (express a condition)
   My brother likes to read them.
   The electricity goes out.

4. (express a relationship of effect-cause)
   I think my brother likes to do this.
   He likes to scare me.

**Sentence Combining with Subordinators—Emily Dickinson**

Join the sentences that follow using carefully chosen subordinators. Use as many different subordinators as possible. Your final product will be one paragraph. Include the italicized sentences when you write out your paragraph.

*Emily Dickinson was born in 1830.*

1. Growing up she was exposed to a large, powerful social circle.
   She grew up in a politically active family concerned with civic issues.

   *In fact, her family had a role in founding the Amherst Academy and the Amherst College.*

2. She was ready for school.
   She attended Amherst Institute and Mount Holyoke Female Seminary.

3. She completed her education.
   She spent most of her time in her room in the family home.

4. She did not enjoy visiting in person.
   She kept up a constant correspondence with a number of friends.

**Notes**

5. She wrote poems throughout her life
   No one realized how many until after her death.
   Her sister found 1,147 poems in a dresser in Dickinson's room.

6. She wrote almost two thousand poems as an adult.
   Only two poems were published in her life.

***Sentence Combining with Subordinators—Reading Dickinson***
Join the sentences that follow using carefully chosen subordinators. Use as many different subordinators as possible. Your final product will be one paragraph.

1. I love reading Dickinson's short, intriguing poems.
   They are very challenging.

2. I can't understand them.
   I read them several times.

3. I read them aloud.
   I get a clearer idea of what she is saying.

4. I'd like to take a class on Dickinson.
   There's so much to learn about her and her poems.

**Your Own Work**   Create three sentences that you might use in an essay about music or poetry. These sentences must contain a subordinated clause and an independent clause.

## ▲▼▲ Coordinator and Subordinator Review

***Sentence Combining with Coordinators and Subordinators—Maya Angelou***
This is a *coordinator and subordinator review* exercise. Carefully choose the best joining words and combine the sentences below. Use a variety of joining words and be sure to punctuate your sentences correctly. Your final product will be two paragraphs. Be sure to include the italicized sentences in your final paragraphs.

1. Maya Angelou was born in 1928.
   Her name was Marguerite Johnson.

2. She was very young.
   Her parents divorced.
   She moved to Arkansas with her brother Bailey.

3. She was seven years old.
   She was sexually assaulted.

4. She told who assaulted her.
   He was killed.
5. She felt guilty for what she thought her words had done.
   She quit talking for six years.

   (new paragraph)
   *When she was older, she lived with her mother in San Francisco.*

6. Angelou ran away.
   She lived with other homeless children in a junkyard.

   *Later she became the city's first black streetcar conductor.*

7. She was sixteen.
   She had a son.

   *However, poverty, trauma, and an unstable family life hasn't stopped her from enjoying life and trying new things.*

8. She has worked as a Creole cook, a singer, a songwriter, dancer, and actress.
   She has been an educator, a social activist, and a writer.

   *She read her poem "On the Pulse of the Morning" at President Clinton's inauguration.*

**Sentence Combining with Subordinators and Coordinators—**
***Listening to Maya Angelou***
This is a *coordinator and subordinator review* exercise. Carefully choose the best joining words and combine the sentences below. Try to use a variety of joining words and be sure to punctuate your sentences correctly. Your final product will be one paragraph.

1. I have read Angelou's *I Know Why the Caged Bird Sings*.
   I enjoyed it.
   I enjoy her poetry even more.
2. I could listen to her read aloud.
   That is the ultimate in enjoying her words.
   She has a stunning, deep, rich voice.
3. I heard her speak once.
   I was in college.
   I have never heard a voice that magical since.
4. I heard her in person.
   I bought some audio recordings of her telling stories about her life.

**Notes**

5. She will always be a person I admire greatly.
   She has strength, compassion, humor, a sense of joy, and a beautiful voice to tell us all about life.

*Your Own Work*   Create three sentences that might show up in an essay about music or poetry. (You might use sentences you wrote in response to Questions for Critical Thought.) These sentences must have a dependent clause beginning with a subordinator and an independent clause. (The dependent clause may come first or second in the sentence.)

## ▲▼▲ End of Term Progress Journal

Completing a college writing course is an admirable accomplishment. Take time in this final journal to reflect on your growth as a writer, reader, and critical thinker. (Draw comparisons between your skills and processes at the beginning of the term to your skills and processes now at the end of the term. Be specific.)

- How has your reading process changed?
- How has your writing process changed?
- Have your critical thinking skills improved? Explain.
- Have your attitudes toward reading, writing, and critical thinking changed? Explain.
- Which specific writing skills have improved the most? (Think about your ability to focus, organize, and develop ideas.)
- How have your sentence skills changed?
- What skills and processes do you still need to work on?
- What writing assignment from this term are you most proud of? Why?

We recommend that you share this journal with your classmates. We hope that your class has become a community of writers who are interested in each other's progress.

Good luck in your future writing, reading, critical thinking endeavors!

# Supplemental Readings

## SECTION III

*This section of* Connections *offers you a selection of supplemental readings that connect to the themes in this book. Your instructor might assign readings from this section and/or you might choose to read these pieces to strengthen your reading and critical thinking skills and deepen your knowledge about a particular topic.*

**FAMILIES, ROLES, AND RELATIONSHIPS**
"Recipe for the '90s"
"Spare the Rod? Maybe"
"Spare the Chores, Spoil the Child"

**THE POWER OF LANGUAGE**
"The Most Precious Gift"

**HEROES AND ROLE MODELS**
"Look Past Rapper for Real Heroes"
"It's a Rap the Young Don't Deserve"
"Who Is Great?"
"The Wrong Examples"

**TELEVISION AND THE MEDIA**
"Child's Play"

**MUSIC**
"Look Past Rapper for Real Heroes"
"It's a Rap the Young Don't Deserve"
"Family Ties Put a Face on the Faceless Issue of Free Speech"

Notes

**Reading Assignment**

*"Recipe for the '90s"*

*Preview*   Read paragraphs 1–3 of this journalistic piece.

*Anticipate*   What do you think this article will be about? Record your thoughts in the "Notes" column.

*Read and Reread*   Read the entire article, marking unknown terms. Then reread more slowly and use the "Notes" column to interact with the essay. Mark important and interesting points and define unknown terms.

## Recipe for the '90s

*(Associated Press)*

This article was published in the *Sacramento Bee*, 3/15/92.

1   Once upon a time, a white picket fence neatly separated the home from the office.

2   Now the fence is falling down.

3   Technology, the changing nature of work and the growing number of women in the labor force are redefining the office and home, experts say. People trying to balance their work and personal lives are also blending the two.

4   "It used to be you never brought your family problems to work and you never brought your work home to your family," said Robert E. Kelly, a business professor and author at Carnegie Mellon University.

5   "Now it goes both ways: People bring their pets and their kids to work, and they bring their laptop computers and their beepers home."

6   The dawn of computers, fax machines and portable phones has made it possible to work anywhere, anytime. That can be a blessing or a bane.

7   "I was skiing one day, and the attorney I was with was litigating on a ski lift," said Michael Fortino of San Francisco. "He dropped the phone and jumped off the ski lift to get it."

8   Fortino, a lifestyle consultant and lecturer, carries a briefcase that has a laptop computer, portable telephone, fax, printer, copier and modem.

9   "This is my office. I can go anywhere," he said in a telephone interview from a Florida beach. "The corporate environment as we know it will become less predominant."

10   Leba Pierce, 42, of Albuquerque, N.M., set up a crib in her family's import store and brought her newborn son to work.

11  When the baby began crawling, Ms. Pierce put an electric typewriter in the sunroom at home and set up shop there. She gets most of her work done when the baby naps in the afternoon.

12  "He loves to wait on the customers," she said of Mark, now one. "He also likes money and checks."

13  Like Fortino, Ms. Pierce says her life is hectic, but she has made choices that make it full and happy. "I do have it all," she said. "I can go down to my store anytime I want to. I can have work at home any time I want."

14  Paula Bern, a syndicated newspaper advice columnist who deals with work issues, says about sixty percent of the thousands of letters she receives from readers concern clashing personal and professional responsibilities.

15  "There's a lot of confusion, bewilderment," she said. "What do you do?"

16  She believes the conflicts are arising largely because so many women have jobs now.

17  "Traditionally, the women have been the care-givers, the nurturers, the people who take care of the children, the dogs, the cats, everything in the house," she said. Suddenly there isn't anyone any longer at home.

18  Slightly more than half of U.S. women with infants were in the labor force last year, compared to about a third in 1980, according to the U.S. Census Bureau.

19  Bern has received letters about child care, office romance, people who sell Tupperware or cosmetics on the side at work, even a woman who kept a poodle named Baby under her desk.

20  The problems aren't confined to the corporate executive. One woman wrote to say her child regularly tags along while she cleans offices on weekends to supplement her income.

21  Bern recently received hundreds of angry letters criticizing her negative response to an attorney who brought her infant to work when her baby sitter was sick; she nursed the child during an office meeting.

22  "Is motherhood so undervalued that we would discourage all attempts by a woman to take care of her child if these actions conflict with antiquated, oppressive office etiquette?" wrote one reader, Teresa Monley of Denver.

23  "The average professional is spending more time at work, about 47.5 hours a week," Fortino said. "The long hours make it tough to find time for personal matters, such as errands or phone calls, so people are devoting more time at the office to those things," he said.

24  Personal packages are delivered at work, and some businesses are offering employees services such as haircuts, manicures and shoeshines at the office.

*Notes*

Notes

25. "When they finally get home, many people have little time or energy for the traditional mealtime gathering where good food and conversation is shared," Bern said.

26. "What they don't finish in the office I find people are finishing at home," she said. "They eat a hurry-up dinner. There's nothing to talk about."

27. Many people are feeling overwhelmed by the stress of trying to manage it all.

28. "If you say to people, 'Hi, how are you?' people used to say kind of rotely, 'I'm fine,'" said Kelly, the Carnegie Mellon business professor. "I don't hear that anymore. People are saying, 'It's been terrible this morning,' or 'My kids were up all night.'"

29. These long days are not entirely new. At the turn of the century, many people worked twelve hours a day, six days a week, Kelly said. The single-breadwinner, eight-hour workday was made possible by the economic prosperity that followed World War II.

30. The days when a plant worker earned enough to raise a large family may have been an anomaly, he said.

31. Today, in less prosperous times, the need to make ends meet motivates many people to push harder. But the great American dream, the need to do a little better and provide the extras is a big factor, Kelly said.

32. Self-worth and social status became tied to work in the past forty years, and the fast-track was born, he said. Baby boomers and their parents bought into that, but now in the shadow of the booming '80s, many people are scrutinizing the myth of upward mobility through organizational ranks, Kelly said.

33. "People are starting to redefine the role of the workplace in their lives," he said. "People have lost touch with their spouses, their nuclear family and they're asking themselves, 'Why am I doing this?'"

34. Time-management concepts in the '70s and '80s focused on using technology and planning to become more efficient and organized, but many people used the extra time to do more work, Fortino said. That left a legacy of burnouts, heart attacks and divorces.

35. Now Fortino preaches the importance of balancing career and financial considerations with health, family, social, recreational, spiritual and intellectual needs. He likens the modern person to a juggler trying to keep rubber and crystal balls in the air.

36. "If one of those balls that are rubber falls it bounces," he said. "If the crystal balls health and family fall, they shatter. And you can't bring them back."

## ▼ Questions for Critical Thought

### "Recipe for the '90s"

1. What changes in society are causing the blending of home life and work? Give two examples of how the lines between work and home are becoming blurred.
2. In what ways has technology allowed for this blending of work and home responsibilities?
3. What are the statistics mentioned on the number of working mothers in the U.S. today, as compared to 1980?
4. What are the statistics on the average number of hours people today spend at work each week? At what other time in American history did people have such long work weeks? Approximately how many hours did the average American work at that time?
5. What are the motivating factors today that cause Americans to push themselves to work so hard?
6. What recommendations or warnings are made in the article regarding the average American's future and health?

## Reading Assignment

### "Spare the Rod? Maybe"

*Preview*   Read the introduction and topic sentences in this essay.

*Anticipate*   What do you think this article will be about? Use the "Notes" column to record your thoughts.

*Read and Reread*   Read the entire article, marking unknown terms. Then reread more slowly and use the "Notes" column to interact with the essay. Mark important and interesting points and define unknown terms.

### Spare the Rod? Maybe

*by Michael D. Lemonick*

Reported by Alice Park/New York and Jacqueline Saviano/Los Angeles. This article was published in *Time* magazine, 8/25/97.

1    One of the toughest parts of parenting is the seemingly endless series of decisions you have to make. Breast-feeding or formula? Cloth or

Notes

disposable? Day care or the mommy track? It is not as though there is an absolute right answer to any of these questions—yet parents often feel the wrong choice could be disastrous. That is especially true when it comes to spanking. Every parent has been in a situation where a whack on the rear seems like the only recourse to little Janie's or Johnny's tantrum. But at least since the 1960s, the conventional wisdom propounded by parenting gurus has been that hitting is generally unwise because it sends a message that violence is an acceptable way to solve disputes.

2   Now comes a scientific study that frames the issue in larger societal terms. Writing in the journal *Archives of Pediatric and Adolescent Medicine,* University of New Hampshire sociologist Murray Straus and his colleagues report that "when parents use corporal punishment to reduce [antisocial behavior], the long-term effect tends to be the opposite." Not only that—the authors suggest that if you spare the rod, you will help reduce the overall level of violence in American society.

3   Straus' study, first presented at a conference in 1994 and now appearing in formal publication with a more careful analysis of the data, is highly controversial. It may prove something, say critics, but not what Straus thinks it does.

4   The problem has to do with who was in the study. Straus and company culled their information from telephone interviews conducted by the U.S. Bureau of Labor Statistics beginning in 1979 with 807 mothers of children ages six to nine. They were asked how many times they had spanked their children in the past week and what the kids' behavior was like—did they lie, cheat, act up in school? Then the bureau polled the same group two years later. Sure enough, the kids who had been spanked had become increasingly antisocial.

5   But when you look a little closer at these findings, they start to seem a bit murky. To begin with, observes Dr. Den Trumbull, a Montgomery, Ala., pediatrician who is vocal in the spanking debate, the mothers ranged in age from fourteen to twenty-one. That is hardly a representative slice of American motherhood. Moreover, those who spanked did so on average twice a week. These factors, says Trumbull, plus the fact that some of the kids were as old as nine, "are markers of a dysfunctional family in my mind, and in the minds of most psychologists and pediatricians."

6   Trumbull also observes that limiting the study to six-to-nine year-olds skewed the results: by then kids can understand the consequences of their actions. For them frequent physical punishment is likely to be humiliating and traumatic—and might well lead to worse behavior down the line.

7     Straus disagrees. He writes, "It is plausible to argue that [corporal punishment] of toddlers will have a greater effect [than it does on older kids] because it occurs at a crucial developmental stage."

8     Plausible to Straus, anyway. According to Trumbull, more sophisticated studies have consistently shown that corporal punishment is effective and not harmful to long-term development if it is confined to youngsters between eighteen months and six years. Younger children have a poor understanding of the consequences of their behavior. If inappropriate behavior gets out of hand—especially if it poses a danger to the child or to others—a smack on the bottom may be the only way to control it.

9     Trumbull, a pro-spanking partisan, adds that he favors corporal punishment only as a last resort, after putting a child on time out—a few minutes of inactivity—then warning him or her that the next miscue will bring a whack. Still, he says, punishment should be limited to one or two mild slaps on the buttocks. His views are widely shared. More than two-thirds of pediatricians in recent polls approved parental spanking in certain situations.

10     "The usual example," says child-abuse authority Mary Ann Mason, who teaches a course on Children and the Law at the University of California, Berkeley, "is when a kid races across the street in front of a car. The slap literally imprints on him the need for safety. No one would consider that child abuse."

11     It is the legitimate fear of child abuse that Trumbull believes is largely behind the anti-spanking movement. The backlash started in the 1960s, he says, with the advent of more permissive parenting. But in the past decade or so, a shocking rise in child-abuse cases has had public-health officials scrambling for an explanation. Blaming spanking made sense; the notion that violence begets violence has a certain touchy-feely logic. Besides, most parents feel terrible after spanking their kids. What better reason to cut it out?

12     Trouble is, while spanking is down, child abuse is still up. It appears that well-meaning professionals have been using the wrong whipping boy—and Straus' study offers little reason to change that assessment.

## ▼ Questions for Critical Thought

### "Spare the Rod? Maybe"

1. In paragraph 2, we're told that a new study reports that "when parents use corporal punishment to reduce [antisocial behavior], the long-term effect tends to be the opposite." Explain in your own words what this study suggests.

*Notes*

2. The article presents two very different views on the issue of spanking. What are the two views presented and who represents each view in the article?
3. Why are Straus' findings about spanking being questioned?
4. In what situations does Dr. Trumbull advocate spanking? What does he believe is behind the anti-spanking movement?
5. What other expert opinions are included in this article?
6. After reading the article and thinking about the issue, what is your position on corporal punishment?

## Reading Assignment

"*Spare the Chores, Spoil the Child*"

***Preview*** Read the first sentences of the first ten paragraphs of this book review.

***Anticipate*** What do you think this book review will be about? Respond in the "Notes" column.

***Read and Reread*** Read the entire article, marking unknown terms. Then reread more slowly and use the "Notes" column to interact with the essay. Mark important and interesting points and define unknown terms.

### Spare the Chores, Spoil the Child
*Jennifer Bojorquez*

This article was published in the *Sacramento Bee*, 8/21/95.

1   A few years ago, William Damon attended an international conference for child development experts in Germany and heard something that shocked him.

2   Household chores for children are out of fashion.

3   This news was delivered to the group by an expert who had completed a study on children and household chores. He said things-to-do lists hanging on the refrigerator door are from another era. The proportion of children doing chores—especially in Western countries—is decreasing, according to the study. That means that soon there might be no more nagging your kid to take out the garbage or to vacuum the living room. No more hassles over the cleaning their rooms.

4   The expert then gave the reason: Parents have simply given up.

5   Damon, listening as the expert spoke with an approving voice, noticed that the other people in the room seemed to agree that the study's findings were positive. One person said it was about time that adults realize that kids' time is valuable, too.

6   "The parents said it was easier to do the chores themselves than to get their kids to do them," says Damon. "I couldn't believe it. . . . Everybody was acting as if this was right."

7   Damon says he then stood and listed the benefits of having children do household chores. But when he started talking about the work ethic, responsibility and the importance of helping in the community, he noticed that few seemed to agree with him.

8   "Everybody looked at me as if I was from Mars," says Damon. "It hit me: We have come too far. Our children are running our homes, and in the long run, it hurts them. We are bringing up a generation of self-indulgent, spoiled kids who whine to get their way. . . . Parents are giving in to this type of behavior because child care experts have told them that's the way it should be, and it starts with something as simple as household chores."

9   Damon himself is one of those experts. He is a professor in the education department at Brown University, and is considered a leader in his field. That conference, however, convinced him that there is something very wrong with the way we are bringing up our kids.

10  In his 246-page, highly praised book, *Greater Expectations* (Free Press, $23), Damon argues that dangerous misconceptions about children's developmental needs have resulted in an increase in youth violence, suicide, delinquency, teen pregnancies, poor social conduct and low academic achievement.

11  "Children need discipline. They need to be told 'no,'" he says in an interview. "But parents are afraid of hurting their children's self-esteem or hurting their feelings. . . . This is what they've been told by popular culture child care experts, and they are wrong."

12  Damon argues that children thrive on challenges because their abilities are tested, that children are capable of understanding serious discussions, that children must be taught morals early and that parental discipline, when applied thoughtfully, is good.

13  In other words, instead of lowering standards, we should increase standards, and have greater expectations of our children.

14  Our children, he argues, will adjust accordingly.

15  "Despite what parents may hear, children will not be scarred for life if you tell them 'no,'" says Damon. He emphasizes that he recognizes that there is abuse—that too many parents put too much pressure on

their kids—but says that in the majority of the cases, parents and educators have lowered standards.

16  He particularly criticizes the self-esteem movement.

17  "We are telling children that they are great, but they haven't earned it. Yes, it's important to tell your children positive things, but telling your child everything he does is great is not good for him. It lowers his expectations and instills a sense of entitlement."

18  Damon's views are shared by a growing number of people in the child development community.

19  "We are telling them they are great for doing the minimal," says Daina Bluett, child development specialist for In-Charge, a national program that teaches parenting skills. "Children develop this sense that they are great and they are owed something without working for it. . . . The end result is that they feel they are entitled to $90 tennis shoes."

20  Damon blames a lot of this on baby boomers' belief that children should have the freedom to make their own decisions. Damon says a certain amount of such freedom is good, but it has gone too far. He says parents must return to a common-sense approach.

21  "I'm a parent. I know it's not easy . . . . but we as a society can't afford this. But it is something we can change."

22  The next time your child tries to get out of a chore, he says, talk to him or her about why it's important to do it. And make them do it. . . . Be consistent. After a while, probably a shorter time than most parents think, children will change."

23  And they'll be cleaning their rooms themselves.

## ▼ Questions for Critical Thought

### "Spare the Chores, Spoil the Child"

1. According to Damon, why have chores for children gone "out of fashion"? Why have parents taken over their children's chores in many cases?

2. What does Damon think of children not having chores? What are some other views regarding children and chores expressed in the article?

3. Why does Damon criticize the self-esteem movement? What other experts agree with this view? Why?

4. Damon suggests that parents should increase their standards, not lower them. Explain what he means. Do you agree or disagree with his view? Why?

5. After reading this review, what do you anticipate Damon's book to be about?

## Reading Assignment

*"The Most Precious Gift"*

***Preview***   Read the first three paragraphs of this journalistic article.

***Anticipate***   What do you think this article will be about? Use the "Notes" column to record your thoughts.

***Read and Reread***   Read the entire article, marking unknown terms. Then reread more slowly and use the "Notes" column to interact with the essay. Mark important and interesting points and define unknown terms.

### The Most Precious Gift
*by Hank Whittemore*

This article was published in *Parade Magazine*, 12/22/91.

1   "Sometimes I do wonder where I came from," muses Robert Howard Allen of West Tennessee, who had never seen the inside of a classroom until, in 1981 at age thirty-two, he entered college. No, he was not a late-blooming genius; but last May, after just a decade of school, he graduated from Vanderbilt University in Nashville with a master's degree and a Ph.D. in English. A gentle, unworldly spirit who plays the banjo and loves to make puns, he adds with an enigmatic grin, "Maybe I just fell out of the sky."

2   When Allen first appeared on the campus of Bethel College, a small Presbyterian school in McKenzie, fifteen miles from his backwoods home, administrators were even more baffled. Here was a grown man who had never been to grammar school or high school, yet he had "blown the lid off" his college placement test. He stood six feet tall, with unkempt red hair, and his tattered sweater was held together by safety pins. There were holes in his shoes and his front teeth were gone. He had rarely set foot outside Carroll County, 120 miles west of Nashville, where he was born. He lived in a ramshackle farmhouse—one of three

homes in the tiny hamlet of Rosser—without indoor plumbing. He had never ridden a bicycle or been inside a movie theater or out on a date.

3   With an aura of innocence, however, Allen's blue eyes sparkled from behind his steel-rimmed glasses as if he had a secret. And it turned out that he did—a secret that amounts to a triumph of faith.

4   From the age of seven, Robert Allen read books. Not just several books or even a few hundred, but thousands of every description—from Donald Duck comics to the Bible, from Homer to James Joyce—to the point where his head was filled with history and classical literature. The scope of his learning was far greater than that of any professor at Bethel, where he was invited to skip most of his freshman courses and enter as a sophomore. Yet, having spent his whole life in virtual isolation with elderly relatives, Allen himself had no idea how special he was.

5   He turned up at Bethel on a whim. "I'd started my own upholstery business in the back of the house," he recalls, "but when the 1980 recession came on, there was no more work. So I thought I'd give education a whirl. I didn't think I could succeed at it, though. I just assumed that people in college knew more than I did.

6   In three years, he graduated summa cum laude.

7   Without realizing it, Robert Allen had proved the power of reading to transform an individual life. In circumstances that otherwise would have been unbearable, he had read as an unconscious act of sheer survival. "Books were my great comfort," he says simply. "They were my pastime and my playmates." Reading whatever he could get his hands on, he traveled freely across time and space, meeting the world's greatest philosophers and poets down through the ages.

8   "He's at home in mythological Babylon and in eighth-century Judea," says Dr. William Ramsay, one of his Bethel advisers. "He became a citizen of the world without ever leaving Tennessee."

9   "Robert retains everything," says Prof. Vereen Bell, who teaches English at Vanderbilt, "so his head is just full of all this historical and mythological stuff that he has accumulated. In a sense, he missed the 20th century. He's in a kind of time warp, and I think he forever will be."

10  Allen's triumph had its seeds in suffering. His parents were divorced a few months before he was born. He yearned for his father but, to this day, has never seen him. His mother, Hazel, worked as a waitress and all but ignored him. "She was in the generation between the farmers and me," he says, "so I think she felt caught in that condition." When Robert was six, his mother abandoned him, running off with a traveling shoe salesman. She left him to be raised by elderly relatives—his grandfather and three great-aunts and a great-uncle—living in the same household.

11. Even today, Allen can express his youthful pain only through his poetry, as when he writes that the mother "had no love for her stray mistake of a child" and that his grandmother "died just one spring later, too soon to fill my childhood with any love." It was Uncle Eddie Jones, his guardian, who decreed that school was "a waste of time" and blocked authorities from enrolling him.

12. "I never entirely understood it," Allen says, adding that he was also told that his father might return "to kidnap me, even though there was no evidence that he even knew I existed." In any event, he adds, "They kept me home. I really was pretty much isolated."

13. The county sent teachers for the homebound twice weekly for a year, but from age seven the boy's formal education was over. In a house where at least one of his relatives was always sick or dying, growing up without friends, Allen listened to endless family stories; and Aunt Bevie Jones, Uncle Eddie's wife, began reading to him. "She had gone up to the eighth grade," he says, "but that was the only education in our family." Aunt Bevie taught him to read; his grandfather taught him to write; and the boy, in turn, read the King James Bible to his blind Aunt Ida, going through it twice from cover to cover.

14. Allen's male ancestors had been farmers, but since the 30s the men had become carpenters and house painters. The boy was destined to pick up these trades; but at age twelve, while he was helping care for sick relatives at home, he began reading an old set of Shakespeare's works. "I opened it up and just about read it through at a sitting," he says, and today he'll quote long passages from *King Lear* and *The Tempest*—to name just two of his favorites—at a moment's notice.

15. Hungry for more, he began picking up books at yard sales for pennies apiece—works of mythology, history, poetry and anything else he could find. By his early 20s, Robert had some 2000 volumes and a goal: "I followed a vague, overall plan, which I more or less fulfilled," he recalls, "to study literature in the context of history from the earliest times to the present."

16. When he saw the Carroll County Library in nearby Huntingdon, it was like discovering gold. "Sometimes his Grandfather Jim and Aunt Bevie came with him," recalls Claudine Halpers, the staffer who eventually encouraged him to try for college. "They showed up every week or two, regular as clockwork. They were poor but not ashamed. Robert was his own person—unassuming, but very bright with a keen sense of humor."

17. On the shelves, Allen found the complete set of Will and Ariel Durant's *The Story of Civilization* and spent the next two years wading through its ten massive volumes, simultaneously reading histories and

*Notes*

classics for each period. Out of pure enjoyment, he worked his way through the entire library, also teaching himself to read Greek and French to better absorb original versions. The works of Milton, Burns, Keats, Whitman, Wordsworth and other poets continued to feed his insatiable appetite for knowledge and what he now calls "language used to its highest potential."

18   At age thirty, Robert Allen took a high school equivalency test and easily earned his diploma. Two years later, when Bethel College officials saw his placement scores, they eased his way with a work-study grant combining scholarship funds and a campus job.

19   By 1984, after three years as an amiable, older and unquestionably "different" figure on the Bethel campus, he topped his senior class with straight As in all but typing. He scored 3.92 out of a possible 4.0 grade-point-average. As graduation presents, the faculty bought him his first suit—which he accepted reluctantly, saying they should give it to "someone who really needs it"—and a set of new front teeth. Aunt Bevie, by now 77, attended ceremonies where he received his diploma. The newspaper ran a story about him.

20   The publicity, however, led to a crushing blow. One Sunday, while attending the local Baptist church, Allen recalls in a soft tone of wonderment, "The pastor got up and preached a sermon on 'the sinfulness of these arrogant people who get their picture in the paper,' obviously meaning me. It was a very unpleasant experience."

21   Accepting a fellowship from Vanderbilt, with an eye toward ultimately teaching, Robert Allen packed up his belongings that fall and moved with Aunt Bevie to Nashville. It was his first venture beyond the green hills of West Tennessee and his entrance into the modern world of a "big city," where he took his first elevator ride.

22   While coping with noise and traffic, along with adjusting to university life, Allen decided it was time to reconcile with his mother, who had remarried and settled in Missouri. For three years, he had phoned her on Mother's Day, although she always seemed annoyed and even hostile. He told his friends, "There's a new chance for us, because I can finally forgive. I just want to be a son to her." Near Christmas in 1984, he and Aunt Bevie drove to Missouri uninvited.

23   The incident is still hard for him to discuss. "We spent about an hour with her," he recalls, "and basically she was angry. She blamed everyone for not treating her well. I think she felt guilty. It was a tirade about how badly she had been raised." Allen left with Aunt Bevie while his mother was still shouting from the doorway. He cried all the way back to Tennessee.

24   The following summer, no longer able to take care of ailing Aunt

Bevie, he was forced to put her into a nursing home in Huntingdon. He drove to visit her every other weekend until she died in 1988, leaving him to face the rest of his remarkable odyssey alone.

25. Aunt Bevie had lived long enough to see him earn his master's degree at Vanderbilt in 1986. Allen's thesis was a collection of his poetry, most of it autobiographical or based on the family tales he had heard as a child. For his doctoral dissertation, he began studying an early poem by William Butler Yeats, "The Wanderings of Oisin."

26. In 1990, on the verge of earning his Ph.D., he drove alone to Missouri to see his mother and try once more. He called from a nearby pay phone to announce his arrival, only to be told that she had died ten days earlier. No one had notified him. He visited her grave, then drove back to Nashville.

27. During the first half of 1991, aside from attending graduation ceremonies at Vanderbilt, Robert Allen taught a semester of English at Bethel College. During the summer, he continued to live alone in McKenzie. There, he set aside a copy of *War and Peace* one afternoon to talk about the future. "I'd like to continue teaching and writing poetry," he told me. "In the past year I've been turning family history into a long series of poems, loosely linked together." What does the Ph.D. mean to him? "Well," he shrugged, "it means I can get a job." Any thoughts of eventually getting married? "No," he said with a smile—as if that were a possibility too far down the road to see.

28. "Robert is struggling with great courage to make himself more a part of the contemporary world," says Professor Bell, "so his story is going to go on and on."

29. At the doorway of his small, rented home, Robert Allen, age 42, stands with his Tolstoy edition in one hand, waving with the other. He smiles his enigmatic smile before turning and disappearing, at least for a while, into a distant time and place. Reading is what saved him; writing poetry about his family is both an exorcism of painful experiences and a bold journey of personal evolution. His secret seems to lie at some unfathomable depth, as if he were not only destined but determined, to finally solve the mystery for himself—to keep on falling out of the sky.

## ▼ Questions for Critical Thought

### "The Most Precious Gift"

1. Why did Robert Allen read so much as a child? What purpose did reading serve?

2. Why does Robert Allen write poetry now?

*Notes*

3. Have you ever used reading or writing in ways that are similar to how Allen used reading and writing? Explain.

4. What did you find most interesting about Allen's life?

## Reading Assignment

*"Look Past Rapper for Real Heroes"*

***Preview***   Read the first four paragraphs.

***Anticipate***   What do you think this article will be about? Write your response in the "Notes" column.

***Read and Reread***   Read the entire article, marking unknown terms. Then reread more slowly and use the "Notes" column to interact with the essay. Mark important and interesting points and define unknown terms.

### Look Past Rapper for Real Heroes
*by Fahizah Alim*

This article was published in the *Sacramento Bee*, 3/13/97.

1   You can bet that the vast majority of Americans didn't know a thing about Notorious B.I.G. until his murder last week made headlines in newspapers and on TV newscasts across the country.

2   Today, even more people will learn about the slain rapper—his family plans to drive to his funeral procession through Brooklyn neighborhoods he grew up in, while blasting his music and further glamorizing a life and a message that deserve no glamour.

3   The death of B.I.G. (born Christopher Wallace) introduced to millions of Americans the hulking image of an ex-dope-dealing black man rapping about apparently living a "gangsta" life.

4   His is a harmful, misleading image that has captured the adulation and respect of too many adolescents—of all races. But, most significantly, it undermines the reality of millions of young African American males who are living decent, productive, even exemplary lives.

5   It's a negative image that I want to juxtapose with another.

6   And that is the image of young black men who, like my 22-year-old son, Sherod Thaxton, are far removed from gangsta rap's highly promoted, fatalistic culture.

7   This week, my son graduates from UC Davis and joins the growing ranks of black men earning bachelor's degrees.

8. It doesn't make the front page, but black men earned 30,086 bachelor's degrees in 1994—a 19.6 percent increase from 1977, according to a report released last week by the United Negro College Fund. Black enrollment in college also is at a historically high 10.1 percent.

9. I want the image of my son spending his evenings reviewing offers of full scholarships from Ivy League colleges and law schools across the country to counterbalance the image of black gangsters counting their dollars.

10. I want young black men trapped in this "to-die-for-materialistic-culture" to know that rappers, athletes and drug dealers are not the only black men who can make money.

11. When the public sees a young black man, I also want them to think of 18-year-old Kenyatta Muhammad, a senior at Luther Burbank High School who is receiving offers from every college he applied to. An excellent student raised by a single mother, Kenyatta spends his spare time reaching out to disaffected youth—when he is not working at his part-time job at the Department of Education.

12. Maybe not all youths can be scholars like Sherod or Kenyatta. But the millions of hard-working black males who hand out burgers and stock warehouses and serve in the armed forces deserve to be recognized far more than a guy who makes his living spewing out misogynistic filth.

13. I want millions of Americans who last week became acquainted with the black gangsta rapper to become more acquainted with the black scholar and the black soldier, the black factory worker, and the black banker, all of whom make up the majority of black men.

14. The life of Notorious B.I.G. is a dangerous exception, and his highly publicized image reinforces negative stereotypes and promotes criminal behavior.

15. We should be ashamed to have radio stations across the country stop regular programming for hours to salute him. These stations cater to our impressionable youth.

16. And what was Los Angeles Assemblyman Kevin Murray thinking last week when he proposed that the Legislature commemorate the passing of B.I.G.?

17. Was B.I.G. the most worthwhile black man he could find to honor? Murray, and everyone else who is intrigued by Notorious B.I.G., need to look beyond the hype.

▼ **Questions for Critical Thought**

"Look Past Rapper..."

1. Why does Alim, the writer of this article, object to the "gangsta" image?

Notes

2. What image does Alim wish would "counterbalance the image of black gangsters counting their dollars"?

3. Why does Alim object to radio stations and politicians commemorating rappers like B.I.G.?

4. Alim suggests those "intrigued by Notorious B.I.G. need to look beyond the hype." Explain what she means. Do you agree or disagree with her position? Why?

## Reading Assignment

*"It's a Rap the Young Don't Deserve"*

*Preview* Skim this journalistic piece by reading the first sentence of each paragraph.

*Anticipate* What do you think this article will be about? Write your response in the "Notes" column.

*Read and Reread* Read the entire article, marking unknown terms. Then reread more slowly and use the "Notes" column to interact with the essay. Mark important and interesting points and define unknown terms.

### It's a Rap the Young Don't Deserve
*by Donna Britt*

This was published in the *Sacramento Bee*, 3/19/97.

1   Even if you never met Brian, Terrance and Nate—or didn't give two snaps about Notorious B.I.G.'s death—the brave new world of black folks could confuse you.

2   I found it strange enough two weeks ago—when Tyra Banks, *Sports Illustrated*'s first black Swimsuit Issue cover girl, inspired a young white man to gush on TV that human cloning might be cool because "we need more Tyra Banks." Then I saw Ralph Lauren's glossy new ads featuring hot black models Naomi Campbell and Tyson and heard of the $5 million that CBS will pay Bryant Gumbel—called by some "the smartest man on TV."

3   Then on Tuesday morning, I turned on the TV. The first image: a muscular black guy leading two buff white women in a workout. Switching channels, I saw an African American anchorman giving sports highlights.

4   I kept switching. Next was a McDonald's ad featuring a young black couple, then a pro-education commercial with a scholarly looking brother. Next station: dreadlocked singer Chic Street Man leading kids in a Calypso song. By the time I got to CBS' "This Morning"—whose black announcer had his arm linked with that of his white female counterpart—I figured I'd slipped into multicultural heaven.

5   But like many blacks, I'm torn between celebrating African Americans' growing presence in high-profile jobs, ads, TV shows and movies and feeling paralyzed by the defeats.

6   Deep-seated racism remains. Nearly half of black children live below the poverty level—on less than $12,980 for a family of three. My son, fifteen, is nearly ten times as likely to die violently as his white pals.

7   My confusion was only heightened by the recent shooting death of Notorious B.I.G. My knowledge of the gangsta rapper was gleaned from articles after Tupac Shakur's slaying in September and a *Vibe* magazine cover story. Pictured with then-wife Faith, B.I.G. flashed a sneer and hefty jewelry; Faith sported sky scraper hair and a hot-mama pout.

8   I wasn't impressed.

9   I wasn't supposed to be. The gangsta image is most appealing to the young. But can kids see through those who rap about being have-nots while flaunting their wealth? Can they see the emptiness in B.I.G.'s and others' macho materialism?

10  The questions led me to the first group of baggy-jeans-wearing, sideways-baseball-cap-sporting black youths I could find. Walking down a suburban street, the kids looked like black teenagers everywhere.

11  Brian Campbell, Terrance Presbury and Nate Williams, all 14, are freshmen at a racially mixed high school in Silver Spring, Md. Each lives in a modest apartment with his single mom and loves rap—including some of B.I.G.'s music.

12  The stereotypes end there. The guys, on their way to tutor middle school students, were courteous, well spoken and stunned by B.I.G.'s death—"Most rappers have a real life they don't talk about and a stage life," Terrance said. "You don't expect them to die." The youths feel too many people, such as salesmen who follow them around stores assuming they're shoplifters, mistake their hip-hop style for substance.

13  "You might dress like rappers, but it doesn't mean you're going to go out and shoot somebody," explained Brian, an aspiring veterinarian.

14  They'd never call women "bitches" or "hos" as some rappers do—"That's just rude," Terrance explained. "And the gangsta lifestyle—that's too dangerous. It's stupid, trying to be big and bad." Nate, who wears cornrows, added, "My heroes are Martin Luther King, my mom and

**Notes**

dad. People who judge the rappers put a name on us.... I'm going to college to be a lawyer. Don't judge me by them."

15   Listening to them, I felt grateful. Like my thankfulness at seeing how far some blacks have progressed, the gratitude was touched by sadness—for kids who aren't as perceptive, and for the culture that forgets young black men such as Brian, Terrance and Nate exist.

16   But Terrance said such attitudes give him something to aspire to:

17   "Being successful—and making all the people who doubted us shut up."

### ▼ Questions for Critical Thought

*"It's a Rap the Young Don't Deserve"*

1. What are some of the images Britt celebrates at the beginning of the piece?

2. In paragraph 5, Britt says that she feels conflicted over the contrasting conditions for African Americans. Explain the conflict as she sees it.

3. How did Britt's encounter with three high school students cause her to reconsider the gangster influence on youth? Do you agree with her assessment? Why? Why not?

### Reading Assignment

*"Who Is Great?"*

***Preview***   Read the first three paragraphs and then all the subheadings.

***Anticipate***   What do you think this article will be about? Write your response in the "Notes" column.

***Read and Reread***   Read the entire article, marking unknown terms. Then reread more slowly and use the "Notes" column to interact with the essay. Mark important and interesting points and define unknown terms.

> *Are the people we call "great" really different from you and me? Here's what experts find when they ask . . .*

### Who Is Great?
*by Michael Ryan*

This article was published in *Parade* magazine, June 16, 1996.

1. As a young boy, Albert Einstein did so poorly in school that teachers thought he was slow. The young Napoleon Bonaparte was just one of the hundreds of artillery lieutenants in the French Army. And the teenage George Washington, with little formal education, was being trained not as a soldier but as a land surveyor.

2. Despite their unspectacular beginnings, each would go on to carve a place for himself in history. What was it that enabled them to become great? Were they born with something special? Or did their greatness have more to do with timing, devotion and, perhaps, an uncompromising personality?

3. For decades, scientists have been asking such questions. And, in the past few years, they have found evidence to help explain why some people rise above, while others—similarly talented, perhaps—are left behind. Their findings could have implications for us all.

4. **Who is great?** Defining who is great depends on how one measures success. But there are some criteria. "Someone who has made a lasting contribution to human civilization is great," said Dean Keith Simonton, a professor of psychology at the University of California at Davis and author of the 1994 book *Greatness: Who Makes History and Why*. But he added a caveat: "Sometimes great people don't make it into the history books. A lot of women achieved great things or were influential but went unrecognized."

5. In writing his book, Simonton combined historical knowledge about great figures with recent findings in genetics, psychiatry and the social sciences. The great figures he focused on include men and women who have won Nobel Prizes, led great nations or won wars, composed symphonies that have endured for centuries, or revolutionized science, philosophy, politics or the arts. Though he doesn't have a formula to define how or why certain people rise above (too many factors are involved), he has come up with a few common characteristics.

6. **A "never surrender" attitude.** If great achievers share anything, said Simonton, it is an unrelenting drive to succeed. "There's a tendency to think that they are endowed with something super-normal," he explained. "But what comes out of the research is that there are great people who have no amazing intellectual processes. It's a difference in degree. Greatness is built upon tremendous amounts of study, practice and devotion."

7. He cited Winston Churchill, Britain's prime minister during World War II, as an example of a risk-taker who would never give up. Thrust into office when his country's morale was at its lowest, Churchill rose brilliantly to lead the British people. In a speech following the Allied evacuation at Dunkirk in 1940, he inspired the nation when he said,

"We shall not flag or fail. We shall go on to the end . . . We shall never surrender." After the war, Churchill was voted out of office but again demonstrated his fighting spirit when he delivered his famous "Iron Curtain" speech at Westminster College in Missouri in 1946. This time, at the dawn of the Cold War, he exhorted the entire Western world to stand up to communism: "We hold the power to save the future," he said. "Our difficulties and dangers will not be removed by closing our eyes to them."

8   **Can you be born great?** In looking at Churchill's role in history—as well as the roles of other political and military leaders—Simonton discovered a striking pattern: "Firstborns and only children tend to make good leaders in time of crisis: They're used to taking charge. But middleborns are better as peacetime leaders: They listen to different constituencies better and make the necessary compromises. Churchill, an only child, was typical. He was great in a crisis, but in peacetime he was not effective—not even popular."

9   Timing is another factor. "If you took George Washington and put him in the 20th century, he would go nowhere as a politician," Simonton declared. "He was not an effective public speaker, and he didn't like shaking hands with the public. On the other hand, I'm not sure Franklin Roosevelt would have done well in Washington's time. He wouldn't have had the radio to do his fireside chats."

10  **Can you be *too* smart?** One surprise among Simonton's findings is that many political and military leaders have been bright but not overly so. Beyond a certain point, he explained, other factors, like the ability to communicate effectively, become more important than innate intelligence as measured by an IQ test. The most intelligent U.S. Presidents, for example—Thomas Jefferson, Woodrow Wilson and John F. Kennedy—had a hard time getting elected, Simonton said, while others with IQs closer to average (such as Warren G. Harding) won by landslides. While political and economic factors also are involved, having a genius IQ is not necessary to be a great leader.

11  In the sciences, those with "genius level" IQs do have a better shot at achieving recognition, added Simonton. Yet evidence also indicates that overcoming traditional ways of thinking may be just as important.

12  He pointed to one recent study where college students were given a set of data and were asked to see if they could come up with a mathematical relation. Almost a third did. What they did not know was that they had just solved one of the most famous scientific equations in history: the Third Law of Planetary Motion, an equation that Johannes Kepler came up with in 1618.

13   Kepler's genius, Simonton said, was not so much in solving a mathematical challenge. It was in thinking about the numbers in a unique way—applying his mathematical knowledge to his observations of planetary motion. It was his boldness that set him apart.

14   **Love your work.** As a child, Einstein became fascinated with the way magnets draw iron filings. "He couldn't stop thinking about this stuff," Simonton pointed out. "He became obsessed with problems in physics by the time he was sixteen, and he never stopped working on them. It's not surprising that he made major contributions by the time he was twenty-six."

15   "For most of us, it's not that we don't have the ability," Simonton added, "it's that we don't devote the time. You have to put in the effort and put up with all the frustrations and obstacles."

16   Like other creative geniuses, Einstein was not motivated by a desire for fame, said Simonton. Instead, his obsession with his work was what set him apart. Where such drive comes from remains a mystery. But it is found in nearly all creative geniuses—whether or not their genius is acknowledged by contemporaries.

17   "Emily Dickinson was not recognized for her poetry until after her death," said Simonton. "But she was not writing for fame. The same can be said of James Joyce, who didn't spend a lot of time worrying about how many people would read *Finnegans Wake*. Beethoven once said, when confronting a musician struggling to play some of his new quartets, 'They are not for you, but for a later age.'"

18   Today, researchers have evidence that an intrinsic passion for one's work is a key to rising above. In a 1985 study at Brandeis University conducted by Teresa Amabile, now a professor of business administration at Harvard University, a group of professional writers—none famous—was asked to write a short poem. Each writer was then randomly placed in one of three groups: one group was asked to keep in mind the idea of writing for money; another was told to think about writing just for pleasure; and a third group was given no instruction at all.

19   The poems then were submitted anonymously to a panel of professional writers for evaluation. The poetry written by people who thought about writing for money ranked the lowest. Those who thought about writing just for pleasure did the best. "Motivation that comes from enjoying the work makes a significant difference," Amabile said.

20   **What price greatness?** Many great figures have had poor personal relationships, perhaps a result of their drive to excel, said Simonton. And great people, he added, often can be unbearable: "Beethoven, for instance, was tyrannical with servants and rude to his friends. His

*Notes*

personal hygiene was not particularly great either. When working, he would go for days or weeks without bathing."

21   Yet one common belief about greatness—that it often is accompanied by mental imbalance—seems unfounded.

22   "Certain types of psychopathology are more common in some professions than in others," explained Dr. Arnold M. Ludwig, a psychiatrist at the University of Kentucky Medical Center and author of a new book, *The Price of Greatness*. "Poets, for example, have high rates of depression. But architects as a group are very stable. Fiction writers and jazz musicians are more likely to abuse drugs and alcohol. But when you go outside the artistic fields, you find phenomenal creative achievements among scientists, social activists, and politicians. It is certainly possible for people to achieve great things without corresponding mental illness."

23   Dr. Ludwig did some personal research on the issue as well. "I have two children who are very creative and artistic," he said. "I decided to find out whether they would have to be crazy if they were to grow up to be geniuses. I was happy to find out that they would not."

### ▼ Questions for Critical Thought

#### "Who Is Great?"

1. Referring back to the reading, list some of the "great" people mentioned. Who were they, and what did they do?
2. Now list some of the qualities of a "great" person.
3. If you are currently working in the *hero* chapter (Chapter 5), explain which qualities a "great" person and a hero have in common.
4. In paragraph 2, the author, Michael Ryan, asks three questions. Why does he ask all of these questions? How do they help him communicate with us?
5. In paragraph 4, Ryan tells us about Keith Simonton. Ryan tells us where Simonton works and the title of a book. Why did Ryan choose to include this information?

### Reading Assignment

#### "The Wrong Examples"

*Preview*   Read the introduction and the topic sentences.

*Anticipate* What do you think this article will be about? Write your response in the "Notes" column.

*Read and Reread* Read the entire article, marking unknown terms. Then reread more slowly and use the "Notes" column to interact with the essay. Mark important and interesting points and define unknown terms.

## The Wrong Examples
*by David L. Evans*

This article was published in *Newsweek*, 3/1/93.

*An engineer and a native of Helena, Arkansas, Evans is a senior admissions officer at Harvard.*

1. As a college admissions officer I am alarmed at the dearth of qualified black male candidates. Often in high schools that are ninety percent black, *all* the African-American students who come to my presentation are female! This gender disparity persists to college matriculation where the black male population almost never equals that of the female.

2. What is happening to these young men? Who or what is influencing them? I submit that the absence of male role models and slanted television images of black males have something to do with it.

3. More than half of black children live in homes headed by women, and almost all of the black teachers they encounter are also women. This means that most African-American male children do not often meet black male role models in their daily lives. They must look beyond their immediate surroundings for exemplary black men to emulate. Lacking in-the-flesh models, many look to TV for black heroes.

4. Unfortunately, TV images of black males are not particularly diverse. Their usual roles are to display physical prowess, sing, dance, play a musical instrument or make an audience laugh. These roles are enticing and generously rewarded. But the reality is that success comes to only a few extraordinarily gifted performers or athletes.

5. A foreigner watching American TV would probably conclude that most successful black males are either athletes or entertainers. That image represents both success and failure. Success, because the substantial presence of blacks in sports, music and sitcoms is a milestone in the struggle begun almost fifty years ago to penetrate the racial barriers of big-league athletics and television. It is a failure because the overwhelming success of a *few* highly visible athletes, mu-

sicians and comedians has type-cast black males. Millions see these televised roles as a definition of black men. Nowhere is this more misleading than in the inner city, where young males see it as "the way out."

6   Ask a random sample of Americans to identify Michael Jordan, Bo Jackson, Magic Johnson, Hammer, Prince, Eddie Murphy or Mike Tyson. Correct responses would probably exceed ninety percent. Then ask them to identify Colin Powell, August Wilson, Franklin Thomas, Mike Espy, Walter Massey, Earl Graves or the late Reginald Lewis and I doubt that ten percent would respond correctly. The second group contains the chairman of the Joint Chiefs of Staff, a Pulitzer Prize-winning playwright, the president of the Ford Foundation, the secretary of agriculture, the director of the National Science Foundation, the publisher of Black Enterprise magazine and the former CEO of a multi-million-dollar business.

7   The Democratic National Convention that nominated Bill Clinton brought Ron Brown, Jesse Jackson, David Dinkins, Kurt Schmoke and Bernard Shaw into living rooms as impressive role models. Their relative numbers at the convention were in noticeable contrast to the black baseball players who made up nearly half of the All-Star teams on the Tuesday night of the convention.

8   This powerful medium has made the glamour of millionaire boxers, ballplayers, musicians and comedians appear so close, so tangible that, to naive young boys, it seems only a dribble or dance step away. In the hot glare of such surrealism, schoolwork and prudent personal behavior can become irrelevant.

9   Impressionable young black males are not the only Americans getting this potent message. *All* TV viewers are subtly told that blacks are "natural" athletes, they are "funny" and all of them have "rhythm." Such a thoroughly reinforced message doesn't lie dormant. A teacher who thinks every little black boy is a potential Bo Jackson or Eddie Murphy is likely to give his football practice a higher priority than his homework or to excuse his disruptive humor.

10  **Neck jewelry:** Television's influence is so pronounced that one seldom meets a young black man who isn't wearing paraphernalia normally worn by athletes and entertainers. Young white men wear similar attire but not in the same proportion. Whites have many more televised role models from which to choose. There are very few whites in comparison to the number of blacks in the NBA. Black males are twelve and one-half percent of the American male population but constitute seventy-five percent of the NBA and are thereby six times overrepresented. That television presents poor role models for *all* kids doesn't wash.

11     These highly visible men's influence is so dominant that it has redefined the place of neck jewelry, sneakers and sports apparel in our society. The yearning to imitate the stars has sometimes had dire consequences. Young lives have been lost over sneakers, gold chains and jackets. I dare say that many black prison inmates are the *flotsam and jetsam\** from dreamboats that never made it to the NBA or MTV.

12     Producers of TV sports, popular music and sitcoms should acknowledge these "side effects" of the American Dream. More important are the superstars themselves. To a man, they are similar to lottery winners and their presence on TV is cruelly deceptive to their electronic protégés. Surely they can spend some of their time and resources to convince their young followers that even incredible talent doesn't assure fame or fortune. An athlete or performer must also be amazingly lucky in his quest for Mount Olympus.

13     A well-trained mind is a surer, although less glamorous, bet for success. Arthur Ashe spent his whole life teaching precisely this message. Bill Cosby and Jim Brown also come to mind as African-American superstars who use their substantial influence to redirect young black males. At this time, when black men are finally making some inroads into the upper echelons of American society, we need more than ever to encourage the young to look beyond the stereotypes of popular culture.

### ▼ Questions for Critical Thought

#### "The Wrong Examples"

1. What is Evans' reason for writing this essay? What do you believe he hopes to accomplish?

2. What kinds of media images is Evans concerned about and why? Do his concerns seem legitimate to you? Why? Why not?

3. What kinds of heroes would he like to see young black males look up to? List them.

4. Choose a well-developed paragraph from this essay and explain the kinds of evidence Evans uses to support his paragraph point.

### Reading Assignment

#### "Child's Play"

**Preview**    Read the opening paragraph.

---

\* *Flotsam and jestsam:* shipwrecked objects floating aimlessly.

Notes

*Anticipate* What do you think this article will be about? Write your response in the "Notes" column.

*Read and Reread* Read the entire article, marking unknown terms. Then reread more slowly and use the "Notes" column to interact with the essay. Mark important and interesting points and define unknown terms.

### Child's Play
*by Calvin Trillin*

This article was published in *Time* magazine, 12/30/96.

1. HERE IS WHAT NOBODY HAS BOTHERED TO MENTION IN ALL THE TALK ABOUT how V chips are going to protect our kids from the smut and violence on television: in most American households, the only people who understand how to program modern electronic devices are the children. So the V chip will presumably have to be managed by the very people it is meant to control.

2. You're thinking that it won't work that way. From what you've read, you understand the V chip to be so simple to use that a grownup can do it. That's what was said about VCRs. Yet we all know people like Bennett and Linda Weber, whose travails I reported on a year or two ago. The Webers thought they were pleased that their 26-year-old son Jeffrey had finally moved out of the house, and then they realized they had lost the ability to tape.

3. Someday, of course, people of Jeffrey's generation will be the parents in control, and they will be casually hooking up V chips to CD-ROMs and the Internet so that their children can play nonviolent, smut-free, four-dimensional Parcheesi with friends in Bangalore while listening to symphonic background music. Until then, though, any attempt at a techno-fix like the V chip will put the inmates in charge of the asylum.

4. This hadn't occurred to me until last week, when I was talking to a television reporter about the controversy over the rating system that will be used to offer parents guidance about which programs they may want to block. The television industry, which is in the enviable position of writing its own warning label, has resisted the content-based system favored by virtually everybody else, presumably on the theory that warnings of violent or suggestive content could scare off viewers and advertisers.

5. Having decided on a fuzzy, age-based rating system similar to the one used by movies, the networks are having their flacks write op-ed

pieces that extol the Aristotelian virtues of vagueness. In a similar position, the tobacco industry would favor a cigarette-pack warning label that says, "Some people sort of think that cigarette smoking may not be the absolutely best thing you can do for your health, although some others may disagree."

6   Networks may also dread a content-based rating system because of the potential embarrassment of seeing most of their programs listed in the paper with an accompanying *V* for Violence or *L* for Language or *S* for Sex. Think about what could happen if the industry ever lost control of the ratings, and someone like the editor in charge of the television listings decided to offer absolutely honest appraisals. The daytime talk shows would be rated *PE* for Pathetic Exploitation; the shopping channel would carry a *UA* for Untrammeled Acquisitiveness; and most sitcoms would be rated *MT* for Mindless Trash.

7   Even without those improvements, I told the reporter, I thought content-based ratings might be specific enough to serve some purpose. Liberals could block violence, and conservatives could block sex; and in a desperate attempt to see plenty of both, their children might visit each other's homes often enough to make a start on getting along with each other when they grow up.

8   But then, I could envision a younger version of Bennett Weber trying to block, say, programs that contained strong language and instead doing something that caused the set to transmit nothing but cooking shows. "Do something!" he says, turning to the child he's trying to protect. That child is Jeffrey at fourteen, who says, with a sly grin, "don't worry, Pop. I'll take care of it."

## ▼ Questions for Critical Thought

### "Child's Play"

1. What is the V-chip?
2. What similarities does Trillin see between the V-chip and VCRs? What is Trillin's main concern about the V-chip?
3. Trillin presents two kinds of rating systems: the age-based system that has been adopted by the television industry and the content-based system. Which system does Trillin seem to prefer? Why? What system would you prefer? Why?
4. Trillin uses humor and detail to get his points across. Look at paragraph 3. At what point does the example in this paragraph start to become a little unbelievable and humorous? Explain.

Notes

Notes

5. In the topic sentence of each of his paragraphs, Trillin uses a word or phrase that connects back to the previous paragraph. Highlight the words and phrases that create effective transitions.

## Reading Assignment

*"Family Ties Put a Face on the Faceless Issue of Free Speech"*

*Preview*   Quickly read the first eight paragraphs of this newspaper column.

*Anticipate*   What do you think this article will be about? Write your response in the "Notes" column.

*Read and Reread*   Read the entire article, marking unknown terms. Then reread more slowly and use the "Notes" column to interact with the essay. Mark important and interesting points and define unknown terms.

### Family Ties Put a Face on the Faceless Issue of Free Speech
*by Eric Slater*

This article was published in the *Los Angeles Times*, 4/18/98.

1   Newspaper writers and rap stars, it is not widely known, have much in common.

2   Stereotypically speaking, both groups are almost impossibly bad dressers—rappers opting for gold, gold, Armani and gold; journalists for lightly stained Dockers. Both work with language and, on the rare fine day, spin mere words into music. And most notably, both are frequently saved from a societal whipping behind the woodshed by the protections of the First Amendment.

3   Brothers of a sort, we are.

4   What, then, to make of my dilemma with rapper Shawn Thomas? In a song called "Deadly Game," Thomas, my free speech brother, advocates the killing of cops.

5   But I hear his words with new ears because now my real brother *is* a cop.

> It's a deadly game of baseball
> So when they try to pull you over
> Shoot 'em in the face, ya'll.

6   Thomas' song is of course not the first by an angry young rock 'n' roller to lash out at police officers, the symbol and sometime instrument

of real oppression, racism and brutality. Bob Marley shot the sheriff, but spared the deputy, in his spare, deceptively mellow classic.

7   Ice-T rose to the status of gangsta rap demigod when, in 1992's "Cop Killer," he declared:

> I'm 'bout to bust some shots off.
> I'm 'bout to dust some cops off.

8   But my younger brother Blake wasn't a cop then, he was a high school kid. And when a group of Texas lawmen threatened to disrupt a Time Warner shareholders meeting if the label didn't drop the Ice-T album, I derided them as simple, predictable reactionaries. I defended the rapper with a simple predictable free speech mantra: art does not beget violence. Today, I defend Shawn Thomas, who records under the name C-BO, with equal fervor but more thought, and—whether art begets violence or not—with the image of my little brother lying by the side of a road, shot in the face.

9   It was a year ago that the shades of gray began mottling my black and white mental canvas of artistic expression.

10   Two other reporters and I had stopped at the Tower Records in Northridge on our way back to the office from lunch. I don't recall which albums I picked up, or which the other passenger picked up. I only recall that the reporter who was driving that day grabbed Ice-T's 5-year-old album, "Body Count." Back in the car, he slid it into the CD player and punched up the song that made Ice-T a star, "Cop Killer."

11   We all cackled—not at the notion of killing cops, certainly, but because this rant of true and deep urban anger seemed a little silly now, having become a hit in Toledo and Yakima as well as South-Central L.A., and because Ice-T had become a well-paid movie actor with a television sitcom in pre-production.

12   My laugh, though, was not as hearty as it might have been. My little brother had become a cop by then, a deputy sheriff in Boise, Idaho. I figured I could still chuckle because Blake had drawn jail duty, where not even the officers carry firearms. He broke up brawls and held down screeching, flailing mental cases until they could be ushered off to safer facilities.

> Cop killer, I know your family's grievin'
> Cop killer, but tonight we get even.

13   By late last year, Blake was itching to get out of the Ada County Jail and onto the street. He was quickly hired by the police department in Nampa, a suburb of Boise and a nice quiet place to settle in with his wife and two young, ballet-dancing daughters.

*Notes*

Notes

14. He had been at his new job thirty minutes—half an hour into his very first day—when a call came.

15. A white Mercury Cougar matching the description of one driven by a federal fugitive was flying through town. The driver should be considered armed and dangerous. He had vowed never to return to prison.

16. After a high-speed chase, the suspect high centered his car on the tracks at the railroad yard and ran. Blake was close enough to see that the gun in the man's hand was a .45-caliber semiautomatic, the classic 1911 model Army pistol.

17. Blake drew his Glock .40-caliber and sprinted after the man. The fugitive ran to an old railroad car, and turned. He saw Blake closing on his left, two state troopers on his right. He raised the gun to his right temple. And as Blake watched through the sights of his own weapon, the man killed himself.

18. Later at the hospital, when the physicians had officially declared the fugitive dead and left the room, Blake stayed with him for a few minutes. He wasn't trying to understand why he'd done it. That would be impossible. He wasn't questioning his actions or those of the other officers.

19. He was just trying to take in a little death, he told me later. He wanted to quietly immunize himself, just a bit, against the violence that would become part of his daily life.

20. Then he went home.

21. I stopped the other day at the same record store where my reporter friend had picked up Ice-T's album. A couple of weeks had passed since the state parole board decided that C-BO had violated parole with the anti-law enforcement lyrics in "Til My Casket Drops"—a decision the board swiftly and properly reversed. I wanted to hear the CD.

22. It wasn't selling so well, an employee said, and they had knocked $4 off the price.

23. In the album's liner notes, before he thanks his parents for giving him "the motivation and talent to go after what I want, which is millions," C-BO thanks God for giving him 25 years of life.

24. My brother Blake, who will defend C-BO's right to rap about shooting cops until the day he dies, is just 25 himself.

## ▼ Questions for Critical Thought

*"Family Ties..."*

1. Slater doesn't clearly state his thesis in this journalistic-style piece. In your own words, state what you think his thesis is.

2. What are your thoughts about music and free speech?

SECTION

# IV

# Skill Builders

*This section of* Connections *offers you information and exercises to help you sharpen some important skills.*

- **DISCOVERING YOUR LEARNING STYLE**

- **USING THE DICTIONARY**

- **BUILDING YOUR VOCABULARY**

- **SPELLING MATTERS**

- **READING ALOUD: A TRICK OF THE TRADE**

- **WRITING IN CLASS / WRITING THE ARGUMENT**

Notes

### ▲▼▲ Discovering Your Learning Style

Each person has his or her own **learning style**—a method that makes learning easier. Researchers have found that there are basically three styles: **visual, auditory, tactile (or kinesthetic)**.

- **Visual learners** learn best when they see the material.
- **Auditory learners** learn best when they hear the material.
- **Tactile (or kinesthetic) learners** learn best when they can touch the material.

If you know what your learning style is, you will have an advantage in college because then you can study in the way that is best for you. For example, if you are a visual learner, you will want to use charts, and review cards and pictures when you are studying. However, if you know that you are an auditory learner, you know that lecture classes will be easier for you, and you might even tape record information to play back to yourself. If you are a tactile learner, you will want to find ways to learn information that involves physical movement: building models, organizing ideas by organizing note cards, and so on. (You'll notice in this textbook that we offer activities/approaches that work for all three kinds of learners: charts to express and organize ideas about heroes, reading aloud to help you edit your essays, manipulating idea cards to learn more about organizing your thoughts in an essay, and many more.)

No one learns *only* one way. You may learn best with visual materials, second best with auditory materials, and third best with tactile materials. The key is knowing how you learn best, making the most of that method, and strengthening your other styles as you go along.

### Take the Test

Take the test that follows and find out what your strongest learning style is. Then carefully review the study tips for each learning style.

> **Barsch Learning Style Inventory**
> *Jeffrey Barsch, EdD*
>
> To gain a better understanding of yourself as a learner you need to evaluate the way you prefer to learn. We all should develop a style which will enhance our learning potential. The following evaluation is a short, quick way of assessing your learning style.

This is not a timed test. Try to do as much as you can by yourself. You surely may, however, ask for assistance when and where you feel you need it. Answer each question as honestly as you can. There are twenty-four questions.

When you have finished, transfer each number to its proper place on page 435. Then, total each of the three columns on that page. You will then see, very quickly, what your best channel of learning is. At that point you will know whether you are a visual, auditory, or tactile learner. By this we mean, whether you as an individual learn best through seeing things, hearing them or through the sense of touch (writing).

For example:
- If you are a **visual learner**, that is, you have a high visual score, then by all means be sure you see all study materials. Use charts, maps, filmstrips, notes, and flashcards. Practice visualizing or picturing spelling words, for example, in your head. Write out everything for frequent and quick visual review.
- If you are an **auditory learner**, that is, have a high auditory score, then be sure to use tapes. Sit in the lecture hall or classroom where you can hear lectures so that you can review them frequently, tape them frequently. Tape your class or lecture notes. After you have read something, summarize it on tape. Verbally review spelling words and lectures with a friend.
- If you are a **tactile learner**, that is, have a high tactile score, trace words, for example, as you are saying them. Facts that must be learned should be written several times. Keep a supply of scratch paper just for this purpose. Taking and keeping lecture notes will be very important.

Discuss the results of this test with your teacher or counselor. You will develop, through conversation, other helpful ways to study and learn more efficiently. Good luck for a more intelligent study pattern.

Place a check on the appropriate line after each statement.

Notes

|  | Often | Sometimes | Seldom |
|---|---|---|---|
| 1. Can remember more about a subject through listening than reading. |  | X |  |
| 2. Follow written directions better than oral directions. | X |  |  |
| 3. Like to write things down or take notes for visual review. | X |  |  |
| 4. Bear down extremely hard with pen or pencil when writing. |  |  | X |

## Notes

|  | Often | Sometimes | Seldom |
|---|---|---|---|
| 5. Require explanations of diagrams, graphs, or visual directions. | | | X |
| 6. Enjoy working with tools. | X | | |
| 7. Are skillful with and enjoy developing and making graphs and charts. | X | | |
| 8. Can tell if sounds match when presented with pairs of sounds. | | | X |
| 9. Remember best by writing things down several times. | | X | |
| 10. Can understand and follow directions on maps. | | X | |
| 11. Do better at academic subjects by listening to lectures or tapes. | | X | |
| 12. Play with coins or keys in pockets. | | X | |
| 13. Learn to spell better by repeating the letters out loud than by writing the word on paper. | | | X |
| 14. Can better understand a news article by reading about it in the paper than by listening to the radio. | | X | |
| 15. Chew gum, smoke or snack during studies. | | X | |
| 16. Feel the best way to remember is to picture it in your head. | | X | |
| 17. Learn spelling by "finger spelling" the words. [Writing in the air.] | | | X |
| 18. Would rather listen to a good lecture or speech than read about the same material in a textbook. | | X | |
| 19. Are good at working and solving jigsaw puzzles and mazes. | X | | |
| 20. Grip objects in hands during learning period. | X | | |
| 21. Prefer listening to the news on the radio rather than reading it in a newspaper. | | X | |
| 22. Obtain information on an interesting subject by reading relevant materials. | | X | |
| 23. Feel very comfortable touching others, hugging, handshaking, etc. | | X | |
| 24. Follow oral directions better than written ones. | | | X |

**Scoring Procedures:**

OFTEN = 5 points
SOMETIMES = 3 points
SELDOM = 1 point

Place the point value on the line next to its corresponding item number. Next, add the points to obtain the preference scores under each heading.

*Notes*

| Visual | | Auditory | | Tactile | |
|---|---|---|---|---|---|
| No. | Pts. | No. | Pts. | No. | Pts. |
| 2 | ___ | 1 | ___ | 4 | ___ |
| 3 | ___ | 5 | ___ | 6 | ___ |
| 7 | ___ | 8 | ___ | 9 | ___ |
| 10 | ___ | 11 | ___ | 12 | ___ |
| 14 | ___ | 13 | ___ | 15 | ___ |
| 16 | ___ | 18 | ___ | 17 | ___ |
| 20 | ___ | 21 | ___ | 19 | ___ |
| 22 | ___ | 24 | ___ | 23 | ___ |

VPS = _____      APS = _____      TPS = _____

VPS = Visual Preference Score
APS = Auditory Preference Score
TPS = Tactile Preference Score

## Study Tips for Different Learning Styles

Directions: Use the study tips outline for your first learning preference and then reinforce what you are learning with tips from your second preference.

### I. Tips for Visual Learners (Print, Pictorial)

1. Write down anything you want to remember, such as a list of things to do, facts to learn for a test, etc.

2. Try to write down information in your own words. If you don't have to think about the material and restate it in your own words, you won't really learn it.

3. Underline or highlight important words you need to learn as you read.

4. When learning a new vocabulary word, visualize the word.

5. When you have a list of things to remember, keep the list in a place where you will be sure to see it several times a day. Suggestions:

*Notes*

bulletin board by your desk at home, in your notebook, on the mirror in the bathroom, etc.

6. Try drawing a picture of any information you want to learn. Try making a diagram, a chart, or actually drawing people, things, etc.

7. Always read any material in the textbook before going to class so you have a chance to visually connect with the information before hearing it.

## II. *Tips for Auditory Learners (Oral, Interactive)*

1. Use a tape recorder to record notes when reading instead of writing facts down. Play it back while you are riding in the car, doing dishes, washing the car, jogging, etc.

2. Subvocalize—that is, talk to yourself about any information you want to remember. Try to recite it without looking at your notes or the book.

3. Discuss with others from your class and then quiz each other on the material. Really listen to yourself as you talk.

4. When learning a new vocabulary word, say it out loud. Then spell it out loud several times. See if it rhymes with a word you know. You could even try singing the word in a song.

5. To learn facts, say them out loud, put the facts to music or read them into a tape recorder. Then listen often to what you have recorded.

6. When writing, talk to yourself. First, tell yourself what you will write, say it out loud as you write it, and then read aloud what you have written or tape record it.

7. Always read material in your textbook to be learned after hearing the information first in the class lecture (unless the instructor assigns the reading first before class so you can participate in class discussions).

## III. *Tips for Physical Learners (Haptic, Tactile, Kinesthetic)*

1. Try to study through practical experiences, such as making models, doing lab work, or role playing.

2. Take frequent, short breaks (5–10 minutes) in study periods.

3. Trace words and letters to learn spelling and to remember facts.

4. Use the computer to reinforce learning through the sense of touch.
5. Memorize or drill while walking, jogging, or exercising.
6. Try expressing your abilities through dance, drama, or sports.
7. Try standing up when you are reading or writing.
8. Write facts to be learned on 3"x 5" cards, with a question on one side and the answer on the other. Lay out the cards, quiz yourself, shuffle them, lay them out again and quiz yourself again.
9. When working with a study group, think of T.V. quiz games (*Jeopardy,* etc.) as ways to review information.

IV. **Tips for Multisensory Learners (*Any Combination of the Above Styles*)**

Use any combination of the above study tips. It may take some experimentation before you find the best techniques for you.

▼ *Activity*

### Making the Most of Your Learning Style

Find other classmates who share your learning style. (If you don't get the chance to do this with classmates, work individually or with a tutor.) Review the study tips for your learning style and try to rewrite each tip so that it applies specifically to the work you do in this class. Then choose another class you are taking and rewrite the tips so that they specifically work for that class. You may want to do this for your second learning style.

*Notes*

## ▲▼▲ Using the Dictionary

The following section on using the dictionary will help you see what an important tool the dictionary is to the writer, the student, and the person in the work world.

Every college student should own (and carry, if possible) a good dictionary, because the dictionary can help you

- spell
- define words
- find the right verb forms
- find other forms of a word.

The next four sections will help you understand how the dictionary works and how you can use the dictionary for the purposes listed above.

### Using the Dictionary to Spell

Imagine that you are working on an essay about Anne Frank's diary. You have typed the following quote into your essay and returned Frank's diary to the library. You're editing your essay, and you want to make sure you've spelled *recapture* correctly.

> I can shake off everything if I write; my sorrows disappear, my courage is reborn. But, and that is the great question, will I ever be able to write anything great. Will I ever become a journalist or a writer? I hope so, oh, I hope so very much, for I can recapture everything when I write, my thoughts, my ideals, and my fantasies.
>
> —Anne Frank (1929–1945)
> *diary entry 4/4/44,* Diary of a Young Girl

A word like *recapture* is fairly easy to look up in a dictionary. By sounding out the word, you know to begin by looking up words beginning with *re*. Then you can narrow your search to words beginning with *reca* or *reka*, and by scanning the entries on the page, you will find *recapture*.

Other words might be more difficult to find when you are unsure of the spelling. Do your best to sound them out and then scan the dictionary pages. Other options include asking a tutor, instructor, or friend to help you get started. You can also try using an electronic dictionary or a computer dictionary. The advantages to these two kinds of dictionaries is that you can type in a word by the way it sounds to you, and often, but not always, the electronic or computer dictionary can figure out what you are looking for.

Be aware, too, that sometimes you may look up a word in the dictionary and not find it because it is in a form that is not listed. For example, if you looked up *recapturing*, you would not find it listed in bold print in its own entry in the dictionary. With *recapturing*, you would simply look for a form of the word that is listed in bold print. Then check that entry to see if the form you want is listed. In other words, you'd look up *recapture* and find *-turing* toward the front of the entry. This tells you the word is spelled *recap + turing*. In other situations, you may find the form you want listed at the end of an entry.

Finally, if you are using a computer to complete your essays, you can use spell check. This is a program that will check your writing for you. But be careful of relying on it too much. A spell check program cannot catch wrong word errors. (For example if you typed in *recapturing* instead of *recaptures,* spell check would see nothing wrong with your work. A more common problem is when a writer mixes up words like *their/there* or *to/too* or *its/it's*. Spell check does not help in these situations.)

## ▼ Activity

### Spelling

Look up the following misspelled words in a dictionary to find the correct spellings. If you can, use an electronic or computer dictionary for three of them. Write down the correct spelling next to each word and where you found it (book, computer, electronic dictionary).

assend (to climb upwards)

bankrupped (having no money)

filanthropist (someone who gives to charities)

rationnaly (reasonably)

gord (like a squash or pumpkin)

cresent (shape of a partial moon)

seperate (to keep apart)

perpatrator (someone who commits a crime)

Notes

## Using the Dictionary to Find Word Meanings

Imagine that you're unsure just what *recapture* means in the Frank quote. You want to find the meaning in the dictionary.

> I can shake off everything if I write; my sorrows disappear, my courage is reborn. But, and that is the great question, will I ever be able to write anything great. Will I ever become a journalist or a writer? I hope so, oh, I hope so very much, for I can recapture everything when I write, my thoughts, my ideals, and my fantasies.
>
> —Anne Frank (1929–1945)

The dictionary says,

transitive verb ⟶

noun ⟶

**recapture** (rē-kăp'chər) *tr.v.* -tured, -turing, -tures. **1.** To capture again; retake or recover. **2.** To recall: *an attempt to recapture the past.* **3.** To acquire by the government procedure of recapture. –n. **1.a.** The act of recapturing. **b.** The condition of being recaptured. **2.** International Law. The retaking of booty or goods. **3.** Anything recaptured. **4.** The lawful taking by a government of a fixed amount of the profits of a public-service corporation in excess of a stipulated rate of return.

When you look at a dictionary entry you can't just pick any part of the entry and apply that information to the word and sentence you are interested in. *Recapture*, for example, can be a transitive verb or a noun. The *tr.v.* and the *–n* above tell us that. You have to figure out how the word you want to define is being used. In the quote above, *recapture* is being used as a verb, so you should pay attention to the first three definitions. The first definition seems to suggest that someone is actually taking some object back. That doesn't really fit what Frank is saying. The second definition, however, seems perfect because Frank is discussing *thoughts, ideals, and fantasies*. According to this definition, writing helps her recall, remember, recapture things from the past.

So, remember when you are looking up words for meaning, look carefully at the other words in the sentence and surrounding sentences. These other words are the **context** that you must study so that you can choose the right definition in the dictionary.

 **Activity**

### Finding Meanings in the Dictionary

Find definitions for the eight words in italics in the following reading. This is part of the introductory section to Marie Winn's essay "The Trouble with Television." Make sure that the definitions you write down fit how the words are used in this *context*.

1   Of all the wonders of modern technology that have *transformed* family life during the last century, television stands alone as a universal source of parental *anxiety*. Few parents worry about how the electric light or the automobile or the telephone might *alter* their children's development. But most parents do worry about TV.

2   Parents worry most of all about the programs their children watch. If only these weren't so violent, so sexually *explicit*, so *cynical*, so unsuitable, if only they were more innocent, more educational, more worthwhile.

3   Imagine what would happen if suddenly, by some miracle, the only programs available on all channels at all hours of day and night were delightful, worthwhile shows that children love and parents wholeheartedly approve. Would this eliminate the nagging anxiety about television that troubles so many parents today?

4   For most families, the answer is no. After all, if programs were the only problem, there would be an obvious solution: turn the set off. The fact that parents leave the sets on even when they are *distressed* about programs reveals that television serves a number of purposes that have nothing to do with the programs on the screen.

5   Great numbers of parents today see television as a way to make childrearing less *burdensome*. In the absence of Mother's Helper (a widely used nineteenth-century patent medicine that contained a hefty dose of the *narcotic* laudanum), there is nothing that keeps children out of trouble as reliably as "plugging them in."

## Using the Dictionary to Find Verb Forms

I can shake off everything if I write; my sorrows disappear, my courage is reborn. But, and that is the great question, will I ever be able to write anything great. Will I ever become a journalist or a writer? I hope so, oh, I hope so very much, for I can recapture everything when I write, my thoughts, my ideals, and my fantasies.

—Anne Frank (1929–1945)

Assume that you are writing an essay, and you want to relate your own experiences to what Anne Frank says in her diary entry. You like the way she says, "I can shake off everything if I write." You want to say, "I too have shaked (?) off troubles when I write." The problem is that you're not sure if *shaked* is the right form of the verb. Dictionary entries list verb forms so that you can easily find information like this.

Notes

The dictionary says,

**shake** (shāk) v. **shook** (sho͝ok), **shaken** (shā'kən), **shaking, shakes.**
–tr. **1.** To cause to move. . .

Dictionaries generally follow the same format. With an irregular verb like *shake*, a dictionary will first give its *base form* (**shake**), then its *past tense form* (**shook**), then its *have form* or *past participle form* (**shaken**), and (sometimes) its *present participle form* (**shaking**), and (sometimes) its *-s form* (**shakes**).

You can now see that the sentence is incorrect: "I too have shaked(?) off troubles when I write." The dictionary says that after the helping verb *have* you should use **shaken**. The correct sentence would read: "I too have shaken off troubles when I write."

▼ *Activity*

### Verb Forms in the Dictionary

Look up the following irregular verbs in the dictionary and make a chart that shows their base form, past tense form, and have form.

(Note: with some irregular verbs, the past tense and the have form are the same. For example, *lose*—base form, *lost*—past tense form, *lost*—have form.)

| | |
|---|---|
| arise | hold |
| bid | keep |
| burst | leave |
| forget | prove |
| hide | slide |

## Using the Dictionary to Find Other Forms of a Word

I can shake off everything if I write; my sorrows disappear, my courage is reborn. But, and that is the great question, will I ever be able to write anything great. Will I ever become a journalist or a writer? I hope so, oh, I hope so very much, for I can recapture everything when I write, my thoughts, my ideals, and my fantasies.

—Anne Frank (1929–1945)

---

*See the Irregular Verb Chart in Section V for more information.

One effective way to improve your vocabulary is to pay attention to the different forms a word can take. If, for example, you added the word *ideal* (from the Frank quote) to your vocabulary notebook, you might notice in the dictionary all the words listed before and after *ideal*: *idea, idealism, idealist, idealistic, ideality, ideally*. Being aware of and studying word forms is key to communicating clearly, and your dictionary can help you.

Consider the following sentences where writers have used the wrong form of a word:

1. He is headed down a *destructional* way.
2. People are judged by what they *product* on the job.
3. He works without *supervise*.

(from Errors and Expectations, *Mina Shaughnessey*)

In sentence (1) the writer needs an adjective to describe *way*. In sentence (2) the writer needs a verb for the subject *they*. In sentence (3) the writer needs a noun to follow *without*.

These writers may have sensed that they weren't using the correct form of the word they wanted. When a writer knows or thinks that she has used the wrong form of a word, the dictionary is a perfect resource.

## ▼ Activities

### Correcting Word Forms

In the dictionary, look up the misused words in 1–3 above and list the different forms you find. Choose the correct forms for sentences 1–3 and rewrite the sentences.

### Studying Word Forms

Write down the definitions of words 1–5 that follow and the different forms you find in the dictionary. Write down what part of speech each form represents: n. (noun), v. (verb), adj. (adjective), adv. (adverb). Make sure that the new words you write down connect at least loosely in meaning to the word you look up.

*Example:*

a) organize: *verb—to put together in an orderly fashion*
organizer *(noun)* [found at the end of the entry defining *organize*]
organization *(noun)*

*Notes*

[But don't include organist. It looks similar, but doesn't connect in meaning.]

1. illusive:

2. glorify:

3. simplify:

4. violent:

5. empathy:

## ▲▼▲ Building Your Vocabulary

Writing, reading, and critical thinking grow more interesting, more complex, and more rewarding as your vocabulary grows. With a larger vocabulary you'll do all of the following:

- understand your readings more easily and more completely
- express your own thoughts more clearly and accurately
- think through complex concepts defined with difficult vocabulary more easily.

In this section you'll study the steps to building a better vocabulary.

### Read and Recognize Vocabulary Choices

The first step in working on your vocabulary is to read as much as you can. This is the most natural (and painless) way to improve your vocabulary. If you don't currently read much, begin by reading materials that seem easy and interesting to you. Make reading a regular part of your day. Periodically, push yourself to read something different or something that seems more difficult. This way you'll be exposed to a larger variety of words.

Enjoying what you read is key to improving your vocabulary because if you don't relax and enjoy, you probably won't read much. You should also get into the habit of recognizing the choices writers make when selecting their words. Writers want their writing to be clear and compelling, and, fortunately, the English language offers many word choices.

Consider what it would be like if we only had "good" and "bad" as our adjectives. ("Dinner was good. The band was bad. The dancing was bad. The dessert was good.") Not only would our language be repetitive, but we would be incredibly limited in the feelings and information that we could relate to others.

John Krakauer, author of *Into Thin Air*, demonstrates in the following paragraph the powerful results of making good vocabulary choices. He is describing how exhausted he was when he reached the top of Mount Everest and, consequently, how he couldn't quite appreciate the moment.

> Straddling the top of the world, one foot in China and the other in Nepal, I cleared the ice from my oxygen mask, hunched a shoulder against the wind, and stared absently down at the vastness of Tibet. I understood on some dim, detached level that the sweep of the earth beneath my feet was a spectacular sight. I'd been fantasizing about this moment, and the release of emotion that would accompany it, for many months. But now that I was finally here, actually standing on the summit of Mount Everest, I just couldn't summon the energy to care.

Instead of saying "standing at the summit," he says, "Straddling the top of the world, one foot in China and the other in Nepal." The image he paints with these words is clearer and more interesting. Instead of saying he "looked down into Tibet," he says, he "stared absently down at the vastness of Tibet." With these words we get a better sense of the incredible sight in front of him and, importantly, his inability at that time to really appreciate the view.

By noticing other writers' choices, you will deepen your understanding of how certain words are used, and you will become more aware of the choices you make in your own writing. You will begin to see opportunities to clarify your thoughts through your choice of vocabulary words.

## Defining Words through Context Clues

Of course, recognizing and admiring the choices other writer's make is just the first step in building your vocabulary. The next step is for you to learn new words as you read, and contrary to what you might think, going to the dictionary is not the first step to understanding unfamiliar words.

It is important to be able to figure out the meanings of unfamiliar words by considering the *context* in which they appear. This means that you should consider the entire sentence and nearby sentences

*Notes*

when trying to figure out the meaning of a word. Other words and other sentences will often give you clues as to what the unfamiliar word means. Doing this well will save you time—since you won't have to reach for the dictionary so often—and you are more likely to develop a deeper understanding of the word in question by studying how it is used.

For example, the word *banal* in the following paragraph might be unfamiliar to you. Read the entire paragraph, highlight the word *banal* and study the rest of the paragraph for clues to the meaning of *banal*.

> [Krakauer has just reached the summit of Everest and has realized he is out of bottled oxygen; he is worried about how he will make it down the mountain with no extra oxygen.] I removed my now useless [oxygen] mask, planted my ice ax into the mountain's frozen hide, and hunkered on the ridge. As I exchanged banal congratulations with the climbers filing past, inwardly I was frantic: "Hurry it up, hurry it up!" I silently pleaded. "While you guys are [goofing around] here, I'm losing brain cells by the millions!"

Krakauer tells us clearly that he is frightened about what will happen to him. He is "frantic," "pleading," yelling at people in his mind. What kind of congratulations would he offer other people when he is feeling this way? Well, he wouldn't be offering sincere, joyful congratulations. He would probably be saying what was expected without really feeling the happy emotions. *Banal* is an adjective you can use to describe something unoriginal, worn-out, flat.

### ▼ Activity

**Context Clues in Textbooks**

Find a reading in this textbook that you have not read yet that has at least three words you are unfamiliar with. Read the entire selection. Write down the words that are unfamiliar to you, the clues you find, and the meanings you figure out on your own. (Also, write down the name of the reading, page numbers, and paragraph numbers.) Then compare your definitions to the dictionary definitions.

### Keeping a Vocabulary Notebook

Whether you are confident that you have figured out what a word means through context clues or whether you have used a dictionary, the next step should be to record the new word and information about the new word. Simply writing down information helps you remember it. Then referring back to and studying what you have written brings you even closer to the point when these "new" words will become a part of your everyday vocabulary. (Be sure to enter in your notebook all unfamiliar words you come across in *all* of your classes—not just your English class.)

An entry in your vocabulary notebook should look like this:

*demure* ──────────────────────── vocab. word

"Demure and reserved, the forty-seven-year-old Namba was forty minutes away from becoming the oldest woman to climb Everest..." ── sentence it showed up in

I think it means quiet. ──────────── meaning in context

It is an adjective.
Pronunciation: dĭ-myo͝or′
Other forms of the word: demurely (adverb),
　demureness (noun)
Definition: Sedate in manner or behavior; reserved, shy

─ information from dictionary

▼ *Activity*

### Vocabulary Notebook

Go back to the activity on page 446 where you selected words out of a reading in this textbook. Put those words into your vocabulary notebook (or on your vocabulary notecards). Be prepared to share your work with your instructor and classmates.

---

Writing out all this information will help you learn new words, but don't stop there. You must actually *use your notebook*. Study the words you enter in your notebook. Study words while brushing your teeth, riding the bus, ironing clothes, and so on. Quiz classmates.

Also, take a chance now and then and *use your new words* when you speak and write. The words might feel a little awkward at first, but you must use them for them to be truly in your vocabulary.

## Special ESL Vocabulary Concerns

If English is not your first language, then you may have special vocabulary concerns. Consider the following suggestions:

Notes

a. Read and write in English as often as possible. Of course, you'll have required work in college, but you should also read for pleasure in English. Find a magazine or novel that interests you and read. Begin keeping a journal in English. You can write about what happens during your days; you could focus on your school experiences; you could write about what you're reading for pleasure. A journal simply gives you another opportunity to use your English.

b. Speak English as often as possible. Join study groups at your college. Work with an English speaking tutor.

c. Listen to English. Television is helpful for this, but an even better choice is to listen to books on tape. You can rent these from libraries and video stores or purchase them at book stores. Sometimes you can find unabridged novels on tape, and you can then read while also listening to the tape.

Here are some suggestions for audio books:

*Into Thin Air: A Personal Account of the Mount Everest Disaster* by Jon Krakauer

*To Kill a Mockingbird* by Harper Lee (story about race relations in the South, a young girl growing up, and the trial of a black man)

*A Night to Remember* by Walter Lord (sinking of the *Titanic*)

*Wouldn't Take Nothing for My Journey Now* by Maya Angelou (Angelou reflects on some of the lessons she has learned in her life.)

Note: Most contemporary best sellers are on audio tape (see books by Stephen King, John Grisham, and so on.)

d. Keep an idiom notebook. There are many English idioms, and the only way to learn them is by memorization since rules don't apply.

An **idiom** is an expression that may not make sense if you translate it directly word by word. Here are some sample idiom notebook entries.

*kicked the bucket:* died

*got up on the wrong side of the bed:* means woke up in a bad mood

*caught a movie:* watched a movie

*caught a bus* or *took a bus:* rode a bus

*dumped that class* or *dumped that girl(or boy):* stopped attending that class or stopped dating that girl (or boy)

*tie the knot:* marry

## ▲▼▲ Spelling Matters

*Notes*

Developing spelling skills is an important part of your progress as a student, writer, and employee because often your writing meets people before you do:

- You may send a resumé or letter of inquiry about a job.
- You may fill out an application for college admission.
- You may communicate through letters or e-mail.

First impressions are important. Whether you think it's fair or not, you may be judged in the business world and in college by the number of spelling errors appearing in your writing as many see the ability to spell as an indication of intelligence and literacy.

In the age of computers and spell check, employers and professors consider spelling errors avoidable and unacceptable. In the business world, misspellings detract from the overall quality of an employee's work and could cost the company a client or business opportunity. In college, misspellings could result in a student receiving a lower score on an essay or project.

The fact is that many people struggle with spelling and dread the thought of memorizing endless lists of spelling words in order to improve. However, there are some strategies that you can learn and practice to improve your skills and reduce the number of spelling errors.

This chapter offers a combination of explanation and action strategies to help you strengthen your spelling skills:

- You'll discover why spelling errors occur.
- You'll learn some practical strategies for overcoming individual spelling issues.
- You'll review the spelling of plurals, verbs, homophones.
- You'll learn when to use the apostrophe.

As you begin this section it's important to recognize that spelling difficulties are unique to the individual. There is no one-size-fits-all solution, but there are some basic things that you can do to help yourself become a more accurate speller.

### Understanding Spelling

English is a language that has been evolving over centuries. As written English developed, people were fairly relaxed when it came to spelling

*Notes*

and simply spelled out words according to sound. However, spelling according to pronunciation posed a communication problem, since the pronunciation of words varied from region to region. As the language evolved, some people began to fear that words would lose their connection to sounds.

By the late eighteenth century, Benjamin Franklin and others had begun to lobby for a standardized and more simplified system of spelling. Today, many still believe that spelling should be simplified. But for now, here are some basic facts that may help to explain why spelling can be difficult:

- In English, a single sound may be spelled in several different ways. For example, examine the different spellings of the sound *sh* in *shell, sugar, ration, anxious, occasion, pressure,* and *champagne.*
- Some letters in English are silent in certain situations. Think about the silent *k* in *k*nife as opposed to the spoken *k* in *k*ite, or the *p* in *p*neumonia as opposed to *p*arty.
- Spelling in English is less consistent than in some other languages, such as Spanish in which letters and sounds are often matched.
- English contains many words which sound alike but have different spellings and meanings. Consider the difference in meaning between *here* and *hear*, or *one* and *won*.
- English is a blend of many languages, which helps explain why our spelling system is inexact.

Even though English contains some irregular spellings, you should also know that most English spellings follow basic, rational patterns or "rules." Only a few vary completely from the patterns and must therefore be memorized.

## Why Spelling Errors Occur

As you've seen, there are some reasons why spelling can be difficult in general. However, there are also reasons why spelling may be difficult for the individual.

- Those with less reading experience may have trouble recognizing misspellings in their own writing.
- Those with less writing experience may sometimes scramble letters within a word.

- Those with less experience speaking English or those who do not fully pronounce words may find it difficult to spell by sound.
- Those who don't know how to break words into syllables or form word variations (such as plurals or verb tenses) may be making spelling errors that otherwise could be avoided.

## Overcoming Spelling Problems

While it may seem too easy to suggest that by writing, reading, and speaking more, your spelling will improve, the fact is that it will. Just as reading skills improve as you read more and writing skills improve as you write more, your spelling will improve as you read and write. But there are many other things you can do to develop your spelling skills.

***The Spelling Log*** Perhaps one of the easiest ways to help yourself become a better speller is to carry a small 3 x 5 spiral notebook with you. In it, you would keep a list of problem words—words that cause *you* trouble—spelled correctly. When faced with a situation in which you must write, you would have your personal spelling list with you. Of course, you would add to this list as you begin to be more aware of your spelling and the kinds of spelling errors you're making consistently.

- While editing essays in a workshop, a classmate finds a misspelling (not a typo) in your essay. You would add it to your list.
- When you receive your essay back from your instructor, you would check for any misspellings your instructor found and then add them to your list.
- As you're reading, you notice a word that you realize you've been misspelling. You would add it to your list.

Keeping a personal spelling list means that you're taking responsibility for your spelling and becoming more aware of your own repeated spelling errors.

***Spell Check*** Most computer writing programs today come with spell check, a program which identifies possible misspellings in papers and documents. Basically, spell check works by searching the computer's dictionary and highlighting any words that don't appear in the dictio-

Notes

nary. In most cases, when spell check highlights a word, it will offer a list of suggested spellings. It's likely that the correctly spelled word is in that list. If so, you only need to select the correct spelling, and the program will replace the incorrect spelling in the paper. Spell check also identifies possible capitalization errors and repeated words errors. We recommend that you use spell check whenever you write on a computer, especially during the editing stage of the writing process. If your spelling skills are particularly weak, we suggest that you type out all of your homework on a computer and then use spell check before turning it in. (There are many variations of spell check. If you're working in a computer lab, ask the computer technician to show you how to use it the first time.)

Spell check does have a few drawbacks, however. When a misspelling is highlighted, and you've been given a list of suggested spellings, don't assume the correct spelling for the word will always be on the list. It may not be. If it isn't, you'll need to go to the dictionary to find that word. Also, spell check will not catch words that sound alike but have different meanings (*to, too, two*). If you're trying to decide between using *hear* or *here*, for instance, go to the dictionary or to "Using the Right Word" in Section V of this text and look up the meanings of the words. Finally, spell check won't identify errors in proper names and places, so when editing your paper, be sure to check these spellings yourself.

***The Dictionary*** The dictionary is an invaluable spelling tool. Not only does the dictionary give you the spelling of a word, but it offers the plural of nouns, and for verbs, the basic tenses. When in doubt about how to spell a word, you can always look it up in the dictionary.

But how do you look up a word if you don't know how to spell it? Usually you do so through trial and error, looking up the word by pronunciation and then trying slightly different variations of spelling until you find the word. If you find looking up words in the dictionary nearly impossible, however, you might benefit from a misspeller's dictionary.

***The Misspeller's Dictionary*** A misspeller's dictionary contains two columns of words: one column lists words as they are typically misspelled and a corresponding column lists the same words spelled correctly. For instance, in such a dictionary, you might see the following entries:

| Incorrect | Correct |
|---|---|
| eco | echo |
| eightteen | eighteen |

Often this type of dictionary also contains a section on **homophones** (words that sound alike but have different meanings) and their meanings such as *find* (locate) and *fined* (given a penalty).

*The Spelling List*  Another speller's tool is a pocket-size spelling list. In it, words have been broken into syllables so that they're easier to look up according to pronunciation:

bi•og•ra•phy        re•cant        ty•po

Such spelling lists include the correct spellings for the most commonly misspelled words.

Both the misspeller's dictionary and the spelling list are light and small enough to carry with you everywhere.

## A Review

The spelling log, spell check, dictionary, and misspeller's dictionary will certainly help you cut down on the number of spelling errors in your writing. But there are a few areas of spelling that students find particularly troublesome. In this section we'll review the spellings of plurals, past-tense form and have form of verbs, homophones, contractions, and possessives.

*Plurals*  Change a noun from singular to plural according to the following rules:

- To form the plural of most nouns, add *s* to the word: tree to trees, action to actions.
- To form the plural for nouns ending in *s*, *ss*, *sh*, *ch*, *x*, *z* (a hissing sound called a **sibilant** sound), add *es* to the word: church to churches, hush to hushes, box to boxes, kiss to kisses.
- To form the plural for nouns ending in *o*, add *s* or *es* to the word, depending on the word: hero to heroes, stereo to stereos. (Note: Since some of the words ending in *o* are followed by *s* and some are followed by *es*, you should look them up in the dictionary when you're uncertain.)

**Notes**

- To form the plural of a noun that ends in *y* when preceded by a vowel, add *s*: toy to toy*s*, monkey to monkey*s*.
- To form the plural of a noun that ends in *y* when preceded by a consonant, change the *y* to *i* and add *es*: party to part*ies*, rally to rall*ies*.

Not all plurals are formed by adding *s* or *es*. Some words are adopted from other languages and keep their original plural spellings. Others are simply irregular plurals, exceptions to the rules mentioned above. Here are a few examples:

| **Singular** | **Plural** |
|---|---|
| analysis | analyses |
| child | children |
| criterium | criteria |
| datum | data |
| foot | feet |
| goose | geese |
| man | men |
| medium | media |
| moose | moose |
| mouse | mice |
| tooth | teeth |
| woman | women |

When in doubt about forming a plural, look up the singular form of the word in the dictionary. You'll find the plural form of the word listed after the singular form.

***Verb Tense*** The past-tense form and the have form of verbs pose spelling problems for students only when these forms are irregular. In most cases, the past-tense form and have form are easy to spell. Simply add *ed* to the end of the base form or add just *d* if the base form ends in *e*.

Examples of regular verbs:

| **Base** | **Past** | **Have** |
|---|---|---|
| generate | generate*d* | generate*d* |
| talk | talk*ed* | talk*ed* |

Examples of irregular verbs:

| Base | Past | Have |
|------|------|------|
| drive | dr*o*ve | driv*en* |
| sing | s*a*ng | s*u*ng |

When you have questions about verb forms, you can look up the base form in the dictionary. After the base form, you'll find the past-tense form, the have form, and finally the *-ing* form. (If the past-tense form and have form are the same, the dictionary will list that form once.) Or you can check the Verb Chart in on pages 476 and 477 of the text for spellings of the most common irregular verbs.

*Homophones* Homophones are words which sound alike but are spelled differently and have different meanings. Homophones cause problems for students who may believe they're spelling words correctly when in fact, they're spelling the *wrong* words correctly. This is another instance in which your dictionary is an invaluable tool. When in doubt about which spelling to use, look it up. Another resource in this text is "The Right Word" on page 478, which contains a listing of words that are often confused such as **to, too, two. To** means toward a particular direction. *I traveled to Paris to see the Mona Lisa.* **Too** means also. *My husband went, too.* **Two** is the number. *We discovered two can travel for the price of one.*

*Apostrophe* The **apostrophe** is used in two very different ways in English. It's used to form possessives—my *daughter's* new car—and contractions—she *can't* drive yet. Because the apostrophe is used in such different ways, students are often confused by when and how to use the apostrophe. We'll examine both uses.

*Contractions* A **contraction** is a word with an apostrophe in it. The apostrophe indicates where letters have been left out.

1. it + is = it's
2. had + not = hadn't
3. she + would = she'd

Notice that in example #1, *it's* is a contraction of the words *it* and *is*. Also note that the apostrophe shows where a letter has been left out.

Notes

Notes

In example #2, *hadn't* is a contraction of the words *had* and *not*. In this case, too, the apostrophe shows where a letter is missing. And in example #3, *she'd* is a contraction of *she* and *would*. The apostrophe shows where several letters have been left out. *In a contraction, the apostrophe indicates where a letter or letters have been left out.*

### ▼ Activity

#### Practice in Forming and Using Contractions

Change the following word combinations into contractions. Look up any you're unsure of in your dictionary.

a) he + would = _____  b) what + is = _____

c) can + not = _____  d) will + not = _____

e) should + have = _____  f) I + have = _____

g) you + are = _____  h) do + not = _____

i) it + will = _____  j) we + are = _____

Now write a sentence using each of the contractions.

**Possessives**  A **possessive** is a word that shows ownership. In English we often use the apostrophe to form possessives of nouns and pronouns.

1. Anthony's goal is to become a doctor.
2. Chris' house is three doors down from mine.

Forming Possessive Nouns
- To form the possessive of a noun that does not end in *s*, add *'s*: *children* to *children's*, Tim to Tim's. We showed possession by adding *'s* to Anthony in sentence 1. (Note: Do not worry about whether the noun is singular or plural. If it does not end in *s*, then add *'s*.)
- To form the possessive of a noun that ends in *s*, add only an apostrophe: ladies to ladies', Jones to Jones'. In sentence 2, the apostrophe alone is needed to indicate possession since Chris already ends in *s*. (Note: Do not worry about whether the noun is singular or plural. If it ends in *s*, then only add an apostrophe.)

## ▼ Activity

### Practice Forming Possessives

Change the following nouns into possessives:

a) lady to _____        b) ladies to _____

c) man to _____         d) men to _____

e) child to _____       f) children to _____

g) Harris to _____      h) Gomez to _____

i) actress to _____     j) actor to _____

k) twins to _____       l) instructors to _____

Once you've formed the possessive of each noun, use the possessive form in a complete sentence.

### Forming Possessive Pronouns

There are two basic types of pronouns, personal and indefinite. **Personal pronouns** (which refer to specific persons, places, or things) *do not need* apostrophes to show ownership, but **indefinite pronouns** (which refer to nonspecific persons or things) *do need* apostrophes to indicate ownership.

- Personal pronouns *do not need* apostrophes to show possession. They include: *hers, his, its, mine, ours, theirs,* and *yours.* Consider this sentence: Samantha earned *her* degree. Because *her* is a personal pronoun, no apostrophe is necessary.
- Indefinite pronouns *do need* apostrophes to show possession. Add *'s* to indefinite pronouns when showing possession: *anybody's, anyone's, each's, everybody's, nobody's,* and *somebody's.* Study this sentence: *It was anybody's game.* Because *anybody* is an indefinite pronoun, an *'s* is must be added to show possession.

## ▼ Activity

### Practice Using Personal and Indefinite Pronouns

Write five sentences that include personal pronouns (no apostrophes) and five that include indefinite pronouns (with apostrophes) which show possession.

Notes

### ▲▼▲ Reading Aloud: A Trick of the Trade

Most professional writers routinely read their own writing aloud. They know that reading aloud will help them identify weaknesses in their writing.

Here is a writing scenario that might be familiar to you:

*A student works hard on her essay.*
*She follows all the process steps.*
*The student is proud of the final version of her essay: it is interesting, thoughtful, carefully created.*
*The student takes the time to proofread and is sure that the essay is nearly perfect.*
*The instructor reads the essay and appreciates the thoughtful meaning in the essay. The instructor responds to the ideas and offers suggestions about how to keep improving writing skills. The instructor sees places where the student needs more information and needs to delete or move information. The instructor also notes <u>many</u> spelling, grammatical, and typographical errors.*
*The student appreciates the instructor's writing suggestions, and wonders why she didn't see those spots that clearly need some improvement. And the student is shocked at the number of minor errors in what she thought was a perfect paper. How did the student miss all those spelling, grammar, and typing errors?! The student feels discouraged.*

This scenario is fairly common. Sometimes writers are surprised that they didn't see the weak spots in their papers. Mostly, this is a normal part of acquiring good writing skills, but it can also be a sign that the writer hasn't been able to see her paper objectively.

Now, the mechanical errors (spelling, typing, and grammar errors) may seem minor, but they can confuse the reader, and they certainly ruin a professional image.

Being a good reviser and proofreader takes time and practice. The more you read and write the better you will get, provided you don't rely on a tutor or friend to do your revising or proofreading work for you. However, there are a few ways to acquire good revising and proofreading skills *more quickly*. One method is to *read aloud*.

### Reading Aloud Helps When You Revise

Students at California State University, Sacramento, were required one semester to read all of their essays aloud into tape recorders. Students were amazed at all the problems and errors they found in their essays. On the tapes they would say things like, "American students don't study enough. That's why they score lower than students in other countries. Hmm . . . I bet I need some proof here." Or, "The man murdered her husband. She is against capital punishment. Oh, that sounds funny. That doesn't flow." Reading aloud helped these students see their writing more clearly, more objectively.

There are, in fact, many benefits to reading aloud. If you read your essays aloud frequently, you will find places

- to add information
- to delete unnecessary information
- where transitions must be added or information moved.

And reading aloud while writing your essay will help you get going again if you lose focus or run out of things to say. Reading aloud is a tool professional writers rely upon:

> We spoke before we wrote, historically and individually. Writing is not quite speech written down but it is speech transformed so that it may be heard. The voice lies silent within the page, ready to be turned on by a reader.
>
> We know our language best by hearing it and speaking it. Writing is an oral/aural act and we do well to edit out loud, hearing the text as we revise and polish it. Should we add this, slow that down, speed it up here, take time to define this term, use this word, this construction? What is traditional and expected by the reader? What best supports and communicates the meaning of the draft? These questions can often be answered by reading the line out loud, taking something out and reading it out loud, putting something in and reading it out loud. Hand, eye, and ear, a constant interplay.
>
> —Donald Murray, American novelist, poet,
> Pulitzer Prize-winning journalist, writing instructor

## *Reading Aloud Helps When You Edit*

Finally, when you are proofreading (editing) your essay, read aloud frequently. Don't leave this to the last minute because you may find areas where you left out a whole sentence, or you may find minor errors that you want to fix on the computer or typewriter before handing in your work. Look for these kinds of errors:

- misspelled words
- missing words/sentences
- wrong words
- words repeated or used too often
- punctuation errors

*Notes*

- subject-verb agreement errors
- verb tense errors
- run-ons, comma splices, fragments

### ▼ Activity

**Reading Your Own Writing Aloud**

Read aloud a piece of your writing that has not yet been seen by anyone else. (Ideally, you should read a draft of an essay, but a journal or even answers to reading questions will do.) Read your writing several times. Mark any errors or problems that you see now that you hadn't seen before.

## Reading Aloud Helps You Develop a Writer's "Ear"

Experienced writers, like Donald Murray, quoted earlier in this section, have what we call an "ear" for language. They know what *sounds* good. By reading material aloud they can easily hear punctuation errors, awkward sentences, weak spots in focus/development/organization. You can improve your "ear" for language by reading aloud good pieces of writing.

Here are some recommendations:
- Choose an essay out of this textbook each week and read it aloud at home.
- Participate in class when your instructor wants to read an essay aloud.
- Choose something you really like to read (a newspaper, magazine, novel, poem) and read aloud to your spouse, significant other, or children.
- Listen to books on tape (available at video stores and libraries.)

If you do some or all of these activities you will
- improve your vocabulary,
- improve your sense of how sentences should flow, and
- improve your sense of how writers can focus, develop, and organize writing.

## Some Final Notes about Reading Aloud

- When a piece of reading is very difficult to understand, try reading it aloud. (Students find it especially helpful to read aloud such things as famous speeches, poetry, and Shakespeare because these were meant to be "heard.")

- Read to your children. Your "ear" for language will improve and, besides, study after study shows that reading aloud to children helps children build their vocabularies, their "ear" for language, their problem solving skills, and so on.
- When you read aloud in private, you will be preparing yourself for those situations at school and work when you must present oral reports.
- When you read aloud, note words that you are unsure about pronouncing. Look in a dictionary and study the pronunciation information. Ask a tutor or instructor how to pronounce these words—they are bound to show up again (perhaps when you need to make an oral report).

### ▼ Activity

#### Reading Angelou Aloud

The following reading is a chapter from Maya Angelou's *Wouldn't Take Nothing for My Journey Now*. Angelou, poet and writer, is well known for the "voice" in her writing. Her vocabulary and sentence structure make her meaning nearly sing off the page. Read this aloud and enjoy the power of Angelou's voice. (Her book is available on audio cassette.)

#### Complaining

When my grandmother was raising me in Stamps, Arkansas, she had a particular routine when people who were known to be whiners entered her store. Whenever she saw a known complainer coming, she would call me from whatever I was doing and say conspiratorially, "Sister, come inside. Come." Of course I would obey.

My grandmother would ask the customer, "How are you doing today, Brother Thomas?" And the person would reply, "Not so good." There would be a distinct whine in the voice. "Not so good today, Sister Henderson. You see, it's this summer. It's this summer heat. I just hate it. Oh, I hate it so much. It just frazzles me up and frazzles me down. I just hate the heat. It's almost killing me." Then my grandmother would stand stoically, her arms folded, and mumble, "Uh-huh, uh-huh." And she would cut her eyes at me to make certain that I had heard the lamentation.

At another time a whiner would mewl, "I hate plowing. That packed-down dirt ain't got no reasoning, and mules ain't got good sense. . . . Sure ain't. It's killing me. I can't ever seem to get done. My feet and my hands stay sore, and I get dirt in my eyes and up my nose. I just can't stand it."

*Notes*

And my grandmother, again stoically with her arms folded, would say, "Uh-huh, uh-huh," and then look at me and nod.

As soon as the complainer was out of the store, my grandmother would call me to stand in front of her. And then she would say the same thing she had said at least a thousand times, it seemed to me. "Sister, did you hear what Brother So-and So or Sister Much-to-Do complained about? You heard that?" And I would nod. Mamma would continue, "Sister, there are people who went to sleep all over the world last night, poor and rich and white and black, but they will never wake again. Sister, those who expected to rise did not, their beds became their cooling boards and their blankets became their winding sheets. And those dead folks would give anything, anything at all for just five minutes of this weather or ten minutes of that plowing that person was grumbling about. So you watch yourself about complaining, Sister. What you're supposed to do when you don't like a thing is change it. If you can't change it, change the way you think about it. Don't complain."

It is said that persons have few teachable moments in their lives. Mamma seemed to have caught me at each one I had between the ages of three and thirteen. Whining is not only graceless, but can be dangerous. It can alert a brute that a victim is in the neighborhood.

## ▲▼▲ Writing In Class / Writing the Argument

Notes

So far in this text you have been using the writing process to develop your writing skills in out-of-class writing assignments. But there may be times when you will be required to write essays in class within a specified period of time such as an hour or two.

- Timed essays are a key part of many college courses.
- Timed essays may be used as part of an entrance evaluation into a particular area of study.
- Timed essays may be used to determine entrance into or exit from a writing class.
- Timed essays may be used to determine basic writing proficiency for graduation.
- Timed essays may be used by writing instructors to gauge students' development as writers at various points of the semester.

### The Writing Process in Timed Situations

While the thought of writing an entire essay in an hour or two may make you feel uneasy, you should know that the very same strategies you have learned and practiced this semester in your out-of-class writing assignments will serve you in your in-class writings as well. This chapter will teach you how to use the same process you have practiced in your out-of-class essays in timed-writing situations in class.

### Preparing to Write

In order to write well in timed situations, you must be mentally and physically prepared for the task. You must be as well rested and relaxed as possible. It's a good idea to arrive early to class on these days. Then you'll have a few minutes to get out paper and pen, think about the task, and envision yourself writing. It may help to do a quick five-minute freewrite. Any topic will do. You could freewrite on how you're feeling about writing in class. Or if you have an idea about what the topic might be about, you could get the juices flowing by listing ideas or by writing on the topic in general.

*Notes*

## Utilizing the Writing Process in In-Class Writings

When writing an out-of-class essay, writers have ample opportunity to rethink ideas, revise, and make their essays better. However with an in-class essay, writers are required to complete their essays in a set amount of time. Because of this time limit, writers sometimes panic and make one of the worst mistakes they could make—they just start writing. Writing without a plan is like traveling in unknown territory without a map.

In order to write a successful in-class essay, a writer must read and understand the prompt, brainstorm ideas, decide what main idea to present, and list supporting points—all before writing the essay. Experienced writers have learned to set aside a portion of class for these activities. (Be careful, however, not to spend so much time on these activities that there's no time left for writing. Students should spend no more than 20-25% of the time on these planning activities.)

The bulk of writing time, anywhere from 60–75%, should be devoted to proving the main idea set up in the first few minutes of class. At this time, the writer jots down the introduction and thesis, and then begins addressing the supporting points one by one. (When a reading has been assigned, the writer should bring it to class with important points and interesting quotations highlighted for easy reference.)

The final portion of class should be devoted to revision and then editing. While you don't necessarily need to rewrite your entire essay (though some students do), you should go back and revise words, phrases, and sentences. If you've written on every other line, you can easily revise by drawing a line through a sentence that doesn't work and rewriting that sentence in the blank line above. For those on computers, the revision process is much easier. You need only go back to certain spots to insert new text and delete what doesn't work.

Editing is the very last stage of the process. Be sure to leave the final few minutes of time to read for errors in spelling, capitalization, sentence boundaries, and verb tense. Since you know your own grammar weak spots, you should look carefully for those kinds of errors in your essay. If you use a computer, also use spell check before printing your essay.

### *Tips for Writing the In-Class Essay*

- Ask your instructor for a sample of a previous essay exam to study and practice.
- Try to anticipate the kinds of questions that might be asked.

- If you know the topic beforehand, discuss it with classmates or friends.
- Arrive early so you can mentally prepare.
- Think positive thoughts—envision yourself writing a strong essay.
- Outline, list, or freewrite on potential topics.
- Neatness counts, but don't worry too much about penmanship.
- Write on every other line to allow for changes and revision.
- If writing on computer, use spell check before printing your essay.

## Anticipating the Writing Prompt

Even if you have no idea what the writing prompt will be, you can still prepare to write. If you are taking a content course like sociology, for instance, you could review sections of your textbook and any lecture notes you had taken. Then you would be in a better position to *anticipate* the kind of essay question your instructor might assign. If your instructor had been lecturing on dating and how technology has entered into courtship, and if she had recently assigned the class an article to read entitled, "Love Online," you might anticipate that your instructor would be assigning an essay on contemporary dating trends.

You might even complete a cluster to see what area of the topic you would be most interested in writing on.

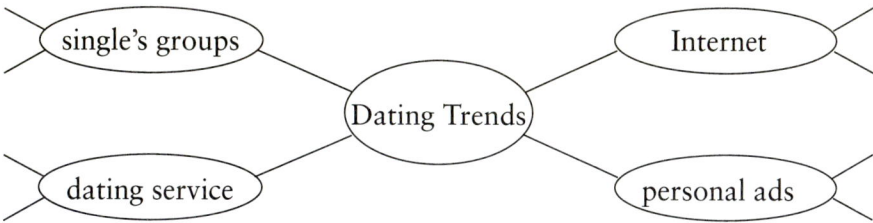

If you had been in a class in which controversial issues were being discussed, you could complete a pro/con list on a topic from class:

| Should High Schools Provide Students with Condoms? | |
|---|---|
| *Pro (For)* | *Con (Against)* |
| —Yes, this would help ensure that children would practice safe sex. | —No, this is the equivalent of giving children permission to have sex. |

*Notes*

It's important to do as much preparatory work as possible before an in-class essay. If you have read and done some brainstorming ahead of time, you'll feel much more confident about the in-class writing experience. And even if you haven't been given a reading and don't have an idea of what the writing topic will be, remember you can still "warm up" by brainstorming, summarizing chapters, studying your notes, and anticipating essay questions.

▼ **Activity**

**Warm-up Topics**

If you have no idea what the writing prompt will be, you can still practice your brainstorming and writing skills before the day of the in-class writing. Here are a few topics to practice on:

- favorite or most interesting class
- your hero
- the best or worst job you ever had
- your view on gun control
- your first love
- your view on living together before marriage
- your favorite hobby
- your view on censoring music lyrics
- the best or worst lesson you learned

## Understanding the Writing Prompt

Once you're in class and the writing prompt has been handed out, your most important task begins. For in the first few minutes of class, you must read and break down the prompt to make sure that you understand it so that you can address its parts.

This first prompt has not been connected to an outside reading, so students would receive this topic "cold" on the day they write.

*Write about what you see as one of the most serious problems in your city or state today. First, explain the problem. Then, discuss what you think can and should be done to try to solve it.*

Section IV  Skill Builders  **467**

Notes

Breaking it down:

- Note the opening general statement. Students are being asked to write about "one of the most serious problems in your city or state today." (Notice *one* not two or three, *today* not yesterday, *your city or state*, not somebody else's.)
- That general statement is followed by two steps. The first asks students to *explain* or define one of the most serious problems.
- Students are then asked to *discuss* what they think *can* and *should* be done to solve the problem. In other words, they are being asked for a solution to the problem.

In the next prompt, students have been given a cartoon to consider and then analyze in an essay.

*Prompt: Write an essay in response to the comic strip, "Why Johnny Can't Read."*

For this prompt, students haven't been given much in the way of direction. What they have been told is "to write an essay in *response* to the cartoon," which means that students are expected to offer their opinions (agreeing or disagreeing with the comic strip's message).

- Before beginning to write, students should carefully consider the title of the piece, the picture, and the artist's message.

*Notes*

- They should also brainstorm (listing ideas or writing down their reactions to the cartoon), focus on the most important issue or idea they see, then develop a thesis *before* writing.
- In developing the body of the essay, students should draw support from their own observations or experiences with television. Students should also refer to any articles on television they might have read.

### Utilizing the Reading Process in In-Class Writings

Sometimes students will be given a reading ahead of time and will be expected to write about an issue in the reading during class. If this is the case, then you would read the piece as soon as possible so that you would have time to reread, think, and talk about the topic. You would be wise to practice your reading process and summary skills in preparation for writing.

Let's say that your instructor announces that you'll be writing an in-class essay during your next class period. She then assigns, "Spare the Chores, Spoil the Child," by Jennifer Bojorquez, which appears on pages 406–408, and she tells you to be prepared to write about the ideas expressed in the article. How would you prepare for such an event?

Well first, you would follow the PARTS of the reading process to make sure that you understand the article. You would preview the article first, looking at the title, publication information, and main ideas. Next you would read quickly, anticipating what would come next, highlighting key terms and ideas, but not looking anything up yet. Then you would reread the article more slowly, looking up unfamiliar terms and making notes in the "Notes" column so that you would remember the main ideas. You would respond to the reading questions, too, which would give you a bit of practice writing about various aspects of the article. You would think about and discuss the reading and the ideas in the reading with classmates, friends, or family members. And finally, you would write a summary of the piece, restating the most important points in your own words. By this point, you would know the article very well, so well in fact that you would probably have some strong opinions to express on the topic of children and what parents expect.

## ▼ Activity

*Preparing to Write*

1. You're preparing to write an essay in your next class on a topic taken from "Spare the Chores, Spoil the Child," by Jennifer Bojorquez, pages 406–408. Follow the reading process as you read the article.

2. Summarize the article.

3. Finally, take time to anticipate what the essay prompt might be about. Brainstorm ideas for possible prompts.

When reading a prompt, look for *key words* that indicate a certain kind of approach:
- If you see *take a position, take a stand*, or *argue for or against*, then you can be sure you're supposed to be persuading an audience to believe as you do about an issue.
- If you see *examine the sides* or *discuss*, you're being asked to provide a more balanced view of both sides of the issue.
- If you see *explain, describe*, or *define*, you're being asked to help your reader see and understand through your explanation.

## ▼ Activities

*Analyzing the Prompt*

An in-class writing prompt for "Spare the Chores, Spoil the Child" follows. Your job is to analyze and then paraphrase the prompt.

In the article "Spare the Chores, Spoil the Child," Professor William Damon argues that while children thrive on challenge, American children aren't challenged enough. He uses the example of children not being required to complete chores as proof that not much is expected of them. Do you agree or disagree with Damon's view that today's children need more discipline and responsibility?

*Write an essay in which you discuss the issue of parental expectations and children. In America do parents have appropriate expectations for their children? Or do children need more discipline and responsibility? Support your view with evidence from the reading or from your own experiences and personal observations.*

Notes

### Writing the In-Class Essay

Set aside a two-hour period to write an essay on the prompt for "Spare the Chores, Spoil the Child" which you paraphrased in the last activity. Be sure to divide your time wisely so that you have time for prewriting, writing, revising, and editing.

## Writing the Argumentative Essay in Class

Argument is an important part of many of the discussions you'll engage in as college students. When you argue, you try to persuade an audience to believe as you do about a cause, an issue, or an idea. Handling an argument in an essay can be tricky. On the one hand, you need to get across your point of view. On the other hand, you need to represent the opposition fairly without cancelling out your own arguments. So how do you accomplish such a feat in a timed writing situation? In this section, you'll learn the strategies for writing an effective argument in class. But first you'll examine the essential elements of an argument.

### In the Argumentative Essay

- The writer establishes a clear position on the issue.
- The writer presents the opposing view fairly. The writer doesn't ignore the opposing view but presents it, then tries to refute it (argue against it). (The writer who doesn't mention the opposing view has written a one-sided argument.)
- The writer supports his or her own position with evidence in the form of facts, examples, or experience.

***The Writer Takes a Stand*** When you've been given a writing prompt that asks you to argue an issue, you've been given a very specific task—take a position and prove your point. Consider the following writing prompts:

- Argue for or against testing college athletes for drug use.
- Argue for or against condoms being distributed to students at local middle schools and high schools.
- Argue for or against stricter handgun regulations.
- Argue for or against mothers nursing their babies in public.
- Argue for or against children being required to wear uniforms at school.

- Argue for or against censorship of pornography on the Internet.
- Argue for or against [add your own issue].

Before you could take a position on any of these topics, you would need to spend some time brainstorming. The pro/con list is an excellent tool for brainstorming argumentative topics.

| Should College Athletes Be Drug Tested? ||
|---|---|
| *Pro (For)* <br> —Yes, college athletes should be tested because they represent the school. | *Con (Against)* <br> –No, it's a violation of privacy. |

Once you've listed as many pros and cons as you can think of, you should be in a better position to decide where you stand on the issue. Have you come up with more pros than cons? Are some arguments more important than others? (Draw a line through less important ones.) At this point ask yourself which side you agree with most. This will be the side to take in your argument.

**The Writer Organizes the Arguments** Once you've established your position, you should identify and highlight the top two or three arguments on each side of the issue. These are the arguments you'll address as you write your essay.

Consider organizing your arguments in one of the following ways:

- least important ideas first, most important ideas last

Notes

- (alternating pro/con arguments) pro argument, con argument, pro argument, con argument, and so on
- pro arguments (divided into different paragraphs) and then con arguments (divided into different paragraphs)

To avoid a one-sided argument and to show your audience that you are fair and well-educated, you should present your opponents' view as well as your own. You may even admit that your opponents have some legitimate points. However, you will want to point out that your points are more important, more persuasive, and probably more in number. How do you address the opposition without weakening your own argument?

Here are a few methods:

- Mention fewer of your opponents' ideas compared to the number of your ideas.
- Mention your opponents' ideas early and then focus the rest of your essay on your ideas.
- Mention your opponents' ideas and then explain why these ideas are not as strong or why your ideas are better.

### Strategies for Writing the Argument in Class

As discussed earlier in this chapter, sometimes students will be given a writing prompt at the start of class and will be expected to write an essay on the topic from their general knowledge. Such is the case with the argument prompt that follows.

> *Some people believe that spanking is an effective method of disciplining children. Others feels that spanking is cruel and only teaches children to be violent. In your opinion is spanking a good way to punish children? Argue your point of view and support your reasons with facts and examples.*

Action Strategies:
- Read and analyze the prompt.
- Develop a pro/con list on the topic.
- Establish your position.
- Highlight the most important points on both sides of the issue.
- Decide on an organizational pattern to follow.

- Draft the essay, presenting pros and cons, but make sure your position is clear and well supported.
- Revise your essay.
- Edit your essay.

### ▼ Activity

#### Writing the In-Class Argument

Using the action strategies mentioned, respond to the argument prompt on spanking. Set a time limit of two hours to complete the essay.

At other times, students will be given an essay to read, think about, and discuss as preparation for writing an argument in class.

### ▼ Activity

#### Writing the In-Class Essay

1. In preparation for writing an in-class essay, read "Family Ties Put a Face on the Faceless Issue of Free Speech," by Eric Slater, pages 428–430. Be sure to follow the prereading instructions and answer the questions at the end of the piece.

2. Using the action strategies for writing in-class arguments, *write an essay in which you argue for or against rappers' and other musicians' rights to publish violent lyrics.* Be sure to support your position with evidence, example, or observation. Set a time limit of two hours to complete the essay.

## A Final Note

Not all of your in-class writing will be done in writing classes. Many instructors across the disciplines use the in-class essay to test students' knowledge of the course material as well as students' writing ability. The things you've learned in this chapter should help you with in-class writing in all your courses.

# SECTION V

# Easy Reference Rules

*This section of Connections offers rules that you can easily and quickly refer to when necessary.*

**COMMON IRREGULAR VERBS**

**THE RIGHT WORD**

**CAPITALIZATION**

**USING OUTSIDE SOURCES**

**PUNCTUATION RULES**

**GRAMMAR RULES**

## Notes

**The Three Columns:**

- The first is the *base form* of verb, the form you'd look up in the dictionary for meaning.
- The second is the simple *past form* (remember—an action completed in the past).
- The third lists the *have form*. (See p. 442 for review.)

Note: The dictionary lists verbs in this same order—base form, past form, have form—See "Utilizing the Dictionary" in Section IV for more information.

## ▲▼▲ Common Irregular Verbs

| BASE | PAST | HAVE FORM |
|---|---|---|
| awake | awoke | awakened |
| be | was | been |
| become | became | become |
| begin | began | begun |
| bite | bit | bitten, bit |
| blow | blew | blown |
| break | broke | broken |
| bring | brought | brought |
| build | built | built |
| buy | bought | bought |
| catch | caught | caught |
| choose | chose | chosen |
| come | came | come |
| cost | cost | cost |
| cut | cut | cut |
| dive | dove | dived |
| do | did | done |
| drag | dragged | dragged |
| draw | drew | drawn |
| dream | dreamed, dreamt | dreamed, dreamt |
| drink | drank | drunk |
| drive | drove | driven |
| eat | ate | eaten |
| fall | fell | fallen |
| feel | felt | felt |
| find | found | found |
| fit | fit, fitted | fit, fitted |
| fly | flew | flown |
| freeze | froze | frozen |
| get | got | got, gotten |
| give | gave | given |
| go | went | gone |
| grow | grew | grown |
| hear | heard | heard |
| hit | hit | hit |
| know | knew | known |
| lay [to put or place] | laid | laid |

| BASE | PAST | HAVE FORM |
|---|---|---|
| lead | led | led |
| let | let | let |
| lie [to recline] | lay | lain |
| pay | paid | paid |
| put | put | put |
| ride | rode | ridden |
| ring | rang | rung |
| rise | rose | risen |
| run | ran | run |
| say | said | said |
| see | saw | seen |
| set [to place] | set | set |
| shake | shook | shaken |
| shine | shone, shined | shone, shined |
| shrink | shrank | shrunk |
| sing | sang | sung |
| sit [to be seated] | sat | sat |
| speak | spoke | spoken |
| spring | sprang | sprung |
| steal | stole | stolen |
| swim | swam | swum |
| take | took | taken |
| teach | taught | taught |
| tear | tore | torn |
| throw | threw | thrown |
| wake | woke, waked | waked, woken |
| wear | wore | worn |
| win | won | won |
| write | wrote | written |

## Notes

**The Three Columns:**

- The first is the *base form* of verb, the form you'd look up in the dictionary for meaning.
- The second is the simple *past form* (remember—an action completed in the past).
- The third lists the *have form*. (See p. 442 for review.)

Notes

## ▲▼▲ The Right Word

Sometimes words that are close in sound or meaning can be confusing. Yet using the right word in a paper can mean the difference between being understood or misunderstood. This section includes a list of commonly confused words (like *to, too, two*) and their basic meanings. For additional information on these words, consult your dictionary.

**a, an**   Use **a** before words beginning with any consonant sound even if the word actually starts with a vowel: *a horse, a unicorn, a Cadillac.* Use **an** before words beginning with any vowel sound even if the word actually starts with a consonant: *an honor, an act, an evergreen tree.*

**accept, except**   **Accept** is a verb meaning to receive. *Hal accepted the invitation.* **Except** means but. *Everyone ate ice cream except Cheshire.*

**advice, advise**   **Advice** is an opinion about a problem or issue. *His advice helped me make a decision about which car to buy.* **Advise** is a verb meaning to suggest. *He advised me to wait until interest rates are lower.*

**advise, advice**   See **advice, advise.**

**affect, effect**   **Affect**, a verb, means to have an influence on. *Studies suggest that TV violence affects behavior.* **Effect**, as a noun, means a result. *The negative effects of cigarette smoking have been documented.*

**effect, affect**   See **affect, effect.**

**hear, here**   **Hear** means to be able to listen. *I hear knocking at the door.* **Here** means present at this time. *I arrived here this morning.*

**here, hear**   See **hear, here.**

**its, it's**   **Its** is the possessive form of it. *The canary chirped its song.* **It's** is a contraction meaning it is. *It's time to go.*

**know, no**   **Know**, a verb, means to understand. *I know how to study well.* **No** means not so. *No, I'm not eating now.*

**no, know**   See **know, no.**

**one, own, won**   **One** means a single thing. **Own**, a verb, means to possess. *Chandra owned one cat.* **Won** is the past tense of the verb win. *We won the tennis tournament.*

**own, won, one**   See **one, own, won**.

**their, there, they're**   **Their** is the possessive form of they. *Their faces turned in unison.* **There** means place. *The lid is there on the counter.* **They're** is a contraction for they are. *They're our favorite guests.*

**there, they're, their**   See **their, there, they're**.

**they're, their, there**   See **their, there, they're**.

**to, too, two**   **To** means toward. (Also part of an infinitive—**to** eat, **to** sleep) *I traveled to Paris to see the Mona Lisa.* **Too** means also. *My husband went, too.* **Two** is the number. *We discovered that travel for two is cheaper than travel for one.*

**too, two, to**   See **to, too, two**

**two, to, too**   See **to, too, two**

**your, you're**   **Your** is the possessive form of you. *Your heroism is inspiring.* **You're** is a contraction of you are. *You're going to receive a promotion.*

**you're, your**   See **your, you're**.

**wear, where**   **Wear** is a verb meaning to put on something. *Sandra wears her baseball cap.* **Where** means at or in what place. *Where is the morning newspaper?*

**which, witch**   **Which** refers to choice. *Which of these would you prefer?* A **witch** is a female sorcerer. *The witch cast a spell.*

**win, when**   **Win**, as a verb, means to achieve victory. *We win every year.* As a noun **win** is the victory. *Andre enjoyed a spectacular win.* **When** means at what point. *When will we take our vacation?*

**when, win**   See **win, when**.

**where, wear**   See **wear, where**.

**witch, which**   See **which, witch**.

**won, one**   See **one, won**.

*Notes*

*Notes*

## ▲▼▲ Capitalization

**Capitalize Proper Nouns** (naming *specific* people, places, things)
   San Francisco       Texas
   Whitney Houston   *New York Times*
(But not common nouns: songwriter, newspaper, book, state, class)

**Capitalize the days of the week, months, and holidays.**
   Monday         November        Thanksgiving

**Capitalize the first word in a sentence.**
   She traveled to Philadelphia by train.

**Capitalize the first word of a quoted sentence.**
   The instructor said, "Essays are due Thursday."

**Capitalize *specific* courses** (but not subject areas: history, geography).
   Art 101         Biology 1A

**Capitalize *I* when used as a personal pronoun.**
   My writing improved as I learned to revise.

**Capitalize language, nationality, ethnicity.**
   Native American   Asian American   Swiss
   French           Hispanic         African-American
   German          Welsh            Caucasian

**Capitalize the names of celestial bodies:**  Mars    Milky Way

**Capitalize the first and last words and other significant words in titles of books, films, movies, television series, compact discs, magazines, journals.**
   *The Color Purple*   *South Park*   *A Short History of the World*
   *GQ*                *Vogue*         *The Bridges of Madison County*
(Don't capitalize *a, an, the* or prepositions unless at the beginning of the title or the last word in a title.)

**Capitalize names of wars and historical events.**
   the Vietnam War              the American Revolution

**Capitalize names of government agencies, corporations, institutions.**
   Bank of America            Microsoft
   Department of Defense      Stanford University

**Do not capitalize the seasons:**  summer, fall, winter, spring

**Do not capitalize centuries:**  the twenty-first century

## ▲▼▲ Using Outside Sources

Notes

The guidelines here will help you use outside information for this class. Other classes may require you to learn more about citing sources. Ask your instructor about the appropriate handbook for you to refer to. Citing sources can get very complicated and must be done with precision.

### Introduction to Outside Sources

An **outside source** is a person or publication that supplies you with information.

**Outside information** is any fact or idea that someone other than you came up with.

Writers often use information from other sources when writing their own essay, book, or article. Sometimes a writer will use something she heard on television or in a speech. Sometimes a writer will use something she read in an encyclopedia, a newspaper, a textbook, or a magazine. There are many places to get useful information.

Guidelines A–E will help you get started on using outside sources.

#### A. Why Writers Use Outside Sources

- A writer may hear or read something interesting and want to discuss it in more detail.
- A writer may come across an idea she disagrees with and want to argue against it.
- A writer may find information that supports something she already wants to discuss.

#### B. Source of the Source

Of course, a writer can't use information from just anywhere. The source of the information must be one that readers will respect. For example, a writer should use information from a reputable publication or a recognized expert. Readers might not believe information that comes from a gossip magazine, and they might not be too interested in what your neighbor down the street once dreamt about aliens from outer space. Choose your sources carefully. When doing research, keep careful notes on where you get your information from. Write down the following source information whenever possible:

author

title (of essay or article and the title of the magazine or newspaper it was published in) or (of book)

date
page number
volume number (when the source is a journal or encyclopedia)

### C. Quantity of Outside Sources

You can use a little outside information or a lot of outside information, depending on what you are writing. In a cover letter for your resumé, you probably wouldn't use many (if any) outside sources. In a scientific report, you would probably use many outside sources. Most of the college essays you write will call for *some* outside information. Here's a good general rule: outside information should play a supporting role to what you have to say. That is, your ideas should come first and take center stage. (If you are ever worried about having too many pieces of outside information in your writing, highlight all information that you borrowed from an outside source. If you highlight more than a third of your essay, you've probably got too much outside information and too few of your own original ideas.)

### D. Where to Use Your Outside Sources

Generally, you want to use the quotes and borrowed information in the body of a paragraph. Sometimes you can start a paragraph with a quote, but usually you need your own topic sentence. Rarely, you can put outside information at the end of a paragraph. Usually, you, as the writer, must interpret outside information. You must explain it and analyze it for the reader. Otherwise, your reader might interpret the information in ways you don't expect.

### E. The Most Important Thing to Remember about Outside Sources

Interpret, explain, and analyze your outside information. Readers don't want a bunch of quotes. They want your well-supported ideas.

## Using Outside Information

When you use ideas and information that belongs to someone else, you must give that person credit. If you do not do this, you'll be guilty of **plagiarism**. In some cultures, it is common practice to copy the words of an expert without mentioning the expert. Such a practice stems from the idea that copying these words is the writer's way of saying, "These are better words/ideas than I could ever come up with." However, in American colleges and businesses, writers are expected to give credit to the person who first came up with the idea/information. Plagiarism can be grounds for being dismissed from a college or job, so it is important that you know how to use outside information and give credit to the person who first stated the information. Giving credit to the original sources is called **citing your sources**. (The information that follows focuses mainly on how to use quotations. However, even if you put someone else's ideas into your own words and you don't use quotation marks, you must still say where you got these ideas from.)

First, you should know that information that is considered "general knowledge" doesn't have to be cited. For example, if you are writing an essay about George Washington and you find his birth date in an encyclopedia, you do not have to cite this encyclopedia. Washington's birth date can be found in many different sources: it is considered general knowledge.

However, if you want to use a piece of information that cannot be found in many different places, you must say where you got the information from.

There are many ways of incorporating a quote into your essay. Here are five common patterns. (Note: when you introduce a quotation, put a comma after the introductory phrase and capitalize the first word in the quotation. Pattern #5 is different because of the word "that.")

Pattern #1: *Dennis Denenberg, a professor of education at Millersville University of Pennsylvania, explained this very well:* "*Like junk food, popular . . . .* "

[Author's name], [author information], explained:

Pattern #2: *In "Move Over, Barney" Dennis Denenberg, a professor of education, explained this very well:* "*Like junk food, popular . . . .*

In [name of the article] [author's name], [author's info.], explained:*

Pattern #3: *According to Dennis Denenberg, a professor at Millersville University of Pennsylvania,* "*Like junk food, popular. . . ."*

---

*Nothing in a prepositional phrase can be the subject of a sentence. So, if you begin a sentence with "in" as shown in Pattern #2, you must supply a subject after that introductory phrase. In Pattern #2, the subject is *Dennis Denenberg*.

**Notes**

According to [author's name], [author's info.],

*or*

According to [name of article],

If the writer had already introduced Dennis Denenberg and explained his status as an expert, the writer could have just said the following:

Pattern #4: *Denenberg noted, "Like junk food, popular . . . ."*

[Author's last name] noted,

Pattern #5: *Denenberg said that "like junk food, popular . . . ."*

[Author's name] said that [no capital letters at the beginning of the quote]

Note: The first time you use a source, it is a good idea to explain who/what your source is. If your source is a person and the person is an expert, what is this person's job title? Where does he or she work? If the source is a journalist, for what magazine or newspaper does the journalist write for? If you are using statistics, from what government agency or private company did you get the statistics? Your reader is more likely to trust your information with these kinds of details included.

## ▲▼▲ Punctuation Rules

**Punctuation Rule #1** (see pages 219 and 341)
Put commas between items in a series.
Example:
*The exhausted, confused, and frustrated writer leaned back in his chair.*
(The comma before the *and* is optional with a list like this.)

**Punctuation Rule #2** (see pages 277 and 394)
When you <u>begin</u> a sentence with a subordinated or dependent clause, you must put a comma after the subordinated clause.
Example:
*If he could just remember that great opening line, the rest would flow.*

**Punctuation Rule #3** (see pages 277 and 394)
If the subordinated clause comes *after* the independent clause, you do not need a comma.
Example:
*The rest would flow if he could just remember that great opening line.*

**Punctuation Rule #4** (see pages 280 and 282)
You may use a semicolon to separate two complete sentences.
Example:
*He needed to find the words now; his editor was waiting for his work.*

**Punctuation Rule #5** (see page 283)
Put commas around interruptive words/phrases in a sentence.
Example:
*For two long hours, **however**, no words came to his mind.*

Notes

> **Punctuation Rule #6** (see page 388)
>
> When you join two complete sentences with a coordinator (FANBOYS), you must put a comma after the first sentence.
>
> Example:
>
> *At midnight he finally remembered his thrilling opening line, and he began to type.*
>
> ("Once upon a time. . .")

*Note: When checking punctuation in your writing, don't use commas unless you can cite one of the rules here. Unnecessary commas can confuse your reader.*

## ▲▼▲ Grammar Rules

> **Subject-Verb Agreement Rule** (see page 157)
>
> Subjects and verbs must agree in number. This means that single subjects must have single verbs. Plural subjects must have plural verbs.
>
> Remember, in the present tense, when the subject is *he*, *she*, *it*, or another word that could be replaced by *he*, *she*, or *it*, the verb must have an *s* on the end.

> **Preposition Rule** (see page 158)
>
> Prepositional phrases, or anything in the prepositional phrase, cannot be the subject or the verb of the sentence.

> **Pronoun Reference Rule** (see page 211)
>
> A pronoun must always have a noun to refer to. The noun the pronoun refers to is called the *antecedent*.

> **Pronoun Agreement Rule** (see page 212)
>
> If an antecedent is singular, you must use a singular pronoun. If an antecedent is plural, you must use a plural pronoun.
>
> Remember, indefinite pronouns such as *someone*, *everybody*, and *anybody* are singular.

# Glossary

**activities:** work that puts into practice new writing concepts or ideas (24).

**action verb:** a word that expresses activity or movement. Example: Jake *jumps* rope (107).

**adjective:** a word that describes a noun (161).

**adverbs:** words that describe verbs, adjectives, other adverbs, and whole groups of words (348).

**analyze:** to break down a complex concept into smaller, less complex pieces and then study the pieces (354).

**and:** one of the seven coordinators. It expresses a relationship of addition (387).

**anticipate:** a step in the reading process when the reader guesses what the reading will be about based on his or her preview of the reading material. Readers also anticipate (or guess what will come next) while reading the entire piece for the first time (73).

**apostrophe:** a punctuation mark used to show possession. Example: *My dad's car is new.* An apostrophe can also be used in a contraction (two words joined as one). Example: *can + not*, can't (455).

**audience:** any person or persons you are communicating to (10).

**body:** the middle section of an essay or paragraph that supports the claim established in the introduction or topic sentence (30).

**body paragraphs:** paragraphs that appear after the introduction of an essay and before the conclusion. They contain information that helps support the claim established in the introduction (33).

**brainstorm:** a piece of writing written freely without concern for grammatical correctness or form. The purpose of a brainstorm is to let the writer explore ideas (133).

**but:** one of the seven coordinators. It expresses a relationship of opposition (387).

**citing your sources:** giving credit to the original source of information (216).

**clause:** a group of words with a subject and predicate (276).

**coherence:** in a coherent essay, all the ideas fit together and support the thesis (142).

**column:** a piece of writing in which a columnist (the writer) expresses his or her own views (49).

**columnist:** a writer of a column (49).

**columns:** long vertical rows of newsprint in a newspaper (42).

**comma splice:** an error that is created when two complete sentences are joined as one with only a comma to separate them (280).

**command sentences:** sentences that give someone work to do. This type of sentence has the implied subject *you* (156).

**completer:** a word or phrase that completes the meaning of the sentence (220).

**con argument:** an argument *against* something (226).

**concessions:** words that create bridges between ideas and emphasize one idea over another. When they attach to an independent sentence, concession words create dependent clauses (283).

**conclusion:** the final paragraph in a piece of writing. It sums up the most important points, restates the writer's claim, and draws the piece to an end (30).

**conjunctive adverbs:** words that help writers build bridges between ideas. For example—*however, therefore, consequently* (282).

**context:** the surrounding words, sentences, and ideas in which another word/idea appears (81).

**487**

**contraction:** a word with an apostrophe in it that indicates where letters have been left out. Example: *they* + *are*, they're (455).

**coordinators:** seven different words that can be used to join independent sentences: *for, and, nor, but, or, yet, so* (387).

**dependent clause:** a group of words containing a subject and verb and preceded by a subordinator. It cannot stand alone. (276).

**development:** the process of moving from a basic idea to a fully expressive, well-supported main idea that communicates to a specific audience for a specific purpose (287).

**embed:** to insert phrases into sentences to add more meaning (340).

**essay:** an organized, multi-paragraph piece of writing in which the writer focuses on and develops a particular issue or theme for a specific audience for a specific purpose (25).

**essay prompt:** the essay assignment instructions (134).

**excerpt:** a selected piece of a longer reading (36).

**feature story:** a newspaper article that presents and discusses a timely issue (41).

**figurative language:** language that compares two things. For example: *The moon, a silver platter in the sky, lit our way.* (The moon is being compared to a silver serving dish.) (358)

**focused:** sticks to one point (162).

**focused essay:** an essay with a clear thesis and body paragraphs that directly support the thesis (164).

**focused paragraph:** a paragraph with a clear topic sentence and information that connects directly to the topic sentence (168).

**for:** one of the seven coordinators. It expresses a relationship of effect-cause (387).

**fragment:** an incomplete sentence (220).

**fused sentence:** two sentences incorrectly joined as one with no punctuation separating them (278).

**helping verbs:** verbs that work with another word to create a verb. Example: We *are* laughing. The *are* is a helping verb (110).

**homophones:** words which sound alike but have different spellings and meanings (453, 455).

**idiom:** an expression that may not make sense if it is read literally or translated word for word (448).

**implied subject:** a subject that is not stated. Command sentences have the implied subject *you* (155).

**imposters:** words that look like verbs but really aren't (114).

**indefinite pronoun:** refers to nonspecific persons, places, things (457).

**independent clause:** a group of words that can stand alone as a sentence (276).

**infer:** to draw a conclusion based on evidence (354).

**infinitives:** *to* + verb combination (116).

**introduction:** the opening paragraph or two of a piece of writing. It explains what the piece will be about and may suggest the order and direction of the body paragraphs that follow (29).

**journalism:** news writing and reporting (41).

**journals:** "free writing zones." They are an opportunity to explore ideas on paper without fear of judgment (23).

**kernel sentence:** the basic subject and predicate of a simple, non-descriptive sentence (340).

**lead:** the opening statement of a journalistic piece of writing designed to "hook" the reader (45).

**linking verb:** a verb that connects or links parts of the sentence (107).

**meter:** a specific, formal rhythmic pattern used in poetry (357).

**nor:** one of the seven coordinators. It expresses a relationship of negative addition (387).

**nouns:** words that name people, places, things, or ideas (160).

**or:** one of the seven coordinators. It expresses a relationship of alternatives (387).

**outline:** a formal and thorough list of all major points and supporting points in an essay, *or* a quick list of just the major points (134).

**outside information:** any fact or idea that someone else came up with (213).

**outside source:** a person or publication that supplies you with information (213).

**PARTS:** the five stages of the reading process—*preview, anticipate, read and reread, think critically, summarize* (73–74).

**personal narrative:** a piece of writing in which an individual recounts an event or series of events from his or her life usually to make a point or to help the reader better understand an issue (84).

**personal pronoun:** a word that can stand in the place of a noun (457).

**phrase:** a group of words that is missing a subject or predicate or both (276).

**plagiarism:** using information that belongs to someone else without giving that other person credit (215).

**plot line:** a concise summary that retells the major events or actions in a story or a film (206).

**plural:** more than one (157).

**possessive:** a word that shows ownership (456).

**predicate:** in a sentence, the verb *and* all the words that are not part of the subject (154).

**prepositional phrase:** a group of words consisting of a preposition and its object (116).

**preview:** the first step in the reading process in which the reader looks at author, title, length, topic sentences, headings, subheadings, charts, pictures or diagrams in order to get a sense of what the reading will be about (73).

**pro argument:** an argument *in favor* of something (226).

**process package:** a collection of work—including class notes, a brainstorm, an outline, a draft, and more (122).

**pronoun:** a word that can be used instead of a noun (210).

**purpose:** the author's reason for writing (10).

**Questions for Critical Thought:** questions that follow the readings in this book. These questions are designed to help you understand and analyze your readings and to help you consider the writer's message and strategies (25).

**Questions for Development:** a set of questions used by writers and journalists to "flesh out" ideas (293).

**read and reread:** the act of reading through a selection quickly (only marking unknown terms and interesting points) and then rereading a second time more carefully (responding to the text and looking up unknown terms) (73).

**reading:** an essay, article, book excerpt presented to give you information on a theme and to help you strengthen your reading, writing, critical thinking skills (25).

**reading assignments:** assignments that help you engage in the steps of the reading process (25).

**reading process:** a series of stages readers go through to help them comprehend (understand) and retain (remember) what they have read. There are five stages in this process: preview, anticipate, read and reread, think critically about, summarize (73).

**response:** a written, thoughtful reaction to what you have read. It is a commentary on the most important or intriguing ideas presented in a piece (78).

**revise/revising:** reseeing what you have written and then rewriting it to strengthen focus, organization, or development (61, 137).

**run-on sentence:** two sentences incorrectly joined as one with no punctuation separating them (278).

**sibilant sound:** a hissing sound (453).

**singular verb:** a verb that works with *one* person or idea (157).

**so:** one of the seven coordinators. It expresses a relationship of cause-effect (387).

**stanzas:** paragraphs in music lyrics and poems (357).

**subject:** the person or thing the sentence is about. The subject is performing the action expressed by the verb, or it is being linked to other information by the verb (154).

**subject-verb agreement:** subjects and verbs agreeing in number. For example, a single subject needs a single verb. A plural subject needs a plural verb (156).

**subordinators:** words that when added to an independent clause, make it a dependent clause (276).

**summarize:** putting the main ideas of a piece of writing into your own words; also the last stage of the reading process (74).

**summary:** a concise retelling of the main point of a longer piece of writing (54).

**technology:** a broad term encompassing anything that science has created, usually relating to industry and commercial items (230).

**tenses:** tell what time the action of a sentence is taking place in (present tense, past tense, or future tense) (113).

**test of time:** the act of placing *yesterday, today,* or *tomorrow* at the beginning of a sentence to see which word (or words) can or must change tense. The word that changes is the verb (114).

**thesis statement:** the overall main idea of an essay, chapter, or article (32).

**think critically:** to look beyond the surface of an issue or action and examine the purpose or motivation behind it (8).

**topic sentence:** general statement that introduces the main idea of a paragraph (33).

**transitions:** words that strengthen coherence in an essay (*however, therefore, consequently,* and other words) (142).

**verb:** the word that acts as the heart of the sentence. It may tell what action is occurring or it may act as a connector to descriptive information. It will tell when the action (or connecting) is taking place (68).

**writing assignment:** academic essay assignment (25).

**writing process:** the steps a writer takes when completing a writing assignment. There are six stages: *discuss and engage; read, discuss, think critically; explore the writing assignment; draft; revise; edit* (120–121).

**writing-reading-critical thinking connection:** the act of using your writing, reading, and critical thinking skills to understand an issue and communicate your ideas about the issue (3).

**yet:** one of the seven coordinators. It expresses a relationship of opposition (387).

# Acknowledgments

**CHAPTER 1**

**p. 7:** Abigail Van Buren, taken from the "Dear Abby" column by Abigail Van Buren. © 1996 Universal Press Syndicate. Reprinted with permission. All rights reserved; **p. 89–91:** James Kirby Martin, Randy Roberts, Steven Mintz, Linda O. McMurry, and James H. Jones, from *America and its People*, 2/e. © 1993 by Harper-Collins College Publishers. Reprinted by permission of Addison-Wesley Educational Publishers, Inc; **p. 14:** Joshua Meyrowitz, from "Television: The Shared Arena," *The World & I*, July 1990, pp. 465–481. © 1990 by Joshua Meyrowitz. Reprinted with permission of the author; **p. 12:** Mortimer J. Adler, from essay, "How to Mark a Book," 1940;

**p. 15–16:** William H. Armstrong, from *Study is Hard Work*. © 1995 by William H. Armstong. Reprinted by permission of David R. Godine, Publisher, Inc.

**CHAPTER 2**

**p. 30–32:** Frank D. Cox, from *Human Intimacy: Marriage, the Family, and its Meaning*. St. Paul, MN: West Publishing Company, 1979; **p. 36–38:** Alex Thio, from *Sociology: A Brief Introduction*, 3/e. © 1997 by Longman Publishers. Reprinted by permission of Addison-Wesley Educational Publishers, Inc.; **p. 42–45:** William R. Macklin, "Modern Marriage" as appeared in *The Sacramento Bee*, 1/30/99. Reprinted with permission of Knight Ridder/Tribune Information Services; **p. 49–51:** Maggie Bandur, "Women Play the Roles Men Want to See," *The Daily Northwestern*, 1/23/96. By permission of *The Daily Northwestern* at Northwestern University, Evanston, IL; **p. 56:** James Kirby Martin, Randy Roberts, Steven Mintz, Linda O. McMurry, and James H. Jones, from *America and its People*, 2/e. © 1993 by HarperCollins College Publishers. Reprinted by permission of Addison-Wesley Educational Publishers, Inc.; **p. 58–59:** William E. Thompson and Joseph V. Hickey, from *Society in Focus: The Essentials*. © 1996 by William E. Thompson and Joseph V. Hickey. Reprinted by permission of Addison-Wesley Educational Publishers, Inc.; **p. 62–64:** Anastasia Toufexis, "Sex Has Many Accents," *Time*, 5/24/93. © 1993 by Time, Inc. Reprinted by permission.

**CHAPTER 3**

**p. 75–77:** Elizabeth Wong, "The Struggle to Be an All-American Girl" originally appeared in *The Los Angeles Times*, 1980. Reprinted by permission of the author, Elizabeth Wong; **p. 85–87:** Jim Bobryk, "Navigating My Eerie Landscape Alone" from *Newsweek*, 3/18/99. All rights reserved. Reprinted by permission of *Newsweek*; **p. 89–91:** James Kirby Martin, Randy Roberts, Steven Mintz, Linda O. McMurry, and James H. Jones, from *America and its People*, 2/e. Copyright © 1993 by HarperCollins College Publishers. Reprinted by permission of Addison-Wesley Educational Publishers, Inc.; **p. 93–95:** William E. Thompson and Joseph V. Hickey, from *Society in Focus: The Essentials*. © 1996 by William E. Thompson and Joseph V. Hickey. Reprinted by permission of Addison-Wesley Educational Publishers, Inc.; **p. 97–99:** Kavita Menon, from "In India, Men Challenge a Matrilineal Society," *Ms. Magazine*, September/October 1998. Reprinted by permission of *Ms. Magazine*, © 1998;

**p. 101–104:** Dave Murphy, "Not a Two-Bit

Problem," *San Francisco Examiner*, 4/11/99. © 1999 San Francisco Examiner. Reprinted with permission.

## CHAPTER 4
**p. 141:** John Macionis "When Advertising Offends" from *Sociology 5/e*, © 1995 by Prentice-Hall, Inc. Reprinted by permission of Prentice-Hall, Inc., Upper Saddle River, NJ; **p. 146–147:** "The Most Evil Character," author unknown. Every attempt has been made to identify an author or original source. If the author/source can be identified, please contact the publisher listed on the title page of this text.

## CHAPTER 5
**p. 184–186:** Sandy Banks, "It's Good to Know Real Heroes Are Still Revered," *Los Angeles Times*, April 20, 1998. © 1998, *Los Angeles Times*. Reprinted by permission; **p. 192–194:** Megan Burroughs, "A Hero in My Family." 1999 (with permission from Elaine Roberts and Geoffrey Burroughs.) By permission; **p. 177–183:** Dennis Denenberg, "Move Over, Barney," *American Educator*, Fall, 1997. By permission of Dennis Denenberg; **p. 187–191:** David Wallechinsky, "How One Woman Became The Voice Of Her People," *Parade*, 1/19/97. Reprinted with permission from *Parade* and David Wallechinsky. © 1997; **p. 195–198:** Darlene R. Stille, "Florence Rena Sabin," from *Extraordinary Women Scientists*. © 1995 Children's Press, Inc. Used by permission of Grolier Publishing Company.

## CHAPTER 6
**p. 234–236:** Amy Wu, "Stop the Clock" from *Newsweek*, 1/22/96. All rights reserved. Reprinted by permission of Newsweek; **p. 227–228:** John J. Macionis "Modernization and Women: A Report from Rural Bangladesh" from *Sociology 5/e*. © 1995 by Prentice-Hall, Inc. Reprinted by permission of Prentice-Hall, Inc., Upper Saddle River, NJ; **p. 244–247:** Abby Goodnough, "Internet Access Puts Burden of Control on Schools," *New York Times*, 4/19/97. © 1997 by the New York Times Co. Reprinted by permission; **p. 248–250:** Seth Schiesel, "On Web, New Threats to Young Are Seen," *New York Times*, 3/7/97. © 1997 by the New York Times Co. Reprinted by permission; **p. 250–253:** Tina Kelley, "School District Organizes Itself Around Internet," *New York Times*, 4/23/97. © 1997 by the New York Times Co. Reprinted by permission; **p. 237–239:** Peter King, "Resistance to Internet Grows Weak," *The Sacramento Bee*, 4/26/98. © *The Sacramento Bee*, 1998. By permission; **p. 256–257:** Joanne Cleaver, "Leveling the Playing Field" from "Class Acts: How Three Schools Use New Technology to Empower Students." Web Site http://www.connect-time.com, August 1997. By permission of Joanne Cleaver/Winston-Taylor Associates, Inc.; **p. 254–256:** Marie Faust Evitt, "Forging Global Connections" from http://www.connect-time.com, August 1997. © 1997 by Marie Faust Evitt. Used by permission of the author; **p. 265–267:** Susan Swartz, originally published as "Words from Up Close and Non-Virtual," *The Press Democrat*, 1/2/98. By permission of *The Press Democrat*.

## CHAPTER 7
**p. 288:** Joshua Meyrowitz, from "Television: The Shared Arena," *The World & I*, July 1990, pp. 465–481. © 1990 by Joshua Meyrowitz. Reprinted with permission of the author; **p. 289:** Douglas Gomery, from "As the Dial Turns," *The Wilson Quarterly*, Autumn, 1993, pp. 41–46. © 1993 by Douglas Gomery. Reprinted by permission of the author; **p. 289–290:** Neil Hickey, from "How Much Violence," *TV Guide Magazine*, August 22, 1992. Reprinted with permission from *TV Guide*. © 1992 TV Guide Magazine Group, Inc. *TV Guide* is a registered trademark of TV Guide Magazine Group, Inc.; **p. 291–292:** Nancy Signorielli, from "Television, the Portrayal of Women, and Children's Attitudes" in G. Berry and J. Asamen (Eds.) *Children and Television: Images in a Changing Sociocul-

*tural World,* pp. 229–242. © 1993 by Sage Publications, Inc. Reprinted by permission of Sage Publications, Inc.; **p. 297–306:** Marie Winn, "The Trouble With Television" from *Unplugging the Plug-In Drug.* © 1987 by Marie Winn. Used by permission of Viking Penguin, a division of Penguin Putnam Inc.; **p. 314–317:** Daniel R. Anderson, "How TV Influences Your Kids," *TV Guide Magazine,* March 3, 1990. Reprinted with permission from *TV Guide.* © 1990 TV Guide Magazine Group, Inc. *TV Guide* is a registered trademark of TV Guide Magazine Group, Inc.; **p. 324–326:** Kathryn Doré Perkins, "V-Chip: Can it Protect Kids?" The *Sacramento Bee,* 3/29/96. © The *Sacramento Bee,* 1996. By permission; **p. 327–329:** Diana Griego Erwin, "What You Can Do About Violent TV," The *Sacramento Bee,* 6/30/96. © The *Sacramento Bee,* 1996. By permission; **p. 330–332:** Michael Kilian, "V-Chip Will Add to Parental Chaos," *Sacramento Bee,* 3/6/96. © Chicago Tribune Company. All rights reserved. Used with permission.

## CHAPTER 8

**p. 355–356:** From *The World Almanac and Book of Facts 1998,* reprinted with permission. © 1997 PRIMEDIA Reference Inc. All rights reserved; **p. 359–360:** Langston Hughes, "Evenin' Air Blues" from *Collected Poems* by Langston Hughes. © 1994 by the Estate of Langston Hughes. Reprinted by permission of Alfred A. Knopf, Inc; **p. 362–363:** Roger Waters, "Time," words and music by Roger Waters, Nicholas Mason, David Gilmour, and Rick Wright. TRO- © 1973 Hampshire House Publishing Corp., New York, NY. Used by permission; **p. 363–364:** Joe Chambers and Larry Jenkins, "Old 8 x 10." Words and music by Joe Chambers and Larry Jenkins. © 1988 Universal—MCA Music Publishing, Inc., a division of Universal Studios, Inc. (ASCAP) International Copyright Secured. All rights reserved. By permission of Universal Music Publishing Group; **p. 365–366:** Bonnie Raitt, "Tangled and Dark." © 1991 by Kokomo Music (ASCAP). All rights reserved. Used by permission of Bonnie Raitt, administered by Gold Mountain Management; **p. 367:** Alanis Morissette and Glen Ballard, "Perfect." Words and music by Alanis Morissette and Glen Ballard. © 1994 Universal - MCA Music Publishing, Inc., a division of Universal Studios, Inc. (ASCAP) International Copyright Secured. All rights reserved. By permission of Universal Music Publishing Group; **p. 368–370:** Melissa Etheridge, "Silent Legacy." © 1993 M.L.E. Music (ASCAP). All rights administered by Almo Music Corp. (ASCAP). All rights reserved. Used by permission of Warner Bros. Publications U.S. Inc., Miami, FL 33014; **p. 375:** Jessicah Pratt, "What I Saw on the Bus" from "Words of Wisdom" by Stephanie McDade, The *Sacramento Bee,* 3/6/98. © The *Sacramento Bee,* 1998. By permission; **p. 376–377:** Adria Conley, "Take Wing" from "Verse & Versatility" by Gwen Schoen, The *Sacramento Bee,* 4/11/97. © The *Sacramento Bee,* 1997. By permission; **p. 378:** Lorna Dee Cervantes, "Refugee Ship". Reprinted with permission from the publisher of *A Decade of Hispanic Literature: An Anniversary Anthology.* (Houston: Arte Publico Press—University of Houston, 1982); **p. 379–380:** Robert Frost, "The Road Not Taken," 1915; **p. 381:** Marge Piercy, "A Work of Artifice" from *Circles on the Water: Selected Poems of Marge Piercy.* © 1982 by Marge Piercy. Reprinted by permission of Alfred A. Knopf, Inc.

## SUPPLEMENTAL READINGS

**p. 400–402:** Associated Press, "Recipe for the '90s" appearing in The *Sacramento Bee,* 3/15/92. By permission of The Associated Press; **p. 403–405:** Michael D. Lemonick, "Spare the Rod? Maybe," *Time,* 8/25/97. © 1997 by Time, Inc. Reprinted by permission; **p. 406–408:** Jennifer Bojorquez, "Spare the Chores, Spoil the Child," The *Sacramento Bee,* 8/21/95. © The *Sacramento Bee,* 1995. By permission; **p. 409–413:** Hank Whittemore, "The Most Precious Gift." First published in *Parade,* 12/22/91. © 1991 by Hank Whittemore. Reprinted by permission of *Parade* and Scovil Chichak Galen Literary Agency on behalf of the author; **p. 414–415:** Fahizah Alim, "Look Past Rapper for Real Heroes," The *Sacramento Bee*, 3/13/97 ©, The *Sacramento Bee*, 1997. By permission; **p. 416–418:** Donna Britt, originally published as "Hip-Hop Guys Who Break the Mold" in *The Washington Post*, 3/14/97. © 1997, The Washington Post Writers Group. Reprinted with permission; **p. 418–422:** Michael Ryan, "Who Is Great?" First published in *Parade*, 6/16/96. © 1996 by Michael Ryan. Reprinted by permission of *Parade* and Scovil Chichak Galen Literary Agency on behalf of the author; **p. 423–425:** David L. Evans, "The Wrong Examples" from *Newsweek*, 3/1/93. All rights reserved. Reprinted by permission of *Newsweek*; **p. 426–427:** Calvin Trillin, "Child's Play," *Time*, 12/30/96–1/6/97. © 1996 by Time, Inc. Reprinted by permission; **p. 428–430:** Eric Slater, "Family Ties Put a Face on the Faceless Issue of Free Speech," *Los Angeles Times*, April 18, 1998. © 1998, Los Angeles Times. Reprinted by permission.

**SKILL BUILDERS**
**p. 432–437:** Jeffrey Barsch, EdD, *Barsch Learning Style Inventory*. © 1980 by Academic Therapy Publications. Used by permission of Academic Therapy Publications; **p. 461–462:** Maya Angelou, from *Wouldn't Take Nothing For My Journey Now*. © 1993 by Maya Angelou. Reprinted by permission of Random House, Inc.

# Sources

## SECTION I

### Chapter 2:

Blum, Deborah. 1995. "Monogamy: Till-Death-Do-Us-Part is Rare for Mammals; What About Us?" *The Sacramento Bee,* 16 October, A16. [Sources in Alex Thio's "Preparing for Marriage" from *Sociology: A Brief Introduction,* 3/e. 1997.] Kephart, William M., and Davor Jedlicka. 1988. *The Family, Society, and the Individual,* 6th ed. New York: Harper & Row. Simpson, Jeffrey A., Bruce Campbell, and Ellen Berscheid. 1986. "The association between romantic love and marriage: Kephart (1967) twice revisited." *Personality and Social Psychology Bulletin,* 12, pp. 363–372. Strong, Bryan, and Christine DeVault. 1992. *The Marriage and Family Experience,* 5th ed. St. Paul, Minn. Whyte, Martin King. 1992. "Choosing mates—The American Way." *Society,* March/April, pp. 71–77. [Sources in William E. Thompson and Joseph V. Hickey's "Sexual Revolution, Cohabitation, and the Rise of Singles" from *Society in Focus: The Essentials.* 1996.] Beeghley, Leonard. *The Structure of Social Stratification in the United States.* Boston: Allyn and Bacon, 1989. Bumpass, Larry L., and James A. Sweet. "National Estimates of Cohabitation." *Demography* 26, 1989:615–625. Bumpass, Larry L., James A. Sweet, and Andrew Cherlin. *The Role of Cohabitation in Declining Rates of Marriage.* NSFH Working Paper No. 5. Madison: University of Wisconsin, 1989. Gwartney-Gibbs, Patricia A. "The Institutionalization of Premarital Cohabitation: Estimates from Marriage License Applications, 1970 and 1980." *Journal of Marriage and the Family* 48 (May), 1986:423–434. Hofferth, Sandra L., Joan R. Kahn, and Wendy Baldwin. "Premarital Sexual Activity Among U.S. Teenage Women over the Past Three Decades." *Family Planning Perspectives* 19, 1987:46–53. Lamanna, Mary A., and Agnes Riedmann. *Marriage and Families: Making Choices and Facing Changes,* 3d ed. Belmont, CA: Wadsworth, 1988. Masters, William H., Virginia E. Johnson, and Robert C. Kolodny. *Human Sexuality,* 3d ed. Glenview, IL: HarperCollins, 1988. Masters, William H., Virginia E. Johnson, and Robert C. Kolodny. *Heterosexuality.* New York: HarperCollins, 1994. Miller, Brent C., and Kristin A. Moore. "Adolescent Sexual Behavior, Pregnancy, and Parenting: Research Through the 1980s." *Journal of Marriage and the Family* 52 (November), 1990:1025–1044. Seltzer, Judith A. "Consequences of Marriage Dissolution on Children." *Annual Review of Sociology* 20, 1994:235–266. Spanier, Graham B. "Married and Unmarried Cohabitation in the United States, 1980." *Journal of Marriage and the Family* 45 (May), 1983:277–288. Stengel, Richard. "Resentment Tinged with Envy." *Time,* July 8, 1985:56. Surra, Catherine A. "Research and Theory on Mate Selection and Premarital Relationships in the 1980s." *Journal of Marriage and the Family* 52 (November), 1990:844–865. U.S. Bureau of the Census. *Population Studies.* Washington, DC: Government Printing Office, 1990b. U.S. Bureau of the Census. "Marital Status and Living Arrangements." *Current Population Reports.* Series, P-20, No. 478. Washington, DC: Government Printing Office, 1993a

### Chapter 3:

[Sources in William E. Thompson and Joseph V. Hickey's "Feminism: The Struggle for Gender Equality" from *Society in Focus: The Essentials.* 1996.] Andersen, Margaret L. *Thinking About*

Women: Sociological Perspectives on Sex and Gender, 3d ed. New York: Macmillan, 1993. Faludi, Susan. *Backlash: The Undeclared War Against American Women.* New York: Crown, 1991. Laslett, Barbara, and Johanna Brenner. "Gender and Social Reproduction: Historical Perspectives." *Annual Review of Sociology* 15, 1989:381–404. Lips, Hilary M. *Women, Men, and Power.* Mountain View, CA: Mayfield, 1991. Lips, Hilary M. *Sex and Gender: An Introduction,* 2d ed. Mountain View, CA: Mayfield, 1993. Vance, Carole S., and Carol A. Pollis. "Introduction: A Special Issue on Feminist Perspectives on Sexuality." *Journal of Sex Research* 27 (February), 1990:1–5. Wood, Julia T. *Gendered Lives: Communication, Gender, and Culture.* Belmont, CA: Wadsworth, 1994.

### Chapter 4:
Elbow, Peter. 1995. *Peter Elbow on Writing,* Media Education Foundation. "The Most Evil Character," author unknown. Every attempt has been made to identify an author or original source. If the author/source can be identified, please contact the publisher listed on the title page of this text. Simpson, Janice C. "Buying Black." *Time.* Vol. 140, No. 9 (August 31, 1992):52–53. Westerman, Marty. "Death of the Frito Bandito." *American Demographics.* Vol. 11, No. 3 (March 1989):28–32.

## SECTION II

### Chapter 5:
Frears, Steven. 1992. *Hero.* Motion Picture. Winik, Lyric Wallwork. 1996. "I Just Reacted—I Don't Know How.'" *Parade,* 2 June, 4–6.

### Chapter 6:
*The Whole World Book of Quotations.* 1995. Ngugi wa Thiong'o. New York: Addison Wesley Longman, 320. Alam, Sultana. "Women and Poverty in Bangladesh." *Women's Studies International Forum.* Vol. 8 No. 4 (1985):361–371. Mink, Barbara. "How Modernization Affects Women." *Cornell Alumni News.* Vol. III, No. 3 (April 1989):10–11. Mumford, Lewis. *Camp's Unfamiliar Quotations from 2000 B.C. to the present,* Wesley D. Camp (New Jersey: Prentice Hall, 1990) 385.

### Chapter 7:
Gomery, Douglas. 1993. "As the Dial Turns." *The Wilson Quarterly* (autumn): 41–42. "FCC Approves TV V-Chip That Can Block Programs." The Salt Lake Tribune, 13 March 1998. http://www.sltrib.com/1998/mar/03131998/nation_w/27553.htm. Stern, Christopher. "V-Chip Marches Forward At FCC." *Reuters/Variety,* 26 September 1998. http://www7.yahoo.com/text/headlines/970926/entertainment/stories/television_vchip_1.html

### Chapter 8:
Bergreen, Laurence. 1997. *Louis Armstrong: An Extravagant Life.* New York: Bantam Books. Holman, C. Hugh, and William Harmon. 1986. *A Handbook to Literature,* 5th ed. New York: MacMillan. *The New Encyclopedia Britannica.* Vol. 1. 1997. Louis Armstrong. Chicago: Encyclopedia Britannica, Inc. *The World Book Encyclopedia.* 1999. Louis Armstrong. Chicago: World Book Inc. *Knowledge Adventure Encyclopedia.* 1998. Louis Armstrong. http://www.letsfindout.com/subjects/art/louis-armstrong.html

## SECTION IV:
## SKILL BUILDERS V

**Building Your Vocabulary:**
Frank, Anne. 1967. *The Diary of a Young Girl.* Translated from the Dutch by B.M. Mooyaart-

Doubleday. New York: Doubleday & Company, 218. Shaughnessy, Mina P. 1977. *Errors & Expectations: A Guide for the Teacher of Basic Writing.* New York: Oxford University Press, 190. Krakauer, John. 1997. *Into Thin Air: A Personal Account of the Mount Everest Disaster.* New York: Anchor Books, 3 and 7.

**Spelling Matters:** Shaughnessy, Mina P. 1977. *Errors & Expectations: A Guide for the Teacher of Basic Writing.* New York: Oxford University Press, 164–175. Bryson, Bill. 1990. *The Mother Tongue: English & How It Got That Way.* New York: Avon Books, 120, 129.

**Reading Aloud:** Murray, Donald M. 1991. *The Craft of Revision.* Chicago: Holt, Rinehart, and Winston, Inc. 143.

# Subject Index

## —A—

A/an rule, 342
Action verb. *See* Verb
Active reading. *See* Listening
Activities, 24
Adjective, 161
    *-ing* words as, 161
    using adverbs and adjectives, 348–350
    using *have* form, 345
    using to improve sentences, 341–347
Adverbs, 348
    using adverbs and adjectives, 348–350
    using to improve sentences, 348
Advertisements, writing about, 122–145
Agreement
    subject-verb, 156–157
    pronoun, 212–213
Analogy, 332
Analysis
    in essays, 355
    in paragraphs, 355
Analyze, 354
Antecedent. *See* Pronoun
Anticipate. *See* Reading process
Apostrophe, 455
Argument
    pro and con, 226
Argumentative essay, 470–473
    organizing the, 471–472
    strategies for writing the, 472–473
Audience, 9–10, 34
    in journalistic writing, 47–48, 52–53

## —B—

Base form of verb, 345–346, 442, 476–477
Body of an essay, 30, 38
Body paragraphs
    of an essay, 33
    of a newspaper article, 46
Brainstorm, 133

## —C—

Capitalization, 480
Citing your sources, 213–217
Clause, 276
Coherence, 142, 283
Cohesion, 210
Column, 49
Columnist, 49
Columns (in newspapers), 42
Command sentence, 156
Commas. *See* Punctuation rules
Comma splice, 280
Completer, 220
Computers, 21
Con argument, 226
Concession words, 283–285
Conclusion of an essay, 30, 34, 39
Conjunctive adverb, 282
Context, 81–82
Contractions, 455–456
Coordinating conjunctions, 387–392
Coordinators, 387
Creating expressive sentences, 340
Critical thinking. *See* Think critically

## —D—

Dependent clause, 276
Detail, 195
Developed essay, 290–291
Developed paragraph, 288–290
Developing the focused essay, 293

Development
    defined, 287
    points to remember about, 295
    questions for, 293–294
    in writing, 287
Dictionary usage, 79–81, 438–439
Draft. *See* Writing process

—E—

Easy reference rules, 475–486
Embed, 340
Essay, 25
    assignment, 134
    prompt, 134
Evil character, writing about the most, 145–153
Excerpt, 36

—F—

FANBOYS. *See* Coordinating conjunctions
Feature story, 41
Figurative language, 358
Focus, 167
    points to remember about, 172
Focused essay, 169–170
Focused paragraph, 168
Fragment, 220, 275
Fused sentence, 278

—G—

General information
    in academic writing, 56–57
    in journalistic writing, 62
Gerunds. *See -ing* words as nouns and subjects
Grammar rules, 486
    Preposition rule, 158
    Pronoun agreement rule, 212
    Pronoun reference rule, 211
    Subject–verb agreement rule, 157

—H—

*Have* form of verbs, 346, 476–477
Helping verb. *See* Verb
Heroes, writing about, 166–209

Homophone, 453, 455

—I—

Idiom, 448
Implied subjects, 155
Imposter, 114–116
    *-ing* words 114–115
    to + verb combinations, 116
Indefinite pronouns, 457
Independent clause, 276
Infer, 354
Infinitive, 116
    as verb imposter, 116
*-ing* words, 114–115, 159–162
    as adjectives, 343–344
    can describe, 161–162
    as nouns and subjects, 160–161
    as phrases, 344
    as verb imposters, 114–115
Internet. *See* Technology
Introduction of an essay, 29, 32–33, 38–39
Irregular verbs, 476–477

—J—

Journal assignments, 23–24
Journalism, 41

Keeping a notebook, 17–18
Kernel sentence, 340

—K—

Learning style, 432–437
Lead, 45
Linking verb. *See* Verb
Listening, 15–16
Lyrics. *See* Music and poetry

—M—

Main points, 60
Meter, 357
Music and poetry
    effect, 358
    form, 357

language, 357–358
responding and interpreting to, 358–359
writing about, 353–386

—N—

Nouns, 160, 341
    *-ing* words as, 160

—O—

Organization, 222–230
    of notebook, 17–18
    one approach to, 228–230,
    patterns of, 223
    points to remember about, 230
Outline, 134–135, 201–202
Outside information, 213
Outside sources, 213–217
    using, 481–484

—P—

PARTS. *See* Reading process
Participles. *See -ing* words can describe
Personal narrative, 84
Personal pronoun, 457
Phrase, 276
Plagiarism, 215
Plot line, 206
Plural verb, 157
Poetry. *See* Music and poetry
Possessive word, 456
Predicate, 154, 275
Prepositional phrases, 116–117
    cannot be subjects, 158–159
Preposition rule, 158
Preview. *See* Reading process
Pro argument, 226
Process package, 122
Pronoun, 210–213
    agreement rule, 212
    antecedent, 211
    reference rule, 211
Punctuation rule
    #1, 219, 341
    #2, 277, 394
    #3, 277, 394
    #4, 280, 282
    #5, 283
    #6, 388
Purpose, 9–10, 34
    in journalistic writing, 47–48, 52–53

—Q—

Questions for critical thought, 25
Questions for development, 293–294

—R—

Read and reread. *See* Reading process.
Reading
    active, 12–15
    aloud, 458–462
    assignments, 25
    magazine and newspaper articles, 96–106
    the personal narrative, 84–88
    textbook chapters, 88–96
Reading process
    anticipate, 73
    PARTS, 73
    preview, 73
    read, 73
    reread, 73, 77
    summarize, 74, 78
    think critically, 74, 77
Response to reading, 78–79
Revise. *See* Writing process
Revision, points to remember about, 137
Right word, 478–479
Run-on sentence, 278–280

—S—

Sentence combining
    using adverbs and adjectives, 348–350
    using the have form adjective, 345–347
    using *-ing* adjectives, 342–347
    using prepositional phrases to improve sentences, 351–352
Sentence work, 26–27
Sentences, shaping, 217–220
Sibilant sound, 453

Singular verb, 157
Skill builders, 431–473
Specific information
    in academic writing, 56–57
    in journalistic writing, 62
Spelling, 449–462
Stanzas, 357
Structure
    in a newspaper column, 49
    of academic writing
        body, 30
        conclusion, 30, 34, 39
        introduction, 29
        overview, 29–30
    of an essay
        body, 30, 33, 39
        conclusion, 30, 34, 39
        introduction, 29, 32–33, 38–39
    of journalistic writing, 41–42
        body paragraphs, 46
        conclusion, 47
        lead, 45–46
    of a textbook
        body paragraphs, 39
        conclusion, 39
        introduction and thesis, 38
Subject, 154
    identifying a, 154–156, 218–219
    implied, 156
    -*ing* words as, 160
    in *there* sentence, 162–163
Subject-verb agreement, 156–157
    rule, 157
Subordinating conjunctions, 276, 393–398
Summarizing
    essays and textbook chapters, 53–61
    journalistic writing, 61–65
    as the last step in the reading process, 74
Summary, 54

—T—

Taking notes, 12–17
Technology, 230
    writing about, 221–274

Television, writing about, 286–339
Tense. *See* Verb
*There* sentence, 162–163
Thesis statement, 32–33,
    create your, 134, 201
Think critically, 8–10
To + verb combination. *See* Infinitive
Topic sentence, 33
Transitions, 142
Transition words, 281–283
Tutors, 19–20

—V—

V-Chip, writing about the, 323–338
Verb, 68, 218–219
    action, 107
    helping, 110–111
    identifying, 107
    irregular, 476–477
    linking, 107–108
    tense, 113–114
    test of time, 114
    understanding, 68–71
Verbal phrase. *See* Fragment
Vocabulary building, 79–84, 444–448
Vocabulary notebook, 83

—W—

Writing assignments, 25–26
Writing in class/writing the argument, 463–473
Writing process, 120–122
    developing an effective, 121
    points to remember about, 121
    the stages of an effective, 120–121
        discuss and engage, 120, 122
        draft, 120, 135–136, 202
        edit, 121, 138
        explore the writing assignment, 120, 131
        read, discuss, think critically, 120, 124
        revise, 61, 120, 137
Writing-reading-critical thinking connection, 3–11

# Index of Authors and Titles

Alim, Fahizah, "Look Past Rapper for Real Heroes," 414–415

Anderson, Daniel R., "How TV Influences Your Kids," 314–317

Associated Press, "Recipe for the '90s," 400–402

Bandur, Maggie, "Women Play the Roles Men Want to See," 49–51

Banks, Sandy, "Rosa Parks Joins Children's Wall of Heroes," 184–186

Bobryk, Jim, "Navigating My Eerie Landscape Alone," 85–87

Bojorquez, Jennifer, " Spare the Chores, Spoil the Child," 406–408

Britt, Donna, "It's a Rap the Young Don't Deserve," 416–418

Burroughs, Megan, "A Hero in My Family," 192–194

Cervantes, Lorna Dee, "Refugee Ship," 378

"Child's Play," (Trillin), 426–427

"Class Acts: How Three Schools Use New Technology to Empower Students," (Evitt and Cleaver), 254–257

Cleaver, Joanne, and Marie Faust Evitt, "Class Acts: How Three Schools Use New Technology to Empower Students," 254–257

Conley, Adria, "Take Wing," 376–377

Cox, Frank D., "Romantic Love," 30–32

Denenberg, Dennis, "Move Over, Barney," 177–183

Etheridge, Melissa, "Silent Legacy," 368–370

Evans, David L., "The Wrong Examples," 423–425

Evitt, Marie Faust, and Joanne Cleaver, "Class Acts: How Three Schools Use New Technology to Empower Students," 254–257

"Family Ties Put a Face on the Faceless Issue of Free Speech," (Slater), 428–430

"Feminism: The Struggle for Gender Equality," (Thompson and Hickey), 93–95

"Florence Rena Sabin," (Stille), 195–198

Frost, Robert, "The Road Not Taken," 379–380

"Gender Role Images on Television," (Signorielli), 291–292

Goodnough, Abby, "Internet Access Puts Burden of Control on Schools," 244–247

Griego Erwin, Diana, "What You Can Do about Violent TV," 327–329

"Hero in My Family, A," (Burroughs), 192–194

Hickey, Joseph V., and William E. Thompson, "Feminism: The Struggle for Gender Equality," 93–95;
"Sexual Revolution, Cohabitation and the Rise of
Singles," 58–59

"How One Woman Became the Voice of Her People," (Wallechinsky), 187–191

"How TV Influences Your Kids," (Anderson), 314–317

"In India, Men Challenge a Matrilineal Society," (Menon), 96–97

"Internet Access Puts Burden of Control on Schools," (Goodnough), 244–247

"It's a Rap the Young Don't Deserve," (Britt), 416–418

Kelley, Tina, "School District Organizes Itself around Internet," 250–253

Kilian, Michael, "V-Chip Will Add to Parental Chaos," 330–332

King, Peter H., " Resistance to Internet Grows Weak," 237–239

Lemonick, Michael D., "Spare the Rod? Maybe," 403–405

"Look Past Rapper for Real Heroes," (Alim), 414–415

Macionis, John J., "Modernization and Women: A Report from Rural Bangladesh," 227–228; "When Advertising Offends: Another Look at Aunt Jemima," 141

Macklin, William R., "Modern Marriage," 42–45

Martin, James Kirby, et al., "Seventeenth Century Roles for Puritan Men, Women, and Children," 89–91

Menon, Kavita, "In India, Men Challenge a Matrilineal Society," 97–99

"Modern Marriage," (Macklin), 42–45

"Modernization and Women: A Report from Rural Bangladesh," (Macionis), 227–228

Morissette, Alanis, "Perfect," 367

"Most Evil Character, The," (author unknown), 146–147

"Most Precious Gift, The," (Whittemore), 409–413

"Move Over, Barney," (Denenberg), 177–183

Murphy, Dave, "Not a Two-Bit Problem," 101–104

"Navigating My Eerie Landscape Alone," (Bobryk), 85–87

"Not a Two-Bit Problem," (Murphy), 101–104

"Old 8 x 10," (Travis), 363–364

"On Web, New Threats to Young Are Seen," (Schiesel), 248–250

"Perfect," (Morissette), 367

Perkins, Kathryn Doré, "V-Chip: Can it Protect Kids?" 324–326

Piercy, Marge, "A Work of Artifice," 381

Pink Floyd, "Time," 362–363

Pratt, Jessicah, "What I Saw on the Bus," 375

"Preparing for Marriage," (Thio), 36–38

Raitt, Bonnie, "Tangled and Dark," 365–366

"Reality Writes—Web Is but a Tool," (Swartz), 265–267

"Recipe for the '90s," (Associated Press), 400–402

"Refugee Ship," (Cervantes), 378

"Resistance to Internet Grows Weak," (King), 237–239

"Road Not Taken, The," (Frost), 379–380

"Romantic Love," (Cox), 30–32

"Rosa Parks Joins Children's Wall of Heroes," (Banks), 184–186

Ryan, Michael, "Who Is Great?" 418–422

Schiesel, Seth, "On Web, New Threats to Young Are Seen," 248–250

"School District Organizes Itself around Internet," (Kelley), 250–253

"Seventeenth Century Roles for Puritan Men, Women, and Children," (Martin, et al.), 89–91

"Sex Has Many Accents," (Toufexis), 62–64

"Sexual Revolution, Cohabitation, and the Rise of Singles," (Thompson and Hickey), 58–59

Signorielli, Nancy, "Gender Role Images on Television," 291–292

"Silent Legacy," (Etheridge), 368–370

Slater, Eric, "Family Ties Put a Face on the Faceless Issue of Free Speech," 428–430

"Spare the Chores, Spoil the Child," (Bojorquez), 406–408

"Spare the Rod? Maybe," (Lemonick), 403–405

Stille, Darlene R., "Florence Rena Sabin," 195–198

"Stop the Clock," (Wu), 234–236

"Struggle to Be an All-American Girl, The," (Wong), 75–77

Swartz, Susan, "Reality Writes—Web Is but a Tool," 265–267

"Take Wing," (Conley), 376–377

"Tangled and Dark," (Raitt), 365–366

Thio, Alex, "Preparing for Marriage," 36–38

Thompson, William E., and Joseph V. Hickey, "Feminism: The Struggle for Gender Equality," 93–95;
"Sexual Revolution, Cohabitation, and the Rise of Singles," 58–59

"Time," (Pink Floyd), 362–363

Toufexis, Anastasia, "Sex Has Many Accents," 62–64

Travis, Randy, "Old 8 x 10," 363–364

Trillin, Calvin, "Child's Play," 426–427

"Trouble with Television, The," (Winn), 297–306

"V-Chip: Can It protect Kids?" (Perkins), 324–326

"V-Chip Will Add to Parental Chaos," (Kilian), 330–332

Wallechinsky, David, "How One Woman Became the Voice of Her People," 187–191

"What I Saw on the Bus," (Pratt), 375

"What You Can Do about Violent TV," (Griego Erwin), 327–329

"When Advertising Offends: Another Look at Aunt Jemima," (Macionis), 141

Whittemore, Hank, "The Most Precious Gift," 409–413

"Who Is Great?" (Ryan), 418–422

Winn, Marie, "The Trouble with Television," 297–306

"Women Play the Roles Men Want To See," (Bandur), 49–51

Wong, Elizabeth, "The Struggle to Be an All-American Girl," 75–77

"Work of Artifice, A," (Piercy), 381

"Wrong Examples, The," (Evans), 423–425

Wu, Amy, "Stop the Clock," 234–236